Mad Wives and Island Dreams

MaD WiVEs AND ISLAND DREAMS

Shimao Toshio and the Margins of Japanese Literature

Philip Gabriel

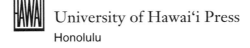

University of Hawai'i Press

Honolulu

© 1999 University of Hawai'i Press
All rights reserved
Printed in the United States of America

04 03 02 01 00 99   5 4 3 2 1

Library of Congress Cataloging-in-Publication Data
Gabriel, J. Philip.
    Mad wives and Island dreams : Shimao Toshio and the margins of
Japanese literature / Philip Gabriel.
      p.   cm.
    Includes bibliographical references and index.
    ISBN 0–8248–2012–6 (cloth : alk. paper). — ISBN 0–8248–2089–4
(pbk. : alk. paper)
    1. Shimao, Toshio, 1917–   —Criticism and interpretation.
I. Title.
PL838.H57Z63   1999
895.6'35—dc21   98–16634
                                                   CIP

Text design by Dennis Anderson
Cover design by Bob Nance

To Mika

Contents

Acknowledgments

MANY PEOPLE have aided me during the years it took to bring this project from initial germ of an idea to dissertation to the present book. Prof. Kageyama Tsuneo first brought Shimao's literature to my attention in 1986, as I was about to leave Japan for graduate school. His encouragement and advice, especially in the beginning stages of my study, were invaluable. In graduate school my dissertation adviser, Dr. Brett de Bary, provided critical feedback and support in countless ways. I am forever grateful to her for three wonderful, challenging years, and for her continued friendship. In Japan my research went as smoothly as it did due to the encouragement and help of Prof. Asai Kiyoshi of Ochanomizu Women's University, who went far beyond the bounds of academic adviser. Professor Asai always found time in his busy schedule to listen to and encourage a struggling foreign scholar. The other members of my dissertation committee—Profs. Karen Brazell, J. Victor Koschmann, and Naoki Sakai—aided me in countless ways. Their insights during the early stages of dissertation research, and at my defense, have served as valuable springboards for thought over the years. I am grateful to them all.

In Japan, Takeuchi Emiko, formerly of Ochanomizu Women's University, patiently read *Shi no toge* and the *byōinki* stories nearly line by line with me. The staff of the literary journal *Genten*—Prof. Yonaha Keiko, Enomoto Masaki, and Prof. Tsuge Teruhiko—provided insights into Shimao's work as well as the opportunity to participate, through interviews, panel discussions, and conferences, in the world of literary studies in Japan. At Hōsei University, my official sponsor during the year of dissertation research, Prof. Nishida Masaru helped me gain access to materials in the university library system, as did Prof. Higa Minoru of Hōsei's Institute of Okinawan Studies. The novelist Saegusa Kazuko and her husband, Morikawa Tatsuya, author of the first full-length study of Shimao's work, provided personal insight, particularly into Shimao's early career. Fieldwork in Amami and Kakeromajima was aided by many wonderful people, especially Shimao's former assistant, Motome Tetsuji. Shimao's widow, Miho, opened up her home, her library, and a wealth of information regarding her husband and his work, and I am forever grateful to her for this, and for her continued encouragement.

Research in Japan was made possible through two grants, a Fulbright Graduate Research Fellowship and a Fulbright-Hayes Dissertation Research Grant. I especially wish to thank the staff of the Japan-U.S. Educational Commission in Tokyo for their assistance. The University of Arizona provided a Humanities Research Initiative Grant that made research in Okinawa possible, as well as a semester leave during which a portion of this book was written. I am thankful to Prof. Brian McKnight, head of my department, and to my colleagues, especially Profs. Kimberly Jones and Elizabeth Harrison, for their warm support over the years. I am grateful to the University of Hawai'i Press staff, particularly my editor, Sharon Yamamoto, my copy editor, Susan Biggs Corrado, and the two anonymous readers whose valuable comments helped me rethink many portions of the book. Naturally, any conclusions reached in this book remain my own.

Junko and Mika provided, on a daily basis, the answer to what this was all about.

Mad Wives and Island Dreams

Introduction

SHIMAO TOSHIO (1917–1986) once summed up his life as a failure to experience. Having left the Kanto region days before the 1923 earthquake, he escaped the horrific natural catastrophe that leveled Tokyo and Yokohama. Likewise, as a naval lieutenant in World War II in charge of a kamikaze squadron of "suicide boats," Shimao was just one radio message away from oblivion when the emperor's words of surrender on August 15, 1945, put an end to the conflict.[1] Despite Shimao's assessment, the reader of his fiction and essays is left with quite the opposite impression, of a writer whose life was amazingly rich. In many ways Shimao's life and the writings based on it form a history in miniature of contemporary Japanese experience of the past half century. In a collage of images and scenes scattered throughout what is, in effect, a lifelong saga, his fiction addresses the traumatic experiences of the war and survival, of attempts to readjust to a "normal" postwar reality, of urban life and the fragility of the newly dominant social unit of postwar Japan—the nuclear family—and the stresses and strains of both the female and male roles within it.

Shimao's fiction thus shares much with the contemporaries with whom he is often grouped, the early 1950s writers—Kojima Nobuo, Shōno Junzō, Yoshiyuki Junnosuke, and Yasuoka Shōtarō—collectively called the *Daisan no shinjin* (Third group of new writers). As Van Gessel deftly summarizes this group's accomplishments in his study, *The Sting of Life*, these writers

> passed through the inferno of complete loss—the loss of spiritual home, the ravages of war, the humiliation of defeat, and the collapse of the familial order.[2]

For Morikawa Tatsuya, too, Shimao is preeminently a representative of a single generation, the *senchūha*, the lost generation whose youth was spent in wartime.[3] As I will argue in this book, however, Shimao's work goes far beyond the boundaries staked out by these novelists and makes him one of the most fascinating and exciting of postwar Japanese writers. In dealing with war, recovery, and the family, Shimao's work coalesces on larger questions of Japan's modernity and its failures, and ultimately catches glimpses of salvation in a social—and personal—unconscious found on the margins of experience. Hidden behind the facade of a homogeneous nation marching in lockstep to economic dominance, Shimao reveals to us, is an unexpected diversity; the only *healthy* future is one that accepts—and embraces—this reality.

Perhaps surprisingly for a writer so caught up in narrating the war experience, there is much in Shimao's work that makes him a very contemporary writer, one whose works should be read as proto-postmodern: the chaotic, fragmentary, and nonlinear nature of his fictional world, its "anti-structure" stance, its irrationality, its challenge to conventional literary genres, and the juxtaposition of two or multiple worlds—the way normality and abnormality are unstable, shifting concepts, the subtle overlap of dream and reality. If, as David Harvey notes, the "most liberative and therefore most appealing aspect of postmodern thought [is] its concern with 'otherness,'" Shimao's work is thoroughly postmodern, because its appeal and power are found precisely in its discovery of the Other.[4] Speaking of Shimao's masterpiece, *Shi no toge* (The sting of death), for instance, the feminist critic Ueno Chizuko notes that, although it appears on the surface a typical I-novel, it includes an element marking it as a decisive break from this major genre, namely the "Other" *(tasha)*, who is crucial to the narrator's salvation.[5]

Shimao's fiction is generally classified into three groups—stories about the war, dream stories, and writings on the madness of his wife—a system this book follows for its first three chapters. While Japanese critics tend to treat these groups more or less independently, I see them as bound together in their search for the Other of postwar Japan: that which has been suppressed, marginalized, and silenced in postwar society (and arguably in the creation of the modern Japanese state). Shimao confronts war responsibility and trauma, the displaced and marginalized of postwar Japan (including women and the insane), and cultural difference. Through his wartime experience, the madness of his southern-island wife, and his twenty-year residency on the small southern island of Amami, Shimao discovered a suppressed diversity, a cultural unconscious antithetical to what he saw as the stagnation of Japanese modernity. His long-term study of Ryukyu culture and history, his so-called *Yaponesia* writings, placed him in the forefront of those debating the place of Okinawa and other peripheral areas on the margins. These writings, in turn, fed into his fiction, producing a series of "island stories" that explored the island and its people. And coloring all his fiction is a gradually developing style that subtly provides a meeting place for the conscious and unconscious, the rational and *something else*.

The war experience looms large in Shimao's life and work and is the subject of chapter 1. Hurriedly graduated a year ahead of schedule in 1944, Shimao, like many college graduates of the time (particularly humanities graduates), was immediately conscripted into the military, in his case the navy. Given the choice of specialties to choose from in officer candidate school, Shimao listed kamikaze duty third, but soon found himself training to be commander of a squadron of *shinyō* boats. These little-known suicide weapons were the surface equivalent of the infamous kamikaze airplanes and proved a dismal failure in combat. Assigned to an inlet on the island of Kakeromajima, halfway to Okinawa, Shimao and his squadron were placed on standby alert three times from November 1944 to the end of the war. The war experience, particularly the final three-day wait for the mission of death, became the subject matter of nearly twenty short stories, including one of the high points of Japanese war literature, Shimao's incomplete war novel, which begins with the 1949 story "Shutsu kotōki" (Departure from a lonely isle). From his earliest postwar stories down to the story he was writing at the time of his death, the war underscored Shimao's career. While many Japanese wished—and continue to wish—to confine the war to the realm of a collective amnesia, for decades Shimao insistently and painfully dissected the traumas of the war. Arguably no other Japanese writer known for war literature has so intensely examined, through a variety of literary genres (the fairy tale, the romance, surrealistic and realistic fiction), the personal and collective consequences of World War II, including the kamikaze experience. (To this day Shimao's war stories remain the only major fictional study of this experience.) Despite his protestations, Shimao continues to be read as spokesman for both the kamikaze victims and the generation of "failed kamikaze" *(tok-kōtai kuzure)*. If, as Ōe Kenzaburō maintains, even today the war hangs like a dark cloud over the Japanese landscape, then Shimao's literature, with its ruthless focus on both the victimized *and* victimizing side of Japan's wartime experience, does much to confront this shadow.

The lingering traumas of war find no better expression than in Shimao's stories of the late 1940s–early 1950s, which I examine in chapter 2. In a series of surreal stories based on the narrative logic of dreams, the best known being "Yume no naka de no nichijō," (1948; trans. 1985, Everyday Life in a Dream), Shimao propelled himself to the forefront of postwar avant-garde writers. Writing, language, experience, authority—the very fabric of contemporary Japanese life and its expression— are called into question in Shimao's dream stories. The chaotic and fragmentary, an undercurrent of repressed memories of wartime victimization, and the concern for those who lie on the social margins all belie the standard postwar linear narrative of stable progress of a nation of homogeneous wartime victims. Hovering on the horizon in Shimao's fiction of this period is an ominous note of impending doom, a vision of both a continued decay of Japan's modernity and an apocalyptic view of a future destruction that, in our nuclear age, makes his work extraordinarily contemporary. Shimao visualizes modern Japan as corrupt, stifling, and deathly. With its overwhelming desire to seek out the margins of experience and of society, to move centrifugally toward the excluded, Shimao's fiction of this period moves in unfocused, faltering steps, toward an alternative to what we know as modern Japan.

The mental illness of Shimao's wife, Miho, descended on his family in 1954, and his fiction now focused exclusively on his domestic troubles. Some critics saw this as an unfortunate "literary retreat" into the established parameters of the I-novel. On the surface this view has some merit, because Shimao's fiction at this point does seem to join that of writers of the time—Shōno and Yasuoka in particular—in focusing primarily on the fragile nature of the postwar nuclear family through examining the details of the writer's daily life. Through the mid-1950s stories of his and his wife's experiences in a mental ward, however, and especially through his sixteen-year composition of *Shi no toge* (The sting of death, 1960–1976), Shimao clearly moved beyond the narrow boundaries of the I-novel. Fiction of this experience—collectively called his *byōsaimono* (stories of a sick wife)—reflects a stylistic maturity that brings together the surreal and the real, the unconscious and conscious, in sophisticated and meaningful ways. That which has been left on the unconscious level now bubbles to the surface of consciousness: the suppressed aspirations of women, the lingering traumas of war, and most important for Shimao's work, the discovery of Otherness. As I examine in chapter 3, the *byōsaimono* are searing, haunting depictions of one woman's descent into madness and her battle to claim a self in the midst of her torment. Shimao carefully depicts the strains and inequalities inherent in the position of women in postwar Japan in ways no other male writer had done before, opening up the claims of women to a heretofore unseen legitimacy. At the same time, *Shi no toge* reinvigorates Shimao's focus on the war and its legacy. As I argue, the novel, part of what one critic calls Shimao's "literature of the victimizer," not only overturns the stance of the standard I-novel with its focus on the protagonist as victim, but shatters the postwar "victim mentality" that, as Oda Makoto sees it, stifles the possibility of real selfhood and growth for postwar Japanese. To borrow from Shimao's well-used image, his literature points toward a way out of the "abyss." A third element of *Shi no toge* indicates directions Shimao's career was to take for its final two decades. Here, the sufferings of the character Miho are intimately linked to the marginalized area from which she comes. As one Okinawan critic puts it, *Shi no toge* depicts the discovery of *place* and its importance in Miho's cure. Difference and diversity—and the tragic consequences of their suppression—became for Shimao lifelong concerns.

In his fiction and essays beginning in the late 1950s, what had been an unfocused narrative desire to uncover the marginalized now became focused on a real place and a real people—the islanders of the Ryukyu Islands. Shimao's literature of the islands—his numerous *Yaponesia* essays, his short stories set in the islands, and his last major piece of fiction, the two-part diary-like *Hi no utsuroi*—all involve the struggle to deal with the islands as Other. As I discuss in chapter 4, *Yaponesia* became both a powerful concept for those in Okinawa seeking to define their identity and a way of recovering a lost cultural diversity within the confines of all of Japan. In the words of Tanigawa Ken'ichi, in the creation of the modern Japanese state, a "multi-layered, heterogeneous" time and space were "twisted together" into a "single strand," and Shimao's *Yaponesia* points the way toward its unraveling. The broader sweep of the essays is balanced by the highly personal focus of Shimao's island fiction. Here, through the mediation of the wife (now revealed in her guise as guide and healer), the male protagonist is drawn into a variety of confrontations with the island and its people. Over a series of stories his shattered and disjointed sense of time and space are gradually restored, the discovery of the Other of the islands proving to be the impetus for him finally to shake free from the baleful influence of a stagnant and alienating modern mainland.

On a personal note, throughout the seven years I have been working on this study I have been heartened by the remarks of the critic Karatani Kōjin, who judges Shimao as one of the major figures of Japanese literature since the war. Shimao's dream stories, Karatani writes, succeed in capturing a nightmarish quality of postwar Japan in ways no other writer has done. Further, for his war literature and other work, Karatani told me, literary history will view Shimao ultimately as more important, his works more lasting, than that of his more illustrious contemporary, Mishima Yukio.[6] This book extends the argument to include Shimao's importance on a number of other levels, including that of cultural critic. As with any writer, only the passage of time will determine Shimao's place in Japanese literary history; in the meantime, I hope readers in the West will search out and discover for themselves not only the work of Shimao Toshio, but that of the myriad exciting and important Japanese writers who—as far as our collective consciousness of Japanese literature is concerned—still lie on the margins.

OnE

Self-Apocalypse:
Tales of the *Tokkōtai*

WHO WERE the kamikaze? In the West these suicide warriors have been seen as everything from fanatical, inhuman automatons to thoughtful inheritors of a "noble" historical tradition of self-sacrifice who willingly, even eagerly, gave up their lives. During World War II, unsurprisingly, the kamikaze (hereafter *tokkōtai*)[1] were viewed by the Allies as one more example of Japanese "barbarous and fanatical behavior" by which the Japanese "forfeited all right to be treated like human beings."[2] "Suicide tactics," Ivan Morris writes, "instead of overawing the Americans as had been confidently expected, produced indignation and rage" and left no compunction on the American side when it came to the decision to employ atomic weapons on civilian populations.[3] This view contrasts starkly with wartime Japanese rhetoric of purity of purpose and selfless sacrifice that surrounded much of the *tokkōtai* ritual:

> [V]irtually every act in which they engaged in one way or another connoted purity. The falling cherry blossom became the best known symbol of the young flyers, appearing in their poems, their songs, their farewell letters, and in the hands of the virgin schoolgirls who assembled to see them off on their final missions. . . . In addition to their white Rising Sun headbands and white scarfs [sic], the pilots often wore white *senninbari* or "thousand-stitch belts," long strips of cloth in which one thousand women had each sewn a stitch — and thus, symbolically, joined the men as they sacrificed themselves. They donned clean clothes for their last flights, and some units drank a ritual cup of water as a further act of purification.[4]

Wartime abhorrence in the West with what was seen as Japanese fanaticism quickly eased into postwar fascination, evidenced in the popular press with such publications as Kuwahara and Allred's 1957 book, *Kamikaze*. This book was one of a series of mass-market paperbacks designed to feed the American public's interest in the other side of the story, namely enemy exploits related by German and Japanese veterans themselves. *Kamikaze* details the brutal methods by which one young Japanese flyer is beaten into submission and total obedience. After repeated, sadistic sessions of beatings with a bat, of which Kuwahara writes, "Never in my life had I felt such pain," this young man, still a teenager at the time, remembers:

> In one week my entire life had changed—my entire consciousness of man, of good and bad, of right and wrong. . . . The initial shock had produced a numbness, a psychological paralysis. And emerging from it all was a continual dread. It was absolutely impossible to obey the injunction not to fear a superior. We became as furtive as rats that have suffered electric shock. It was impossible at first to find even one moment when we could relax. We were always crouched, awaiting the next shock.[5]

Stories like this of decent young Japanese compelled to die meshed well with the occupation, and post-occupation, narrative of the wartime Japanese not as nation of fanatics but as an essentially well-meaning, pliant populace under the thumb of a tyrannical few. Thus a distinction between leaders and led, one made for the Germans during the war, was finally applied to the Japanese.

By the mid-1970s, however, and the publication of books such as Morris' *The Nobility of Failure: Tragic Heroes in the History of Japan* (1975), the Western view of the *tokkōtai* had come full turn. No longer either wartime fanatic or well-meaning, hapless victim, the *tokkōtai* in Morris' revisionist rewriting is resurrected as the inheritor of a heroic Japanese tradition of noble self-sacrifice in a lost cause. Compulsion and brutality are replaced by the image of eager volunteers culturally conditioned to die not through corporal punishment, but rather through belief in the "Japanese metaphysics of death as expressed both in traditional samurai philosophy and in religion."[6] This rehabilitation of the *tokkōtai* in the West, not surprisingly, comes precisely at the beginning of Western awe over Japan's emergence as an economic superpower, and parallels attempts to account for Japan's dominance in cultural terms—"group think," the high value placed on education, a national stoicism reflected in a brutal work ethic, and a Confucian emphasis on social harmony.

Significantly, a substantial portion of Morris' argument rests on the words of the *tokkōtai* pilots themselves found in final letters sent home, the majority of which express calm acceptance of their situation and gratitude toward their parents. Morris never raises the issue of wartime censorship and the fact that eyes other than those of the soldiers' family would first be reading these missives.[7] The extent to which these public, bland, usually stereotypical pronouncements reflect the true feelings of these condemned men is, at best, problematic.

Interestingly, in writing of the *tokkōtai*, each side has gradually appropriated the other's wartime image. Western rewriting of the wartime fanatic into noble hero is paralleled by a decided, although still incomplete, Japanese rejection of such an image in favor of a more clear-eyed view of wartime brutalities. Ienaga Saburō's condemnation of the horrors of war in his *The Pacific War 1931–1945*, for instance, includes a scathing attack on any mythologizing of the wartime *tokkōtai*. Only a "military psychology insensitive to human life, to the individual's right to survive," he writes, "conceived the special attack idea."[8] Morris' use of the depiction of *tokkōtai* as falling cherry blossoms[9] is answered in kind by Ienaga, who conceives his task as exposing the "sordid reality behind this cherry blossom myth"—the way so-called "volunteers" were psychologically pressured to join, the ostracism and derision directed toward those who failed in their mission and returned to base, and the "terrible mental anguish" of the pilots.[10]

Fifty years after the war, understandably in a world grown edgy in the wake of continued terrorist attacks (suicidal and otherwise), the *tokkōtai* continue to hold our imagination. Yet the images of fanatic follower, brutalized victim, and heroic warrior are all incomplete stereotypes of a complex experience irreducible to a simple formula. The question remains: what *was* the reality of the *tokkōtai* experience? For all the writing on the *tokkōtai*—histories, reminiscences, interviews, and collections of letters—there remains but one sustained attempt to recreate this complex experience, made doubly valuable in its status as literary project by a professional writer who himself was a survivor of the *tokkōtai*: the war stories of Shimao Toshio. Shimao's work is particularly compelling in the way it incorporates all three of these images—fanatic, victim, and hero—as components of a shifting, multidimensional reality. Shimao's *tokkōtai* commander abhors his position while simultaneously understanding the depths of his complicity in the structure of "voluntary" death. The heroic rhetoric of the time is echoed throughout, only to be undone by the absurdity and hopelessness of the mission, as well as the *tokkōtai* commander's position as both sacrificial victim and victimizer of all around him. The tunnel vision of the Shimao narrator, so expressive of the alienation the *tokkōtai* experience engendered in the individual, as we will see, only serves to underscore the more social aspects of the *tokkōtai*—the myths and belief system that were its enabling conditions. In Shimao's literature the *tokkōtai* experience and wartime ideology of death are read as part of a repressive ethos of sacrifice, the "dark" culture of modern Japan that suppresses life in favor of death. Shimao's war literature must be read for its insights into the traumas of war, but at the same time it serves as introduction to his lifelong personal and literary search to an alternative to the dominant culture. This search takes him on an extended journey to the margins of experience, to that which the dominant ethos suppresses in order to construct itself. Voices of the excluded are filtered through Shimao's own unique literary voice, one that speaks to us in language that itself has been excluded—the language of the unconscious.

WHILE THE popular image of the *tokkōtai* is that of fighter pilots crashing their bomb-laden planes into Allied ships (or, more likely, being shot out of the sky just beforehand), a whole range of lesser-known weapons was employed by the Japanese military in similar last-ditch, suicidal tactics during the final two years of World War II. And it was to one of these lesser-known weapons that Shimao was assigned. Among them were a group of five naval weapons: *kōryū* (the mini submarines employed in attacks at Sydney Harbor and Pearl Harbor); *kairyū* (submarines one-third the size of the *kōryū*); *kaiten* (long, human torpedoes); *fukuryū* (frogmen equipped with underwater breathing apparatuses and mines on poles, used to fend off enemy amphibious landings); and *shinyō* (small wooden motorboats.) The *shinyō*, five meters long and outfitted with an inboard motor (a refitted car engine) and over two hundred kilograms of explosives in their bows, were both the most numerous of these naval suicide weapons and the least effective.[11] Some estimates say two-thirds of the *kōryū* deployed were effective against the enemy (the rate given for *kaiten* and *kairyū* is one-third, for airplanes one-sixth). On the other hand, only an estimated one in ten *shinyō* deployed ever fulfilled their mission of wreaking havoc with enemy shipping, due to its exposed position as the only surface naval *tokkōtai* weapon.[12]

The first time Shimao heard of the *shinyō* (literally, ocean shaker)—in the summer of 1944 as he and other student-corps torpedo boat trainees were asked to volunteer for *tokkōtai* duty—he imagined a high-tech "flat, steel *tokkōtai* boat in the shape of a whirligig beetle, racing along as if rending the surface of the sea."[13] The reality could hardly have been more different. Derisively dubbed "suicide boats" by Allied sailors, the boats under Shimao's command were flimsy plywood contraptions, too slow to catch retreating enemy ships, equipped with too little explosive to do an effective job, and, in the sweltering tropical heat of the southern island base, gradually decaying. Moreover, hurried and perfunctory training at mainland bases was followed by an almost total lack of drills at their island base due to the necessity of conserving fuel and fear of discovery by Allied bombers. The result was the forced absurdity of a mission doomed from the start to ineffectiveness.[14]

After his training at Yokosuka and Ōmura in 1944, chronicled in *Gyoraitei gakusei* (Torpedo boat student, 1985), Shimao, now a naval lieutenant, was slated to be sent to the Philippines to participate in a massive frontal attack in the war zone where the *tokkōtai* were most employed. As the front line moved closer to mainland Japan, in November 1944 he was reassigned to Kakeromajima, a small island just south of Amami Ōshima. Told to expect an already-built base, he instead found a placid, bucolic inlet where he and his troops had to hastily unload their *shinyō* and frantically construct shelter for themselves and their boats to lessen the chances of detection by enemy aircraft. Shimao's squad, the 18th *Shinyō* Squad, was typical, consisting of just over 180 men and nearly 50 boats, divided into four attack groups. Except for the four boats assigned to the four group leaders (Shimao being one, as well as the overall commander; group leaders had their own pilots), the *shinyō* were one-man boats. Thus the *tokkōtai* troops made up slightly less than one-third of the squad, the bulk of which were ordinary seamen assigned to remain behind after the departure of the *tokkōtai* to defend the island from enemy invasion.

From November 1944 to the end of the war on August 15, 1945, then, Shimao's mission was to prepare and wait for orders to depart on his suicidal mission—a mission that, in the words of his best-known war story's title, "finally never came." As the battle for Okinawa was fought and lost and the forward line of defense drew nearer to the Amami Islands, Shimao's squad was put on standby. Finally, they were placed on red alert on August 13, and remained poised for the final departure for the next two days, until news of the surrender reached them. In September 1945 the *tokkōtai* troops, Shimao among them, were hastily repatriated to the mainland ahead of the ordinary sailors. Shimao returned to his father's home in Kobe and six months later married his island lover, Ōhira Miho, and began his career as fiction writer.

Over a forty-year writing career Shimao produced some eighteen stories based on his *tokkōtai* experiences.[15] The wartime experience had repercussions on his writing far beyond the chronicling of wartime events and underlies much of his subsequent work: his early postwar short stories; the "dream" narratives that placed him at the forefront of experimental and avant-garde writers of the early postwar period; his series of *byōsaimono* ("sick wife stories," most notably the novel *Shi no Toge*) based on the mental illness of his wife, which brought him his greatest public acclaim; and his lifelong concern with the culture of the southern islands (his so-called *Yaponesia* writings) and their possible role as Japan's Other, a fascination that propelled him into the role of leading spokesperson for cultural diversity within Japan. Beyond his personal obsession with relating the *tokkōtai* experience (which he pursued to the end of his life), Shimao's war literature (and, as I argue throughout this book, his other literature as well) constitutes a powerful critique of the postwar "victim mentality" that marginalizes all but the experience of Japanese as victims. Shimao's argument is, in essence, a two-pronged attack, because the mentality that suppresses discourse on past victimization is the same that condones present-day victimization. Shimao, seemingly anachronistic in his focus on events of the war, is thus quite contemporary, his work a continued exposure of a story that lies at the heart of modern and postwar Japan.

The War Novel: 1949–1986

Shimao's wartime stories generally are divided into the realistic, the "pastoral," or "fairy tale-like," and the "dream-like," or "surrealistic."[16] Here I will first examine the realistic stories, in particular the three stories that, collectively, were considered by Shimao to be one linked story or unfinished novel—"Shutsu kotōki" (Departure from a lonely isle, 1949), "Shuppatsu wa tsui ni otozurezu" (The departure finally never came, 1962), and "Sono natsu no ima wa" (1967; trans. 1985, "This Time That Summer")—and the incomplete "(Fukuin) Kuni yaburete" ([Repatriation] The country defeated, 1986). Next I will discuss several stories from the pastoral and fairy tale-like, in particular "Hamabe no uta" (Song of the beach, 1945), "Shima no hate" (1948; trans. 1985, "The Farthest Edge of the Island"), and "Yoru no nioi" (The fragrance of the night, 1952). These stories, focused more tangentially on the *tokkōtai* mission, introduce the notions of myth making and the rewriting of experience and reveal a gradual politicizing of Shimao's approach. His work shows an awakening to the political dimensions of his role in the war, a turning away from earlier myth making that concealed these dimensions. In more concrete terms a lyrical, romantic narrative is steadily reworked into a narrative cognizant of the political effects of colonialism, victimization, and war responsibility. I will also briefly touch on a work of Shimao's last years, *Gyoraitei gakusei* (1985), which treats the training leading up to his *tokkōtai* deployment, and return to a discussion of three early to mid-1950s stories that introduce the vital notion of the southern islands as an unassimiliated Other.

Just days before his death in November 1986 Shimao was at work on what he envisioned as the final chapter of his war novel.[17] He finished but a handful of pages, and as the double title indicates—"(Fukuin) Kuni yaburete" ([Repatriation] The country defeated)—one detects an uncertainty, as if Shimao were feeling his way toward an ending to this lifelong project. The personal narrative of repatriation, in other words, vies with the more general tale of the historical fate of the nation. The few pages that do exist reveal a more matter-of-fact, reportorial style than the earlier chapters, more chronicle or historical record than psychological study. This orientation links the chapter less with the earlier work (the three realistic stories) than with the posthumous *Shinyō hasshin* (Shinyō departing, 1987), Shimao's attempt at a more comprehensive history of the *tokkōtai* experience based on interviews with survivors, examination of documents (including court records of war crimes trials), and visits to the sites of former *tokkōtai* bases. No doubt it is this stylistic shift to more neutral recorder that prompted Shimao's widow to undertake the completion of this final chapter herself based on notes left behind, a project that as of this writing remains unfinished. This incomplete final chapter, chronicling the period of late August and early September, covers the repatriation of the *tokkōtai* troops from their island base. Ironically, the departure spoken of in the first chapter ("Shutsu kotōki")[18]—that of the final, suicidal mission to save the nation—is displaced in the end by a guilt-ridden departure of defeated *tokkōtai* troops toward an uncertain future on the mainland, where they fear imprisonment, or even execution, by the Allied Command. Where Shimao saw this story ending, we can only guess.

The three completed stories that make up Shimao's war novel of the *tokkōtai*, written over a period of eighteen years, cover an abbreviated, albeit crucial, period of the war—the final three days, August 13–15, 1945, and the aftermath of the surrender at noon on the 15th. "Shutsu kotōki" covers the morning of August 13 to dawn of August 14, "Shuppatsu wa tsui ni otozurezu" from the morning of August 14 to the evening of August 15, and "Sono natsu no ima wa" the morning of August 16 through a few days later.[19] Yoshimoto and others have spoken of Shimao's inability to come to grips immediately in his fiction with the traumatic moment of surrender, and see him returning to this question of moving from death to life only after confronting similar traumatic emotions in dealing with his wife's mental illness and recovery.[20] Be this as it may, the 1949 "Shutsu kotōki" stops short of this moment, and it is not until 1962—some seventeen years later—that Shimao revisits the narrative to confront the crucial events of August 15.[21]

The three stories comprising Shimao's war novel can be summarized as follows. "Shutsu kotōki" opens with a lengthy inner monologue of the protagonist, the unnamed naval lieutenant of all three chapters. A long description of the "suicide boats" is followed by news of the atomic bombings, thoughts of death mixed with those of possible survival, and meditations on the mission and his role as commander. This is followed by the lieutenant's walk around the cape separating his camp from the village to see N, his village lover. The walk is remarkable because it is the first time the lieutenant has visited N during the day, and as he walks the reader is presented with flashbacks of earlier, nocturnal visits. Arriving at her home, he catches her unawares and realizes how little he knows about her, in particular what she does during the day. The description of their meeting is abbreviated but takes some time, because by the time he arrives back at camp it is already sunset. Soon afterward the message to place the squadron on standby alert arrives; the lieutenant addresses the assembled troops, then sends them out to prepare the boats for launching. Suddenly an explosion is heard in the encampment, which turns out to be a detonating charge exploding. Miraculously, none of the main charges in the boats exploded. After investigating the accident the lieutenant orders everyone to sleep, but is unable to himself. A letter arrives from N, who is waiting by the guardhouse for him. He goes to see her and tells her his squadron is merely practicing. Dawn of August 14 comes, and with it a certain feeling of relief, because the chances of a daytime departure are slim.

"Shuppatsu wa tsui ni otozurezu" also opens with an extended meditation on their mission, and death. The lieutenant feels a sense of frozen time, and a split in himself, his body happy at any reprieve, his emotions unfulfilled at this wait. We learn about the different treatment accorded the *tokkōtai*, who are allowed to sleep on as the ordinary troops tiptoe around trying their best not to wake them. Evening comes, and the villagers assemble to entertain the troops with song and dance in a final farewell. Thinking this night will be the time of departure, the lieutenant decides to visit his lover one last time.[22] He meets briefly with her (here she is called Toë) and tells her their practice is finished. Returning to the camp, he is ordered to report to headquarters; walking there, he speculates on war developments, wondering if Japan has successfully driven off the enemy. Thoughts about the planned mass suicide of the villagers is mixed with clues he sees of a changed situation: people are removing camouflage from a gun battery, and the locals he meets seem to have lost their obsequiousness in front of the military. At the main base he learns of Japan's surrender, and hears the surrender broadcast. He is ordered to keep his men on alert in case the enemy attempts to violate the truce, and wonders how he can possibly control any troops who might want to oppose the surrender by making a final, unauthorized attack. At sunset on August 15 he announces the surrender to his troops and tells them not to defuse their warheads—a direct violation of the orders he was given earlier. The final scene is an extended dialogue between the lieutenant and a noncommissioned officer who visits him; the noncom argues that officers will bear the brunt of responsibility for the war, and that the lieutenant should consider suicide. Now nighttime again, the lieutenant decides to sleep with his sword beside him, presumably out of fear of what his troops might do. He ends by considering his cooled thoughts toward Toë and a "bloodthirsty feeling" directed toward something he cannot identify.

The final complete chapter of the novel, "Sono natsu no ima wa," is remarkable for its concentration on villagers other than N/Toë. The story begins with several villagers, now seemingly unafraid of the military, demanding the return of property given to or appropriated by the lieutenant's squadron. A rush of messy, complicated details and legalities now surround the lieutenant, who had always felt every entanglement would be wiped clean as long as they left on their suicide mission.

As he put it in the second chapter, "Crashing into death was to be a release from all of the past"; now, denied the chance to die, the past comes rushing in on him: "The attack mission was to have bleached everything to transparency. Now that I could no longer anticipate such an effect, the past resurrected itself and began going through all its paces."[23] In the face of rumors flying about that the enemy army will rape and pillage, the villagers have mostly fled deeper into the hills, and in order to deny these rumors and allay their fears the lieutenant decides to read aloud the Imperial Proclamation of Surrender in the village square. As he reads he becomes increasingly emotional about the surrender, as do many of the villagers. He tells the villagers to "not abandon [themselves] to despair" but to think of "building the future."[24] In his own duties, however, the lieutenant shows great reluctance to let go of the past order, becoming easily angered at what he views as a shameful breakdown in military discipline within the squadron following the surrender. Making his rounds, he berates the soldiers' laxity, incurring their enmity all the more. The lieutenant is invited to the deputy mayor's home for a meal, and the reader views glimpses of a return to a normal routine, as well as an increasingly condescending view of the military by civilians. Meanwhile, the squadron begins the task of defusing their warheads, and as the military's task winds down, it is paralleled by increasing hostilities and tensions within the squadron. The tension comes to a head in the final scene, in which the lieutenant, shocked and angered by rumors that someone has attacked his lover, interrogates three officers who know about the incident. Harsh words are spoken and fists fly as the lieutenant struggles to cope with a hopeless breakdown in discipline.

Finally, the lieutenant is informed he will be the first officer sent back to the mainland to arrange for transportation for all suicide pilots off the island. The story ends:

> I had made up my mind to stay on the island after seeing the last of my men off to the mainland. Even were I to go back, my house had been burned, and I had a feeling that my father, the only other member of my family, was dead. Despite my resolution, though, I could not refuse to be transport officer, and since I had received no communication from the senior commissioned officer, I did not know what was happening at Sasebo Command and would have to go there at some point. Suddenly, as if a dam had burst, I wanted to go home. After I had discharged all my duties, I could come back to the island by myself. The strange incident of that morning faded like an old photograph. A desire to jump for joy welled up from the depths of my being, and I could hardly wait for the authorities to fix the schedule for our departure. But

in that case, I thought, I must go to see Toë's aged father and convey to him my intentions.[25]

Notably absent from Shimao's unfinished novel is the very event one would expect it to portray: the war itself. Unlike modern Japanese war classics familiar to Western readers—Ōoka Shōhei's *Nobi* (trans. 1957, *Fires on the Plain*) and its depictions of starving soldiers in the Philippines, Sakaguchi Ango's vivid and terrifying account of the firebombing of Tokyo in "Hakuchi" (trans. 1962, "The Idiot"), and Ibuse Masuji's account of the sufferings of Hiroshima victims, *Kuroi Ame* (trans. 1969, *Black Rain*)—Shimao's stories of the *tokkōtai* depict the actual war in only the faintest of terms: a muffled explosion far in the distance, the sound of an enemy plane on the horizon, radioed reports of the destruction of Hiroshima and Nagasaki. The physical pain and agony, the fighting and bombings, the starvation and bloodshed of war are entirely missing. Not a single Japanese dies. Physical agony is replaced by the psychological, the events and action of war by a complex mix of often stagnant time and the ever-fluid inner world of the protagonist as he waits for his inevitable end.

This orientation should not be surprising, since for *tokkōtai* soldiers war could only, by definition, be a one-time, unrelatable event. The *tokkōtai* experience, naturally, includes the death of any potential narrator of such an experience, and as such excludes the possibility of narrating. One is left with only the margins of the experience. Shimao remarks that while he experienced the daily life of the *tokkōtai* squad, he never experienced war, and thus felt torn between a desire to narrate his unique experience and the knowledge that this narration would always fall short. Shimao instead viewed himself less as a *tokkōtai* than as a *"tokkōtai kuzure"*: a failed *tokkōtai*[26] whose fate it was to narrate these margins, and increasingly to memorialize and remember—but never speak for—the dead. We detect in his stance a cautionary tone, one that should color any reading of war literature, including his own: namely, that the literature of war is always the literature of survivors, never that of war's greatest victims, the dead.

Shimao's war novel, in fact, begins with the *end* of war, a winding down of activity signaled by a weird quiet. "Shutsu kotōki" begins with these words:

> For three whole days I couldn't hear the roar of a single enemy airplane. A very unusual feeling, considering the last six months. Strangely, this made me disappointed. (234)

This sudden lack of sound only serves to highlight the text's emphasis—in flashbacks—on senses normally secondary in novels (sound, and later smell) and is coupled with an abrupt reversal of time and events, with action previously taking place under cover of darkness now occurring in broad daylight. (The presence of enemy planes made any drills or military maneuvers safe only at night, and the lieutenant's visits to the village and his lover also have taken place only at night.) A world of darkness, and of the senses associated with that state—the auditory and olfactory—gradually give way to daylight, and the visual. These changes hint at a return to normality, of a world of peace where people move about freely during the day, yet as seen time and again in Shimao's texts, normal and abnormal are problematic; here it is the abrupt change to a normal state of affairs that strikes the protagonist as most clearly odd and abnormal.

Just as the opening lines of "Shutsu kotōki" hint at the approaching end of war and a return to normality, the reader is brought up short with the knowledge that the world has entered a new age—the nuclear age—that promises even greater war and destruction:

> We'd already learned on the shortwave of the atomic bombs being dropped on Hiroshima and Nagasaki.
>
> I had no confidence in my sense of time then. Was time advancing, retreating, or standing still, I did not stop to ask. I just felt that the progress of history had stalled. Day by day I was getting younger. In other words, I wasn't getting any older. My world tapered off in the direction of the end of the southern sea. This end of the southern sea suddenly became a precipice, and the water froze darkly; dripping water plunged down this bottomless cliff.
>
> In order that I might drop off from there, every day I was getting younger. (239)

Although at first glance this passage suggests that the atomic bombing is a pointless bit of news that can in no way affect the lieutenant's inevitable suicidal death (his dropping off into the abyss), the remarkable reversal of time—the way he feels himself getting *younger* with each passing moment—carries further implications. He is, as one critic points out, already viewing himself as dead.[27] And, combined with the news of the atomic bombings and the unspoken wish that they may mean an end to the war, the narrator, then, glimpses the possibility of reversing an inevitable narrative of death—that is, he is already dead, but is moving backward toward, and finally away from, the moment of extinction. As is so often the case with Shimao's texts, however, this moment is soon countered by an opposing move, in this case viewing the atomic bombings as the beginning of an apocalypse, one in which all Japanese, civilians as well as soldiers, will perish. The narrator, heretofore straining to find meaning in his sacrifice, is released from the need to explain his suicidal mission. In this "crazy age" (Ibuse's term from his story, "The Crazy Iris") of the dawn of the nuclear age the search for meaning is itself meaningless:

> Strangely enough, the news of the atomic bombings made me feel cheerful. I could die easily now. An embarrassing thought. But secretly I felt that way, aware of a sense of guilt at not being able to tell anyone. (240)
>
> [I]n the face of the atomic bomb, all orders were no doubt nonsense.
>
> This new type of bomb had extraordinary power, and since no air defense facilities would be of any use, when the order came down from defense headquarters that all squads should take immediate precautions, I was able to laugh it off.
>
> A strange sense of liberation came over me. (241)

Shimao at times seems a backward-looking writer, one who literally until his dying day was obsessed with reliving, and reworking, the events of 1945. Some, however, such as Ōe Kenzaburō, view Shimao as very much a contemporary writer. For Ōe, himself concerned with the ever-present threat of nuclear destruction, Shimao's war stories, in particular the second passages above, create a kind of time tunnel connecting the summer of 1945 with our present-day nuclear age. Shimao does not merely meditate on the ushering in of the nuclear age in the destruction of Hiroshima and Nagasaki—a score of Japanese writers have chronicled the effects of these events more convincingly and in far greater detail. Rather, Shimao's work throughout his career continued to resist accommodation with postwar Japan; more specifically, he maintained a steadfast and remarkable sense of incongruity and dread in the face of the "normality" of our MAD (Mutually Assured Destruction) age.[28] As I examine in chapter 2, this linking of war and a continued apocalyptic vision are prominent features of many of Shimao's dream stories. He simultaneously writes of the war that was and the apocalyptic war to be. One story in particular, "Yume ni te" (In a dream), illustrates this contemporary quality, opening with a favorite Shimao dream motif, the sudden sound of an explosion and a fearful object flying through the air. In this case, a kind of "lacquered, insect-like object" appears and lands in the middle of the narrator's town. Out of the flying object come several Caucasians, holding threatening-looking cylindrical objects:

> Though this scene which suddenly appeared before me was out of the bounds of the everyday, I was overwhelmed at the graphic way in which what I had

envisioned might actually happen had materialized before my very eyes. The strength left my knees, and all I could think of was that the citizens had to quickly organize a defense group; but my thoughts raced ahead and I couldn't move.[29]

Rushing home to see that his family is safe, the narrator is confronted by his wife, who tells him they must all quickly stuff mud into their noses since it "neutralizes the poison."[30] Written in December 1962, only two months after the Cuban missile crisis, this is not merely a re-working of World War II imagery, but an abstract, yet chilling, expression of the sense of dread the missile crisis engendered. It is precisely the linking of present and past Ōe detects in Shimao's work—the dawn of the nuclear age and the eschatological crisis that continues to this day as a kind of repressed unconscious.

By far, however, the most obvious attraction of Shimao's *tokkōtai* novel for the ordinary reader is the way it answers some simple yet compelling questions: what did it feel like to be a *tokkōtai* soldier? How did one resign oneself to inevitable extinction? What were the psychological adjustments made by survivors after the reprieve of the surrender and the return to life? Shimao's stories have many answers, with the climax and boundary—Japan's surrender—coming at the physical middle of the text, neatly dividing it to give equal weight to both issues of extinction and survival.

In sharp contrast to the wartime Japanese rhetoric of youth, purity, and freshness, Shimao's *tokkōtai* world is, from the beginning, one of decay. Physical decay of the instruments of death—the *shinyō* boats as they rot deep within their dank, cave-like shelters—reflects a similar sense of a rotting away within the squadron and within the mission itself. Paradoxically in a world where one's sense of time is skewed, with one's temporal sense reversed, or stagnated, the lieutenant's conviction that there is but one genuine point when the departure can be accomplished willingly, with no self-doubt, serves as a single anchor in a world in decline. If only the order for departure can come at the opportune psychological moment, he thinks, "My life will be able to complete its ending" and everything will serve as "paean to a glorious death" *(sōretsu na shi)* (307).[31] "We, or rather I," he says, "did my best to remain true to my duty of being a glorious crew member of the suicide boats" (237). Shimao's text is liberally sprinkled with such militarist terms as "glorious death," "glory," the "beauty" of death (295), and a "death full of dignity" (306). Combined with the lieutenant's oft-stated desire to rush toward death, the casual reader might detect a nationalist sentimentality in Shimao's work, the sort of atmosphere of uncritical nostalgia latent in the recent rise of right-wing rhetoric. What makes Shimao's work so complex and interesting is that this kind of one-dimensional sentiment—the surface rhetoric, after all, of the era portrayed—is not entirely expunged from the text, nor openly challenged, as it might be in early postwar antimilitaristic assaults on the war. Rather, it is positioned so that it is negated by that surrounding it. The foundations supporting the *tokkōtai* mission here—the boats themselves, the tactics involved, the impact the mission will have on the war, the military order holding the squadron together—are all shown as corrupt and spurious while the narrator simultaneously depicts his mission in "glorious" terms. One detects here the oft-ignored sense of humor and the absurd in Shimao's writing that Karatani and others have pointed out, the way Shimao's protagonists are depicted as sympathetic persons struggling with all their might in the face of an absurd situation.[32] One senses, too, that occupation censors of 1949 (the year "Shutsu kotōki" was published), in the midst of their own mission to root out veiled militarist sentiment, felt much the same way, allowing Shimao's work to stand and readers to make these connections.

Despite this strong element of the absurd—or perhaps *because* of it—Shimao's war novel *is* a serious study of the psychology of the *tokkōtai.* How did it feel to be a *tokkōtai* soldier, condemned to certain death? Shimao's lieutenant, in his wait for the inevitable departure to death, feels foremost bound by a duty to keep a certain "promise":

> Finally the hour of the festival for us mass suicides was near. I couldn't believe our actions would turn the war situation around, but even so we loyally kept faith to our promise, a promise to whom we had no idea. We set ourselves up as victims in a tragedy, or as standing at the apex of some makeshift pyramid, darkness before us, countless instinctive antennae moving about in time and space, trying somehow to maintain our balance. (238)

A word repeated often is "weariness" *(kentai),* the weariness of the wait; as one might expect, the lieutenant has no appetite and feels his body falling apart (249). He feels alienated from both the natural surroundings of the island and from other people, as well as from himself: he experiences an internal division, his self split equally into body and mind. This divided self constantly pulls him in two directions—both toward and away from death—as illustrated, for instance, soon after the news about the atomic bombings. A single enemy plane, appearing as a sur-

real "jellyfish-like monster" in the sky, drops something silver that
flutters toward earth (which turn out to be leaflets with news of the
Potsdam Declaration). The lieutenant instantly perceives it as another
atomic bomb:

> [T]hough I expected the atoms of my flesh to be completely destroyed and
> dribble down and turn into dirt, my mind turned to unseemly thoughts of
> escape. (242)

Here, his body expects, even welcomes, self-immolation, while the mind
pulls him away from the abyss, roles that are later reversed as his mind
is set on death while his body, in its normal demands for sustenance and
rest, serves as a reminder of life.

The strong sunlight of the southern island, an ever-present reminder,
like the lush vegetation around him, of life-sustaining forces, is covered
with shadow; furthermore, his body is drained of strength, the details
of everyday life are annoying, and the day of attack is at once feared and
hoped for:

> A shadow was part of the strong sunlight; from the four corners of my vision
> the film was burnt and in the center dark soot poured in. Like the fear that
> strikes you when the ground shakes, after this time [when they should have
> attacked] passed, I lost all strength in the muscles beneath my skin; this spread
> to my whole body, and I lost all interest in life. Fearful of the day of the raid,
> I waited, thinking the sooner it comes the better; and though it had come as
> I had hoped, I was still made to wait in vain. Every aspect of living was now
> annoying to me, and all strength left my arms, as if my body temperature had
> fallen. (299–300)

The part translated as "in vain" above is actually more complex than the
English indicates. The Japanese expression *fuhatsu no mama*, literally,
"in a misfired state" (as with a bomb), is linked to both the voiced *hatsu*
in the "shup*patsu*" (departure) of the title "Shuppatsu wa tsui ni otozurezu" and the fact that the departure never came, and to the unex-
ploded state of the bombs themselves in the bows of the *shinyō*.[33] More
interestingly, this image of remaining in a "misfired state" connects this
passage with an earlier one and some subtle sexual imagery wherein the
tokkōtai soldier, denied his chance to die, is left in a state of near sexual
frustration:

> [T]here was not a single day I did not think of how I would be sucked into
> the bottom of the sea. But the movement of everything around me abruptly
> seemed to come to a halt. Like the revenge of something unseen, this threw

me into a strange state of stagnation. A spring wound up and, its purpose lost, tossed aside still tightly wound, a blood-engorged fatigue *(ukketsu shita ken-tai)* spread over me, and a frustration of not knowing where to turn blew through my body. Certainly a contradictory sense of irritation, happy on the one hand that for a while my body was off the track that led towards death, my feelings were engulfed in frustration. The completion of my goal was put off, and between the standby alert and departure lay an infinite distance, and the faces of the two were in no way similar. (294)

One feature of Shimao's war literature, indeed of all his fiction, is a strong concern with temporality and the ways in which time is both pliable and fluid, as if time is always a subjective phenomenon. This multivalency of time, not surprisingly, is a feature, too, of Shimao's dream stories, where the logic of the unconsciousness wreaks havoc with any attempt to discover a "normal" chronology of events. Even in such realistic work as his war novel, however, we witness time's fluidity. Stagnation is a key feature of time here, with the protagonist feeling captive in an endless wait for the closure of death; but the flow of time is also flexible and can reverse itself. Similar to the sense of time depicted in the above quotation, in the war novel events of the present are already seen as part of the past, an immediate distancing of self and events that further the protagonist's sense of alienation. "Weirdly," he thinks, "time stopped its progress and the events of everyday fell like they were already written down in some history book" (239). Recent events, the tenuous links of the text with the world outside the *tokkōtai* camp, are viewed as already part of long-past history. The Potsdam Declaration leaflets dropped from the sky seem like something the narrator read about in a "junior high school textbook." "Why is that stale matter brought up now, and a summary of it dropped on us from the sky?" he wonders (242). Earlier news of Germany and Japan's defeat evoke a similar response:

> No matter what happened, I couldn't be surprised by it. I couldn't grasp the meaning of Mussolini's slaughter, or Hitler's disappearance; it was nothing more than reading old items on a chart of historical events. I couldn't think at all that a history was beginning that this was a part of, and that something else would happen afterwards. My head was an intensely spiritless, blank whirlpool. Yesterday did not connect up to today, and today did not seem to connect up with tomorrow. (239)

These temporal orientations provide insight into two types of related psychological defense mechanisms employed by the *tokkōtai*. The alienation from present-day events allows the protagonist to distance himself from an unspoken event, namely his own death, and to view even his death in retrospect, much as one is able to do in a dream. Thus even this self-apocalypse can be viewed as just one more piece of "old news" from which one is disconnected. Second, the schizophrenic sense of fractured time, of independent moments in a disrupted linearity, erects a psychological barrier to admitting any connection between oneself and *future* events—in fact, it denies any sense at all of the future and the extinction that lies there. Underlying all these defense mechanisms, naturally, is an emotion the texts underscore just as much as they do the willing rush toward death: the protagonist's overwhelming and understandable fear of death and of the great void represented by the abyss of the southern sea falling away into nothingness. Paralleling such death wish sentiments as his "strange sadness" that the "cruel confusion of flesh and blood" he pictures as his death may pass him by (292) are a profusion of expressions of a more expected abhorrence and fear of extinction. The text alternates, sometimes at almost blinding speed, between the two apparently contradictory poles—the desire to die and the desire to escape, to "fly away" like some "small bird" (300). As I will show, however, death is also portrayed as a means of escape.

THE PERVASIVE sense of alienation, the distancing of oneself from events, nature, and other human beings,[34] seeing the world through the eyes of only one limited consciousness (which is the overwhelming *mood* of Shimao's war novel) only serve to reveal the other side of the story: how Shimao's war novel is very much a story of connectedness and the social—of the structures, beliefs, and myths that were the enabling conditions of the *tokkōtai* situation. The lieutenant's alienation fails to mask how he is totally involved with others and serves as a defense mechanism to deny his own involvement in maintaining the structure that victimizes himself and others and allows him to be a victimizer.[35]

The lieutenant's position and role are bound up with power and the maintenance of a social hierarchy both within the military and without. The memorable image above (see p. 21) of the *tokkōtai* "standing at the apex of some makeshift pyramid, darkness before us . . . trying somehow to maintain our balance" seems to be yet another picture of men balanced on the fearful abyss before their mission, yet the imagery speaks to other aspects of the story—the maintenance of power through force, the power of victimization, and the belief system holding this all together. This mythology is both powerful and fragile. The pyramid is that of military hierarchy, the fifty-odd *tokkōtai* members at the apex; the balance they try so hard to maintain is that of the entire wartime enterprise of which they are a part and their privileged position within it. As the lieutenant acknowledges, the *tokkōtai*'s privileged position and his own position alone at the apex of this pyramid rest on a "strange myth" *(kimyō na densestu)* of the *tokkōtai* as sacrificial victims and his own position as the first to depart as victim (238). This wartime novel, with the actual war absent and the departure never coming, in many respects is a study in miniature of wartime power dynamics—exploring the national mythology underlying the enterprise of war and, as Naoki Sakai puts it, supporting the formation of national community as a "community of 'unnatural' death."[36] The state and emperor are noted only briefly in Shimao's war stories, in particular in the noontime broadcast of August 15. Instead, the emperor's localized representative, the lieutenant himself, reads the Imperial Proclamation of Surrender aloud to the villagers and explains the terms of the surrender to the troops. The power of the imperial/state mythology is internalized within the lieutenant, in his eagerness to fulfill a "promise" to die, to race to become a victim, despite his acknowledging the emptiness of the promise and, from a military standpoint, the pointlessness of his death. Not mere fanatic, nor hero, nor simple victim, the protagonist is implicated in, and supportive of, the very system he also attempts to deny.

Underscoring this is the way in which the lieutenant (as with many Shimao protagonists) is carefully positioned *in-between*—as a character who partakes of both being victim and victimizer. This one aspect clearly distinguishes Shimao's work from that of other Japanese writers of the war who, in the words of Oda Makoto, portray only the "literature of the victim."[37] Ōoka's starving Private Tamura, Ibuse's A-bomb-scarred Shigematsu and Yasuko, even Sakaguchi's Izawa and his idiot companion fleeing the flames of a burning capital are clearly positioned as victims, even tragic victims, of war.[38] Unlike the mindless militarist title figure, say, of Ibuse's "Lieutenant Lookeast," who is the mere conduit for an ideology from above that he does not doubt in the slightest, Shimao's lieutenant is recipient of *meirei* (orders) from above, producer of *meirei* himself, and conscious converter of *meirei* into *unmei* (fate)—the process by which political imposition of one's will on another is naturalized. In other words, one will die because it is one's "destiny." Shimao's contribution, in short, is the way he opens up a literature of victimization. Many critics have discussed how the story of Shimao's lieutenant and his island lover are a rewriting of Amami island mythology of the Nirai Kanai god from across the sea who comes to rescue the island in time of great need.[39] That Shimao—so absorbed in the legends and folktales of Amami—was cognizant of the outlines of this myth is a given. What is most illuminating is how these critics emphasize the positive side of this "god"-like figure to the exclusion of the negative. Whereas the lieutenant's ostensible mission was, like the god in legend, to sacrifice himself so that others may live, in the realities of 1945 Kakeromajima his protective powers are overwhelmed by his power to *destroy*. As one soon pieces together from the war stories, the lieutenant has control over who will live and who may die among the *tokkōtai* (as he can decide the order of departure), as well as among the villagers. In the case of the villagers, the *tokkōtai*'s departure will not signal the salvation of the island, but rather its total annihilation, because the villagers, mainly the elderly, women, and children, are assembled in trenches to await their mass suicide.[40]

Plans for mass suicide of civilians were not uncommon at the time, the slogan "*Ichioku tokkō*" (literally, "One-hundred million as special attack [fighters]") reflecting how this became viewed as part of government policy. Mass suicides took place throughout the Okinawan campaign, a period, in Shimao's words, in which Okinawan civilians feared the Japanese military as much as—or more than—they did the enemy.[41] As one Okinawan writes:

> Japanese strategists essentially sacrificed Okinawa to free more resources for the defense of the Japanese mainland. Okinawans were dragged into a losing battle, which reduced the whole Ryukyu chain to ruins. Citizens, who should have been protected to the last, were the first to die. . . . More than 150,000 islanders—one-third of the entire population at that time—were killed. The number of Japanese regulars killed there was less than half that number.[42]

Perhaps the most infamous example of mass suicide (after the war, *shūdan jiketsu*, "group suicide"; during the war, *gyokusai*—a "grandiose militaristic euphemism signifying the 'crushing of jewels'"[43]) came in March 1945 at Tokashiki Island, some twenty miles off mainland Okinawa near a *tokkōtai shinyō* base much like Shimao's. As one survivor, a child at the time, recalls, grenades distributed to the civilians did only part of the job:

> Those who had blades, or scythes, cut their wrists or severed arteries in their necks. But we didn't do it that way. We might have used a string. When we

raised our hands against the mother who bore us, we wailed in our grief. I remember that. In the end we must have used stones. To the head. We took care of Mother that way. Then my brother and I turned against our younger brother and younger sister.

As this survivor recalls, the *tokkōtai shinyō* soldiers, denied the opportunity to attack the enemy because of the swiftness of the American offensive, fled into the hills: "The residents committed suicide quite early, gathered in one place as if they were mice in a sack. On other isolated islands, where there were no soldiers, there were no group suicides."[44]

Iwaya Seisho has pointed out the importance of Shimao's 1970 "Naha ni kanzu" (Thoughts on Naha) in understanding his feelings toward Amami, its people, and his role in the war.[45] In this essay Shimao notes his shock at reading in the newspaper of a former army lieutenant, back for the first time in twenty-five years, who stops at the Naha airport on his way to his former wartime post, Tokashiki, to attend a memorial service for the victims of the mass suicide discussed above. The man is met by demonstrators protesting his visit because he had ordered some three hundred villagers to die. Although Shimao notes his difficulty in understanding the man's motives for returning (perhaps, he thinks, the man returned there to die), he notes that, "What hung over my thoughts was the notion of how the man's environment in the war and my own too closely resembled each other."

> In the same Ryukyu chain, he was at Tokashiki and I was at Kakeroma. What's more, the villagers who lived near our squad had dug air-raid shelters to take cover in when and if the enemy landed, and which in the end, they understood, would be where they destroyed themselves. For instance, even after the *tokkōtai* squad took off and the squad left behind was separated from my directions, the fact remained that those strange air-raid shelters had been dug with the help of our squadrons.[46]

After ruminating on how very easily he could have been in the other lieutenant's position—if he had departed on his mission and had been taken prisoner, for instance—he notes:

> But did he really think he could go over to Tokashiki Island and take part in the memorial ceremony without anyone accusing him? Did he really believe that deep down? No way that I could comprehend this, I fell into a deep, dark chasm.
> But no matter what, a strange embarrassment made my body hot, and a dark self hatred made me crumple up, and there was nothing I could do about it. Something was so ugly I couldn't stand it. When I tried to think about what I would have done in his shoes, I felt even more despair, and this situation, too, was ugly, a thought I couldn't escape.[47]

The mass suicide planned for the villagers is mentioned only briefly in Shimao's war novel, with the lieutenant noting only that according to rumor the villagers would "commit mass suicide (*jiketsu*) by blowing themselves up" (313). Shimao Miho, a survivor of the ordeal, recalls the two sides of the real-life Lieutenant Shimao: both the idea many villagers had of him as their "guardian deity" and the darker, more malevolent side. Whereas the lieutenant had the power to protect the village, he also, as with gods, had the power to destroy:

> It had been arranged that after the suicide pilots had departed on their mission, the men of the island, in cooperation with those left on the base, would take up their bamboo swords; the young women had been instructed to serve on the battlefield as nurses; and *the elderly, the women, and the children were to gather in one place and commit mass suicide*. This was to be done in a U-shaped tunnel in the valley near the barracks, which the unit and the villagers had joined forces to dig. The order to assemble in that tunnel was given late on the night of 13 August, and the people came, resolved to die. But the Shimao squadron remained on standby alert all that night, and they were still there to greet the dawn. One more night passed, and the war was over.[48]

As if unable to confront this directly in the war novel, Shimao makes this traumatic experience known tangentially in other areas of his literature, and it underlies an intense sense of guilt directed toward the people whose lives the real-life Shimao controlled. The dream-like 1949 story, "Asufuaruto to kumo no kora" (Asphalt and the baby spiders; see chapter 2), finds the wartime narrator attempting to stop a similar mass suicide. The 1959 story, "Kawa ni te" (discussed in chapter 4), is set in an island river, where the narrator bathes with the villagers, only to be overwhelmed by his guilt and dread that his "past" will be revealed—engendered by seeing this group of women and elderly gathered in a group. And in one key section in *Shi no toge* the wife, Miho, describes a vivid and frightening dream she has had that, in part, reveals the nightmarish scene of villagers dead in a hole in the ground (see chapter 3).

Although Shimao's war novel mostly eludes the entire possible mass suicide, in some mostly unsubtle ways we learn of the lieutenant's desire that others may suffer as he does, and even die as he will. An old farm couple, for instance, scrambles fearfully into their bomb shelter as he watches from above: "It felt good to watch this couple," he notes, "wrinkled austerely by time, tremble at the sound of bombs" (252–253). The lieutenant hands his lover a dagger; in "Shima no hate" this is a cross-like, religious symbol, but in the war novel it is given to her for the obvious purpose of self-destruction. The lieutenant's feelings for his lover, one can imagine, are the most complex of all. As with himself, he desires her both to die—and live:

> N. All I could imagine now was the figure of N, hair all disheveled, half-crazed. For some reason the only thing I could picture was N, shameless and mad. No doubt she would fall victim to the fires of war and lose her life. I wanted her to die. But I also hoped that, like a weed, she would tenaciously live on. (273)

Yet despite his desires he recognizes the realities of the situation: N will fall victim to himself and the military he heads.[49]

And, as we have seen earlier, news of the atomic bombing brings with it relief that *everyone* will die. If everyone would perish in the war (civilians as well as soldiers), the lieutenant's own death would become easier, since he no longer would be singled out to die while others remained behind.[50] And with the power he has over the village, on a localized level he does not need to wait for this to happen, but can instigate it on his own. The lieutenant recognizes that it is fully within his power, on the microcosmic level of the village, to imitate what happened at Hiroshima and Nagasaki by ordering total death and destruction.

Although the mass suicide never occurs, this does not mean the wartime relationship between the military and the villagers was entirely one of potential, but never actualized, victimization. Suppressed resentment bubbles to the surface as soon as the wartime order begins to break down. This is most clearly depicted in "Sono natsu no ima wa" in the immediate aftermath of the surrender. Much of this story depicts the sudden changes in relations within the military itself, too, and between the military and the civilians under its jurisdiction, all of which the narrator sees as the beginnings of an uncontrollable collapse *(kuzure)* of order, a collapse he himself resists. In the opening scene of the story, even before the lieutenant has assembled the villagers and read the Imperial Proclamation of Surrender, the villagers' attitudes have changed:

> The next morning, I noticed a man from the village, standing in the assembly area directly below headquarters, facing the inlet. I walked by him, but he gave no sign of acknowledgment. His dull complexion, his broad but thin shoulders, his gravity and solidity oozed defiance. He wore a torn undershirt, and his almost equally shabby trousers were a little too short, exposing spindly legs and bare feet. His very appearance seemed a demonstration that he could withdraw no further from the spot. Something that would have

been unthinkable until yesterday was happening here, I thought, with a mixture of annoyance and fear. (31)[51]

The villager had come to get back two boats that had been lent to the
squadron. As the officer on duty notes:

> In the space of a single day here they are already demanding we return their
> boats. They're only thinking of their own self-interest. The instant they re-
> alized we had been defeated, they started talking as though they were taking
> a loss by letting us use the boats for one more hour—it makes you wonder
> why they lent us the boats in the first place. (31)

This matter of returning the boats is just the beginning of the collapse
in the power relationship between military and village, with the military having now lost the "power to refuse." Its "secret" off-limits base
can now be freely breached, boundaries have collapsed, and even the
question of the legality of their entire confiscation of the inlet—in fact
their present and past raison d'être—looms on the near horizon.

The changed attitude and exposed resentments of the villagers toward the military in the first half of the story are paralleled by the increase of repressed hostilities *within* the squadron itself. The narrator
must deal with fanatics who still want to attack, soldiers spreading rumors about the violence the Allies will commit against the village (as
one soldier comments, "All those guys can think of is what they themselves did in China"), and sullen, uncooperative soldiers who ignore his
orders. He fears smoldering "misunderstandings and collisions of temperament among men from various regions of the country" and feels
"at a loss how to deal with this atmosphere of tension in which the four
flotillas . . . in total one hundred and eighty-four men—might at any
moment spring into independent action."[52] All around him he sees the
collapse of the order maintained during the war, and he feels powerless
to stop this: "I was afraid that my authority with the rest of the men
might be undermined, but I could do nothing now to offset my loss of
dignity" (44). He has the "desire to stand firm, to rebel against the soft-
ening current [he] felt beginning to rush through" him (44).

This "return to the everyday world" (36) brings with it a host of
complications the commander had hoped his suicide mission would
wash away. "The attack mission," he notes, "was to have bleached
everything to transparency. Now that I could no longer anticipate such
an effect, the past resurrected itself and began going through all its
paces" (51). One personal aspect of this past, of course, is his relation-

ship with his villager lover. "There was the expectation," he notes, "that our inevitable departure [on the attack mission] would sooner or later wipe out all traces of my misconduct" (36). His misconduct involves having abandoned his post nearly every night in order to pursue his affair with a woman, always with the knowledge that the vital orders to attack could come in his absence (a dereliction of duty). Now he must face this misconduct, as well as the more legalistic aspects of the male-female relationship he has entered—aspects that also should have been "bleached to transparency" by his final mission.

But much more significant than negotiations over boats and love affairs is the additional burden the lieutenant must bear, now that the war is over and he has failed to die. As local representative of the Japanese military and state (and emperor), he must also be one of those who bear responsibility for the course of the war and its consequences. In a scene near the end of "Shuppatsu wa tsui ni otozurezu," just after the troops hear of the surrender, one of the lieutenant's noncoms visits him:

> "Commander, are you planning on returning to the mainland?" he said, suddenly lowering his voice.
>
> "...."
>
> "*The responsibility for the war is something the officers will have to bear.* Noncommissioned officers are not responsible. *That's what it means to be an officer. That's why officers have had special privileges.* It doesn't matter that you were an officer for just a short time, or that you're a reservist; sorry to say it, but you have to take the responsibility as an officer. And the Americans will definitely try to hold you to that. I've been in the military for a long time so I know this is true. You'd better prepare yourself. All the officers may end up punished. Unless they do that, such a large-scale war like this won't be settled properly." [53]

In the war stories the past, which death will obliterate, includes guilt at dereliction of duty, of having "used" N and the villagers, of being a "phony" protector, of being in a position that gave him the power to victimize others to the point of ordering their deaths. All of this, however, is acceptable to the lieutenant as long as he can sacrifice his own life. As long as he becomes a victim in the end, the slate will be wiped clean, thus the shock that, ironically, surviving the war brings: "The life to which I had submitted in total earnest, obediently surrendering my body to preparations for a suicide mission, now seemed like a counterfeit, a phony." [54] This is not merely the shock of the sudden reversal of common sense and logic brought on by the abrupt end to the war. It is also his shock at realizing he must now live with the responsibility for his part in the war—that the slate of the past *cannot* be so easily wiped clean. Time and again Shimao's work reminds readers of what they wish to forget—the issue of war and responsibility.

In wrestling with this issue, Shimao's *tokkōtai* lieutenant remains, in the end, a complex figure. Just as the militaristic vocabulary of a "glorious and beautiful death" is negated by the absurdity of the death these words purportedly describe, the lieutenant's seemingly transparent death wish is not the simple acceptance of the wartime ideology of death. In almost mantra-like fashion, the reader is reminded repeatedly that he seeks death for one overriding purpose: to *flee* from entanglements of "everyday life." Suicidal death, then, can be turned to his own purpose, as the only possible escape from the structure of power and victimization in which he is totally implicated. And paradoxically, when he is unable to die, with military discipline and order quickly beginning to collapse, he desperately seeks to maintain this order. By keeping a lid on the seething forces and desires the system (of which he is a part) keeps suppressed, then, he can deny its oppressive nature. Powerless to change the system of oppression, he can only die. Denied death, he is left only with the power of denial.

Three Pastoral Stories: "Hamabe no uta" (1945), "Shima no hate" (1948), "Yoru no nioi" (1952)

If Shimao's war novel is his attempt to deal in a decidedly realistic manner with the crucial events of August 13–15, 1945, a second strand of stories of the *tokkōtai* deal with the war in a very different fashion. This group, the "pastoral" or "fairy tale"-like, is identifiable by its lyrical, romanticized content, and in some cases by a pared-down style more appropriate to a children's story than to a modern psychological novel.[55] There is a formal distancing in these stories absent from the war novel, a shift from the immediacy of the first person to that of the third, and a distancing between the time of events and the time of narration. The war novel, most of which was written some twenty years after the war, returns to a stylistic immediacy to relate events of the past. In contrast, the pastoral stories—written only a few years after the war's end (and in one case *during* the war)—maintain a discrete distance from recent events. "Shima no hate," the best known of these early stories, opens with an introductory sentence set off from the rest of the text: *"Mu-kashi, sekaijū ga sensō o shite ita koro no ohanashi na no desu ga—."* The English translation—"This story takes place long ago, when the whole world was at war"—fails to capture the way this opening echoes the standard beginning of Japanese fairy tales: *"Mukashi, mukashi,"* "Long, long ago." "Hamabe no uta" opens with a separate frontispiece that reads *"Hamabe no uta—Ashita hamabe o samayoeba mukashi no koto zo shi-nobaruru,"* translatable as "Song of the beach—If tomorrow I wander the beach I will recall things of the past." The sense of past events is further reinforced by the somewhat archaic grammatical ending, *shinobaruru*, as well as by the structure of the first sentence of the story, *". . .ga ari-mashita* ("there was a . . .")—which, like the opening of "Shima no hate," is a standard rhetorical device of fairy tales.[56]

Why this deliberate distancing from recent events? As Kawamura Sō argues, the traumatic events of the *tokkōtai* experience produced in Shi-mao the need to "create myths and legends out of reality" as one way of dealing with them.[57] The trauma Shimao suffered first had to be filtered through other modes of expression, other genres—here, the mythic, in the next chapter the dream-like and surreal—before it could be brought to the surface and directly confronted. And indeed to a great extent Shimao's fiction follows this trajectory. One should be cautious, however, not to understand trauma as wholly a personal and individu-alized sense of alienation brought on by a sentence of death followed by a last-minute reprieve. The intensely subjective, alienated perspec-tive of Shimao's war novel does not fully mask, and in fact is an incom-plete attempt to neutralize, the social and historical forces at work—forces of victimization, exploitation, power, colonialism, and national ideology—and the ways in which the individual has internalized and acts on what he abhors. This internal division is the mark of the Shimao protagonist's trauma.

Trauma has many effects in Shimao's stories—distancing of events, mythologizing and romanticizing experience, and recoding experience in the language of the unconscious. Here I would like to examine the second group of effects by looking at three early war-related stories: "Hamabe no uta" (1946), "Shima no hate" (published 1948), and "Yoru no nioi" (1952). As I will argue, in the reworking and rewriting of ex-perience Shimao moves from myth to hard reality, with "Yoru no nioi" standing as the link, or transition, between the pastoral and the more realistic.

"Hamabe no uta" (1946)

Most *tokkōtai* soldiers left behind final letters to family. Shimao left behind a story. Fittingly, one can see "Hamabe no uta," the one story actually written during the war at the *tokkōtai* camp at Kakeromajima, as his substitute last will, a final statement from this self-styled "literary youth." Almost entirely mute on the subject of the war, and presenting an overly romanticized view of the *tokkōtai* life, one wonders how Shimao intended this story to be read. With its overall simplicity of style and purity of emotion the story conforms well to the predominant wartime public persona of the *tokkōtai*. Yet, seen as a substitute final *tokkōtai* letter, the story's focus on the lyrical, the feminine, the life of the villagers who were treated as marginal, even suspect, incomplete Imperial subjects—all at odds with the wartime rhetoric of *bushidō* (the samurai ethic) and *yamatodamashii* (the "Yamato spirit")—makes it a form of willful verbal protest, through exclusion, of all the *tokkōtai* supposedly stood for. One could argue that wartime censorship precluded any mention of the wartime situation, let alone even a hint of criticism, and that how Shimao intended the story to be read is unimportant because, unlike his other stories, "Hamabe no uta" was written for an audience of one and never intended for publication.[58] Nevertheless, Shimao's exclusion of this story from the 1962 edition of his Collected Works is doubtless because, like his critics, he saw his later story, "Yoru no nioi," as essentially a more polished rewrite, as well as a strategic move to substitute a more clearheaded view of the grim realities of the war and the *tokkōtai* for one that ran the risk of aestheticizing it.[59]

The pastoral stories bring to the forefront what in the war novel is a parallel, but understated plot: the relationship between the lieutenant and his island lover. The war story is reworked into the romance genre. The focus shifts substantially as the island is highlighted instead of the war; instead of the *tokkōtai* soldiers, we experience the islanders and their lives. The war novel, of course, does not ignore the lives of the villagers nor the lieutenant's lover. In the opening of "Sono natsu no ima wa," for instance, with the surrender the villagers literally make their appearance, coming down out of hiding in the hills and confronting the military with sudden demands. Likewise, a running subplot of the novel is the lieutenant's concern for his lover and his visits to her. In "Shutsu kotōki," as the lieutenant makes his way around the cape separating the base and her village and is sprayed by the sea's waves, he suddenly shifts from the stagnant, eerily quiet base, a place where he is alienated from his surroundings, to the natural world. Likewise, catching sight of her for the first time in daylight, crouched in her house wearing a slip and chewing on brown sugar candy, he realizes how she is able momentarily, unlike himself, to be oblivious to the war.

Shimao sets up a clear dichotomy in his war stories: the *tokkōtai* base as place of constriction, of death and alienation from nature, and the village as the opposite—a place of freedom, life, and closeness to the natural world. It is in this sense that one should read the recurring motif of the lieutenant's journey toward the village. At one point he labels these trips a *michiyuki*; it is, in fact, a "reverse *michiyuki*"—a reversal of the classical sense of this word found in the Tokugawa period plays of Chikamatsu, that is, the journey of two lovers toward a rendezvous with double suicide. In Shimao's works the recurring *michiyuki* is a journey not *toward* death, but *away* from it.

"Hamabe no uta" opens with one of the most lyrical depictions in Shimao's entire ouvre. For readers accustomed to his usual dread of the outside world and dissociation with the natural world, the opening passages come as something of a shock—especially considering the time and circumstances of composition. The story begins with an extended description of the island and its inlets, of other far-off islands "like paintings," of the sound of the waves and the "rustle of the pines along the peaks"—enough to make anyone there "feel as if in a dream" (9)—while in the villages themselves the waves gently lap at the shore, illuminated at times by the glow of phosphorescent creatures, and the laughter of children is heard behind the high shrubbery of the homes (10).[60] The idealized, romanticized view of the island and village, told in the simple style of a folk tale, is an attempt both to expunge the war and to view the situation not from the military standpoint, but from that of the villagers. Both attempts are only partially successful, because the shadow of war, found in the dislocation of the islanders lives, lies just below the surface, just as hidden among the lyrical descriptions of the setting are hints of the fate of both the villagers and the *tokkōtai* in war: under the moonlight, the two villages look "exactly as if sunken on the bottom of the blue, blue sea" (10).

The narrative next shifts to the simple plot of the story, again through a deliberate distancing. This section begins: "*Sate, itsu no koro datta ka* . . ." (Well, when was that, exactly . . .) (10). The story centers around dislocations brought about by the military's presence, focusing on the village children and their problems walking to school over a new road built because the old one was summarily closed to secure the camp from easy outside access. The plot concentrates on one small girl, Kiku Keko (Keiko) and her relationship with the lieutenant. Initially disliking him because she and the other children must now walk a longer, more difficult path to school, she gradually grows fond of him. The story implies greater dislocations. Disruptions of daily routine brought about by the military's impact on the adult population, indeed the village as a whole, are left unexamined, as is a larger issue: the fact that the military's presence on the island does not *create* a secure zone, but rather makes the island a military target and puts the lives of the islanders in jeopardy.

All of these issues are ignored by the simple story of the lieutenant's and Keko's growing affection for each other. The lieutenant teaches the children military songs *(gunka)*, which they readily take to, and the villagers decide their earlier suspicions of the military are unfounded, and hold a party to entertain the troops. These types of parties *(imonkai;* literally, consolation meetings) are mentioned frequently in Shimao's war stories and were the only official times groups of soldiers, banned from fraternization with the villagers, could officially disport themselves with the locals. In "Hamabe no uta" this party is an idyllic feast, a pleasant mingling of two cultures with "unusual southern country food" and drink, music on snakeskin samisen, and local dances (15–16). This contrasts greatly with the later story, "Shuppatsu wa tsui ni otozurezu." There, this sort of gathering is rewritten in a grimmer, darker tone. As the *tokkōtai* are on standby for departure, the villagers come to entertain the troops briefly one final time. As the lieutenant notes, it is not the soldiers trained for death who should be pitied, but the villagers: "Rather it is they, without special privileges *(tokken mo motazu ni)*, who are facing the fear of death unarmed, who should be comforted" (302). Just as the lieutenant feels split in two, so too are the villagers: their faces as they dance are a contrast of smiles and sadness in their large eyes, and in the gathering darkness their eyes seem to him to grow larger and larger, overwhelming the forced smiles. The villagers are divided in another way: "unarmed" *(sude,* literally, naked hand) before death, they are also barefooted *(suashi,* literally, naked feet), a state that comes to represent, in much of Shimao's writings on the islands, an idealized innocence and physical grounding in one's surroundings. As they dance, the villagers' "unrestrained" continuous movement hints at a way out of the stagnation the lieutenant feels. In "Shuppatsu wa tsui ni otozurezu," as if to leave no doubt concerning the ultimate fate of the villagers, Shimao fills the leave-taking between them and the soldiers with Buddhist death imagery. In the fading light the villagers row their boat to the far shore, the glow of the setting sun behind them as they head to the west, the direction of the Buddhist afterlife (304–305).

In "Hamabe no uta," after another performance for the troops by the island children at the local school, the lieutenant gives presents to Keko, whose lyrical dancing so impressed him. This marks the beginning of their friendship, the unusual attachment of adult to small child so common in Shimao's stories. Knowing Shimao's other war stories, one is tempted to see the sweetness and fragility of the child as a contrast to the horrors of war awaiting the lieutenant and thus as an attractive escape for him, a point made more apparent in "Yoru no nioi." Here, however, this is an unwarranted projection, because the story is marked by an almost complete erasure of the wartime mission, of which the reader learns nothing other than that the troops are always busy with their "work." What one *does* learn is the background of Keko and her family, a description that serves to enhance the fairy tale-like mode of the story. They are originally from Satsuko Island, which, legend has it, was visited by angels, a fact accounting for the ability of Keko, indeed all the children from that island, to dance and sing so impressively. Thoroughly taken with Keko, the lieutenant invites her to go with him to visit her teacher, Mie-*sensei*, who lives in the main village. They set off across the hill separating Keko's village (a smaller one closer to the base) from the main village; along the way, Keko rides on the lieutenant's shoulders. He questions her about her dancing and singing, and about the island dialect. After a short visit with Mie, they set off for home; Mie loads them down with roses from her luxuriant garden, and continues to send roses to the lieutenant until his room is filled with them and her garden is empty. "Hamabe no uta" ends as it begins, both lyrical and entirely reticent about what is really at stake:

> All of a sudden the Kiku family of Nijinura went back to Satsuko Island. On that day Keko-chan got on a little boat and went out of Nijinura inlet. The commander stood watching all the while from the shade of an *adange* tree. Keko's big eyes were full of tears.
>
> Not too long after the Kiku family returned to Satsuko Island, the commander and all the soldiers in Nijinura were gone. No one knows where they went to.

> On moonlit nights, in both Ujirehama and Nijinura, the owls cry out
> *Kuhou, kuhou*, and the plovers on the beach flicker about. The end.

"Shima no hate" (1948)

If "Hamabe no uta" is a fairy tale, "Shima no hate" is a romance. It is also
a far richer blend of elements—scenes from the earlier story, sketches
of scenes that appear in the later war novel, elements of island shamanism, local myths and legend, and Catholic belief. Of equal importance
is the way the story introduces the realities of the war in the midst of
a lyrical island setting, as if "Hamabe no uta" and "Shuppatsu wa tsui
no otozurezu" had somehow collided and merged. The story presents a
speedier version of events depicted later in the war novel, minus the
psychological insight into the lieutenant (here named Lieutenant Saku).
Instead the focus of such insight is on the island woman, the lieutenant's
lover, here called Toë.

Toë is both child and woman. The elements of purity and sensuous-
ness divided between two female characters in "Hamabe no uta" are here
combined into one, with an emphasis throughout on what Kathryn
Sparling calls her "pure, almost mythical" characteristics:[61]

> One could say that Toë lived among the roses. . . . All day long Toë's sole
> occupation was to play with all the village children. They came barefoot,
> gathering in Toë's garden, and she taught them songs. . . . Nobody knew how
> old Toë was, but she looked extremely young. Her head was round like a little
> bird's, and she was plump and girlish, although she weighed remarkably
> little.[62]

The reader is told, too, that something about Toë sets her apart: "Among
the people of the village, both children and adults, there were many
who thought that Toë was fundamentally different from themselves."[63]
Toë's difference rests in certain powers she seems to possess that make
her very much a *yuta*, or Amami shamaness;[64] like a *yuta*, she lives alone
in an "isolated sacred dwelling" and possesses "extraordinary auditory
and visual powers." As Sparling writes:

> [B]y putting her ear to the sand on the beach Toë can hear the lieutenant's
> footsteps all the way up the mountainside, and his conversation with the
> watchman at the pass; and somehow or other she knows about the torpedo
> boats hidden in the caves and of the squadron's secret mission.[65]

To this one should add Toë's extraordinary knowledge that the lieutenant, whom she has never seen, will appear; she is waiting for him
with fish dinner ready just as he makes his entrance. As *yuta* Toë is very

much in keeping with the figure of the shamaness who, in the Nirai Kanai legend mentioned above, is the propitiation between the savior god and the islanders, becomes his mistress, and ritually sacrifices herself to join the god in the Nirai Kanai paradise.[66] Other legends add to the richness of this text, in particular the *kenmun* legend of a malicious goblin.

Obvious Christian elements and symbolism abound in "Shima no hate" as well, which is not surprising considering the heavily Catholic population of Amami and surrounding islands. The fish Toë offers the lieutenant is merely one element, a Christian symbol whose association with resurrection makes it appropriate for those about to perish. The dagger the lieutenant presents Toë is another, which she holds "reverently, like a cross, to her breast" as she waits for the departure and death of her lover, who, Christ-like, will give up his life for others. Much more obvious is the leather-bound book, a present from her dead mother, that Toë presses to her cheek as she "prayed to God." The "two narrow intersecting strips of cool gold" are enough to identify this as a Bible, but Shimao leaves no doubt: "That she did this, Toë never revealed to a soul. She was certain she would be told that these were the teachings of an evil Western religion, the enemy's religion" (23). Christian islanders were often rounded up and berated by the military stationed in the islands, hence the secrecy of Toë's practice, which is more evidence of the *in-between* nature of the characters in Shimao's war stories. The islanders, suspect imperial citizens, strain to accommodate themselves to the military, to speak "correct" standard Japanese and hide their "enemy" religious beliefs, and the lieutenant is torn between his Yamato duty (death) and flight—his *michiyuki* toward the island and life.

The language of "Shima no hate" certainly contains elements of "pristine storybook language,"[67] but overall one is reminded less of a child's story than of classical Japanese *monogatari* tales such as *The Tale of Genji*. The story is structured with the interplay of poetry and prose so characteristic of the *Genji*, combined with such strong motifs as the waiting woman, night visits of the socially higher-ranking male lover who must protect his position by concealing the tryst, the leave-taking at dawn, and the frequent exchange of letters. One passage that gives flavor to this text is as follows:

> Suddenly, Toë felt like cursing everything. Why, why, why? Why must he turn his back and leave her? Once, the lieutenant had stayed with her too long. When he saw that the Morning Star already shone over Kyanma Mountain, he turned away and went as fast as he could up over the mountain

pass back to the base. Hadn't she then waited, and waited, lingering in the village square, her eyes on the red earth path up the misty mountainside, hoping to catch sight of him

> On Toë's shore the morning mist
> On the sleeve of his uniform the crimson stain
> Of tears of parting

And the tears welled up anew and rolled down her sleeves. Even Toë was dimly aware that the enemy was coming. She knew why the lieutenant could no longer come to visit her, and she knew only too well what the lieutenant would do when the enemy finally came. (23)

As the final line indicates, the awful realities of war begin to encroach on the idyllic, romantic, and mythologized world of the island—as if the lyrical world of the *Genji* were gradually overrun by the brutal world of *The Tale of the Heike*. The war, however, is still muted, unlike the opening of "Shutsu kotōki," where details of the mission, the boats, and wartime strategy are discussed in almost laconic, objective fashion, as if Shimao were sketching out a military history of the period. In "Shima no hate" Shimao very painstakingly, step-by-step, allows the realities of the war and their mission to intrude upon the peaceful setting of the beginning. Especially to those readers unfamiliar with Shimao's wartime background, a real sense of mystery pervades the text. What is the mission of the soldiers? What exactly is hidden in the caves? The text entices one forward with the promise of answers to these questions, but ultimately leaves the reader half satisfied. One imagines the suicide boats themselves being slowly dragged out of the deep caves where they had been lined up one after another, the bow of the first craft just about to jut out from the entrance when the curtain falls. We first hear of these caves when the squadron is ordered to build a revetment in front "to protect their contents from bombing" (13). "Soon the order would come, and the contents of those caves would be set to water; he and his men would climb aboard and dash themselves against the enemy boats" (15). Toë, as already seen, has intimations of what is to come: "Don't go. I know. I know what you're hiding in the caves. I'm scared. Toë is scared. I know about the fifty-one men" (21). In fact, the word "boats" is first mentioned only at the very end of the story: "Even after the revetment in front of the caves had been completely removed and the boats inside were ready to embark at any moment, much time had passed" (27). Likewise, an image from "Hamabe no uta" reappears, this time unmistakably linked with the coming death and destruction:

Each night when he had soothed Toë and was on his way home, he came to the foot of the banyan tree at the pass. A strange voice from the village below lingered in his ears and stopped him in his tracks. It put him in an unusual frame of mind, *as if the entire village were submerged beneath blue waters and the sorrow of the people of the village crystallized into the cry of a curse.* Presently, very faintly, like methane gas bubbling up from the depths of the pond, the voice assumed the tones of one young girl gone mad, insistently transfixing the youth who was crossing the pass and leaving the village behind. The voice echoed on and on in a melody like no music he had ever heard. The lieutenant put his fingers in his ears and hurried on, but the melody was still with him. It was Toë, who had run barefoot down onto the beach and was singing, singing "I shall never see my love again." (21; emphasis added)

It is these sorrows and cries of the village people that Shimao's work now begins to discover.

"Yoru no nioi" (1952)

"Yoru no nioi" combines elements of the other two pastoral stories. The story is a rewrite of the plot of "Hamabe no uta" with a pronounced awareness of the war, glimmerings of which are seen in "Shima no hate." In short, "Yoru no nioi" transforms the lyrical "Hamabe no uta" into a more realistic narrative, as fully cognizant of the political dimensions of the war as "Hamabe no uta" is willfully ignorant of them.[68]

The title, much like those of the two earlier stories, holds the promise of yet another lyrical, pastoral narrative. Other Shimao stories lead us to assume that the "fragrance of the night" is that of the local flowers, so redolent in the village, or perhaps of the sea. This fragrance, however, is a divided phenomenon: "Not just the fragrance of the tide—the night held another smell, but what it was I could not tell" (362). Within the fragrance of the natural world, the world of the island that pulls the lieutenant (here named Kiji) away from his mission and death, is a competing odor—the very stink of death he wants to flee. This "other smell" he ponders turns out to be that of a dead, burnt U.S. airman shot down and killed, still detectable in the woods (370). This smell, in turn, mingles with other competing smells—his own body, the fragrance of the *hamayū* flowers, the alluring smell of his woman's (Rie) body, like the fragrance of tatami and incense mixed together with that of the native plants. This complex mixture of odors, then, which together make up the "fragrance of the night," is emblematic of the text as a whole, a rich compilation of the idyllic, alluring aspects of the island and the cruel realities of war and the lieutenant's position within it.

The plot of "Yoru no nioi", nearly identical to that of "Hamabe no uta," is simple: the lieutenant, who has taken a liking to both a little girl (here named Keiko) and her teacher (Ikai *Rie* here, not Mie as in the earlier story), carries the little girl on his back over the hill separating the *tokkōtai* camp and the village. Together they visit the teacher and are given a gift of flowers when they leave. Here, however, the resemblance to "Hamabe no uta" ends, with "Yoru no nioi" taking the bare bones plot and adding a rich layer of flashbacks in the lieutenant's mind. All of this demonstrates how, even in his self-styled "moonlit night *michiyuki*," the war and its effects—"the sorrow of the people," as "Shima no hate" puts it—is something he can never escape.

In the series of flashbacks that constitute the main action of the story, the reader is shown the realties of the war: the relations between the military and islanders, the cruelty of the Japanese military, discrimination within the island community, the desire of some islanders to assimilate, feelings of guilt, and death. In "Hamabe no uta" the islanders were represented by a little girl, their language by a series of onomatopoeic words and simple words for objects she teaches the lieutenant. Here, the islanders are adults, with names whose readings are carefully delineated with *furigana*, and who are given a language and a voice with which to speak. One sees here the beginnings of Shimao's attempt to introduce the island language as an unassimilated Other within the text, with several untranslated sentences phonetically spelled out and left to (somewhat) stump the mainland Japanese reader.[69]

Lieutenant Kiji's moonlit *michiyuki* to the village is punctuated by flashbacks to the hard realities of the time. He recalls first his deception of the islanders, telling them that the island will not be attacked, but that if it is he and his men can easily defend it; this belies his knowledge that an attack is imminent and his boats hopelessly unsuited to defense. Unable to drill because of the fear of being detected by enemy planes, his men have spent their time planting potatoes, and Kiji has serious doubts about their abilities (366–367). Kiji next recalls a young girl, Mitsuko, whose father had leprosy, and how the other island girls did not shun her, but were fearful of holding hands with her during dances. Mitsuko, it turns out, is the lover of a sailor in Kiji's unit who, for fraternizing with a village girl against orders, is publicly beaten at Kiji's order. Both incidents underscore Kiji's feelings of duplicity, both toward the villagers and his men, the latter because as he recalls the beating he is on his way to visit his own island lover. In his position he can flaunt the rules, yet must severely punish those who break them.[70]

The enemy is present as never before, in the form of a young pilot shot down over the island and killed as his parachute gets entangled with his plane. Kiji recalls the entire incident, his feelings of "terrible regret," and the particulars of the pilot himself, and for the first time in a Shimao story the enemy, too, is given a name, a face, and a history. Kiji recalls his name, Norman Witledge, found inside the pilot's notebook, and the postcard addressed to him, signed "your beloved, Mary" (370). Feelings of guilt on Kiji's part—the dominant emotion in the story—come to a head with thoughts of the dead pilot, and the resistance of some of the villagers (especially the troublesome village "intellectual," Mori) to having him buried in the village graveyard. In the end the pilot's wooden grave marker is thrown into a stream by someone, and Kiji is left with the frightening thought that, with the pilot's spirit thus unsettled, his severed hand may be walking around, too, ready to seize Kiji (372).

The story, indeed, is heavily populated by spirits of all kinds, all out to punish or chastise Kiji. Islands in the distance appear as evil spirits, while fallen leaves look to him like the "eyes of evil spirits" *(mono no ke no me)* (378). The *hamayū* flowers in Rie's garden are not part of the "sweet sour smell of vegetation" that pulls him toward the village, but instead now resemble the faces of people—the faces, we take it, of the villagers who, because of the military's presence, have been forced to abandon their village to live like animals in "evacuation huts" deep in the hills. The sounds of the owls around him, too, have been transformed. In "Hamabe no uta" the *kuhou, kuhou* cry of the owls that ends the story—the island dialect onomatopoeia Keko taught the lieutenant—is more than just one element of a lyrical scene. With the military gone, the island has returned to its former state, where the language of *its* people is the way to describe its realities. Here in "Yoru no nioi" the owls are something different. As an explosion is heard far in the distance (the war edging closer), the sound of the owls hooting is now a "depressing sound." Rie's eyes, "like those of an owl," reflect the sadness of herself and her people at the edge of extinction (379). From a fairy tale return of the island to its "natural" state we have moved to the edge of the island's total annihilation.

Thus "Yoru no nioi" is everything "Hamabe no uta" is not: any potential lyricism is quickly engulfed by the realities of the war. Shimao has set up, then deconstructed, his dichotomy of village as life/base as death, because both are portrayed as inexorably bound together. Every natural phenomenon holding the potential for escape turns back on the lieutenant, and respite from brutality, subjugation, and victimization is nowhere to be found.

Gyoraitei gakusei (1985)

Very late in life Shimao returned to his wartime experiences to produce two works that, taken together, complete his literature of the *tokkōtai*. *Gyoraitei gakusei*, a realistic, autobiographical account of his *tokkōtai* training, recounts the decision to volunteer for the *tokkōtai* and assignment to Kakeromajima, and brings his personal story full circle.[71] *Shinyō hasshin* (Shinyō departing, 1987) is a piece of reportage, the result of Shimao's investigation of former *shinyō* base sites, interviews with survivors, and readings of official documents.

At first glance *Gyoraitei gakusei* is a disturbing work.[72] The figure of the young ensign (the narrator), fresh and healthy, proudly wearing his new naval uniform (which makes him "strong"), quietly absorbing lectures on master swordsman and tactician Miyamoto Musashi and then, like all his fellow officers, rather calmly deciding to volunteer for the *tokkōtai*, comes uncomfortably close to the image of serenely stoic warriors projected by Morris in *The Nobility of Failure*. Shimao, however, quickly fills in the picture, reminding us that the *tokkōtai* experience was far from one-dimensional. His protagonist here is a complex character, irreducible to a simple formulaic type of fanatic, victim, or hero.

Repeating strategies employed in the pastoral stories, Shimao moves from a dichotomy of nature versus war to a collapse of the two. The natural scenery surrounding the narrator at the training base (at Ōmura Bay in Nagasaki) seems "eternally unmovable" and leaves him confused; death in war, and war itself, are unnatural occurrences at variance with the stolidity of nature. The mountains around him are like a "Japanese-style painting" *(Nihonga)*, and call up pleasant memories of childhood. They are, in fact, his past and indeed his country, yet dying *for* them (for Japan) is a betrayal *of* them, a "death opposed to nature" *(shizen ni han-suru shi)* (94). Soon, however, the nature versus war opposition begins to melt away, with the scenery an active reflection of war and his situation as suicide cadet. The "dark gray" *(nezumi iro;* literally, rat color) scenery, "squatting as if asleep," becomes a narrow bay with an even narrower outlet to the sea. There is no exit; he and the other cadets are "trapped like rats" *(nezumi)*, haze surrounds them, and the sleepy scenery invites one to "eternal sleep"—namely, death. At the end of the story, gazing down at a fishing village and the sights and sounds of ordinary life *(nichijō)*, he thinks:

> The ordinary rose stifling in my heart, and sorrow bubbled up at the ruptured thought that I could never go back again. While somewhat comforted by the croaking voices of the frogs, whose number had increased markedly, I found myself wanting to feel this contemplative sound as mysteriously enveloping the strange position I had chosen for myself. (105)

In a very short space the narrative moves from questioning the wartime enterprise to a feeling of helplessness in the face of it, to a desire to mythologize (make "mysterious") the path one has "chosen" for oneself. This complexity of emotional reaction makes *Gyoraitei gakusei* much more than the nostalgic, simplistic memoir it first appears to be. The same complexity, as seen before, marks the bulk of Shimao's war stories, and achieves for it a very special place in the annals of Japanese—and indeed world—literature on war.

War and Place: (Re)Discovery of the Margins— "Tatakai e no osore" (1955), "Hoshi kuzu no shita de" (1955), "Sotetsujima no jifu" (1950)

Read against the grain, Shimao's war stories are important for one further, often-neglected reason: they depict the genesis of an encounter with an Other on the margins of Japan. The eleven months spent stationed in Kakeromajima became Shimao's introduction to an unknown world, one he continued to explore in fiction, non-fiction, and in his daily life until the end of his life. Amami and the southern islands—and Shimao's lifelong coming to terms with the diverse, the alien, the marginal that these islands represent—are the enabling conditions of the bulk of his fiction. In the pastoral stories this encounter is seen in a shift of attention away from the wartime mission and to the protagonist-village relationship. "Shima no hate," as we have seen, opens up an alien world of island shamanism and folk belief, and it and other stories juxtapose the cold stoicism of the *bushidō* ethic of death with the welcoming warmth and life of the village. In a story such as "Yoru no nioi" Shimao depicts the first pair of oppositions (village; island ethos) being overwhelmed by the second (base; mainland ethos). However, much of his later work remains an extension of the protean search for the truth of the island, the desire to break through to the "heart" of the village—

the very antithesis of the mainland—glimpsed in the midst of war. Shimao himself, as well as his fictional protagonists, are forever on the road to this discovery, all of which begins with experiences of war.

In early 1955, in the midst of the marital discord depicted in *Shi no toge*, Shimao wrote a pair of war stories remarkable for two reasons. First, they rewrite the wartime experience to erase the island lover. This move is understandable considering the obvious parallels between his life in Tokyo ten years after the war, with an outside lover in whom he escapes the stagnation and decay of home (his new "base" of operations), and the way this reversal of roles (Miho, the former lover now standing for decay, and even death) has compounded his wife's misery. The second, and here more relevant, reason is the way in which these two stories—in the midst of Shimao's own discovery of the Otherness of his own wife and her alienation from life on the mainland—revisit his wartime encounters with an alien culture.

The first story, "Tatakai e no osore" (Fear of fighting) underscores in its title the strong motif of many of his stories (war stories or otherwise)—the protagonist's dread of death.[73] I have suggested that death, while depicted as the more commonsensical natural abhorrence of extinction, is at times an almost welcome escape from the "everyday," the system of oppression the protagonist seeks to escape. This fear of death, however—an overwhelming emotional register of Shimao's work—is symbolic of much more. In essays and interviews Shimao speaks of his desire to escape the "dark way of thinking" of mainland culture, "dark" being shorthand for the entire stoic, humorless, samurai-based ethos of post-Meiji Japan[74] that culminated in the *tokkōtai*. Thus the obsessive nature of his *tokkōtai* protagonist's concern with death, and his trembling and dread in the face of it, are not just a reaction against the mainland ethos of sacrificial death in the name of the state and emperor, but by extension, against the central culture in general. Despite some attempts at a heroic stance toward the mission, Shimao's wartime protagonist, with his hypersensitivity, his dread of death, and his complete lack of confidence, is, in the end, the very antithesis of the stereotypical *bushidō*-motivated warrior. Shimao's work might be read as a running commentary on the excessive pronouncements of his early literary rival, Mishima Yukio, whose neo-samurai posturings ended in his own farcical *seppuku* suicide. Mishima, in short, rejected postwar Japan for its *lack* of the ethos centered on a stoic "tradition" of emperor-centered self-sacrifice, Shimao for its lingering *presence*. This is evident throughout Shimao's later, non-wartime-related works, where the discovery of the imminence of "death" in everyday life highlights a dominant culture he viewed as stagnant, stifling, even death-inducing.

Amami, although historically controlled and suppressed by one of the more militant Tokugawa-period realms (Satsuma han), absorbed very little of either Buddhism or *bushidō* and remained, for Shimao, a potential site of freedom from repressive aspects of the mainland ethos. The kernels of such thought lie in his wartime experiences. The repeated motif of the lieutenant's *michiyuki* toward the village, seen yet again in "Tatakai e no osore," and the varied iterations of this motif in later stories, express the desire to turn one's back on the mainland (which equals stagnation and death), and toward the more positive promise held out by the island (which equals life). Shimao complicates matters by clothing the island village in constant darkness. Logically one would expect a movement away from "dark thinking" to be toward *light*. On a practical level this reflects the fact that Shimao himself was only able to visit the village, and his lover, at night. The darkness enveloping the entire wartime island, however, stems from the presence of the mainland ethos, in the guise of the military. The reading of the emperor's surrender proclamation, after all—the last gasp of the mainland ethos—ends with the words swallowed up by a final darkness. And it is only with the surrender, and the collapse of the *tokkōtai* myth, that the village is revealed for the first time in brilliant daylight. As seen in later works, particularly the *byōinki* and *Shi no toge*, this light/dark opposition is between the shadows *(kageri)* of Miho's madness on the mainland and the "cure" that lies in returning to a place without shadow *(kageri no nai)*—her southern island home.

"Tatakai e no osore" is yet another reworking of the simple plot of "Hamabe no uta" and "Yoru no nioi"—the lieutenant's affection for the little girl, Keiko, the trip over the hill at night to visit her teacher in the village—that adds an evening get-together *(imonkai)* between villagers and the military. Here there is a playful, and significant, reversal of roles, with the lieutenant exchanging uniforms with an ordinary seaman and being lightly struck with a bat, all the while crying out and reciting a verse in "island song" *(shima uta)* style. Besides being in island dialect (the first time the Shimao lieutenant has used this), the song introduces several island beliefs: the idea of a *tachigami*, a protective spirit of sorts, usually of someone close, and *ikimaburi*, the spirit of someone who is about to die. One senses, in short, the lieutenant's growing knowledge of both the language and beliefs of the island. At the same time, the obvious carnivalesque role reversal, the symbolic thrashing of the actual commander, speaks to both the frustrations of the sailors and to those of the villagers. The lieutenant, placing himself in this situation, leaves unspoken his desire to flee his mission and to identify with those over whom he has the power of life and death. This sentiment is echoed later, in yet another lyrical description of the nighttime village, when he ends by wondering whether he will "be forgiven" by the village (263).

The second 1955 war story, "Hoshi kuzu no shita de" (Under scraps of stars), traces the protagonist's movement from unawareness of his surroundings to a strong sense of nature, the village, and the differences between himself and the island—and finally to a realization of his ignorance. A series of strange events in the spring of 1945 (strange signal fires, a belt washed up on shore with foreign writing, the sound of an unidentifiable flute) mark the island as the site of mystery, the unknown, a foreshadowing of the appearance on the island of a mysterious man, the character Ginsei. The lieutenant and his cohorts, hearing rumors of the sudden appearance of a suspected spy on the island (part of a "dangerous thought group"), set out to investigate. Their confrontation with Ginsei, who turns out to be a local villager returning to settle an inheritance, constitutes the main plot of the story. The lieutenant and his officers, thinking they are rousting someone who does not belong on the island, come to realize *they* are the ones who do not belong. The narrator (the lieutenant) feels pulled by the village, its night sky and stars so unlike the ones of his hometown (285):

> What made me feel even more a foreignness about the village was the figures of the trees which grew in profusion, ones I was unfamiliar with. Roots hanging down, all twisted together, and shrubs with strong-smelling fruit, the inner part half revealed; all of these enveloped the village and called forth a sweet sensuousness—as if they were an enticing liquor I had never tried. The world was so full of things I did not know. (284–285)

In his interrogation of Ginsei a stark contrast is drawn between the lieutenant, who feels himself a "robot," bound by duty, and the independent, proud Ginsei, insulted by the interrogation and by the military's ignorance of the ways of his island. A lengthy section of this encounter (where Ginsei takes them to see his wife in her evacuation hut) is in Amami dialect, left untranslated, thus placing the reader in the lieutenant's position—feeling entirely out of place, yet pulled in by the strangeness of the words. The lieutenant feels drawn by the life of this couple and is swept by a desire to enter their hut and their lives, yet the dialect words and Ginsei's attitude strike him as "an announcement of resolute refusal." "You have nothing to do with the fate of the people of this island," he interprets the subtext of Ginsei's words. "In no sense of the word can you understand these people. There is a deep chasm separating you and them" (288). He badly wants to speak to Ginsei on his own level and is struck by feelings of emptiness and dissatisfaction and a desire to escape his mission (290). He ends his investigation, his senses reinvigorated and attuned to his surroundings, yet he is painfully aware of the gulf separating his life of waiting to die from the lives of the villagers.

Finally, "Sotetsujima no jifu" (The affectionate father of the sago palm island, 1950), although attracting almost no critical attention, is important in how it hints at the directions Shimao saw his fiction taking, and the ways in which the wartime experience and subsequent exploration of Ryukyu culture were to overlap and find voice in his fiction.[75] Written in a light, sometimes humorous, style, the story (listed as an unfinished work in the Collected Works) is a series of separately titled vignettes depicting a variety of village characters and their interaction with the military. An extended description of the "sago palm" island opens the story and clearly focuses attention not on the war, but on the island. (The sago palm is an important symbol of the southern islands, and significantly the sole illustration on the slipcover of Shimao's final Collected Works.) Here the "affectionate father" is an old village man, Bunshu, who lovingly cares for orphaned children and is concerned about the young soldiers. The main action of the story revolves around the soldiers roasting and eating the sago *(sotetsu)* palm berries, and their subsequent illness. Sago palm berries can be poisonous, particularly when eaten raw, and southern islanders, in times of great poverty, were sometimes driven to eat them.[76] Here the soldiers, thinking the berries are "heavy bomber" versions of the gingko nuts they are used to (242), fall ill, and Bunshu laments to one of the orphan girls, Rie, that the villagers should have taught the soldiers everything about the island beforehand. Thus he invites four or five of the ailing soldiers (including one named Shūkichi) to his home for dinner so he can teach them village customs. In the final vignette the soldiers are walking over the hill separating their base and the village toward the dinner party:

> Under the light of the noonday sun the scattered houses of the village, like some living beings, looked as if they were clumping up together, growing nearer. And in the sighs from that dark clump, there was a Shangri-la *(tōgen*

no kyō) actually existing, waiting there in one spot for Shukichi and the others. (247–248)

Unlike Shimao's other wartime stories, this *michiyuki* to the village takes place in the bright glare of the sun, the soldiers heading toward the light of the village. Rather than a tale of mutual suspicion, resentment, guilt, or fear, "Sotetsujima no jifu," in an unashamedly open way, depicts Shimao's idealized relationship between island and mainland: that of teacher and pupil, of gently prodding mainlanders from a state of ignorance to an encounter with the unknown lying on the margins of their existence. As I will argue, the thrust of Shimao's career lies precisely in the exploration of these margins.

On November 10, 1986, while carrying boxes of books to the study of his new house in Kagoshima, Shimao turned to his wife and told her of his plan for a new novel, one he had been promising his publisher for ten years. As Miho remembers the conversation:

> "Miho, I've finally worked out the idea for the novel," he said. "This New Year's let's go to Okinawa and I'll start writing it."
> "Is it going to be a long one?"
> "Well, a little long."
> "500 to 600 pages?"
> "No, much, much longer. The kind of novel I've never written till now."
> "Is it about dreams?"
> "Well, all kinds of things. It'll be a new-style novel." [77]

Only moments later Shimao collapsed from a brain hemorrhage, and in two days, at the age of sixty-nine, died. What kind of "new-style" novel had he planned? Based on interviews over the years it seems clear he very much wanted to write a novel set in the islands, one centered on a village and the life of various people there—one, in other words, like an extended version of "Sotetsujima no jifu." One can only imagine what Shimao had in mind, but one thing remains clear: like a magnet, Amami and the southern islands drew him back to the intersection of war and two cultures. As I will trace in the chapters to come, from a failed self-apocalypse came the beginnings of a rebirth.

TwO

Dreams and the Alphabet of Trauma

> I want to succeed in writing works of a living
> person. This seems like a spell for me. For
> people to understand me clearly, there must
> first be a greater sacrifice.
>
> Shimao Toshio, 1953

The Alphabet of Trauma

IN THE lexicon of postwar Japanese literature, dreams and the work of Shimao Toshio are nearly synonymous. In a burst of creativity just after the war (1946–1948) Shimao wrote eighteen stories, twelve of them dream narratives, that is, short stories based on the logic of the unconscious. Several of these, most notably "Yume no naka de no nichijō" (1948; trans. 1985, "Everyday Life in a Dream"), have become modern classics.[1] Shimao continued to use the unconscious as a major source for his literature throughout his career. In addition to some thirty stories classified in one way or another as dream stories, he wrote essays on dreams, lectured widely on dreams and the unconscious, and even published two volumes of dream diaries: *Ki mu shi* (Record of dreams, 1973), and *Yume nikki* (Dream diary, 1978).

Okuno Takeo's often-repeated statement that he "staked the future direction of Japanese literature" on Shimao's literary dream project is indicative of the high regard with which critics generally held these early stories.[2] While the stories created Shimao's reputation among the lit-

51

erati as a critically admired "writer's writer," among the general reader-
ship they created an image of a difficult avant-garde writer more concerned with literary experimentalism than the reading public, a reputation that was to follow him throughout his career.[3] The early 1950s
Daisan no shinjin (Third group of new writers) closely associated with
him—Yoshiyuki Junnosuke, Shōno Junzō, Kojima Nobuo, Endō Shū-
saku—soon went on to both critical and public acclaim. However, Shimao would wait until late in his career for acclaim when he adopted a
style even more subtle than the dream stories, a complex mix of realism
and the surreal, coupled with themes the other writers had successfully
exploited: closed-in male-female relations (Yoshiyuki), *shishōsetsu* like
details of domestic life and recovery from crisis (Shōno), sympathetic
characters in time of war (Kojima), and, albeit muted, a concern for
faith and religion (Endō).[4]

Why dream stories, and why the profusion of them at one time? One
answer lies in what Tom Wolfe calls the "damnable problem of material," the notion that "literary genius, in prose, consists more on the
order of 65 percent material and 35 percent talent."[5] As a writer who
felt constitutionally incapable of constructing "tales" *(monogatari)*, Shimao throughout his career found material for fiction a particular problem, and dreams proved a convenient well of inspiration. Weaving together remembered scenes from dreams, often in one sitting, produced
a manuscript, he discovered, of just the right length.[6]

A second answer lies in the influence of Kafka. As Shimao writes in
his essay, "Honyaku bun de yonda Kafuka" (Reading Kafka in translation, 1949), soon after the end of the war he found Kafka's approach to
writing, and his dream-like stories, a revelation. Kafka, it is said, "became a major writer when he discovered his dream narrative,"[7] and the
same can be said of Shimao. Having read a portion of "The Trial" in
translation soon after the war, Shimao was drawn to character Joseph
K's dream-like "field of vision." "Narrow and abrupt" though it was,
this vision held an appealing "symbolic meaning" that, for Shimao,
who was obsessed with the search for ways to connect inner and outer
worlds, provided a model for his own fiction.[8] Intriguing parallels, too,
can be found between Shimao's method of composition and Kafka's.
Kafka wrote "The Judgment," the first story he considered a success, in
one night, "in a kind of seizure in which his ordinary constraints and inhibitions fell away so that the story seemed to write itself."

Only so could Kafka write. What he abominated was "constructions," the deliberate contrivances of the calculating consciousness. . . . Inspiration meant the spontaneous expression of his more intuitive, more unconscious side, with its truer grasp of reality, with its grasp of the hidden living rather than the mentally constructed reality.[9]

Shimao has spoken of his early dream stories as written, much like Kafka's, in an "extremely spontaneous way" *(hijō ni shizenhatsuteki ni)*— "Matenrō," for instance, was written in one night.[10] He also spoke of his inability to construct "tales" turning toward a more active dislike of constructions, what Shimao labeled his "anti-structure stance."[11] Like Kafka's characters, the typical Shimao character is obsessed with being judged and feels as if he is on constant trial. More specifically, one finds interesting similarities between Kafka's "The Judgment" and Shimao's "Yume no naka de no nichijō." Most likely coincidental,[12] these are nevertheless striking—the obsession with a friend's plight, the mounting father-son quarrel (a "Freudian cartoon" of the Oedipal complex),[13] and the final scene where the protagonist leaps into a river to escape.

Shimao's ideas on dreams in some ways overlap with Kafka's and in other ways differ. Kafka saw the inner reality of the unconscious as "truer" than that of the conscious: "For him . . . the dream is the opposite of the hallucinatory, it is truth-telling and creative—the dream reveals the reality."[14] Like Kafka, Shimao also viewed the world of the conscious as a site of bondage; dreams, however, are less a "truer" reality than an escape from the conscious world. Dreams lack "tension" *(kinchōkan)*, contain a "loosening of relentless choice" *(sentaku no kibisha ga yurunde-iru)*,[15] and are a way to escape the fear of daily life, the fear of death and impermanence.[16] Dreams allow escape from the fear of death because one can view oneself as dead, then survive to view this death. One can also escape the fear of impermanence because dreams reveal "ancient genetic information," a kind of collective past of which one is a part, yet which survives the individual.[17] The escapist function of dreams, however, does not mean that Shimao, like Kafka, necessarily valorized the reality of the unconscious *over* that of the conscious. After an initial period of dividing his works into two types—those written "with eyes open" and those written "with eyes closed"—Shimao rejected that distinction, concluding that both are equally a person's "reality."[18] Dreams were, to Shimao, on par with waking reality as valid experience, and with the passage of time one experiences the collapse of a distinction between the two, both dream and reality being equally part of the "totality of experience," both "inner and outer," Shimao sought to grasp.[19] In terms of his literary project, then, expressing this total experience "in a style which is neither dream nor reality" became Shimao's own "unfulfilled dream."[20] The opening lines of one of his first dream stories, the 1947 "Matenrō," might be read as a statement of the sense of overlapping dream and reality Shimao hoped to develop:

> I had no idea what country this piece of work was from, or what it was called, and I'm even unclear whether or not I actually saw it, but by closing my eyes, or rather by feeling they were closed, I was able to complete an intricate piece of work right before my eyes.[21]

One of the major issues raised in this book, in fact, revolves around this very point. As I discuss below, Shimao's style did indeed evolve into one in which dream and reality are inseparable, with this evolving style inseparable from Shimao's political stance—his desire to find a point of contact between the mainstream and that which has been confined to the margins.

A third answer as to why there was such a profusion of dream stories immediately following the war lies in the experience of the war itself. As argued in chapter 1 (see p. 33), the traumatic events of the *tokkōtai* experience produced in Shimao the need to "create myths and legends out of reality" as one method of coping.[22] Thus Shimao's early literature, in which the war is the direct setting or theme, often takes the form of pastoral prose that rewrites the war experience as love story or island idyll or, in the case of more realistic fiction, effectively deflects many of the tragic realities of the war. Arguably, only with the 1952 "Yoru no nioi" (a rewriting of the idyllic "Hamabe no uta") does Shimao begin realistically to confront the grimmer aspects of his war experience. This, in turn, anticipates Shimao's war fiction of the 1960s, which takes up where "Shutsu kotōki" left off and finally begins to address questions of postwar survival and related trauma in a realistic manner.

Wartime trauma thus has many effects in Shimao's early stories—the distancing of events, the mythologizing and romanticizing of experience. To these I would add the recoding of experience in the language of the unconscious. Before Shimao could more directly confront his war experiences (including the surrender and the aftereffects of war), he explored ways of dealing with them in a muted, symbolic, dream-like fashion. One thinks, for instance, of events surrounding the surrender and its aftermath, the questioning of his own "right" to survive, first written about in the 1949 dream story, "Asufuaruto to kumo no kora" (Asphalt and the baby spiders), and only some fourteen years later in the more realistic "Shuppatsu wa tsui ni otozurezu." A number of interpretations have been posited for these early dream stories. They have been seen as part of modern literary experimentalism; as revealing a nightmarish quality of life in postwar Japan; and as a deconstruction of the early postwar debate on subjectivity *(shutaisei)* over a reconstituted, politically responsible individual self.[23] For the most part, however, critics have been curiously silent on attempts to interpret these stories in light of war trauma.[24] One is tempted to ask an obvious question: what sort of stories would we *expect* a *tokkōtai* survivor to write? The answer, I believe, is stories like Shimao's early dream stories. These dream stories, I will argue, must first and foremost be read in the context of a literature of trauma, as attempts to work through the experience of the war and its aftermath in what Kali Tal calls "the alphabet of trauma."

As Elaine Showalter has ably demonstrated, the psychological effects of war on veterans are profound. Writing of World War I and "shell shock," she notes that the causes and effects included

> emotional disturbance produced by warfare itself, by chronic conditions of fear, tension, horror, disgust, and grief; . . . war neurosis was "an escape from an intolerable situation," a compromise negotiated by the psyche between the instinct of self-preservation and the prohibition against deception or flight, which were "rendered impossible by ideals of duty, patriotism, and honor."[25]

Wandering, and the desire for flight or escape are all major motifs of Shimao's early dream stories. The form of male hysteria Showalter identifies as the "body language of masculine complaint, a disguised male protest not only against the war but against the concept of 'manliness' itself"[26] manifests itself in Shimao's stories as both a pervading sense of self-loathing and a physical dissolving of the male body. Further, Showalter notes a strain of "psychic anxiety" that characterized post-World War I literature and literary Modernism, particularly impotence as a central image; such anxiety and impotence are prominent features of Shimao's stories as well.[27] Finally, Showalter comments on the similarities between powerlessness and the subsequent neurosis men experienced in war, and the everyday domestic roles of women.[28] In Shimao's opus this conjunction of the female role, powerlessness, neurosis, and the war comes to a head in his 1977 masterpiece, *Shi no toge.*

In our own post-Vietnam War era, "post-traumatic stress syndrome" has replaced the term shell shock, yet the traumatic effects of war remain equally devastating. Tal, writing of the Vietnam War, the literature it produced, and trauma, argues that a necessary distinction, one ignored until now, should be made between war literature by veterans and non-veterans. War literature by non-veterans is the "product of a literary decision" in which "war is simply a metaphor, a vehicle for their message." In contrast, combat veterans' literature is the "necessary rebuilding of shattered personal myths"

> and demonstrates the unbridgeable gap between writer and reader and thus defines itself by the impossibility of its task—the communication of the traumatic experience.[29]

The veteran, and the veteran-writer, Tal argues, remain "liminal types" whose "symbolic production," based on the traumatic experiences of war, is "readable only to those familiar with the alphabet of trauma; what [the symbols generated by liminality] represent is not common knowledge, and, in fact, symbols that commonly represent a particular idea may be drastically transformed within the mind of the liminal type." Tal gives as an example the "symbolism in the Holocaust survivor's description of a bread oven" being "entirely different from the same invocation by a non-traumatized author."[30] Furthermore, "[t]he problem with traditional literary interpretation is that it assumes that all symbols are accessible to all readers—that the author and the reader speak a common language when in fact they do not."[31]

As Tal's example of the bread oven indicates, overlap *can* and *does* exist between the symbolic world of the trauma survivor and others. Although ordinary readers cannot fully fathom the images and memories such an ordinary item would resurrect in a trauma survivor, enough is shared—through language and historical knowledge—to allow the reader at least partial access. Tal recognizes this point, qualifying the "inaccessible" nature of this type of literature by stating that the "untraumatized" reader who has "paid careful attention to the events upon which these symbols are based" is indeed in a position to interpret them correctly.[32] Shimao's dream stories, I would argue, are part of a literature of trauma as Tal has described it, yet are not as inaccessible as the above might suggest. Here I would like to attempt what critics have not, that is, learning the "alphabet of trauma" with which Shimao worked, and decoding his symbolic world. Shimao's "obsession" with connecting inner and outer worlds, his desire to find a point of contact between dream and waking worlds, bode well for such an "impossible" task, as one attempts to find a common language to help the reader gain access. It must remain, however, an attempt, and never a complete reading. Even so, certain motifs and themes recur with enough frequency to allow us to build a rudimentary lexicon—everything from overt war references (including references to the *tokkōtai*), to wandering, the search for victims, visions of apocalypse, psychological transference, feelings of guilt, and a death wish combined with a desire for regeneration. In addition, Shimao's dream stories deal with shattered narrative conventions and with language. For Shimao the war disrupted and made problematic connections between language and the real, and his dream stories are attempts to explore this rupture and search for alternative ways of communicating, most notably by exploring the unconscious within daily life.

As stories of a failed *tokkōtai*, Shimao's work questions Tal's division between combat veteran and non-veteran. Unlike the combat veteran of Tal's analysis, Shimao never experienced battle; still, his dream stories reveal the lingering effects of war-induced trauma. Tal's division needs to be modified. Equally important is the question of victimization. Showalter speaks of soldiers as purely victims of war; to this Tal adds the traumatizing experience when soldiers become victimizers. Shimao's work is doubly interesting throughout for its combination, in one character, of both victim and victimizer, a concern that becomes a major thematic of his later literature. That the reader witnesses the victimizer in the war veteran so soon after the surrender argues against the common evaluation of Shimao's early work as purely the "literature of the victim," as well as the broader categorization of records of Japanese war experience as entirely synonymous with "experience as victim."[33] Despite the claims of some, literary expression of wartime victimization by Japanese does not begin with Endō's *Umi to dokuyaku* (1959; trans. *The Sea and Poison*); powerful as this work may be, Shimao's early dream stories anticipate it by a decade.[34]

Five Stories of War and Dreams: 1946–1949

Here I would like to examine five early dream stories: "Kotōmu" (Dream of a lonely isle, 1946), "Matenrō" (Skyscraper, 1947), "Sekizō arukidasu" (Stone statues walking, 1947), "Yume no naka de no nichijō" (1948), and

"Asufuaruto to kumo no kora" (1949).[35] Like Shimao's pastoral stories, with their shared plot lines and basic scenes, the dream stories overlap and intertwine in a variety of interesting, intercontextual ways. "Matenrō," for instance, shares its setting (the city of Nagasaki) with "Yume no naka de no nichijō," and like the earlier "Kotōmu" involves the appearance of large, mysterious buildings.[36] Most of the dream stories contrast the dynamics of death, paranoia, and a persecution complex with the powers of regeneration, all fashioned on an ever-shifting montage, a transformation from one scene to the next with often tenuous linkage between scenes.[37] Each story, of course, has its own unique qualities: "Kotōmu," for instance, is the only story to position itself from the start *as a dream*, a device Shimao then abandoned.[38] "Matenrō" is unique in its depicting the *waking* from a dream. More commonly, like "Yume no naka de no nichijō," the stories traverse a course from the waking world, or something closer to it, to an obvious "dream" world of unlikely, even absurd, events.

"Kotōmu" (1946)

"Kotōmu," Shimao's first published postwar story, combines elements of dream with the *tokkōtai* experience in obvious ways. The story begins, as with many Shimao stories, in medias res, the protagonist suddenly finding himself in a situation with no memory of how he got there. Taken out of context, the situation is not out of keeping with the more realistic war tales: the narrator, a naval lieutenant, is on the open sea, steering a naval vessel and ordering its crew about.[39] Uncertainty and fluidity, however, mark this as a dream—uncertainty in the narrator's (perhaps) willful forgetting of his mission, fluidity in the ever-changing vessel, which first "appears to be like a torpedo boat," but transforms itself as it "responds freely" to events (175). This fluidity, again, is a subconscious attempt to escape the *tokkōtai* mission, the hope that the "torpedo boat" will transform into something less deadly.[40] In a reversal of the wartime *tokkōtai* scenario, the departure *from* the island is replaced by the narrator and his boat being pulled *toward* the island. The narrator's fear and unease, dominant emotions among Shimao's protagonists, at first lie not in his mission (which, after all, is unknown to him), but in the approaching confrontation with the island: "I felt like shuddering. . . . This island had to be *that island* people talk about" (177).

The narrator reviews various rumors he had heard about the island while living on the mainland: how the people of this "cursed island" share the same appearance as mainlanders and the same "pictographic" writing (*shōkei moji*, i.e., Chinese characters), but how their spoken language is unintelligible and their last names used only one character, their first names three or four. This final point leaves little doubt that the dream narrative is situated in the southern islands, because one of the characteristics of Amami islanders is just such an arrangement for personal names.[41] Landing perforce on the island and setting off to explore it, the narrator thinks:

> I was anxious that if I voyaged near that island I would be pulled in, and my fate would be sealed. And now it's turned out just that way. (178)

Unease is tempered by feelings of pride verging on arrogance; the narrator is sure the islanders will greet him with a hearty, "Oh! It's our commander!" since he is the "guardian spirit of the islands" *(tōsho no shugosha)* (179). He wanders through a village, and as in many dream stories unexpectedly confronts the incongruous. Here the faces of old women weaving clothes all have small, "beautiful moustaches": "I had a feeling of superiority and a desire to somehow, through pen and camera, introduce to our archipelago this island of women with unusual moustaches" (180). His sense of superiority, of being the one to preserve this island scene before him, is shaded by the knowledge he alone has of the island's fate: it will soon be "washed by waves and disappear from this world forever" (180). This "guardian spirit of the islands" is quickly unmasked, because despite his superior knowledge, he realizes his impotence to save anyone but himself; when the fateful time comes he can only escape with his boat and leave the islanders to fend for themselves (181).[42] His ever-present fear is thus inextricably linked to feelings of "despair" (the word *zetsubō*, repeated on almost every page).

"Kotōmu" next takes the narrator to the office of a mainland-educated dentist, whom the narrator instantly dislikes for his affected ways and prejudice against the island, and ends with the sudden appearance of a huge pylon or gateway, an intricately constructed, well-known structure he remembers having seen in postcards. This giant gate, unique to the islands *(kono shima ni shika nai mono)*, helps dispel the feelings of loathing the narrator had for the dentist and his mainland ways. He purchases a model of it to take with him, and feeling time pressing on him, races to the shore and shouts commands at his sailors to prepare for departure.

More concisely than any other of Shimao's stories, this tiny story (barely eight printed pages) reveals his protagonist's feelings of helplessness in the face of the impending disaster of the war, his despair over the impotence of his position as island "protector," and the dirty secret of much of the Ryukyu campaign—the fact that civilians often became sacrificial victims to allow the military to escape. It reveals as well how early Shimao's unique view of the Ryukyu Islands began to take shape—long before he coined the term *Yaponesia* in 1961 and went on to become a leading spokesperson for Ryukyu cultural studies. The dentist character, born on the island but openly critical of island culture, is linked to an overly assimilationist stance vis-à-vis mainland culture, of which the narrator—and Shimao in his *Yaponesia* writings—is highly critical. As in later Shimao stories, the narrator seeks to preserve the island's uniqueness through "pen and camera." One may in fact attribute the narrator's fear of the island sinking beneath the waves less to the results of war than to the fear that its cultural uniqueness will disappear in the face of a dominant mainland. It is in this sense that the protagonist's words about being "pulled in" by the island and therein finding his "fate sealed" should be read. In a related sense, one begins to connect Shimao's statements elsewhere that the Ryukyus and their culture are the unconscious of Japan;[43] the island in "Kotōmu," indeed, is intriguingly like the unconscious. One can visit this place—where the inhabitants are like oneself, yet somehow different—and want to report on the experience to the mainland (the conscious), but one's visit is always brief, because in the end the island will "sink into the sea" after one awakens.

"Matenrō" (1947)

If in "Kotōmu" the war experience is brought to the forefront, in "Matenrō" it is shaded, less distinct. The first-person narrator (almost all of the stories are so narrated) begins by constructing from scattered dream images an incredibly detailed vision of a city:

> [F]rom small things, like a certain expression on my dead mother's face clearly carved into a white, exposed skeleton, to large things, being able to at once construct, then destroy, something like my own city, one with a definite article in front of it *(kanshi no tsuita)* which, within my imagination at least, surely existed. (74)

He is able to fly at will over and around the city, speak a number of languages (French and Russian), go everywhere, and see everything. Contrasting with these images of power and freedom are feelings of fear and paranoia, of being trapped and unable to escape. The narrator feels himself being pursued by a murderer, then suddenly about to be executed in an electric chair, flanked by a pair of criminals (linking himself, in this last point, with the Crucifixion.) He spends a fearful night with some POWs, paradoxically bemoaning the fact that he *cannot die (shinu koto ga dekizu)* (75). And, as with several other of the dream stories, he feels hovering over every scene a "cataclysm" *(tenpen chi'i)* about to occur. In fact mini-cataclysms do occur, with the sea threatening to sink the island in "Kotōmu" here engulfing the town at one point, yet the city is always able to revive itself and grow. The narrator feels constantly chased because he is "serving an abstract concept" (76), yet at the same time he feels in command of "his" city:

> Moreover, walking around with this feeling of persecution *(higai mōsō)* I could tell that I was indeed walking around my town. I wanted to construct a panorama map of those streets. Giving names to each and every street, painting green on the hilltops, roughly sketching out the characteristics of the buildings, noting down the date and particulars of events that had occurred at various locations, adding more details to add a three-dimensional sense, making puppets of the people I meet, making them walk the streets, and I wanted to refer to it not as "that town" or "my town," but give it a name that would, in one fell stroke, express its special character. (76)

And this he does, calling it (in romanized form) "NANGASAKU," an old spelling of Nagasaki, the city where Shimao attended high school and first began writing and publishing his stories. The city, his creation, soon takes on a life of its own and begins to outrun his control, as one day he discovers a tower, a skyscraper, hovering ominously over "his" city:

> It was a wondrously tall steeple *(tō)*. It was so high you couldn't tell how far the top of it extended. It had countless levels, the top of which pierced the underside of the clouds. And it was always covered by mysterious clouds. . . . This skyscraper *(matenrō)*—yes, it was more like a tower *(rō)* than a steeple *(tō)*. Entirely shrouded by mist, sometimes, like when you're standing on a precipice at a volcano's crater, the wind swirls and the mist is blown away, and you can make out directly through the gaps what each level looks like. Maybe the Tower of Babel had appeared in my city NANGASAKU. But other than a certain arbitrary feeling I got from pronouncing the sounds *To-wer-of-Ba-bel*, I knew nothing else about it. (77)

The narrator reviews his ability to fly, a feat he decides to ration until he needs it to escape, and enters the tower, slowly ascending the various floors. The skyscraper is full of people, of gambling houses, prostitution dens, hot springs resorts, Chinese restaurants—a veritable catalogue of the kind of lower-class entertainments Japanese men sought as relief from the chaotic pressures of early postwar Japan. He discovers a magazine stand selling a journal issue that discusses his own appearance (as a new a writer, we are to take it). The narrator discusses at length an earlier memory of finding himself in a huge warehouse, flying through the air progressively deeper into its "incredibly deep" recesses. Discovering some "persistent will" *(shitsuyō no ishi)* threatening him, he spins and flies out, escaping a series of shutters banging shut behind him. The narrative then returns to the skyscraper, where the narrator passes a goblin *(mamono)* carrying a woman. The narrator realizes he knows this woman, intimately, in fact, as he recalls her four mounds of flesh like rice cakes *(mochi)* (81), and wants to rescue her. His "energy" level, however, is fast sinking, and it is all he can do to support himself as he feels "pulled" downstairs to the exit: "I fell into a strange sadness, knowing that until a moment ago I had been under the illusion that I held hegemony *(hegemonii)* over the skyscraper" (81).

In the final scene of "Matenrō" dawn has come, and the skyscraper has disappeared. The narrator finds himself standing in a town square filled with small food stalls and shops catering to the early morning crowds—"an ordinary scene of common people" (81). Incredibly, he recognizes the faces of the people as those in the skyscraper, including the "goblin," who turns out to be a cigarette vendor. As in many Shimao stories, the narrator contrasts his knowledge with the ignorance of all those around him, for he alone knows the nighttime reality of his NANGASAKU:

> They didn't know the form of my skyscraper at night. They had no idea. But I knew that skyscraper had not completely disappeared. When night came around all sorts of malice and plans and dreams and ventures would stretch out towards the sky. I was absolutely sure of it. I sensed the sound of the waves besides the sea in the harbor, and when I looked into the distance, far off it was as if a mountain was spouting fire, inflaming the sky into a deep red. (81–82)

War-induced trauma produces some obvious—and not so obvious—effects in "Matenrō." The pervading sense of guilt that permeates so much of Shimao's fiction is here expressed by a combined persecution complex and not-so-hidden desire for punishment, both of which are linked to wartime experiences. Pursued by a "murderer," the protagonist paradoxically finds that *he* is the one deserving punishment; the warehouse, in this sense, is a kind of prison from which he barely escapes. We detect the stirrings of Shimao's well-known doppelgänger motif—an internal division in the self that produces a second, less-defined self that shadows the first.[44] With the protagonist strapped to an electric chair, then desiring to die and lamenting the fact that he *cannot*, we understand that the "murderer" pursuing the protagonist is none other than his accusatory doppelgänger. In other words, it is a part of himself that feels *he* is a murderer and seeks punishment. Read in the context of the war and the war crimes trials being held at the time of the story's publication, the POW connection is more than coincidence. Shimao's generation of "failed *tokkōtai*"—in particular the officer corps—for the most part escaped Allied retribution, yet they lived with a continuing dread of a punishment that never came. Shimao's final two pronouncements on the *tokkōtai* experience—the non-fiction *Shinyō hasshin* (1987), the last chapter dealing with a war crimes trial of *tokkōtai* members who executed Allied POWs, and the incomplete final chapter of his war novel, "(Fukuin) Kuni yaburete" (1986), detailing the dread and uncertainty with which the *tokkōtai* officer corps faced repatriation—are evidence that the question of retribution and punishment continued to haunt him.[45] In short, the guilt, mixed dread, and desire for punishment seen here and in other stories are not to be dismissed as some universal sense of "original sin," but are seen as lingering effects of war less than two years after its conclusion.[46]

The choice of Nagasaki as the setting is significant. Shimao spent his high school days in Nagasaki, knew the city well, and returned to it in a number of pieces he wrote over the years.[47] The city is also the site of Shimao's first confrontation with the power of the Japanese state, when he and his fellow students were hauled into police headquarters and interrogated over the allegedly antisocial and disruptive contents of their high school coterie magazine, *Jūyon seiki*.[48] "Matenrō," however, urges the reader to see the setting in light of the city's instant obliteration on August 9, 1945. In "Shutsu kotōki" (1948) the destruction of Hiroshima and Nagasaki brings to the *tokkōtai* protagonist less a sense of fear than of relief, because now—with the total annihilation of all Japanese in the offing—he could stop trying to find meaning in his meaningless, sacrificial death. To repeat this quote:

> Strangely enough, the news of the atomic bombings made me feel cheerful. I could die easily now. An embarrassing thought. But secretly I felt that way, aware of a sense of guilt at not being able to tell anyone.[49]

"Matenrō" anticipates and counters this self-destructive desire in terms of a search for the opposite—the limits of *regenerative* power. Whereas in wartime the Shimao protagonist (or at least part of him) welcomes mass destruction, the postwar "dream" narrator opposes the wartime vision of destruction and death with one of regeneration and rebuilding. Further, the typical Shimao wartime narrator's stance is one of extremely narrowed vision and knowledge, a stance furthered by Shimao's deliberate stylistic choice of eliminating all but what the protagonist could confirm with his limited senses.[50] "Matenrō" answers this tunnel vision with an expanded power to see the *whole* picture, to envision every last detail of an entire world, along with such boundary-shattering abilities as the power to fly and communicate in multiple tongues. If, then, "Kotōmu" directly confronts the protagonist's *wartime* impotence, "Matenrō" suggests such impotence through its depiction of his exaggerated desire for control *after* the war. The protagonist, in short, plays out a desire for control to counteract the powerlessness he experienced in wartime, always fearful, however, that events will spin out of his hands.

The *matenrō* of the title is the major figure in the story, and the protagonist's description of it as a kind of Tower of Babel is key to understanding certain effects of Shimao's wartime trauma. The Tower of Babel, of course, is the biblical site of the breakup of one language into many, the site of a massive, worldwide communication breakdown. One might easily opt for a religious interpretation of "Matenrō," with its protagonist punished for subsuming God-like powers of creation, an interpretation that anticipates readings of *Shi no toge* as an Old Testament-like wrath of vengeance on the sinful protagonist. With the story's concern over language (especially naming), however, the Tower of Babel is best seen as standing for, as in the biblical account, both a breakdown in communication and the *origins* of language. The smallest details of his city, we recall, contain a "certain expression" on the face of his dead mother, a reference to the infant's prelinguistic reading of its mother's facial expression, which in the case of NANGASAKU forms a cornerstone—a building block, even—of creativity. As Shimizu Tetsu notes, the search to grasp the "tongue of dreams" (*yume no shita*, a favorite phrase of Shimao's) in Shimao's dream works is connected to Shimao's search for the "tongue of the mother" *(haha no shita)*. "Through tirelessly chasing 'dreams,' [Shimao] desired a return to the origins of writing, and a oneness with the mother's language."[51] In the search to return to the origins of language, Shimao's *matenrō*, like the Tower of Babel, stands at the point where language is fractured, where a rupture occurs between signified and signifiers and a mythical "natural" one-to-one relationship between the two.

In a story so filled with subtle effects of the wartime experience, it is hard not to conclude that this rupture in language is traceable to the recent events of the war. For Shimao in particular, with his role as wartime *tokkōtai* leader, the status of the order to die constituted a kind of absolute existence, never to be gainsaid. When this absolute was suddenly denied, arguably a certain rupture occurred for him within the relationship between language and the real world. Tal finds war trauma survivors, in their inability to communicate trauma, preoccupied with the "limitations of language."[52] Shimao's work also shows a preoccupation with language; instead of its limitations, however, his work more often emphasizes its *power*, a power his protagonists both are drawn to and flee from. In Shimao's fictional world trauma and language are linked in several ways: symbolic confrontations with the point of rupture ("Matenrō"), an exploration of the materiality of language and alternate means of communication ("Sekizō arukidasu"), and the spiraling back toward the origins of speech and a prelinguistic, pre-Oedipal state ("Yume no naka de no nichijō"). And throughout all the early dream stories the reader sees the denial of ordinary human relations mediated by language—an almost total lack of ordinary dialogue.[53] "Matenrō," the first of Shimaos stories to be "about" language, has for some critics taken on a significance beyond that of his other dream stories. To Haniya Yutaka, for instance, it is the summation of Shimao's essence.[54]

"Sekizō arukidasu" (1947)

Published the same month as "Matenrō," "Sekizō arukidasu" (hereafter "Sekizō") takes up where "Matenrō" left off. The mountain erupting in red flame at the end of "Matenrō" now covers the sky in red, with the sound of massive explosions close at hand sending the narrator into spasms of fear.[55] Whereas "Matenrō" is coy about the protagonist's wartime background, "Sekizō" (again barely eight pages long) brings to the forefront both the war and the protagonist's role in it. One begins to detect a pattern emerging in Shimao's dream stories of war trauma, the fluctuation between stories more openly about war and those in which the wartime experience must be teased out. "I thought the war was over," the protagonist says in the first line, the explosive sounds he hears producing fear that a new war has begun: "I was suspicious. War again? But wasn't the war over? And, sadly, the feeling crossed my mind: *Damn. Tricked again*" (55). He rushes off to the sea, hoping to escape what he fears is the bombing of his city, and finds himself with a crowd on a shallow draft boat "bobbing in the water" not far from a flotilla of illuminated "iron ships of the 'Foreign country'" *(totsuguni)* that had won the war (56). And he finds himself dressed in a strange way for peacetime:

> I was flustered. I had on a strange kind of clothes. I was wearing a naval officer's hat and military uniform. Maybe old habits, being ready for an emergency, made me appear this way in front of people. But these things were no more. Where had I pulled these clothes out from? (56)

He convinces himself that the war has not resumed; the sounds are merely "of some unknown, strange thing" that resembled sounds in wartime. Relief immediately turns to confusion: "If the explosion just now was nothing, then that meant I'd have to get up on the wharf in an outrageous costume" (57).

And this "costume," the naval officer's uniform standing out in the midst of the city crowds, leads to his feelings of "disgust and fear" and to the paranoid conviction that he will be jeered at by the crowds of civilians around him hurrying home at the end of the day. Watching their utter lack of concern, the narrator doubts whether any of them had heard the explosion, and feels a split in himself, one part of him standing apart, "carefully watching [his] navy blue serge uniform and hat" (58). This internal split—the doppelgänger motif first seen in "Matenrō"—is developed further, with the narrator seeing himself "standing apart, sadly looking up at his second self" (60), and feeling his head split in two. The two parts each whisper to him (61), these divided voices anticipating the more extended internal dialogue in "Yume no naka de no nichijō."

The narrator's fear that he will be spotted in his uniform and ha-rangued by civilians is realized as one young man suddenly confronts him, asking, "How long are you going to keep wearing that?" The man grabs him roughly and the narrator fears for his life, only to be saved by a second man, wielding a hammer, who attacks the first. With the sound of the beaten man's cries in his ears, the narrator enters a bar, only to see the "Hammer man" enter soon afterward. This man, in turn, is pursued by a group of two or three "thieftakers" *(torikata)*, who shoot him down as he tries to escape into the depths of a nearby river. As the narrator watches the scene, he is astonished to see other ob-servers nonchalantly applauding, making him conclude that the fore-going was all a kind of "outdoor play" (61).

The doppelgänger motif is not confined to the obvious splits in the narrator (his dreamlike ability to be both actor and audience simulta-neously), but extends to each character with whom he interacts. The first young man, the Hammer Man, and the pistol-wielding men who shoot down the narrator's savior are all examples of transference—of the narrator's evolving projection of his simultaneous desire to be pun-ished and his fear of punishment onto a doppelgänger.[56] "Matenrō's" vaguely menacing "murderer" here becomes a defined, focused series of increasingly threatening characters—from the unarmed young man who grabs him, to the hammer-wielding second man, to the group of armed men at the end.[57]

The final act of transference, which lends the story its title, involves the most unlikely of characters—a stone statue that suddenly begins to walk. The story concludes with the following:

> Since that was a hill, when I reached a corner I should have been able to look down on a portion of the city. Just a little before the corner I caught up with a stone statue so tall it seemed to reach the clouds, which was calmly walking.
>
> I knew the street corner where that statue was placed. A rhythm that came from the statue and went *Sakanouetamuramarō* reached my ears. Why was Sakanouetamuramarō walking around, anyway? I scurried to the front of the statue and looked up at its face, nearly worn flat by the elements over the years. Its thick moustache was strangely distinctive, and it walked slowly on.
>
> "What's going on?"
>
> I asked this. But it was conveyed to him in an odd way. I didn't ask this question aloud. Walking sideways, looking up at Sakanouetamuramarō's face, I merely had that thought for a moment, which was then conveyed clearly to Sakanouetamuramarō. He wearily turned his head, and looked down to his

waist. Quickly looking at the same spot, I saw an old reign-year *(mukashi no nengō)* carved there. I thought that that reign-year must be a sign of some important, secret key that no one knew about. And then a "tsuro" material *(busshitsu)* and an "oma" material appeared before my eyes and disappeared. I can't really explain what kind of things this tsuro and "oma" were, but I understood right away that the name of these two materials appearing one after the other were "tsuro" and "oma." Looking up at his face in a somewhat overbearing manner I said, "You're one character short." Sakanouetamuramarō acted a bit flustered, but soon his answer came to me. My nose was hit by a sharp smell. It was the smell of "su" [vinegar].

As soon as I understood how he was trying to convey his idea, I laughed out loud. Ha ha ha—so it's "tsuroomasu," [which means *tsurai*, painful or bitter] is it? But he didn't appear pained *(tsurasō)* at all. The same as before, carefree, even cheerfully, he kept on walking.

All the stone and bronze statues in my town had begun to walk. I thought of this phrase, then spoke it and became enraptured by it, but finally was flustered by this phrase I had thought of. This was a serious matter. I even felt it was a bit ominous. No doubt some new spirit *(atarashii seishin)* had begun to move. Or was it some extraordinary natural occurrence *(tenpen chi'i)* the statues were walking towards? (61–63)

Sakanouetamuramarō was a historical figure, one of the *Sei'i taishō-gun* (whence the word *shōgun*) sent periodically to do battle with the Ezo (Ainu).[58] The final transference, then, is that of the narrator, still wearing the naval officer's uniform, onto this gigantic stone statue of an earlier defender of the nation. One notes the recurrence of a running motif, the word *tenpen chi'i*, the "natural catastrophe" that lurks just off-stage in many of Shimao's dream stories. The unease and ominous feelings the narrator has are in keeping with the tenor of the earlier stories "Kotōmu" and "Matenrō," both of which end on similar notes. Even in these two stories, however, one is justified in a more positive reading of how Shimao is dealing with his wartime trauma. In "Kotōmu," although the protagonist cannot save the island from its fate and can only flee, the desire remains strong to preserve its differences "with pen and camera"—an early indication of Shimao's later *Yaponesia* project, his attempt to preserve, and in a sense "save," the southern islands' culture through his writing. In "Matenrō" the narrator promises further explorations of the unconscious and the rupture in language; he does not give himself up to the mundane waking world, but dares to—and even looks forward to—the night and his fears.

And in "Sekizō" one senses a growing lightness and humor—from the realization that the supposed murder scene he witnessed is merely a "play," to the verbal play in the final scenes, the choice of name of the statue (*saka no ue* means "on top of the hill/slope," precisely where the narrator first spies the statue), the wordplay on *"su"* (which by itself means vinegar, but here is also the final syllable of the word tsuroo-ma*su*), and the absurd contrast between the statue's "message" of pain and his carefree demeanor. Okuno says the sense of the comic *(kokkeisa)* falls flat,[59] but I prefer to see Shimao's subtle comic sense as a rarely employed weapon to combat the lingering effects of war-induced trauma. This final scene in "Seizō"—where stone and bronze statues of former military heroes and defenders of the realm moved by the "spirit of a new age" walk off and disappear—can be read as a hoped-for final disappearance of the remnants of war and militarism in the "new age" of early postwar democracy. Viewed in light of Shimao's, and the narrator's, wartime past, the statue also constitutes a symbolic transference of the wartime role of defender, and of war-induced trauma, onto a symbolic substitute who will, it is hoped, walk off into the distance and disappear forever.

"Yume no naka de no nichijō" (1948)

Surely Shimao's masterpiece of the dream-story genre is "Yume no naka de no nichijō" (hereafter "Yume no naka"). This story, nearly three times longer than the earlier dream stories, combines motifs seen previously—split consciousness, unspoken communication, and the power of the word—with a plot that can best be described as the search for the pre-Oedipal moment and the origins of one's injection into language. "Yume no naka" leaps from one shattered city (based on Kobe) to another (Nagasaki) in a steady regression, adding a number of new elements to the mix—the protagonist's parents and his role as writer. The story reaches a climax in one of the most memorable images in Shimao's oeuvre, if not in all postwar Japanese literature—the famous scene in which the character reaches inside his stomach and pulls his body completely inside out:

> At the same time I felt a violent pain in my stomach. Like the wolf who had his belly stuffed with stones, I seemed to reel, and I felt unable to walk straight. Gathering my courage, I thrust my right hand into my stomach. Then, still madly scratching my head with my left hand, I tried forcibly scooping out what was in there. I felt something hard adhering stubbornly to the bottom of my stomach, so I pulled at it with all my might. And then the strangest thing happened. With that hard kernel uppermost, my own flesh

followed up after me; I kept pulling. Finally, I had turned myself completely inside out like a sock. The itching on my head and the pain in my stomach were both gone. On the outside I was like a squid, smooth and blank and transparent.[60]

This final scene, and indeed much of the story, has been read as an allegory of postwar Japan and relations with the United States. The story begins:

I had gone into the building of a certain charitable organization in the slums. Having heard that a gang of juvenile delinquents lived on the roof of that building, I had decided to become a member of the gang myself.[61]

The roof of the building, bombed out during the war, is just a "bare shell of reinforced concrete" (58). Later, visiting his mother in what appears to be the city of Nagasaki, the narrator must accept the mother's mixed-blood child as his own brother, and then wanders around the city thinking everyone, including himself, is a "fake," finally turning his body inside out. In one reading, the gang of delinquents in the bombed-out building are the Japanese people themselves, the "charitable organization" sponsoring them the U.S. occupation forces, and the "mixed-blood" "bastard" the narrator must accept as his brother none other than postwar "democratic" Japan. One critic sees the final scene as depicting the narrator's inability to become the sort of humanist demanded by postwar society. But it can also be read as the opposite: not as a rejection of postwar democracy, but as the wrenching reversal made by the Japanese people in order to embrace it.[62] The opposition of the father, who curses the mother and her child as well, suggests something similar: such opposition has to be "neutralized" or "it seemed the entire nation would collapse."[63] The Japanese must accept the new order, the "bastard," or else dire consequences are in store for all of Japan.[64]

Autobiographical details of Shimao's life are particularly evident in "Yume no naka"—not merely the peripheral details so beloved by some critics (e.g., the similarities between the building described in the beginning and the Osaka Nihon Demokurashii Kyōkai building where Shimao briefly worked, and the way the final scene suggests Shimao's chronic stomach problems), but those reflecting his position as struggling young writer.[65] The narrator here is a budding novelist who has published only one story and is worried about having enough to write about for the second. Likewise, Shimao had just made his debut in the *bundan* by publishing his first work, the novella "Tandoku ryokōsha"

(A solitary traveler), in a national literary journal *(Geijustu)*, and was worried about a follow-up story. The second story became "Yume no naka," published in *Sōgō bunka*, a central journal of the *Sengoha* (Postwar writers).[66]

Although hints of the narrator-as-writer motif have occurred before (in "Matenrō"), "Yume no naka" is the first of Shimao's works to focus on the protagonist as novelist and to make the struggle to write the theme (the remarkable "Ōbasami," 1953, is another). Because of this, one is tempted to read it, as Sparling does, as depicting the "formation of a writer and the process of creating a literary work." Read like this, the final scene of physical reversal becomes the necessary exposure of "private pain to the world" in an act subordinating everything to his "art."[67] Such a reading, however, fails to account for the fact that when he sees his name in print, that is, when he receives confirmation of his status as novelist, the narrator is suddenly struck by huge, wildly itching sores from which he desperately seeks relief:

> Hurriedly I picked up the magazine and opened it to the table of contents. Hey, it's really in here. My name is in print. But why didn't they send me a copy, I wonder? Surely I have the right to see this before any one else. My head itched. Then the back of my neck began to itch wildly. So I scratched and clawed where it itched.[68]

It is not that he seeks to expose "private pain" in order to perfect his art; rather, it is his art that causes unbearable suffering and from which he seeks to flee, to cleanse himself. The final scene, of him standing in a stream, is a kind of reverse baptism, a move to reject what the story began with—the desire to define his identity as a novelist. Rather than the formation of a writer, then, one witnesses his *de*formation. In this sense of resistance to writing and being a writer, then, one can read comments that "Yume no naka," while helping to solidify Shimao's status as member of the *bundan*, was, ironically, itself a kind of "anti-*bundan*-like theory of the novelist."[69]

"Yume no naka" is best read as a continuation of Shimao's exploration of language, shaded at all times by the experience of the war. Like "Matenrō," "Yume no naka" deals with both the rupture in language and its origins—the latter less in the narrative of Babel than in the Freudian narrative of the individual Oedipal moment. The story explores the unconscious wherein the search for father and mother becomes a re-creation of the relations that created the narrator's unconscious and inserted him into the realm of language. His return to the "southern city" is a return to the realm of the imaginary, to a pre-Oedipal moment, where he experiences a dissolving of his body, his self, and of the dichotomies of subject/object. Hints of this dissolving of boundaries of self, in fact, come as the protagonist makes the final journey to his parents' house. In a train, he finds himself sitting next to a young woman:

> I sensed the resilient warmth of the body of another human being. At her slightest movement, I was keenly aware of the contours of my own flesh, distinguishing clearly the boundary between my body and the woman's. Then, as though I had been smoking a little too much, my vision blurred. Suddenly, I sensed that since that day my flesh had begun to give way and was no longer sound.[70]

In the loosely evolved plot of the story, the dissolving of the narrator's flesh arguably is the result of his exposure to his leprous friend, an action that leads him to want to declare to his father that he has leprosy (66), and to the vicious itching at the end. Although this plot device serves to link the scenes and give continuity to what are disparate sections, the dissolving of the narrator's body must be read in the context of the father-son-mother struggle, which Shimao depicts as following closely Freud's narrative of the Oedipus complex. After the mother-son interaction the father makes his appearance:

> My father looked on in silence. He seemed extremely annoyed by it all, including my eccentric self-confidence. I had no physical sense of my father's existence. I had brought my father here to my mother's house, but my father had almost nothing approaching a position here. Moreover, it was clear that, mentally, I had awarded him a position with respect to my mother. His fatherliness resided in this position. And this fatherliness looked annoyed. . . . I shrank unbecomingly from my father. A normal family, safe and sound, had been my reality until the war. But what about now? . . . I no longer know what I am. How wonderful! All this is my reality. As the feeling spread over me like pox, I was stung by that simple comment by my father. To me, father seemed like the immovable iron wall of society.[71]

The father finally becomes the dominant figure, beating the mother and whipping the narrator, the son.

"Yume no naka" can, in an interesting way, be read as playing out the wartime mission of death. Shimao, who often defined himself as a man who "failed to die,"[72] is in this story tracing a symbolic method of accomplishing his mission. Here, denied death at one end of the spectrum, the chronological time table is reversed, bringing the protagonist to a confrontation with another kind of death—the state preceding formation of the self. As Yonaha Keiko makes clear, the Shimao protagonist here and elsewhere (e.g., "Tandoku ryokōsha") is pulled *south*, back toward the islands and wartime experience.[73] In "Yume no naka" this involves an abrupt leap from the Kobe-like city of the opening to a city based on Nagasaki. In the midst of expected total devastation, the narrator unexpectedly discovers the city restored, and experiences the possibility of personal restoration. This involves a preparatory dissolution of boundaries of self, followed by the traumatic Oedipal moment, the formation of the sense of self through confrontation with the father, who in Freud's case stands for the law and the "iron wall of society," and in Lacan's for the individual's injection into the realm of the symbolic, of language.

Shimao's exploration of the unconscious is complex. On the one hand his protagonist seeks reintegration into "society," searching for the "normal family, safe and sound" that had been his "reality until the war"—thus his journey back to the seminal formation of his family and his self. On the other hand, the gradual dissolution of the self, the thought that "I no longer know what I am," is a joyful discovery. The protagonist seeks to regain self and to be an integrated part of language at the same time that he resists this. Following Lacan, Shimao recognizes in his exploration of the Oedipal moment something both fearful and hopeful. It is fearful in the sense of the alienation brought on by the rupture between signifier and reality that language entails, hopeful in the sense of the possibilities of that which precedes insertion into the realm of language—that is, a time preceding alienation from reality. As Juliet Flower MacCannell writes, it is not the signifier that connects us, but the "signifier [that] separates us from each other, disrupts any communication we might have with each other."[74] It is in this sense that Shimao's protagonist, in the final scene, reacts so violently to confirmation of his status as novelist, as one who, more than others, is caught up in signification. Critics have identified in Shimao's other writings (in particular *Shi no toge*) an essential "impotence of language," particularly the "fundamental impossibility of reconstructing the past through language."[75] In the early dream stories, however, one finds the Shimao protagonist constantly confronted with the *power* of language. This overlaps in intriguing ways with the protagonist's recognition of his role as victimizer of others; language, one is to understand, is also linked with a kind of victimization—in the way it alienates us from reality.

"Asufuaruto to kumo no kora" (1949)

If overt resonances of war are muted in the 1948s "Yume no naka," "Asufuaruto to kumo no kora" (hereafter "Asphalt"), written the following year, brings us back forcibly to wartime—so much so, in fact, that it has been included in collections of both Shimao's war stories and dream stories.[76] The setting, a southern island at the end of the war, and the narrator, an officer on the verge of extinction, are more than familiar; what is not familiar, however, is the extraordinary knowledge the narrator has—not of the coming suicide mission, but the *end* of the war.[77] The story opens:

> At the time, I could predict, through being notified by someone, the day the war would end; I felt it would be difficult to get past that day and continue to live. That doesn't mean I planned to kill myself. It just may turn out that, due to circumstances I couldn't control, I might be driven to end my life. (112)

Armed with his secret knowledge that the war will end the following day at 1:00 P.M., and separated from his unit, the narrator is obsessed with rejoining his men in time for what he envisions as a crucial moment of "great sound and light" marking the end of hostilities.[78] The story, in typical Shimao dream fashion, is marked by ceaseless movement as the narrator wanders a landscape that shifts in and out of focus. The punisher motif seen in "Matenrō" and "Sekizō" (and indeed in "Yume no naka," with the threatening friend in the beginning and the father at the end) is here played out early on, with the narrator's wandering preceded by his ruthless interrogation (while tied to a chair) by a *kempeitai*, a member of the dreaded wartime military police. Forced by the police to drink a strange liquid that will make him demented, the narrator vomits and has blurred vision, and suddenly finds himself surrounded by a group of young girls. Contrasting the purity *(seiketsu)* of the girls with the way his constant retching dirties their room, he finally falls asleep contemplating the next day's events and their connection to his "fate."

The next morning he oversleeps, then resumes his journey to rejoin his unit. His thought processes muddled by the liquid he imbibed, he is unable to remember how or why he was detained the day before. He walks down to the village to observe the villagers' reactions to a possible invasion by the enemy. As he descends, a sudden shower comes upon him and the smell of asphalt from the road, much like creosote, soothes his stomach. The shower revives his surroundings as well, the greenery of the trees and plants around him taking on an added sheen as they absorb the moisture. The war, however, is never far away:

> In the midst of this natural scenery, my thoughts were heavy as I thought of the near despair the people [the villagers] must have as, their war preparations complete, the enemy ships might show up on the horizon; barring any miraculous natural occurrence *(tenpen chi'i no kiseki)* they would be unable to avoid getting caught up in war. (120)

The narrator feels unqualified to live:

> Though I was able to grasp the revelation, I had spent the days before in ignorance, wearing a military uniform, and in a position of leadership—not just being ordered around but giving orders myself—so I did not have the qualifications to pass on to the other side of that impregnable fortress *(kinjō teppeki)* of one o'clock in the afternoon. (120)

At this point the second half of the title becomes clear. The narrator suddenly finds a clump of newly born baby spiders on his shoulder, and he hurriedly brushes them off, crushing some of them—an action he instantly regrets as "one that cannot be undone":

> They were living things so weak if you held them between your fingers they'd be crushed, as small as the head of a pin, plain dots of color as if dark green paint had been spilled; even so they had arms and legs, mouths spitting out threads, and other organs of life I didn't understand—I was struck by regret that I hadn't let them rest on my shoulder and taken the time to observe them. . . . Why couldn't I spare a few moments to stand for a while on the road and watch the movements of the clump of baby spiders on my shoulder? And that singular moment was now gone forever. (121)

The narrator walks through the deserted village and looks in one of the caves the residents have fled to, feeling the cold stares of its inhabitants, "looking at me as if to say 'What could you possibly want *now*?'" (123). He wanders on, speculating on how at the crucial moment of 1:00 P.M. there must be a way in which the "entire world, in a flash" could comprehend its import. "I wanted to meet that moment, not alone, but together with everyone; and if they were to die, I wanted to die" (124). This sense of wanting to belong, coupled with resignation, leads him to feelings of tolerance, of "magnanimity":

> My heart grew gentle, all irritation subsided, and a quiet resignation welled up that because of the shadow of my past *(kako no kage)* I, too, would join the company of victims *(giseisha no nakama).* In this way, in the midst of the final chaos *(makki no konton),* clearly knowing the day and hour, I felt as though I would be able to die amidst the joy of knowing I had been awake *(Watashi wa mezamete ita to iu yorokobi no naka de shinde ikesō na ki ga shita).* (125)

Looking for a "place to die" he hurries along, coming upon a wooden hut overlooking the bay. Here he finds a group of people, military deserters and their women, huddled in fear of the enemy landing. Realizing that their options include suicide, and emboldened by the fact that he outranks the deserters, the narrator suddenly confiscates their weapons and tosses them outside the hut. "You shouldn't be carrying things like that," he admonishes them. "Don't rush things. At 1:00 P.M. the war will be over. Don't worry about useless things. Above all else you must live" (127).

The penultimate scene is a rarity in Shimao's work, the only scene of massed troops on the move. Standing on a hill overlooking the bay, the narrator sees it is already crowded ("gunwale to gunwale") with enemy warships, their "scientific weapons" *(kagaku heiki)* ready to take aim at the Japanese. The mass of Japanese troops begins charging up the hill toward the narrator, shouting out the "special Japanese soldier's battle cry." Thinking that if this cry is detected by the enemy's "sound detection gear" a tragedy might unfold, the narrator yells at the troops to stop. He fears that his actions might be misinterpreted as that of a still-armed Japanese officer apparently urging on an attack, but he is, in the end, ignored by both sides. Suddenly the warship begins shooting out "arrows of light" *(kōsen no ya),* and the narrator is hit and falls to the ground. He interprets the enemy's actions as punishment for the battle cries that were, he speculates, prohibited by the surrender agreement (129). Lying in the rain that has begun to fall, he is unable to move.

This fades into the final scene in which the narrator awakens to find himself alive, on the "other side" of the divide marked by the surrender:

> My limbs were filled with the joy of life welling up . . . as if a brilliant light were shining in through the window. Outside a bright day had begun. But I was confused. I had crossed over that fateful date and had made it to this side, but how different was this from when I was over there? And did I have the

right to live on, an ordinary look on my face? Hadn't I clearly counted myself then as one of the victims? Yet here I was still alive on this side, immersed
in the joy of life. This lay heavy on my mind. Even if my wounds healed, I had
no idea how I was supposed to start walking *(aruki dasu)*. Was it really all right
for me to live? (130–131)

The narrator realizes he is being examined by a pair of doctors, who note
he has regained consciousness. The final line, one resonating with the
title's "spider children," is this:

In the midst of my confusion, I had no idea how to deal with the itchy feeling of the children of life *(seimei no kora)* within my body stretching out their
fingers and faces toward the light. (131)

Thus, some fourteen years before he confronted the moment of surrender and its immediate psychological consequences in "Shuppatsu
wa tsui ni otozurezu," in "Asphalt" Shimao faced the same questions,
again confirming the trajectory of his war fiction: rewriting trauma in
the language of myth and (in this case) dream before bringing it to the
surface in a more realistic mode.[79] The story touches on a number of
motifs common to earlier stories: the sense of incongruity with one's
body, the mixture of fear of and desire for punishment, privileged status or knowledge, wartime mass suicide, a "natural catastrophe" (the
word *tenpen chi'i* again used), and an apocalyptic vision of the end of
the world. Added to this are some of the most open expressions of the
mixed victim-victimizer stance informing the bulk of Shimao's later
oeuvre.

As Tsuge Teruhiko notes, Shimao's protagonists in the early stories
are filled with a sense of incongruity directed at their physical bodies
that manifests itself in a variety of ailments: nausea, stomachache, and
itching in "Yume no naka"; diarrhea in "Tandoku ryokōsha"; and the
nausea that assaults the narrator in "Asphalt."[80] There is, in short, an
immense self-loathing common to Shimao's protagonists, which, together with the doppelgänger and divided self motifs, suggest the divided protagonist's struggle to be rid of a detested part of himself. In
"Asphalt" this struggle works itself out when the protagonist physically
disgorges the mysterious liquid the *kempeitai* forced him to swallow, a
liquid symbolic of the ideology and wartime mindset instilled in the *tokkōtai*, the bitter pill they were compelled to accept from the state in order to obviate any thoughts of survival or surrender. Significantly, the
protagonist vomits up this liquid in the presence of a group of "pure"

young women and girls; likewise in "Yume no naka" it is in the presence of a young woman and dying child that the itching begins. In Asphalt, however, in the midst of the war, this scene is the first of several attempts by the protagonist to discard his dominant position and join the weakest and most powerless over whom he has had some control. Groups of young women and children, naturally, remind the reader of the planned wartime mass suicide on the real-life Kakeromajima where Shimao was stationed (a tragedy barely averted by the surrender)—an idea developed further in the scene at the hut. Here the protagonist is able to accomplish what he could not in "Kotōmu"—save the islanders from extinction. His exhortation to them to live at all costs is presented as a reaction to his thoughtless crushing of the baby spiders. The two scenes are linked through the description of the villagers, huddled in their caves, as "living lives like ground spiders" *(tsuchi gumo)* (122).

The overwhelming desire of the narrator to "join the company of victims," somehow to slough his privileged position of dominance, is revealed symbolically again and again in the dream stories as a movement from high to low. In "Matenrō" this descent comes with the protagonist's failing "flying power," his descent from the tower to the world of the "common people" in the city square. A similar movement is found in the 1948 dream story "Kōbai no aru rabirinsu" (Labyrinth with slope), where the narrator descends from the hill overlooking the city to submit himself to the cold stares of the physically and economically lowest parts of the town. In "Asphalt" the descent is found as the protagonist's move from the hill—where, as in "Matenrō" and "Sekizō arukidasu," he is able to survey the entire scene—to the village, as well as his aborted attempt to descend to the bay.

With the surrender on the horizon, and with his efforts toward both the islanders and his troops to see that they survive—combined with his desire to "join" them—one expects to see the narrator desiring to join them not in death, but in life. In fact, in the end, he does so, with the struggle to come to terms with survival, to feel that he has the *right* to live on, becoming the story's main focus. Only after he has suffered (by being gravely wounded) does he feel he has regained this right. And significantly, this struggle to come to terms with survival equates the forces of light—and life—with a coded reference to the islanders: the "children of life" *(seimei no kora)* are inseparable from the "baby spiders" *(kumo no kora)*, forces of newborn life he earlier unthinkingly crushed out. One is tempted to reread the narrator's intriguing comment in "Kotōmu" that if he traveled near the island he would be "pulled in, and [his] fate would be sealed" in light of the two major projects that later preoccupied Shimao for a large portion of his writing career: *Shi no toge* and his *Yaponesia* writings. The first is a study of a southern island woman and the gradual discovery that her cure lies in a return to her native cultural sphere; the latter is Shimao's discovery of a cultural Other within Japan centered on the Ryukyus.[81] In "Asphalt" the fate of the Shimao protagonist is, through the experiences of war, to be forever coming to terms with the "children of light"—the island and its people—now a sort of unassimilated Other within him. Looking at Shimao's entire career it is arguably his lifelong attempt to define his relationship with this Other that showed him a way to live beyond his trauma. And finally, perhaps most intriguing in view of our discussion of dreams, is the suggestion of a connection between the island and the unconscious. Whereas death and waking had been equated ("I felt as though I would be able to die amidst the joy of knowing I had been awake"), at the end of "Asufuaruto to kumo no kora," life, one understands, brings on the joy of remaining *in the dream*.

From Dreams to the Domestic: Stories of 1949–1954 —"Chinkonki" (1949), "Kizashi" (1952)

"Chinkonki" (Record of a requiem, 1949) and the later "Kizashi" (Omen, 1952) mark turning points for Shimao and his dream stories of the war experience. The former does so in its open insistence on the *tokkōtai* experience as "nonsensical" and anachronistic, the latter in the way it compartmentalizes the *tokkōtai* experience as but one of several areas Shimao would explore in his later fiction. In the titles themselves (requiem marking an ending, omen a sign of things to come) one senses Shimao's desire to map out new directions for his writing, to somehow free himself from the war experience, combined with the understanding that the war experience will never be erased or fail to underlie, in some very basic way, the writing to come.

"Chinkonki" (1949)

"Chinkonki" follows the narrative path laid out by "Yume no naka," the realistic opening gradually spilling over into a surreal development.[82]

Gone, however, are the physical impossibilities of "Yume no naka" and "Matenrō"—the inside-out bodies and flying stunts—to be replaced by a series of possible but incongruous scenes. In these turn of the decade and early 1950s stories Shimao begins to stake out a more sophisticated and complex narrative project—a complex and subtle overlap of realism and surreal that finds its peak in several of the chapters of *Shi no toge* and such stories as "Shima e" (1962).

The narrator of "Chinkonki," like Shimao himself at the time, is a schoolteacher in one of the schools in the "new system" of early postwar Japan. He is also (unlike Shimao) separated from his wife, who is still living outside the city where she evacuated during the war, and is forced by the severe housing shortage to room at the school. Evocative descriptions of energetic female teachers struggling to survive economically contrast with the unnamed narrator's general "ennui" and desire to fall into the oblivion of sleep. A strong motif of Shimao's early fiction—the sense of unease in the presence of friends and colleagues— appears as two friends unexpectedly drop by the narrator's room. He feels obliged to accompany them on a night out on the town, but goes off on his own when they are accosted by prostitutes. Thus begins his wandering, a motif common to many early Shimao stories—most notably "Tandoku ryokōsha" (1947), "Yume no naka de no nichijō" (1948), "Kōbai no aru rabisinsu" (1948), "Yado sadame" (Picking an inn, 1949), and "Chippoke na aventure" (A small adventure, 1950). Wandering free of the obligation to work, the narrator of "Chinkonki" soon finds himself in the countryside, where he runs across an outlandish scene—a group of young men, dressed as *tokkōtai* pilots, riding bicycles off toward some mountains:

> Altogether there were five of them, all wearing flight uniforms and white *hachimaki* tied around their foreheads. Exactly the same outfits the *tokkōtai* wore in the war when they set out on an attack. This thought crossed my mind: Wow—what outrageous clothes. They were all the same age as I was, and their appearance gave the unmistakable impression of those who had had military experience. But in our informal, present day world, where could they possibly be going all carried away like that? (106–107)

"Infected by the bracing clear morning air," the narrator continues, "I imagined the scene of a brave dawn attack, and was suddenly struck by a sense of nostalgia. I was just about to call out to them" (107). Before he can, however, the *tokkōtai* leader strikes up a conversation with an old man who emerges from a nearby house; the old man, it turns out, was the leader's subordinate in the war ("captain" to the younger man's "admiral"). After a brief exchange, the older man goes back into his house, and the narrator speculates:

> What could it mean when, nowadays when these clothes and relations based on rank were already nonsense, this full-fledged member of society on the verge of old age was pressed hard by these people whose attitudes were unchanged since the war, was thrown off balance and, unable to handle it, fled? (108)

The narrator notes how he, too, was an officer during the war,

> but now the foundation supporting these types of relationships of rank was nothing less than nonsense, a thought which made me cringe. . . . Even so, the fact that in the past I had been an officer made me feel proud *(tokuisa o kanjita)*. What was it urging me to tell them that I had once been one of them, I wondered. No matter what I might think or say officially, in the light of day, I was unable to handle this tail of emotions which rose up in such an unexpected place. I felt friendly towards them, but repentant at the same time, the result of the strong resistance I felt. (108–109)

This sense of resistance reaches a peak as the narrator glances at the young officer's notebook, filled with unusual Sanskrit writing and the owner's name with the "strange" title of "former Naval officer" attached to it. "I could sniff out the flickering consciousness of one of the chosen" *(erabareta mono no ishiki)* (109), a thought that makes the narrator quickly lose all his interest in the young man.

Much as the surrender brought on a return of light to the wartime village, here the disappearance of the *tokkōtai* bicyclists marks the end of darkness, the end of the night. With the dawn, the narrator finds himself wishing to visit a "village where peaches are in bloom" and be swept up in a colorful village festival *(matsuri)*. His wish comes true as he soon comes upon the very type of village he seeks, a place that "makes you want to name it Peach Blossom Village" (110). In typical Shimao fashion, the power of the word is revealed, as this imagined name seamlessly shifts to the actual name of the village. In a scene presaging the later "Kawa ni te" (1959) and "Keiji no tsutome" (1962) (see chapter 4), the narrator discovers the communal bath of Peach Blossom Village, which, after some hesitation, he enters and relaxes in. He finds the nakedness of the villagers, young and old, men and women, as soothing as the hot waters: "Everything looked so natural. It was all so totally unreserved there was no time to feel anything like eroticism" (112). He soon becomes aware, however, of the cold stares of the villagers and his status as intruder, the typical Shimao sense of unease vying with the attraction the protagonist is always quick to have for female beauty. Spying a lovely, completely nude, young woman standing up, he notes, "I thought she was beautiful. Now I felt that no matter what judgment might await me, I was ready to take it" (112).

And his judgment day is not far off. Dressing quickly, he is informed by a young village man of a sign prohibiting outsiders from using the communal bath. The narrator is told he must meet with the village "vice chairman" in order to explain his actions and apologize, and the final scene consists of this interrogation. The narrator is quick to make his apologies, linking his actions with his past:

> I am willing to accept any judgment passed on me. But first I'd like to explain why I felt I had to enter the bath. . . . I won't discuss my unhappy past. You can well imagine the dark days I've spent. I've survived til now, keeping my peace. But I can't stand it anymore. (117)

The interrogation is cut short by the appearance of a beautiful woman, the same one he saw in the bath; she is, he is told, the vice chairman's second wife. After she leaves, the vice chairman hands a message to the narrator, a note from the woman asking him to go away with her. He is urged by the vice chairman to do so ("She's that kind of woman," he explains. "Not your usual type"), whereupon the woman reappears. Her presence reminds the narrator of the "hard body" of his own wife: "An abstracted something, like the spirit of my wife's hard body became a shaft of light and pierced me to the quick. The wound from that shaft was deep indeed" (121). The woman departs again, leaving behind a cloisonné box the narrator knows he must eventually open. He is convinced it is a vaporized "aphrodisiac" that, if inhaled, will make him "be in her possession." Unsure of what awaits him, the narrator lifts open the lid (122).

So ends "Chinkonki." The title is intriguing, the natural question being of whose "requiem" this is a record. Considering the earlier dream stories, one must conclude that the story is conceived of as yet another imaginary sloughing and rejection of the *tokkōtai* experience of the narrator—a putting to death or symbolic burying of that part of himself. The absurd scene of stone statues walking off into the distance in "Sekizō arukidasu" is here rewritten in Shimao's newfound idiom of the less "dreamlike," yet still absurd, scene of *tokkōtai* bicyclists pumping their way to the hills at dawn. As with any Shimao protagonist, the narrator of "Chinkonki" is not one-dimensional in his reaction to this remnant of the war. "Nonsensical" though they may be, a part of him identifies with these remnants of war, is drawn to them, although he ultimately resists and rejects their relevance to him. Significantly, the *tokkōtai* here, despite the narrator's own background, is now represented as outside, an Other. Unlike "Sekizō," it is no longer the narrator who wears the uniform, but *another*.

If Shimao saw this work—and indeed much of his writing—as types of *chinkonki*, what are the implications of this? As Robert Lifton notes, the notion of *chinkon*, literally, "consolation of souls," "suggests a gentle atmosphere of respect and love, and above all *a combination of continued connection with the dead and peaceful separation from them.*"[83] In the case of "Chinkonki" this definition captures in part what Shimao is attempting with his writing. Despite unceasing attempts to resist and erase the past, a connection with the dead—and with the *tokkōtai* experience— does continue to inform Shimao's literature. One detects a lingering attachment and, although certainly not love or respect, at least a kind of sympathy directed toward those placed in a position of absurd sacrifice.

Shimao adds a second, and ultimately for his literature more significant, element, namely the idealized village and the protagonist's attempts to enter into its life. This is not to imply that the war experience is no longer important to him. The experiences of war, which never fade from Shimao's literature, cannot be emphasized enough. As seen in chapter 1, two of his last books were studies of the *tokkōtai* experience, and the completion of his war novel (begun in 1949) occupied him until his death. Likewise, the experience of the war—specifically the *tokkōtai* experience on the small southern island—underlines much of his best non-war fiction, including *Shi no toge*. In much of his fiction Shimao moves back and forth between the dichotomy of wartime base (death) and village (life) set up in the war novel and such pastoral stories as "Hamabe no uta" and "Shima no hate," never excluding one or the other completely, yet always underscoring one side of the equation. In "Chinkonki," with the Peach Blossom Village we see Shimao's early, unfocused delineation of what in later fiction becomes more fixed on the site of the southern islands. The protagonist's rejection of the wartime *tokkōtai* as "nonsense," plus his desire to escape the ennui of postwar existence, leads him to a dreamy site of relief from the tensions of postwar life (including the lingering wartime ethos epitomized by the anachronistic *tokkōtai* bicyclists).

Peach Blossom Village is a kind of free-floating desire for respite and forgiveness, its location unmapped, yet it presages a gradual closing in on a specific place—the southern islands. At first Shimao depicts the island village as a place of respite only in the context of the war. As we have seen, a year after "Chinkonki" the story "Sotetsujima no jifu" depicts the southern island village in wartime as a Shangri-la for the soldiers stationed there. The simplistic, pastoral depiction of the village as respite from war soon gives way to the grimmer realities of the 1952 "Yoru no nioi," in which Shimao challenges his own earlier, clear-cut dichotomy mentioned above. What makes "Chinkonki" so interesting in this regard is its depiction of the desire for such a place of respite, of relief, of "naturalness" and "openness" *not* in wartime, but in the midst of postwar life on the mainland. Five years later, living in Tokyo, Shimao wrote the first of what became his *Yaponesia* essays, a short article arguing the case for the southern islands (specifically Okinawa) as rescuers of a "stagnant," even death-inducing mainland. A year after that, Shimao was back in the southern islands himself and, in the midst of work on stories of his wife's madness (see chapter 3), began to rework the basic elements of "Chinkonki" in the specific setting of the southern island that was now his home. He produced stories that combine the protagonist's desire to enter the island village and to know its life—mixed with the unease and tension inherent in his status as outsider and as a person with a "past," which prevents him from assimilation into the village.

"Chinkonki" has been read as political allegory. Okuno sees the village and the protagonist's encounter with it as connected with the author's "desire for revolution," Shimao's own "ambiguous position" both "desirous of revolution and uncertain towards it."[84] Thus one is to see the vice chairman as stand-in for the postwar left, and the protagonist's interrogation as Shimao's own self-interrogation of his decidedly ambiguous stance vis-à-vis contemporary politics. "Chinkonki" predates the heated debate over Shimao's "Chippoke na aventure" by a year, and in retrospect appears to play out Shimao's defense against the negative reactions to this latter story of some *Shin Nihon Bungaku* readers, who saw it as "petit bourgeois."[85] As I have outlined with "Yume no naka" above, and with "Kizashi" below, Shimao's work is certainly not averse to political interpretation. In fact, Shimao's work *is* highly political, but less so in the immediate sense of commentary on the contemporary debate of the left than in the far-ranging sense of highlighting such broad issues as war responsibility, received gender roles, and cultural diversity. Thus while "Chinkonki" may have overtones of contemporary political debate over revolution and the artist's role, in the context of Shimao's oeuvre it should be read as an early expression of the author's desire for revolution not in any easily defined established leftist sense, but in the broader sense of the radical reversals of accepted ideas encompassed by the word *Yaponesia*.[86]

"Kizashi" (1952)

"Chinkonki" not only hints at a gradual distancing of the wartime experience, but with its ending—the "spirit of [the] wife's hard body" piercing the narrator at the moment of his attraction to another woman—reveals that long before the first *byōsaimono*, Shimao was introducing some of the key motifs of his later work. "Kizashi" takes this much further. Here the wife is actually present (as is the other woman), and the story ends with a sudden change in her that startles the male protagonist and sends a "a sudden chill throughout his body." The story thus marks a point of transition where the focus shifts to the domestic scene and the husband/wife relationship, all of which culminate in the novel *Shi no toge*.[87]

Before "Kizashi" arrives at this point, however, it focuses on several motifs common to Shimao's earlier work. It is the first story Shimao wrote after his move from Kobe to Tokyo, a move that marked his attempt to launch a serious writing career in the capital. This move also overlaps with the end of the U.S. occupation. Kizashi is also notable for its structure, different from any previous ones, with four distinct vignettes (separated by blank space) focusing on, in order, the occupation, the *tokkōtai* experience, relations with friends, and writing and the husband/wife relationship. At this critical juncture in his life Shimao is taking stock of where he and Japan have been—the war and the occupation—while simultaneously beginning to develop new themes.

Unlike the earlier dream stories, "Kizashi" is written in the third person and introduces a protagonist, Kannō Miichi, who appears in four later stories: "Kikō no sakeme" (Cracks on the tortoise shell, 1952); "Mimei" (Before dawn, 1952); "Nenokichi no shita" (Nenokichi's tongue, 1953); and "Kisōsha no yūutsu" (The melancholy of homecoming, 1954), dubbed Shimao's *Miichimono*, or Tales of Miichi. These stories, while gradually gelling around the prototypical four-person nuclear family that forms the narrative core of the later fiction, are only loosely connected. The first vignette of "Kizashi" is an allegorical commentary on the occupation. Shimao, who never had trouble with occupation-period censors, avoids doing so by saving his most biting comments on this period for the months immediately following the transition to Japanese rule. Reminiscent of "Sekizō," the protagonist finds himself in a crowd of people, all streaming in one direction. Unlike the two friends with him, who are skilled at adapting to the new order, Miichi initially resists following along, but finally finds himself swept up in the mass after being told by one member, "We're assembling to be trained by a foreigner" (104). Part of his resistance to this blind obedience, as one might suspect, stems from his past experience; having already undergone such military training, in the war, Miichi resists the need to participate again. He falls in with the crowd, however, suddenly finding everyone around him armed with guns, and soon comes face to face with the "foreigner":

> It was a huge, coarse being. The sort of image people had conjured up of a foreign drill master was, I suppose, that of someone overly trim. But the foreigner who appeared before us was not what they imagined. It was an ugly and bizarre thing. Maybe like the kind of monstrous evil deity Muslims conjure up in their imagination. Its flabby body all swollen, its face all bumpy and pitted. (113)

This evil foreigner is accompanied by four or five women, Miichi's fellow countrypersons, whom the foreigner urges the crowd to attack. When they do not, he exposes his long penis and proceeds to show them how to rape one of the women. At this point the crowd turns on the foreigner, shouting at him to let the woman go. When he does, the crowd is relieved and "[w]aited for the next order to come from somewhere. And then shuffled forward" (117). Miichi finally is roused to take action, standing facing the crowd, which has swelled in size, yelling at them to "Unite! Unite! *(Danketsu seyo, danketsu seyo)* Now is the time, now is the moment." A few brief smiles greet him from the crowd, which ignores him and brushes by, and Miichi is left with a "troublesome" "guilty conscience" (117).

With the possible exception of "Yume no naka," never before or after did Shimao write such an openly allegorical work as this opening section of "Kizashi." Shimao traces the disappointment the Japanese felt at the discrepancies between ideals and the realities of the occupation, heaps scorn upon the sheep-like obedience to postwar rearmament, and criticizes the limits of freedom and resistance in postwar Japan. Miichi, significantly, finds his wartime background less an impediment to action than the bitter experience that provides the motivation to resist, albeit feebly, this so-called "Reverse Course."

As if to fill in the background to Miichi's faintly delineated wartime experience, the second vignette of "Kizashi" returns to wartime, and the *tokkōtai*. This time, however, the protagonist is not a *shinyō* commander, but the officer in charge of a *maruhachi*—another name for one of the small attack submarines employed in suicide missions. Miichi's fears are less of dying than of being too late to attack, of the regrets he would have if he alone survived, and the desire to spare his one fellow pilot from the fate that awaits him. After sealing the hatch, however, Miichi finds himself unable to remember how to operate the craft. When he does recall, the submarine plunges not into the sea, but inexplicably underground, boring deeper and deeper into the earth—another symbolic attempt, one gathers, to "bury" the *tokkōtai* experience. The vignette ends with Miichi contemplating his responsibility as an officer (noting that the machine's malfunction is not his doing), and wondering whether he will be able to face his fellow pilot whenever they emerge from the ground. The initial few pages of this vignette, with Miichi's desire to turn the hopeless war situation around and his strong sense of fellowship with his *tokkōtai* comrades, is a sort of throwback, one might decide, an uncritical defense of the *tokkōtai* experience. As seen before, however, Shimao consistently positions such sentiments beside the absurd, here endowing the inanimate—the attack submarine—with the good sense, which humans lack, to flee a hopeless situation. Equally important is the way the *tokkōtai* experience is now compartmentalized; although underlying the first vignette, and continuing to serve as both subtext and surface theme of a fair portion of Shimao's later fiction, its echoes are contained, its effects less all-embracing. It is as if Shimao, newly ensconced in Tokyo and struggling to establish his career, is cataloguing for himself and his readers the possible range of his literature—of which the *tokkōtai* is but one element—and concluding that new directions lie ahead.

These new directions, touched on in the last two vignettes, include areas one might well expect a struggling writer to focus on: feelings about his profession, relations with fellow writers, and the act of writing fiction itself. With the move to Tokyo in 1952, Shimao graduated from the world of coterie magazines to that of professional writing. In that year he published five stories in leading literary journals and joined three major groups of up-and-coming Tokyo-based writers: Genzai no Kai, Shin Nihon Bungakkai, and the Ichi Ni Kai (the latter included Shōnō Junzō, Yoshiyuki Junnosuke, Yasuoka Shōtarō, and Kojima Nobuo as members). The third vignette in "Kizashi" reflects Shimao's new status as budding member of the literary establishment, with Miichi wandering the city, feeling there is "no place to rest." He meets up and feels uncomfortable with a fellow writer, discussing the ubiquitous writers' meetings and roundtable discussions in which he feels totally out of place. All the while, Miichi's stomach plagues him, feeling heavier and, with each moment, sinking lower into his body, as a kind of "monster" *(obake)* he must carry with him. Drinking cocoa with his fellow writer in a café, he suddenly has a dream:

> Stooped down on a river rock in a beautiful mountain stream, he pulls out his stomach from his belly and is washing it in the water. He scraped off the unpleasant matter, pieces of stone, which clung to the folds of his stomach and intestines, and heaved a sigh of relief; why hadn't he realized this before, he wondered. (131)

Parallels with the final scene in "Yume no naka" are striking. Relief from the uncomfortable status as writer here, as in the earlier story, comes only in a physical deformation, a cleansing of the body. Plagued by the incongruity of his position as writer, uncomfortable with other writers, with his newfound surroundings, and with his own body, Miichi's self-directed violence, one soon learns, is paralleled by his view of literature and writing, because violence and writing are closely linked.

In the final section of "Kizashi" Shimao presents the most extended metafictional discussion of writing in his fiction. In the last scene Miichi is visited at home by a literary critic, Idogawa, and his woman friend, Sumiko. A decided tension animates the relationship between the three, because Miichi feels his writing is belittled by Idogawa, and there is an obvious sexual attraction between Miichi and Sumiko, an "intruder" into the domestic scene who is the forerunner of the other woman developed more fully in *Shi no toge*. After a brief discussion of Miichi's feelings about these two people, he launches into an extended monologue on writing and his views on fiction. Writing novels for him is done in an "entirely inadvertent, spontaneous" way, although this is modified somewhat by being done "half consciously." Military vocabulary abounds in this discussion, with talk of enemies, bombs, and surrender, and the male protagonist, as always, haunted by the war experience. "That's my method," Miichi says, "and if the enemy finds this out, my method will collapse." He has set "bombs" everywhere in his novels that, if detected, will also lead to a "collapse" of his literature (133). "Even I, who have set these bombs, often do not have any idea where I have set them," he tells Idogawa. "But I won't surrender":

[N]ovels are pointless *(tsumaranai koto)*. It's violence done by writing. Reality has no need of writing. So novels are unnecessary. That's what I prove through my novels. That's why I usually have to write about stupid things. So people will stop reading novels completely. With reality living in the present, one hundred per cent, full of energy, writing will withdraw, a pathetic look on its face; after reality has completely been washed by waves of oblivion and forgetfulness, it will remain the sole, yes the sole piece of evidence left behind for people of later years—that's the warped violence of writing *(moji no kussetsu shita bōryoku)*. Revenge, you say? Hold on a minute. My novels, no, histories, in short, histories as records *(kijutsu to shita no rekishi)*, are really not that at all." (134)

In a bizarre ending worthy of the writing of Witold Gombrowicz, the final scene following this pronouncement strikes one as an illustration of some of Miichi's ideas, because the reader is indeed hard put to piece together any point from it. Sumiko is taken by a sort of epileptic fit, her legs flailing, and is carried to a sofa by Miichi, who all the while notes the attractiveness of her thick legs. Miichi's wife, clearly upset, painstakingly prepares and serves tea. Sumiko spits up some grains of rice, several of which stick to Idogawa's face; he doesn't wipe them off, and Miichi notes that this stance was precisely Idogawa's "method of critique" (136). Sumiko yells for a bucket (one assumes she is about to be sick); Miichi commands his wife to bring it, and at this point her attitude is revealed, the sudden change in the wife bringing a chill to Miichi's body. The section is perhaps more meaningful than at first apparent, revealing such areas of Shimao's own life at the time as his lack of confidence while trying to break into a career as writer in Tokyo, his fear of exposing his work to criticism from professional critics, and the way his decision to move to Tokyo and be a full-time writer brought chaos and confusion into his home, particularly in his relationship with his wife. Hints of the sudden, drastic change in his wife presage by some three years the actual outbreak of Miho's madness.

Miichi's theory of literature, of course, is important as a statement— albeit an exaggerated and comic one—of Shimao's thoughts on writing and the fictional enterprise as he stared at the abyss separating him from success or failure as a writer. Clearly much of this theory is tongue-in-cheek, particularly the statements regarding the writing of "stupid things" with the goal of eliminating all readers. Yet Shimao, with his difficult, avant-garde dream writings dominating the public perception of his work to this point, acknowledges how his critically acclaimed work has, indeed, struck many readers as obtuse, even pointless. The move to Tokyo brought with it a reevaluation that, as I will argue, finds Shimao's writing from this point gradually evolving into something less openly dream-like, to the point where, as mentioned in the introduction to this book, critics accused him of a literary "retreat" into the comfortable familiarity of the traditional I-novel. Such evaluations are not without merit, but they miss the ways in which Shimao in his later writings developed a sophisticated blend of the real and the surreal, as if a gossamer veil were thrown over the I-novel.

Be that as it may, the priority of reality, plus the "warped violence" that writing does to reality, and the notion of writing as "historical record" reveal the complex, often contradictory visions Shimao had of the fictional enterprise. I have already outlined his obsession with language in earlier dream stories. In "Yume no naka," for instance, the protagonist journeys to a prelinguistic state, and in the final scene, as fledgling writer he turns to violence against his body to reject his status as novelist, as someone, we can now state, most involved in the "warped violence" of language against the real. Likewise, in "Kizashi"(and throughout his career) Shimao speaks of the goal of writing not fiction, but "records," as if language can be but a transparent recording of events. In Shimao's world, then, the desire for a transparent recording is inevitably at odds with the recognition of the power of language to do violence to the real. "Kizashi" informs us, the readers, of the irreconcilable nature of this tension—that, in the end, we are left with "records" or "histories" of a former reality that pale in comparison to the real, yet are all the "evidence" we can ever have. Writing can, at best, be but a record of loss.

"Ōbasami," "Nenokichi no shita," "Kisōsha no yūutsu" (1953–1954)

Shimao was quite prolific after his move to Tokyo, publishing some twenty short stories and radio scripts in 1953–1954 (the latter in the 1972 collection *Garasu shōji no shiruetto*, Silhouette on the glass door).

Three remarkable stories in particular from this period preceding the outbreak of Miho's illness presage his later fictional concerns. With the war trauma now muted, as with many of the writers of the *Daisan no shinjin* group to whom he was close, Shimao turned to domestic drama. Themes such as gender reversal, female madness, and domestic crisis would preoccupy him in his *byōsaimono*, or "sick wife stories," for the next decade and beyond.[88]

"Ōbasami" (1953)

Published in January 1953, "Ōbasami" (Shears), a decidedly surrealistic, dream-like story, combines Shimao's concern for language with the notion of gender reversal, as the protagonist, through the agency of the devil, is transformed into a woman. By "Nenokichi no shita" (October 1953) and "Kisōsha no yūutsu" (April 1954),[89] both "Miichi" stories, Shimao began the gradual shift from the openly surreal style of his earlier works to the more complex mix of his mature work.[90] All the while he focused on major concerns of his later fiction: the husband's agonizing over his role as father, the wife in the throes of mental anguish—the nuclear family, in short, in crisis. War trauma, although subtext, is displaced for a time by *domestic* trauma.

In "Ōbasami," closed up in his room, curtains drawn, the narrator is unsuccessfully attempting to write a story when the devil appears before him. The devil, described in typical Western fashion as having black skin, pointed ears, and tail with a triangular "harpoon-like" barb at the tip (73), hands the narrator a novel (a Finnish *shishōsetu*, or I-novel), the cover of which resonates with other Shimao works. Its depiction of a soldier with multiple shadows emanating from him echoes the typical Shimao narrator's status as ex-soldier, with the doppelgänger trailing close behind. The narrator feels himself "acting in concert with the devil," producing a "dulling" of the senses, in particular an "insensitivity" to the devil's own "magnanimity towards evil" (73). Finally, totally under the devil's spell, he leaps into a "very abstract" pond to which the devil has led him:

At once I sank deeper and deeper, but there was a strong membrane between me and the core *(shin)* of the pond, and unable to be absorbed into it, the weight of my body formed a depression on the surface of the pond which then tried to regain its original surface and spewed up out into the air.

I turned a somersault and was standing by the edge of the pond. And in that instant I was confident I had been transmigrated *(tensei)*. I couldn't see my own figure, but it seemed it had changed into something completely different. (74)

The narrator discovers he has a magical power to make his "desires and hopes" come true, but he wants first of all to set out on an "ascetic training in observation" *(kansatsu shugyō)* to aid his work as a novelist:

> And through this freedom all the objects of the outside world would steadily be recorded by a seismograph, and translated into words understood by most people, and my novels would be completed one after another.
>
> I wasn't without a desire to read the Finnish person's novel that the devil had whispered about, but more than that I would use this advanced, I guess you'd call it, three-dimensional method *(rittaiteki shuhō)* and take uninteresting, commonplace affairs and crystallize them one after another into literary works.
>
> There was no end to material, and my senses, free and insensitive like the devil's, would take in as much as possible and be in rapture. (75–76)

This emotional "liberation" is accompanied by a surprisingly physical change as well: looking into a showroom window, the narrator finds he has turned into a woman. Significantly, however, the transformation into a woman is incomplete; he feels his "core" is still that of a man. A lengthy scene at the women's side of a bathhouse is followed by the narrator awakening to find that he had been dreaming.[91] He is unable to relax, mutters about a "lost thing," finds himself crying, and finally discovers under his futon a hard object, which turns out to be a pair of shears someone has left there.

"Ōbasami" is remarkable for the directness with which it confronts an undercurrent in Shimao's writing of this period—the need for a drastic transformation in both life and writing. The narrator/writer lives in a stagnant and sterile world, closed off from the outside, unable to write. Released from the closed-in world of his room (his unconscious), he is "liberated" to observe and record the most minute details of everyday life, only if, importantly, his unconscious and the world of everyday reality can find a point of contact. It is crucial to note that Shimao's fictional writer is not simply rejecting a surreal style in favor of a run-of-the-mill *shishōsetsu* approach advocated by the devil. The narrator's transformation, after all, is incomplete, with himself always divided between inner man and outer woman; likewise, Shimao's fiction from this point takes on the sophisticated mix of unconscious narrative logic and real events. "Ōbasami," although something of a swan song for Shimao's purer surrealistic style, is far from a fictional farewell to the world of the unconscious. With works of this period and the *byōsai-*

mono, the unconscious rises to the surface and becomes real in a way it has never been before.

"Nenokichi no shita" (1953)

The shears in "Ōbasami" should be seen as an invitation to castration, a way of fulfilling the dream depiction of casting off the male role. This idea segues neatly into the story "Nenokichi no shita" (hereafter "Nenokichi"). Here the male's genitalia are symbolically severed as the female (the wife) comes to dominate events. The story shares with much of Shimao's later work a simple plot, in this case a quarrel between parents and son that escalates into violence, with the son, Nenokichi, struck by the father. As he falls to the ground, the boy cuts his tongue, and the remainder of the story depicts the parents seeking medical assistance and the operation that reattaches the tongue.

As Miichi dithers at a friend's home, attempting to borrow money to pay for the boy's medical treatment, his wife, Nasu, takes charge, accompanying Nenokichi to a doctor's office in a nearby school, where two doctors prepare to sew the nearly severed tongue back on. In a lengthy and gruesome scene, the operation is performed and appears successful. The story ends with Miichi uncertain about its success: the reattached tongue looks "slipshod," and he feels that "some troublesome calamity will surely befall Nenokichi in the future" (28). At the same time, with the tongue now back in place, the familiar "dull, damp pain" Miichi felt at the beginning of the story returns to "begin to spread heavily through [Miichi's] crotch" (28). Very subtly Shimao links Nenokichi's severed tongue with a symbolic castration of the husband and brief assumption of domestic power by the wife. In contrast to her strength and determination in the face of the severed tongue, now with the tongue sewn back on Nasu is no longer a commanding figure. Instead, she appears small and shabby at the clinic following the operation: "Her shoulders and waist were small, her two legs sticking out of her skirt were thin, and overall she looked pitiful" (27).

Miichi's "pain in the crotch" may also be read as the pain of being a father, that is, of having the responsibility of a family. At the doctor's office, awaiting the results of the operation, Miichi's thoughts turn to the sense of liberation he would feel if free of both wife and son:

> An image suddenly came to Miichi of a quiet home, liberated from strange attachments and responsibilities and troubles. (Without any children even our small house wouldn't seem so small.) (26)

Read after "Ōbasami," the story's implications are intriguing. The invitation to castration implied by the final scene of "Ōbasami" is taken one step further, with Miichi emotionally liberated by thoughts of a life free of the role of "man"—as father and husband. Similar sentiments are common to Shimao's male protagonists of this period: the narrator of "Kawa nagare" (The flow of the river, 1954), for instance, desires the "shudder of a strong stimulus" from outside the family to counteract the "stagnation" he feels at home. Violence done to the son—the snapping off of his tongue—thus represents a disguised act of violence directed in part by the father against his own position in the family.

Nenokichi, however, can also be seen as a substitute for the wife, Nasu, and thus the implications of Miichi's violence against the boy take on an entirely different cast.[92] One understands that the parents, in essence, are quarreling with *each other* through the medium of the son. The father's quarrel with his son, in short, is violence aimed at the wife and any attempts on her part to disrupt male dominance in the family. For readers of Shimao's later works the implications are chilling, because quite obviously severing the tongue brings on the inability to *speak*. If, as Sarah Kofman puts it, woman is that which "does not have the right to speak," the severing of the tongue is a powerful symbol of further violence against a woman's right to her own voice.[93] In this sense, Miho of *Shi no toge* becomes woman's ultimate revenge, because she quite literally has become a tongue that does not cease to speak— that *cannot* be cut. Much like the wartime protagonist divided in his desire both to escape and uphold the oppressive system in which he is implicated, Shimao's domestic male protagonist thus always stands divided. He wishes both to disrupt and transform a stable but oppressive order and, at the same time, attempts the opposite, a suppression of that which threatens this order and his position in it.[94]

"Kisōsha no yūutsu" (1954)

"Kisōsha no yūutsu" (hereafter "Kisōsha"), also featuring Nasu and Miichi, replaces the indirect conflict of "Nenokichi" into the dynamic that dominates Shimao's fiction for the next two decades: the direct confrontation between husband and wife. After the initial quarrel opening the story, Nasu suffers what can only be described as an attack of madness, from which she soon recovers. Miichi goes out to drink and ends up spending the night at a brothel. In the meantime, Nasu worries about him and, late at night, sees someone she takes to be Miichi returning home, standing outside in the alley and then disappearing. Miichi returns home the next day surprised to hear he "returned" during the night. The story ends with Miichi fretting over this second self—his doppelgänger. References to wartime clue the reader in to the characters' status as further incarnations of the wartime lieutenant and his island lover.

Like the Miichi in "Nenokichi", here he contemplates how "wonderful" it would be to leave his wife and children, but Miichi is not decisive enough to do so and thus settles on a few drinks in a nearby bar. Yet he still wonders, "Am I really unable to leave like this and just go someplace far away? Maybe I might to be able to do so" (111). In contrast to Miichi's indecisiveness, Nasu lives in constant fear her husband will leave the house, never to return. She cannot rid herself of the first impression she had of him, that of a "soldier who slips away to have fun," a person ready to go off at any time. She squats at his feet at the entrance and begins to polish his shoes. Miichi reacts by pushing her away, making as if to kick her away, and telling her, "I want to be alone" (112). At this moment Nasu has her first mad fit:

> Nasu leaped to her feet.
> She looked silently at Miichi's face.
> That was the instant when it happened.
> She turned around suddenly and with a weird cry of "Uwaa!" she opened the glass door and was about to leap out.
> Miichi's feelings froze. Instinctively he grabbed Nasu from behind.
> Stopped by his embrace, Nasu banged repeatedly on the glass with both hands and yelled out *"Anma!"* Her voice was strangely childish. In the southern island she was from that was the word for mother. Nasu tried to tear Miichi's arms away from her.
> Her strength was incredible. Miichi had to hold her down hard.
> *"Anmai, wandaka, teretitabore"* [in standard Japanese, *Okaasan watashi o tsurete kudasai*—mother, please take me back], Nasu said, and when she looked at his face her expression was ugly and twisted as if she'd run across an evil spirit, and she struggled to escape from his arms.
> "Nasu, Nasu, it's me. It's me, do you understand, it's me." (112)

Nasu's primal scream in dialect to be returned to her island home is significant, as are Miichi's thoughts and feelings about Nasu's attack:

> At least *that* didn't happen. (I haven't been thinking about Nasu at all, have I?) Or perhaps a different sort of life had approached and let me catch a glimpse, and then changed direction and went away.

All of a sudden, the life he was familiar with rose up from his vacant feelings and spread out, together with an old, stuffy smell. (114)

In Nasu's brief mad fit, Miichi has a "glimpse of another life" and is *dis-
satisfied* that "that hadn't occurred" (115). "That," one is led to believe,
is the great transformation Shimao's male protagonists both fear and
desire.

Time passes slowly and "unbearably" as Miichi waits for Nasu to
sleep. Finally, when she and the children have drifted off, he finds himself jumpy and on edge. He feels he has "crossed to the other side of a
deep abyss and couldn't recall what had happened on the other side. He
was surrounded by a gap which absorbed all memory, and felt hurried
by a desire to get up and move to a different place" (116). The imagery
of the abyss is one encountered time and again in Shimao's works. The
most obvious example is the story "Ware fukaki fuchi yori" (the first of
the *byōinki*, which I will examine in chapter 3), which literally means
"We, from a deep abyss."[95] In the *byōinki* this image takes the form of
the protagonist feeling he must accompany his wife to the very depths
of the abyss of madness in order to be able to climb out again. In the
war stories, the image is associated with impending death as the narrator, awaiting his orders to take off on a suicide mission, envisions the
southern ocean "suddenly becoming a precipice" where the "water
froze darkly, and dripping water plunged down this bottomless cliff."[96]
And in "Shima e" (see chapter 4), at the scene at the cape, the narrator
has a hallucination of an abyss opening up in front of him, which in the
next instant is transformed into a broader vision of limitless scope.

Wandering around the neighborhood in "Kisōsha," Miichi is struck
first by the familiar fear that in his absence something drastic will occur:

Again he thought of the fire in the *kotatsu* and was on the verge of starting
back home. But if he went back and Nasu and the children woke up, it was
likely he wouldn't be able to leave again. So he continued to walk, without really knowing why. Then in his imagination he saw something catch fire, and
in an instant his house was enveloped in a hell of flames; Nasu, without ut-
tering a word, was burned to death, and the children cried out tearfully
through the blankets of smoke.

He could not possibly endure the malicious looks from his neighbors,
whose houses had also caught fire. (118)[97]

Seeing Miichi tormented by "the possibility that his worst nightmares
might become reality"[98] grasps but one part of this character's divided
feelings and divided self. The other half, as we have noted, considers

how "wonderful" it would be to be free of the burdens of family, and thus does not react in the expected way to his own vision, namely by visualizing any subsequent loneliness and sorrow.[99]

In the meantime, in the middle of night Nasu sees Miichi returning home. Standing at the toilet looking outside, she hears footsteps and sees a figure she takes for Miichi, and even hears him call out to her, "Mother, I'm back" (122). She scurries outside to open the gate, losing a sandal down the outhouse-style toilet in her haste, only to hear his "footsteps" receding in the distance. What Nasu "saw" becomes the major concern of the remainder of the story. At first she thinks it must be an illusion caused by her attack, but she soon rejects that interpretation. Listening to the radio news about traffic accidents, she is briefly convinced it was the ghost of Miichi, killed in a traffic accident, "come back to tell her about that" (124). Finally, she settles on calling it an *ikimaburi*. We have encountered this word before, in "Tatakai e no osore," published nine months after "Kisōsha." An Amami term for "living ghost," the living spirit of someone soon to die, reappears in *Hi no utsuroi*, where the narrator and his wife (now in Amami) see a white flash flying in the night air above them, which the wife decides is an *ikimaburi*.[100] As becomes clear in *Hi no utsuroi* through the wife's later tales of *ikimaburi* in her childhood on the island, the ability to see them is often limited to certain select people. And Nasu in "Kisōsha" is one who has the extraordinary power to envision those about to "die."

Returning home in the morning, Miichi laughs off Nasu's comments about seeing his *ikimaburi* the night before. He ad libs an excuse about getting drunk in Asakusa, to which Nasu replies,

> "Father, it's no laughing matter. You really did come back." Nasu's face, too, was pale and she laughed. "Surely nothing happened to you, did it?"
>   "How could it?"

Still, Miichi cannot let go of the image of "one more Miichi standing there, smiling at Nasu" (139):

> Where could that guy be walking now? he wondered, and for no apparent reason, this brought up thoughts of the roof tiles of all the roofs, wet in the moonlight.
>   "Father, are you up? You really slept soundly."
>   Nasu called to him from the kitchen.
>   The children were out playing and nowhere to be seen. Hearing Nasu's voice, Miichi was about to leave the toilet when all of a sudden he thought, 'That guy who came back's a real bother.' (139–140)

By 1954, then, a number of elements are gathered in Shimao's fiction: the focus on domestic life and the marital relationship, increasingly paralleling actual events in Shimao's married life (Miichi and Nasu being replaced by Toshio and Miho); the downward spiral of the husband and wife; the wife's mad fits and pleas to return to her island home matched by the husband's desire to break free of stagnation; fear; and death hovering on the horizon. Add to this the wife's unique powers and the subtext of the war, and all the ingredients of Shimao's most famous work—his *byōsaimono*—are in place. Significantly for his later fiction, the "dream" elements in his stories—here defined as the inexplicable and antirational—are now clearly linked with the figure of the wife, and the island.

At the beginning of this chapter I noted Shimao's 1953 statement of his desire to write works "of a living person" and the necessity of a greater sacrifice for this to occur. In Shimao's fiction—and life—this sacrifice was about to occur. And once again this involved him in the painful, but vital, work of constructing an alphabet of trauma.

THreE

Out of the Abyss:
The "Sick Wife Stories"

> Absolute death (non-being) is the state of being
> unheard, unrecognized, unremembered.
>
> Mikhail Bakhtin, *Problems of Dostoyevsky's Poetics*

The Byōinki Stories (1955–1957)

IN THE spring of 1954 Shimao's wife Miho went mad. As she recalls in a later essay, on the day of her husband's birthday, April 18, Miho took her two small children to greet him at the Koiwa Station in eastern Tokyo, hoping that Toshio, who often spent days away from home, would return for the celebration she had planned.[1] She waited in vain:

> I had prepared a nice birthday dinner of whole bream for the four of us, and the sight of it lying cold on the table under the white cloth I had covered it with pierced me to the quick. I was so lonely I went into my husband's room. My husband's room was a sacred spot I felt guilty about invading even when I cleaned it. I didn't touch any of the things on his table, but my eyes were drawn to a few lines dashed off in the diary which lay open on the *kotatsu*. I casually read these, and in that instant I felt a powerful force shoot through my body. A surge of scorching heat. But soon after, my body shivered and a wave of chills assaulted me, making me unable to stand. I was suddenly down on all fours, roaring in a terrible voice like a lion—Uoo! Uoo!—then running around the room. Put in such extremities a person becomes more like an animal, it would seem. I lost all intelligence and consciousness of being a human and became deranged.[2]

99

The diary entry revealed her husband's love for another woman involved in the Tokyo literary circles in which Shimao was a participant.
The mental condition sparked by the above incident soon became a
chronic jealous rage, which continued throughout 1954 and into 1955,
when Shimao had Miho hospitalized. Miho's condition, defined at first
as schizophrenia and later as a more treatable "psychogenic reaction,"
did not improve, and some time in the summer of 1955 she was admitted to the locked and barred mental ward of Kōnodai Hospital, just
east of Tokyo. Her husband joined her to care for her day-to-day needs.
Finally, in October 1955 Miho was discharged from the hospital, and
she and her husband immediately set off to make a new home in far off
Amami Ōshima, near her home island of Kakeromajima. In one of the
more poignant vignettes in postwar Japanese literary history, the Shimaos were seen off at the dock by a group of writers and critics including Yoshiyuki Junnosuke, Shōnō Junzō, and Yoshimoto Takaaki. Some,
like Shimao himself, wondered whether his self-imposed exile marked
the end of his writing career.

Although he was soon busy with a second career as head librarian of
the Amami Library, Shimao's career as writer was not, as he feared, over;
arguably, it was just beginning. And the experience of his wife's madness, which at one point threatened to put an end to his writing, formed
the basis for his best-known work. Beginning with the series of nine
loosely linked stories collectively called the *byōinki* (literally, record of
a hospital stay; 1955–1957) and culminating in the twelve stories published from 1960–1976 eventually collected in the award-winning 1977
novel *Shi no toge* (covering the ten months from the outbreak of Miho's
madness to their admission into the mental hospital), much of Shimao's
best-known fiction during his twenty years on Amami took as its starting point the decisive period of his wife's madness, from 1954–1955.[3]
The moment of Miho's descent into madness became the black hole
of Shimao's fiction toward which all is else is pulled. The two earlier
strands of Shimao's fiction, his surrealistic dream-based stories and depictions of his wartime *tokkōtai* experience, became secondary to Shimao's new literary preoccupation: Miho's madness and its aftermath.
But these two strands are hardly forgotten. Through these "sick wife
stories" *(byōsaimono)* Shimao was, arguably, able to confront more directly the traumas of war and was able to bring the unconscious world
in contact with the conscious world.[4]

Readers faithful enough to have followed all of Shimao's literary production at the time, including the many short sketches he wrote for radio, were left hanging with the March 1955 story, "Jizō no nukumi" (Warmth of the Jizō), which depicts in some detail Miho's mental illness and the couple's struggle with her condition:

> This winter I've spent strange days. No, you should say I'm spending them still.
>
> My wife and I have had our presence of mind blown away. This is a situation other people can't understand easily. To put it briefly, you could condense it into the following lament of my wife: "How much have you ever done for me as a husband?" Naturally this is something very difficult for people to understand. As the result of the tension of being submissive (ninjū no kinchō) for so long, my wife's nerves snapped.
>
> I am nothing but a selfish man, nothing more. The echo of the last train of the night, the footsteps of the neighborhood night patrol, the crow of the first rooster of the morning, the night air finally beginning to stir, the first train leaving, the milk delivery coming. The anxious, dreary daily routine of my sleepless wife, waiting for her husband, is concentrated in these. Even in the sounds of the mice and wind blowing you can see reflected my wife's endless days of putting up with a grief in which all emotional support has collapsed.
>
> Didn't I do an awful thing, sacrificing my wife so I could build up my own ego? Step by step, people are overcome by fatigue. My wife was exhausted, and began to draw away from me. I was confused, and completely drained of color, clung to her.
>
> Thus our strange battle began. We couldn't stand to be separated from each other even for a minute. Going shopping or even mailing a postcard, we walked together. I tried to regain her affections, while my wife did battle with something like an evil spirit in order to link her heart once again with her husband. Like flesh coming part, her feelings were stripped away and she could only sit in a dangerous corner, holding her head.
>
> My wife was forced to experience a psychological torture new to her. The unusual mixture of attachment and hate for me nearly made her mad. No— those were indeed days of madness. Seeing my wife in such agony, I felt despair at myself for lacking the strength to save her from that hell. *Like the days of that strange war when tokkōtai members spent each day waiting for death, we spent ever narrowing days with vision and feelings fixed.* Like two serpents biting each other's tail. This was surely something an outsider's eye would find unintelligible. But we knew that death had come right next to us. (vol. 7, 334–335; emphasis added)

From March to October 1955 Shimao published not a single work of fiction.[5] One chronology of his life lists the following:

> From the end of the summer [1954] his wife Miho's health worsened and her attacks began in October [1955]: For his wife Miho's treatment [Shimao and

Miho] moved to Sakura, Ikebukuro, and Ishikawa. In June, Shimao entered
Kōnodai Hospital to attend to Miho. While his wife received sleep therapy
(*suiminryō*), Shimao began writing the *byōinki* stories.[6]

Just as there is room to doubt the official chronology of the outbreak of
Miho's illness (the fact that she herself dates it in the spring while most
critics follow the chronology of *Shi no toge* and view it as occurring in
the fall), the impression left by the *byōinki* and the scant biographi-
cal material on the period that Shimao and Miho were under lock and
key in the mental hospital for most of four and a half months (June–
October 1955) has lately come under question. Recent research suggests several points that conflict with the usual chronology of Shimao's
life.[7] Shimao, one should remember, made of his life a body of fiction,
and in doing so manipulated and rearranged the facts to create a more
effective narrative. Thus in the *byōinki* Shimao portrays the characters
Toshio and Miho as almost completely cut off from the world, for most
of their time in a locked ward, with Toshio at Miho's beck and call
twenty-four hours a day. This suffocating world, where they strove to
eliminate anything coming between them, is in great part a fictional reworking of a real-life situation where there was a great deal less intensity and more breathing space. Evidence of the latter can be found in
the production of the stories themselves, the first three actually being
composed in the hospital.

The news that Shimao had entered a mental hospital with his wife
came as a shock to his friends in the Tokyo literary world. Haniya Yutaka recalls that

> [w]hen the news came that Shimao Toshio had moved to the mental hospital
> with his wife, my wife said in admiration that Shimao must be a person with
> an extraordinarily deep love. It was certainly not an easy action to take, and
> is both shocking and moving.[8]

The shock contemporary readers such as Haniya felt was not only that
Shimao would enter the mental ward to help in his wife's recovery, but
no doubt also in *what* he found there in the ward: the closed-off world
of illness and despair no Japanese writer had depicted so knowingly.
Shimao's stories of the mental ward stand in stark contrast to the portrayal of the treatment of mental illness in a more contemporary work,
perhaps the best-selling novel of postwar Japan, Murakami Haruki's
Noruuee no mori (1987; trans. *Norwegian Wood*). The novelist Kaga Oto-

hiko, himself a former psychiatrist, condemns Murakami's depiction of
the treatment of mental illness:

> [He] writes about a hospital that's like heaven, and ignores the reality of mis-
> ery. When I read this I felt—how should I put it—sorry for the author.[9]

If one could feel sorry for Shimao, in contrast, it is because he experienced firsthand the true sorrows of mental illness; unlike Murakami,
his work vividly captures the misery of the mental hospital. Besides the
Toshio-Miho relationship that forms the core of the stories, the *byōinki*
depict the gamut of despair caused by mental illness: a lobotomized,
mute student; a man, his brain and nervous system eaten away by vene-
real disease, who stares into space and bursts into song; another man—
nicknamed the "Priest"—who stands in the hallway, praying day and
night, interrupting himself to proffer a pathetic piece of stale bread. Of
one patient and his family Toshio notes:

> Minoru's life was painful in the extreme. He was a craftsman by tempera-
> ment, a cabinet maker, but the infection in his brain made him blind, and
> there was almost no hope for him. His wife's family was poor, and she'd been
> sent out at age six to earn a living taking care of other children; from a time
> when the children she carried on her back had bigger heads than she did, she
> spent half her life as a maid, never even attending grade school. Only her
> voice through the walls as she recited the Lotus Sutra retained a certain in-
> nocence, like that of a young girl not yet twenty. . . . The father and mother
> both in the hospital, and with three children and the husband's aged aunt to
> support, they just managed to scrape by on the money their eldest son earned
> as a craftsman. (153)[10]

Of course the mental patient described in most detail is Miho. After
undergoing electroshock therapy and constant doses of sleeping medicine, she undergoes sleep therapy and then hibernation therapy *(tōmin
ryōhō)*, both of which employ drugs that lower her blood pressure and
bodily functions in order to combat insomnia and the raging attacks on
her husband. All of this is done to rid her of memories that plague her;
side effects include near blindness and the loss of a sense of time.

The nine *byōinki* stories can be briefly outlined as follows: "Ware fukaki fuchi yori" (trans. 1985, "Out of the Depths") depicts Toshio's and
Miho's move from outpatient to inpatient status and Toshio's first reactions to his new environment. The story ends with a detailed descrip-

tion of an organized folk dance performed by the patients—a dance that serves as a partial framing device for the whole series. Here Toshio merely observes the dance to kill time while waiting for Miho's treatment session to finish, viewing the patients as nameless objects. Later, in the seventh story, "Tensō" (Forwarding), Miho has become a joyful participant in the *obon* dance, and the dance serves as a reunion between Toshio and Miho and the friends they have made. The contrast clearly shows the distance the two have come in adapting to life in the mental ward. "Kyōsha no manabi" (Lessons of the insane) and "Aru seishin byōsha" (A mental patient) are sketches of several patients in the male ward to which Miho and Toshio are assigned.[11] The latter story in particular is a detailed and moving account of a patient, Hanio, whom Toshio is both attracted to and repelled by. "Omoi niguruma" (A heavy piggyback ride) covers the events of one day: Toshio takes a trip outside the hospital to buy fruit for Miho; Miho, seeking revenge for being left alone, attempts to kill herself by deliberately falling off her bed. Of the *byōinki* stories this is the most detailed and concentrated account of the nature of Miho's illness and Toshio's attempts to cope with it. "Chiryō" (Treatment) depicts the sleep therapy Miho undergoes, while the main "dramatic action" of the series comes in "Nogare yuku kokoro" (trans. 1985, "The Heart that Slips Away"), with Miho escaping from the ward and Toshio fearing she has died. (She returns in a few hours after wandering in the fields outside.) "Tensō" depicts the cool attitudes of the staff after Miho's escape, and Toshio's and Miho's forced move out of the locked ward to an open ward—a move that fills them with trepidation. "Nemuri naki suimin" (The sleepless sleep) and "Ichijiki" (A period of time) describe life in their new ward, Miho's "hibernation therapy," and her slow but gradual improvement. The series ends on an upbeat note, with Toshio noting that his wife's treatment "appears to be proceeding smoothly" (204).

FIRST AND foremost, Shimao's stories of the mental hospital are marked by an unresolved tension created by the coexistence of opposites. Toshio attempts to exclude the outside world and create a world of just himself and Miho, all the while realizing that Miho's madness is partly the result of the pure one-to-one relationship he thinks will cure her. Even in the nature of Miho's treatment there is a similar tension created by the paradoxical: her hibernation therapy is a "sleep that is not sleep" *(nemuri naki nemuri)*. Most of all, however, the *byōinki*, and Miho's madness, rest on a foundation of mutual contradiction: Toshio's absence causes her to have an attack—as does his *presence*. Thus the ideal situation for her is one in which he is simultaneously *neither* present nor absent. The closest Toshio can get to resolving this paradox is the following imagined solution:

> [I]t occurred to me that it might be better if the two of us were put in separate little rooms facing each other, a heavy bolt on the connecting door keeping us from opening it at will, and in the center of that door, thick like the door of a refrigerator, would be a small square peephole so we could keep track of each other as we lived our daily lives.[12]

Second, the *byōinki* (and to a great extent Shimao's fiction after this series) are characterized by the difficulty of distinguishing objective reality from the subjective, from what lies in the narrator's consciousness. In the early dream stories the events of the entire narrative—the leaps in time and space, the discontinuities of logical connections, the surrealistic actions and images—make it all too easy to assume the stories are recountings of dream fragments. Readers, then, are able to distance themselves from the events of the story or even dismiss them as preposterous or unreal. With the *byōinki*, however, Shimao's fiction takes a new and subtle turn, projecting the dream world onto the real world.[13] Shimao's literary innovativeness lies in the use of an I-novel framework (characters based on himself and his family, events based closely on those of his real life)[14] combined with a thematic—madness—that both reflects the real (Shimao's wife did indeed go mad) and *demands* the real (Miho's pathological demand for the entire "truth" of her husband's past in *Shi no toge*), as well as a style that very subtly calls into question the difference between objective and subjective reality.

Shimao is typically characterized as a difficult stylist. Sparling writes that

> [Shimao's] prose is uniformly difficult: there are logical gaps; the grammatical subject is often unclear; the sentences are long and full of sudden turns and surprises; and words have double meanings, or hidden meanings, exploited later like implications reinterpreted and only gradually understood.[15]

One principle difficulty of Shimao's prose lies in the way it makes objectivity problematic. One section from the opening of "Ware fukaki fuchi yori," for instance, makes this point clear. Here Toshio and Miho are still outpatients in the hospital, and Toshio is walking outside while he waits for her session with the doctor to finish. Ignoring a sign forbidding unauthorized persons to pass to the other ward, he continues walking, "all the more convinced that some important key was waiting on the other side": [16]

> As I drew close, I felt a chill air beneath the windows. The inside was pitch dark; I could see nothing. It gave the feeling of a storeroom or an attic. I hesitated to look at the creatures wriggling in that darkness. *On the ground beneath the window I half expected there to be bits of broken pottery, knives, and razor blades, on which I might accidentally cut the soles of my feet. But I didn't see anything like that on the ground near me.* Walking on tiptoe, I gradually worked my way around to the other side, afraid all the while that someone would come and reprimand me.[17]

As Sparling notes, her English translation of Shimao's stories edits out much of the ambiguity of the original; the above is a good example.[18] Kawamura points out how the italicized portion in the original is much more misleading and ambiguous than it appears in translation, and is indicative of Shimao's approach to writing. The original reads:

> Chikazuku to mado no shita ni wa hiebie to shita kūki ga aru yō ni omoeta. Mado no naibu wa usugurakute nani mo mienakatta. Monooki no yō na kanji ga shita. Sono kurai naka ni ugomeku mono o miru no wa chūcho sareta. *Mado no shita no atari ni wa setomono ya hamono no kakera, kamisori no ha nado ga ochite ite, omowazu ashi no ura o kirikomisō na kanji ga shita.* Miwatashita tokoro sono yō na mono wa miataranakatta keredomo. (11; emphasis added)

Kawamura notes that the part about the "chilled air" and the feeling that the building is like a "storeroom" are not objective descriptions, but subjective reactions to what the narrator can *actually see*, and thus are not problematic for the reader. The difficulty lies instead with the italicized passage. At first reading the bits of broken pottery, knives, and razor blades appear actually to lie beneath the window, perhaps, one imagines, the results of the patients' violent outbursts and suicide attempts. "*Kanji ga shita*"—"I felt like . . ."—at the end of the passage at first seems to apply only to the narrator's feelings about stepping on these sharp objects—thus he "felt like his soles were being cut" by them, even though, one assumes, he is wearing shoes. The next sentence, however, reveals that "*kanji ga shita*" applies to the entire utterance; one now realizes that the narrator only *felt* that these objects were there, when indeed they were not.[19] Kawamura speaks also of the "two directions" of Shimao's prose—the "grasping of dream as real and, paralleling this, the grasping of reality as dream," which are "constantly mixed, weaving together in the work as a whole a cloth of two qualitatively different colored threads." This prose style, in making objectivity problematic, in turn serves to underscore the philosophical stance of the *byōinki*, namely the limits of individual knowledge of others and the world.

Shimao's prose in the *byōinki* is marked as well by its fluid sense of time, the combination at times of past, present, and future in one instant. In "Tensō," for instance, watching the preparations for the patients' *obon* dance, Toshio feels

> [a] feeling of reminiscence welled up in me, as if they were jovial fairies dancing by the side of the pond, and I felt that sometime before I had, by the side of the pond, watched my wife's preparations for the dance like this, but also that I was viewing the present from much later through eyes which saw it as a sweet memory, and felt too that I was previewing beforehand that future experience. (162)

A further feature of Shimao's prose is the centrality of a careful, even clinical, observation. Toshio feels driven to

> faithfully observe everything about [Miho's] reactions and changes in appearance. Observation *(kansatsu)* is both an act of suffering [*juku*, translated as passion, as in the Passion of Christ] and the only way to get my wife's and my reality moving. (105–106)

The process of "faithful" observation, however, is constantly tempered and tinged by the narrator's emotions and mental state, undercutting the possibility of neutral observation.

Observation is always participation. From the opening paragraphs of "Ware fukaki fuchi yori" Miho's madness is less a condition observed by her husband than a struggle in which he is both observer and participant:

> I was battered, mind and body, by my wife's disturbed mental state. When she was in the throes of one of the attacks that were symptomatic of her illness, her logic was iron-tough, and if I were to submit to that relentless logic, neither my wife nor I could go on living. When she drove me into a corner, I would completely lose my head, and many times I grabbed a sash or a cord and tried to strangle myself. Whereupon my wife, like the *Kenmun*, an amphibious goblin in Ryukyuan legend, would suddenly gain amazing strength in her arms and remove the cord from my throat. When the demonic cloud lifted, my attachment to life was restored. After that, it was my wife who felt the dangerous lure to suicide. My nerves were frayed to a pulp.[20]

In these suicide attempts (more powerfully depicted in *Shi no toge*) there is a constant shifting of roles, with first one, then the other, playing at dying. Yet the text makes it clear that for the most part their roles are not so fluid, and that in the power relationship between them, Miho holds the upper hand. Toshio is her "servant" (30). He hides in her shadow like a "black-hooded puppeteer" (138), submitting to being subordinate to her because only thus can she "control her derangement" and "win back her ego" (144).[21] In a scene that makes explicit one of the subtexts of the story—Toshio's and Miho's experiences in the war—we find Toshio no longer the lieutenant in charge, but the lowliest soldier addressing Miho, now the superior:

> In front of her I became a private, standing at attention and using military language. . . .
> "What a racket. Why don't you just go to sleep?" my wife said to me.
> "Am I granted permission to go to sleep?" I asked.
> "Yes, yes. Why don't you just go to sleep?"
> "But later on, won't you deign to express to me that even though I am supposed to be your attendant I just went to sleep without looking after you?" (40–41)

The translation attempts, but fails, to convey the speech levels of the original, which in Toshio's case is humorous in its exaggerated civility: ". . . *ōse ni naru no de wa gozarimasen de gozarimasu ka.*" Although Toshio calls this "military language," one has trouble imagining even the most browbeaten foot soldier of the Imperial Army speaking this way, which is more reminiscent of an Edo-period flunky addressing his lord, or an exaggerated parody of such. A few pages before this the question of civilian, rather than military, power relations is brought to the forefront. In a reversal of the actual power relations obtained during the war, when Miho and the islanders were the "peasants" and the lieutenant "nobility," Miho insists on her superior breeding:

> When my wife's logic that has it that I, being descended from peasants, am humble, while she, belonging to a legendary noble lineage was thus pure blue-blood, failed to move between us, she mercilessly whipped and kicked that aspect of me. I balled up my fists and struck myself on the face first with one hand, then the other. My nose bled, and the flesh inside my nostrils was cut, my eyeballs ached and the outer corners of my eyes swelled up yellow. In my benumbed head my wife, coldly looking down on me with an embarrassed expression, appeared lovely, and I thought maybe it was an illusion to have felt I could occupy a part of her. (37–38).

In a scene that can be described as alternately touching, pathetic, and even silly, Toshio pushes Miho around the ward in a cart, both because of the physical weakness brought on by her treatment and as part of the pattern of submission and subordination he must play out to help her ease her mental turmoil. "My attitude of service *(hōshi)* to my wife had to be exaggerated," he notes. "Her illness sought this to an extreme extent" (193):

> "Your cart has arrived," I said. My wife's face broke into a smile and putting on airs like a noblewoman, she got down from her bed, gracefully walked toward the cart, and got on with my help. "Walk," she then commanded. With a dull sound, the cart began to move. My wife's weight pressed down on the rubber tires, and I had to press with my arms with just enough strength to accommodate this weight, but the weight made me feel cheerful. . . . "Toshio, it's heavy, isn't it? You can push more slowly if you'd like." It was the first time since her illness began that she called me Toshio. (179)

The scene is representative of a change in Miho's illness found three-quarters of the way through the *byōinki* (an improvement that, like everything else in Toshio's world, has a down side as well) and contrasts with the way he views the "burden" of their relationship earlier in their hospital stay. In the section of "Omoi niguruma" from which the story takes its title, Miho is less the weight he cheerfully pushes than a burden he cannot escape:

> When my wife wakes up I can't remain idle even for a second, and I lose all sense of the passage of time. This feeling is just like that of a sailor setting foot in an unknown land. On his shoulders rides *some thing like a person.* If he stops, the *thing* riding piggyback on him tightens its grip on his head and he can't remain there, he must keep on walking around as much as he possibly can. In that deserted, barren, unknown land, he must wander without destination. The *thing* on his back, moreover, signals him which direction to go in by tightening, then loosening, its grip on his head. . . . Give me time of my own, you plead, even a little time with nothing to harass me. If you can't give me that, then kill me [you cry]. Lead me to down to hell. Kill me, kill me. (81; emphasis in the original)

The passage highlights the notion of time and the image of a journey Toshio must take with his wife through madness, one repeated in the most memorable imagery describing their world—one of ice, a frozen field over which they must travel.

Miho's attacks are a "block of ice" he wants desperately to "break up" and escape from: "I want to shout and cry aloud, but as long as I don't go insane myself, this blank reality will continue to approach me at the same pace" (75). In an image repeated over and over in *Shi no toge*, the constant tension Toshio feels in trying to avoid provoking her attacks leads him to feel he is "walking over thin ice" (93). His inability to answer any of his wife's "detailed questions" leads to a "frozen situation"; "Just imagining this is enough to make my tongue harden and make the world pale and freeze over with cracking ice" (101). This frozen world of Miho's mad attacks contrasts with the image of a grassy plain:

> Maybe everything up till now was all a dream? When she wakes up won't we go back to the peaceful, ordinary life we used to have before we entered the hospital? At any rate, for me our life now, just the two of us in the hospital, was one of wonderful satisfaction. That feeling of satisfaction blew away with the first signs that my wife was waking up. In my memory, a nostalgia came to the fore, and a grassy plain with flowers just beginning to blossom; when reality suddenly showed its face it immediately became a wilderness and froze over, with a hungry living ghost, unable to deal with the contradiction (*hai-han*) it contained, running rampant, spitting up flames of ice. (82)

In a similar way, when Miho, on rare occasion, snaps out of an attack to apologize to her husband, "The frozen stiffness is, with those words of hers, melted away, and the field of ice in an instant becomes a spring field with flowers blooming and birds singing." (170).

Throughout most of the *byōinki* Miho's madness is, for Toshio, a profoundly unsettling, frightening, and confusing experience. He has no one to rely on since "[m]y only companion on this journey, my wife, is insane, and like a pitching boat, just when I think she's approaching me with good intentions, she aims the tip of her anger at me. I couldn't take that incessant exchange" *(kōryū)*. As Miho lies next to him, awakening one morning, he senses "flames of the pain of her delusions," which she "coldly, deliberately suppresses"; she "keeps her breathing quiet in order to tap at and break open my soul" (75). Awakening to each new day means awakening to a repetitive cycle of Miho's verbal abuse, followed by sleep as she succumbs to the drugs she is given. And much of the time this cycle is described in terms we would normally expect—that is, his hatred of and inability to cope with this "incessant exchange," followed by relief when she falls asleep or her attacks are over. He feels "broken into pieces" by her attacks (102), loses a sense of time, feels helpless to determine the course of events as a "thing" on his back crushes his skull if he wavers. He feels "defenseless" sitting on a "bed of needles," always on "standby alert" (89),[22] feels Miho is a "pitiless machine binding" him, a *satori* (enlightened one) who deprives him of a private interior space by reaching into his very thoughts and foreseeing his actions (97).

Toshio, significantly, does not portray himself as mere accidental victim of his wife's insanity. He is convinced that the reasons they are in the hospital lie just as much with *him* as with her. Hints of his infidelity are scattered throughout the text; likewise the text contains thoughts on his childhood depression, the "overly sensitive nature," and the bird-like creature he feels pecking away at his "spirit." These problems of the spirit have continued into adulthood, poisoning his relationships with others. Noting that while Miho is a "mental patient" with psychogenic reactions, he thinks he himself might be a *seishin ishuku byōsha* (141). He coined the term to describe his psychological state, literally "atrophied," unable to cope with the normal demands of society. He has "torn off and discarded the limbs of life in society, but the decay has set down roots in a deeper place," and the more he severs these, the deeper he must cut (141–142), and he finds himself unable to "drive away" the "evil spirits" that plague him (155). He is "poisoned by the stink of [his] past," which "suffocates" him, and is conscious of sin—how "all phenomenon" work to "dig up [his] sin" (143). He has "old wounds" that Miho digs up by "opening up of the graves of the past," and his wife's illness is his "fate," he feels (79), because he has made her suffer "for ten years" (their entire marriage) (142).

Yet Toshio's situation is more complex than that of a man who, having provoked his wife's illness, now plays the victim to placate her. In one of the more memorable scenes of the *byōinki*, after having dozed off next to his wife, Toshio hears a slight sound and awakens. Ascertaining that Miho is still asleep, a "sudden sense of relief spread through [his] veins" (83). Through the glass window he witnesses a scene like a "silent play" that illustrates both the way in which observation in the text is bound up with subjective reactions, and the thematics of victim-victimizer seen in Shimao's other fiction:

> My head all gloomy, I finally turned my gaze to the playground outside; suddenly I found myself stunned. A fierce dog as big as a calf was chasing a ball thrown by a young man. Suddenly the dog sidled up to a little girl who had come up later and was playing there. The girl shooed him away halfheartedly. But she was making a mistake. Dogs are wild animals. (83)

The girl suddenly panics, turning to flee, and the dog bites her on the knee. Blood runs down her leg, and the scene, which Toshio had watched at first "as if it were all a joke," suddenly "freezes [his] blood." Toshio recalls "that inexpressible feeling of despair" he had when he was bitten by a dog, a feeling that is now "assailing the girl" (83). Standing there silent, shivering, and fearful, the girl is berated by the dog's owner, who blames her for the attack because only an "idiot" would run away. "Those two immature, thin legs sticking out of the skirt," Toshio comments, "and the blood on her knee so easily stabbed at the defenseless feelings I had" (83–84):

> A nauseous feeling welled up in me. The straight, strong body of the young man galled me. The girl's despondent, helpless stance tugged at my heart; the young man should, I thought, before anything else, hold the girl close. The girl's expression, injured in an outrageous attack and unable to say a word, looked beautiful. That expression still had a human quality to it. But aren't I just like the young man? My wife's attacks come from a power outside the sphere of human life (*jingai no chikara ni yoru mono*). The one who was outrageously injured is my wife. No matter how much my wife sticks a beak inside my heart and picks and gouges it out, I should silently hold her to me. But instead, whenever she has an attack, a coagulated something surges up inside me and I fall into a raving reaction like hers. I forbid myself to do anything that might provoke her, yet I find myself unable to keep this restriction. That young man's arrogant, threatening face was pasted on my own features, and more than ever, I felt my strength drain away. (84)[23]

The attack comes to stand for the complex relations of victim/victimizer between people, which in Toshio's restricted field of vision is played out not at some higher level but at the level of a single man and woman. Remembering the time he was attacked, Toshio identifies with the victim and feels an empathy that manifests itself in physical reactions of nausea. The victim's "loveliness" and "human quality" stand in stark contrast to the "arrogant and threatening face" of the victimizer; and he identifies with the victimizer as well. What is significant here is the dual aspect of himself, *and* Miho, that he recognizes. Toshio, who knows what it feels like now to be a victim (of Miho's attacks) likewise understands how he has been a victimizer. For her part, Miho is the "lovely" girl bitten by the dog (that is, victimized by Toshio) who has now turned around and begun to "pick and gouge out" the heart of the "dog owner" (who is Toshio). She is both the suffering victim of Toshio's mistreatment and the one who makes him suffer. And Toshio, who desires to purge himself of his victimizer side, remains frustrated at how it remains. He is the victimizer who should comfort his victim (in this case by silently enduring her victimization of him) but who cannot, and who instead finds himself turning his own "raving reactions" back on her. The *byōinki*, and much of Shimao's fiction, is a world in which one cannot escape this dual, always divided, nature of human beings and human relationships.

Despite the cycle of repulsion and relief he depicts over and over—repulsion at Miho's attacks and relief when she's asleep—it is clear that, in a strange way, being the constant victim of Miho's attacks brings a feeling of reality and something positive the Shimao protagonist has missed in his life until this moment. Liberation from Miho's attacks when she falls asleep brings a "return of lost 'time,'" yet time itself and a "normal" sense of its flow are not entirely desirable. As he begins to hear once again the "noise of the 'flow of time,'" Toshio feels "in an instant [he] has aged." "My wife and I since we entered the hospital have grown noticeably younger . . . because we no longer have any feeling of 'time'" (81), yet with the return of time

> I felt my own skin rapidly growing wrinkled. And an unbearable loneliness clutched at my chest. I can't let my wife sleep. Time is revolving too quickly. Wake her up. Strangely, in my wife's crazed attacks I hoped to escape from I'd found a tangible truth *(tegotae no aru shinjitsu)*. It was strange, but that's the way it was. (82)

With Miho asleep, he has again lost his "only travelling companion" across the "endless field of ice." "I thought I would shake her awake," he says, "and shout out Hey! Get up! Get up and attack me even more ferociously" (82).

This feeling of a tangible truth, which he finds difficult to account for, is not the same as the "wonderful satisfaction" he feels with "just the two of us in the hospital," a "feeling of satisfaction" that "blew away with the first signs that my wife was waking up." In fact, the feeling of tangible truth is quite the opposite. Whereas his satisfaction at their life is found only when dialogue with Miho is excluded, the feeling of "truth" is found precisely *in* their dialogue. And indeed the need for dialogue, specifically the reopening of a dialogue with the victims of wartime and postwar Japan, marks the *byōinki*. In the dream stories one finds the incessant wanderer over the postwar landscape, a person in search of, but only tangentially contacting, a variety of the marginalized of postwar Japan. In contrast, in the *byōinki* one finds a man whose physical freedom is denied, an inhabitant of a locked and barred mental hospital ward who desires even more restraint, who desires nothing less than complete isolation from society, and to join the patients in their world. In the milieu of the mental ward, among the most marginalized people, the insane, Toshio finds himself for the first time approaching community. Shimao's fictional world, however, is far from simplistic, and from the beginning one senses that Toshio's desire to understand and integrate himself into this community will remain only partially successful. The primacy of dialogue, in short, is underscored simultaneously with the ultimate unknowability of the Other and the problems inherent in the formation of community.

One question that nags at every reader of the *byōinki* is this: why is Toshio so bound to this relationship with Miho? Why not run away and escape from this living hell? Indeed, in many ways understanding these stories boils down to a search for answers to these questions, ones raised by such diverse critics as Mishima Yukio and Karatani Kōjin. In an often-quoted early essay on the *byōinki* and the early chapters of *Shi no toge*, Mishima asks,

> [W]hen the wife is finally hospitalized, why does the husband send his two children to [Miho's] hometown, and attend to his wife, and together with her begin to live the deeply cruel life of the hospital?
>
> In the irresponsible judgment of an outsider, as soon as the wife's attacks begin to destroy the family one thinks the husband should put his wife in the hospital and devote himself to raising the children. This might be the coldly realistic solution of society, but what is the real reason he doesn't take this realistic solution but adopts the method I've described?
>
> Is it because of human love? If so, what about the innocent children? Is it because of a sense of guilt and is done for atonement? If so shouldn't the atonement be best directed at the children?—These are questions your average person would think of.[24]

Karatani is concerned with much the same point as Mishima, commenting that "[w]hat is strange about these stories is why the [first person protagonist] has to submit to his wife's madness to this extent." What remains in the *byōinki*, Karatani writes, is the "suspension of disbelief," an acceptance of things as they are, of an "absolute order" that is never questioned, a world in which the question of why Toshio must "bow in reverence" to his wife's madness is excluded.

In contrast to Shimao's earlier stories, which record dreams, yet in which "there is not at all an atmosphere of dreams," Karatani sees the *byōinki* as works that capture the "essence of dreams" because, just as we feel when we are dreaming, we find in the stories "no leeway . . . for after-the-fact observation. There is no way to find 'distance' toward the other and toward oneself." And paradoxically these works are also the ones that have, "among postwar literature . . . grasped the real world the most."[25] One can easily see Karatani's point in his equation of the Toshio-Miho world and the "real world" of postwar Japan: postwar Japan society is characterized by a lack of individual freedom, is a sort of nightmarish "absolute order" that one must obey and from which one cannot find critical distance. In this sense he would appear in agreement with Okuno's summation of postwar society as "an evil victimizer against our lives and freedom."[26] But Karatani's essay should also be read as a reply to critics such as Okuno who find the *byōinki* a literary retreat from the avant-garde dream stories of Shimao's early career. Karatani's definition of the dream world as a nightmarish site of bondage and lack of critical distance makes the *byōinki* an advance over the earlier stories, which he sees as merely after-the-fact recountings of dreams. Shimao has not abandoned the pursuit of "dreams," but rather finally begun to capture their *essence*.

Karatani is correct in seeing Shimao as critical of postwar Japan and as viewing the postwar "new order" as imbued with enough residue from the past to militate against personal freedom (one remembers the allegorical first section of "Kizashi" in this regard). However, by equating the Toshio-Miho relationship in entirely negative terms, both Mishima and Karatani miss an important point regarding the *byōinki*. The world of Miho's madness, nightmarish to be sure, for Toshio contains a positive truth that he seeks:

> In my head the world of madness had a heavy, tangible sense to it *(zushiri to tegotae ga ari)*, and my life was satisfying. My wife's madness did not miss a single falsehood of mine, even ones the size of the tip of a needle, and there was something pleasant about that intensity. (105)

What is dredged up by Miho in the course of her interrogations is not left entirely to the imagination. Scattered throughout the text are hints of what constitutes Toshio's "past," which he both fears and desires to confront—including, naturally, his infidelity and victimization of Miho over ten years of marriage. While Toshio's infidelity and marital neglect are easily grasped by the reader, the significance of the war references and reversal of mainland-islander status Miho insists on will seem obscure or unmotivated to the reader unfamiliar with the rest of Shimao's oeuvre. They are, however, critical.

The hospital and its rigid order are in many ways like the military base of Shimao's war stories. It is clearly guarded against outside intrusion, and what goes on inside is unknown to outsiders, the "secrets" of the locked mental ward likened to the "secret mission" of the *tokkōtai*. The rigid hierarchy of the base/hospital must be maintained, and escapees are severely dealt with. Toshio describes Miho as going "AWOL" in her escape attempt. The wait for the order to attack in the war—the order for the suicide squadron to set off for certain death—and the tortured wait for Miho's mad "attacks" are quite clearly linked. Tortured by Miho's condition, "not above praying to stones by the wayside,"[27] Toshio feels that "[i]n much the same way, as a member of a suicide squadron during the war, I had wished for the Okinawan Islands to sink suddenly into the sea."[28] Besides the linking of mental hospital and *tokkōtai* base and the more obvious messages involved (the mad nature of the wartime enterprise and, by extension, of contemporary treatment of the insane), the reversal of wartime roles is crucial. Toshio, playing out the lowly soldier, taking orders from the doctors and staff and Miho, is precisely placed in the position of victim, reversing to a great extent his own wartime position of victimizer of others, specifically the islanders.

Beyond this reversed replaying of the wartime scenario, the broader question is raised of historical relations between a dominant central culture and the periphery, between the mainstream and the marginalized—in other words, the way Miho's people have been historically treated by Toshio's. The entire role reversal Miho and Toshio play out reveals this, too, as does Miho's ardent insistence on her own "noble" lineage in contrast to Toshio's "peasant" background, a statement that bespeaks a desire forcibly to reverse conventional wisdom vis-à-vis center/periphery relations. Although traces of Shimao's exploration of the cultural margins of Japan appear in earlier stories (arguably as early as the 1946 "Kotōmu"), this concern becomes a lifelong one only after the experience of Miho's madness, the move to Amami, and the writing of the *byōinki*.

By reversing, on a personal level, the historical relationship of domination of those at the margins by opening a dialogue with those who have been excluded, Toshio finds his "tangible truth." Not surprisingly this discovery is linked with a renewed sense of life. Thus in contrast to seeing their struggle in "Jizō no nukumi" as bringing them closer to death, in the *byōinki*, after their hospitalization, Toshio begins to see a different side—their struggle itself as a way to *delay* death. Following a pattern established in the war stories, the mainland ethos of death begins to give way to the ethos of the excluded, the *tokkōtai* sense of death replaced by something else—namely life—found, significantly, in dialogue with a native of the southern island who is struggling to assert her identity and worth. In the war stories death was equivalent to acceptance of the mainland ethos, the cultural stagnation linked with such notions as *bushidō* and the stoic, humorless acceptance of self-sacrifice epitomized by the *tokkōtai*. Death for Toshio in the *byōinki* is much more. It is not just the stoic self-sacrifice of the mainland ethos, but the exclusion and suppression of difference, the willful forgetting of other voices confined to the margins of consciousness—the mad, women, people on the peripheries. Shimao's protagonist, in replaying the wartime, has discovered a social unconscious.

Taken together, then, Shimao's war stories and his tales from the asylum constitute a profound questioning of two elements crucial to the construction of the modern Japanese state—the creation of a "community of death" and the suppression of difference, of other voices. Shimao's work from here to the end of his career is marked by the interplay of these two forces. By releasing the marginalized, Shimao tells us—by *un*covering authentic voices of difference and diversity—one is simultaneously released from a kind of living death.

Release from this kind of living death, however, is never simple. Opening oneself to the Other, engaging in dialogue, and forming community involve certain hazards and limitations. Toshio may be reaching out to a community of the excluded, but the notion of community is never a simple one. In a dream Toshio has in "Ware fukaki fuchi yori," the last freedom of movement he has is removed and he is, like the most severe mental patients, "incarcerated behind many locked doors," very nearly completely cut off from the world outside. He feels a "faint satisfaction" at "finally be[ing] treated like the real thing," for he "had come to think that unless I became disturbed like my wife, the two of us would never be able to climb out of the abyss."[29] In the dream a "vicious bacteria" breaks out in the ward, forcing further isolation as all the staff except one nurse is evacuated; Toshio feels anxious at the prospect. Nurse C, the one who will stay behind, is warned by Toshio that it may be dangerous for her to stay behind because the patients "might very well riot."

> C just smiled unconcernedly. Would she be made a helpless victim, I won-
> dered. I felt sorry for her but felt, too, that there ought to be at least one such
> person; it ought to happen so.[30]

As with most Shimao characters, Toshio takes the dream quite seri-
ously. The dream reveals a potential for violence, for victimization of
others. Toshio's feelings about the fate of Nurse C reveal both a sense
of sympathy for the potential victim as well as an acceptance of the need
for someone to be sacrificed for the sake of the community of mad patients. One sees Toshio's unconscious acceptance of the necessity of
victimization in order to create the community he envisions—and of
the knowledge that even in this community of victims lies the potential
for victimizing others. Community, then, is less a simplistic refuge than
a problematic category of human relations.

Toshio's unconscious revelation of the dual nature of the mental patients is paralleled by the final scene in "Ware fukaki fuchi yori," where
the patients are all gathered for a community dance.[31] Toshio, in the
company of Miho, is silent observer of the patients circle dance. "Brilliant color exploded before my eyes," he notes, "as if someone had emp-
tied a box of bright confetti near the edge of my field of vision, but
a calmer look revealed, in fact, no gaudy colors." Toshio finds the
dancers "energetic" and "vivid," the dance "pleasing"; "There was," he
concludes, "a simple purity about them that tugged at my heart and
pulled me in."[32] After Miho is taken away for her treatment, however,
a second group of patients joins the first:

> These were ward patients I had not seen before. Another veil was lifted from
> my eyes. These were the real, unmistakable mentally ill. Compared to them,
> the group until now had been absolutely normal. Had I been delirious? A
> chubby woman in short pants, her hair cut short like a man's and parted on
> one side, a young man walking around with his obi untied and his kimono
> open in front, a little boy with a surgical scar on his forehead, waving his arms
> meaninglessly in the air, an old disheveled hag, a woman with her stomach
> protruding as though she were pregnant. When these newly arrived patients
> let out a yell and joined the circle, everyone became confused: some people
> danced backward, some broke away from the circle, and total pandemonium
> ensued.[33]

Toshio ends up with a headache watching the "utterly haphazard attempt at a dance" and is struck with a feeling of "numbness, as if I had
been anesthetized." The feeling of being "pulled in," the attraction the
first group has for him, is quickly replaced by, if not revulsion, the numb-

ing realization of how little he knows about the mentally ill and how much of an outsider he is in the ward. If the first group of dancers, and Toshio's reactions to it, reflect the ward as a place of mutual understanding and sympathy, the second group is more like something out of his dream; this group is the "unconscious" element of the ward, usually kept out of sight, that emerges at times to shock and surprise with its unpredictability. Like the hidden potential for violence and victimization he feels underlying the ward, the second group is a hidden, foreboding Other of the ward. For the first of many times throughout the *byōinki*, too, Shimao highlights the unknowable nature of the Other.

As the title of "Kyōsha no manabi"(Lessons of the insane) suggests, the insane provide Toshio with a lesson, one that further underscores the limits of comprehending others. As he gazes at Oshō, the "Priest" who day and night stands praying, Toshio feels the familiar mixture of attraction and repulsion. While at first thinking maybe Oshō is really sane and just pretending to be mad,

> [a]fter a moment of doubt I could recognize "craziness" in his look, and felt relieved. Standing near him I sensed a ghostly feeling about his whole body, and while intimidated, at the same time a feeling something like the fear you feel when, with a sense of pity you are watching an elephant from afar and a part of its body, its long trunk or a leg, perhaps, suddenly looms into view at the metal fence right before your eyes. This was no doubt because my heart was struck by the "weariness" that that being shouldered. There was the breath of fate allowed only to that particular being, and myself unable to feel close to elephants, I felt the chill of being unable to be a part of its fate. Yet even now, I recalled the dread of foolishly measuring both the elephant and Oshō by my own standards, and a feeling of dread appeared before me and enlarged. (30)

It is a frightening revelation for Toshio that he will always remain an outsider to the pain and suffering of others, that the "breath of fate" each individual bears means that although one may try to force the Other to conform to one's preconceived image, this is never adequate to understand others.

Similar conclusions are reached in Toshio's observations of a second patient, one named Hanio, depicted in "Aru seishin byōsha."[34] Near the end of the story Hanio comes to tell Toshio that he's being released from the hospital the next day. The next morning Hanio's room is empty save for a large bundle of his possessions; Toshio and Miho never see him again, and Toshio feels "happy for him and happy for me that he's gone" (73). Two or three days later, he hears the truth: two or three of the worst cases had been transferred to another hospital, and among these patients was Hanio. The story ends with Toshio thinking:

> What did it mean when, the evening before he left he came to tell us, so happily, about his discharge from the hospital? Did he really believe it? Or did the hospital deceive him, telling him that? Or, as was his wont, did he understand what was really happening and have some sort of trick up his sleeve? In the end I could never find out a thing about Hanio. (74)

In both extended portraits of these two patients one senses the meaning behind Toshio's statement on the act of observation, its dual nature as both an act of suffering and salvation. As Shimao's stories tell us time and again, one is always under the gaze of the Other, just as one cannot but observe and extend one's gaze to others. Only through this relationship can one gain knowledge of oneself and others (thus the active nature of observation). Yet, as with Toshio, we discover in the process the painful realization of the limits to our knowledge of others, of how they always escape our grasp. We see this in the *byōinki*, in more purified form in *Shi no toge*, where the Other is reduced to the singular (Miho), and in Shimao's stories set in the southern islands (see chapter 4), where the Other is Miho, the island, and its people. Out of what many critics see as narrowly focused, regressive I-novels, then, come the outlines of a moving and important political stand: the necessity of a dialogue with the excluded, always tempered by the knowledge that claims to speak for others must be rigorously called into question.

THREE-QUARTERS OF the way through the *byōinki* one first detects a change in Miho's condition due to her treatment, one that, paradoxically but now quite understandably, strikes Toshio as not entirely desirable:

> [M]y wife's attacks, which wildly swelled up, have now lost their focus, and no longer flare up so; this rather makes me even more lonely. (142)

Once harsh and relentless, Miho becomes weak and fearful. Her attacks were once like a "wild horse"; now she gives in more easily and puts an abrupt halt to their dialogues (165–166), which used to go on for hours at a stretch. One sees hints here that what Toshio fears most—more than the fiercest attacks or the pain of being a victim—is silence, the *end of communication*. Even if it brings him excruciating pain, a part of Toshio wants to hear that other voice—in his case, of a ruthlessly in-terrogative wife "picking and gouging out" his heart. It is in this sense that one must read his feelings that the end of Miho's attacks bring a sense of aging, an "unbearable loneliness" that "clutches at [his] chest"—and the question of why he is so bound to her. For Toshio restarting the "flow of time" that will bring on a return to the world outside the asy-lum leads to aging and death, with death here not physical extinction, but the end of dialogue.

"Tetsuro ni chikaku" (1956) and "Ie no naka" (1959)

As he settled in to his new life on Amami Ōshima and his continued work on the *byōinki* stories, Shimao sensed he was again at a crossroads in his life as a writer. In the afterword to his 1956 collection, *Yume no naka de no nichijō*, Shimao labeled his earlier dream stories a "pile of dead bodies," a style of work he declared he would never write again. Likewise, in the afterword to a collection published the following year, *Shima no hate*, Shimao admits to similar feelings about his other pre-*byōinki* stories:

> I thought that when I opened my eyes I'd get this kind of short story [the ones in *Shima no hate*] and when I closed my eyes I'd end up in the world of *Yume no naka de no nichijō*. However these stories [in *Shima no hate*], which are supposed to be the expression of when my eyes are open, tend toward the "in-side of dreams," which is unfortunate. My writing must move on to a com-pletely different world. And "Tetsuro ni chikaku," as it were, is a sign of this.[35]

With the 1956 story "Tetsuro ni chikaku"(Near the railway), then, Shimao believed himself striking out in new fictional directions. How indeed is it different from what came before? In one sense this "differ-ent world" involves an exploration of his domestic past such as Shimao had not undertaken before—a probing of what was elided between "Jizō no nukumi" and the *byōinki*, namely the outbreak and develop-ment of his wife's illness before the entrance into the mental hospital. As "Tetsuro ni chikaku" suggests from the beginning, this new world is also more subtle and intriguing than that of his earlier dream sto-ries; now the reader is struck by the uneasy feeling that the worlds of "eyes open" and "eyes closed" have become *one*. Simply put, the nar-rator wakes from the dream world to find the waking world nearly the same.[36]

"Tetsuro ni chikaku" follows the male narrator as he frantically searches for his wife in hopes of preventing the suicide scene he has envisioned. It is the first of many stories revolving around the search for the lost wife, a motif that takes on added significance in the search for the elusive essence of the southern islands for which the wife is a symbol. The wanderer is now the wife, not the husband. The husband imagines the process by which his wife's fits run their course, the "sad, pitiful pain" like "raging waves" swelling up inside her as she waits again in vain for her husband to return (300). We are told only that she distrusts her husband, that "suspicions [about him] became like the countless spots on the surface of a rain-dappled pond" (300), that she "once again thinks of the same disgusting thing" (299). But, as with the *byōinki*, the details of the causes of her immediate distress are left veiled. Unable to find any trace of his wife, the husband heads back home, afraid, as in earlier stories, that "[w]hat was going to come has finally come" (304). What is significant here, we see, is the husband's confirmation, one echoed in the *byōinki*, that no matter how much pain her attacks cause him, escaping from confrontation with them is not an option he will take. "No matter how much trouble my wife's fitful actions cause, they are worth the trouble" (304).[37]

Whereas "Tetsuro ni chikaku" centers on one day in the world of the wife's madness before she entered the hospital, "Ie no naka" (Inside the home, 1959) spirals back to the starting point of her condition. This story was originally cast as the first chapter of *Shi no toge;* in it, the wife knows everything about her husband's activities, his extramarital affairs. In contrast, the husband, at the time of the events narrated, knows nothing about this and precious little of her deep and grievous suffering.[38] If Shimao had concluded his *byōsaimono* with "Ie no naka," readers would still be left in the dark about the entire process by which the wife reveals her suffering and the husband becomes aware of how he has victimized her. *Shi no toge* fills this gap, and the direct confrontation, repeated endlessly, gives the latter work its power. Although we as readers are made aware of the wife's suffering in "Ie no naka" in a remarkable stream of consciousness section, the wife herself, until the end of the story, remains fiercely determined to suffer alone, to not reveal her mental state to her husband. Only at the end of the story is she no longer able to restrain herself, and the story segues, albeit incompletely, into *Shi no toge.*

What informs the whole of "Ie no naka" is the profound *lack* of what is the main motif of *Shi no toge:* the direct, even brutal communication of feelings between husband and wife. Instead we see again and again the way the wife and husband avoid direct communication in place of illicit observation of the other partner. Their feelings are communicated, if at all, indirectly through mediating agents such as the children, or even the family cat. The husband secretly observes his wife in a crowded neighborhood of shoppers. She looks "dead," and he is stunned by the side of her that he has never seen before. Imagining that he knows everything about her—that the lusterless woman scolding his children is all there is to his wife—he realizes he does not really know her, and, in a glimmer of enlightenment, that it is *he* who has caused her to become so spiritless. For her part, the wife has secretly observed her husband's outside activities: "She knew down to the wrinkles on his skin when he gave a relaxed smile" (330). She walks all over town at night, trying to learn everything about her husband's actions, and during these times she is "shining and lovely," but her husband "couldn't see this" (330). Seeing him off at the station, she "watches him as if she's sending off someone she'll never see again" because she "knew all" about "what strange place her husband has fallen into" (334).

The husband combines a clear-eyed realization that his life is crumbling beneath him with a less than clear understanding of its effects on others, mainly his wife. As seen time and again, however, the Shimao protagonist is a complex figure, always containing opposing aspects. Although he fears collapse, at the same time a part of him desires to bring it on. The wife senses this, saying that her husband is "intent on creating the cause" of their collapse (335). He is indeed *actively desirous* of bringing a crisis into his household. The reasons are clear: the world to him is "stagnant, set in a solidified form." "[T]he landscape around was like artificial flowers. Because it's like artificial flowers, it never decays." He feels depressed and pinned on a hard and stiff "eternal solidity" with his "injured, easily rotting self" emitting a "stink" (341). The stinging "good feeling" he experiences under Miho's attacks in the *byōinki*—the feeling of having found a "tangible truth" he has not experienced before—is the glimmer of a way out of the stagnation of urban, mainland Japan. As he writes these words, one recalls, Shimao is settled in Amami—beginning the long journey of discovering Miho and the southern islands.

To read "Ie no naka," as most male Japanese critics have read Shimao's *byōsaimono,* as the story of one of their own, a male writer struggling with life in postwar Japan, is to miss the point that it is equally the story of a *woman*. In fact, outside of *Shi no toge*, "Ie no naka" contains one of the most compelling depictions of the problems of being a woman in 1950s Japan—a woman neglected by her husband, sexually abandoned, left without hope that their life will improve, and little chance to express her aspirations. In "Ie no naka" the whole process of her drift into madness is laid out in concentrated, step-by-step form. Madness becomes less an irrational, meaningless state than the inevitable explosion of frustration at one's powerlessness—and an attempt to recoup power and a voice of one's own.

In an extended inner monologue, the wife feels her heart is a "desert." The "endless repetition of housework, the trouble of taking care of the children" makes her taste the "emptiness" of life, a feeling like the "dreariness of chewing on sand" (335). Like her husband, she feels their life is heading toward collapse but she is unable to consult with anyone, since the very person she should expect to be able to consult is the one "intent on creating the cause" of this collapse. She knows everything about the other woman, that her husband is not the only lover she has, and she wants to "unravel" the situation but is fearful of taking the next step—that is, confronting her husband with the knowledge she has. As we see, by the end of the story she is teetering on the edge, but only with *Shi no toge* does she take this next step.

The first sign that something is wrong with her in "Ie no naka" comes one day as she waits yet again in vain for her husband to come back on the last train. As the passengers push their way past her, suddenly "a mysterious, wild power swelled up in her, [and] unconsciously she growled like an animal, and burst into uncontrollable sobbing" (336). She loses control of her body's lower half and falls onto the railroad tracks; two station attendants help her up. In the faces of the attendants she sees signs of a "peaceful, ordinary life," and in the odor of their sweat, the "smell of human beings." "It made her feel she was remembering something far off in the distance. *I haven't been treated as a human being for a long time*" (336; emphasis added). Endurance and submission to "agony" in "silence" are indeed what Miho's role seems to be, although she is soon to abandon it. Finally, however, the excess of *gaman* (forbearance) manifests itself in a recurring cycle of physical symptoms: she begins to have outbreaks of "fits" *(hossa)*, but only at night. They begin with stomach pains, and she writhes on the floor in pain with no relief in sight. Next her heart feels "stuffed up," she can't breathe, and her head feels caught in the grip of an "iron hoop" (340):

> I can't stand it. I want someone to save me. Someone, I say—I mean my husband . . . [who] won't come to save me. . . . My head swells up and up until it's like a gigantic iron pot. It is like the entire world is crushed into that pot. This is what hell must be like. (340)

Still, she feels compelled to bear her pain and not reveal it to her husband. When he asks about her bruises, for instance, she conceals the fact that they're from her fall onto the railroad tracks; instead, she lightly explains that she's clumsy and bumps into things. And again, when her fits start to occur during the daytime, and her husband finally witnesses one, standing over her as she writhes on the floor, she plays down her condition, telling him it's "nothing, just a stomach pain" and urging him to go back to work in the next room. In the final scene of the story the husband is rushing back home on the train, full of unease. His home cannot go on forever "without incident," he feels, but he finds it hard to believe today could be the day the crisis explodes. As he soon finds out, it is. One notes again the undercurrent of the wartime experiences as he nears the house. His footsteps as they echo in the alley "make the sound of walking along a moonlit beach"; the image is that of the husband in the war going furtively off at night to rendezvous with his lover on the beach. As the crisis nears, so do husband and wife approach the past, the wartime.

The husband is brought up short by the scene confronting him at home. His wife and the children are sprawled on the floor of his room, fully clothed. He is as shocked by the scene as by the fact that his special sanctuary—where he writes his stories—has been breached. Previously she entered the room only to clean it; now she lies in a room she has obviously trashed. Bottles of soda pop, snacks, and an empty whisky bottle lie carelessly discarded. The husband's first thought is that they have committed suicide by overdosing, and he wonders if there is an empty medicine bottle somewhere around. By putting his hand near his wife's mouth, however, he discovers she is alive and breathing. She wakes up, her hair hanging down, but she doesn't answer as he calls her name. She stares at him steadily, and he expects her to cast her eyes down as she usually does, but she does not; *he* is the one who will have trouble holding her gaze. "You are really something, aren't you," she

finally says, then laughs uproariously and rolls on the floor. The story
ends as follows:

> Unconsciously he shook her body hard. She thought the tide had swelled
> up. He called her name again. And her expression looked back to normal.
> In a strong tone of voice she said this: "No. Let me go. Don't touch me."
> A trembling came up from the husband's core and he felt his whole body
> droop. (349)

Shi no toge: The Sting of Death

The *byōinki* and the later 1950s stories of Shimao's wife's illness are, in a
sense, preludes to a greater work. Starting in 1960, Shimao began writing what is justifiably called his life work—the novel *Shi no toge*. Publishing the work in loose serialized form (as a series of linked stories—
rensaku—published in a variety of literary journals), Shimao finished
the first half in four years; due primarily to accident and illness, the second half took twelve. Before its publication as a finished novel in 1977,
Shimao issued two short-story collections with the same title, one in
1960, the second in 1963.[39] The critical success of the 1960 collection
(winner of the Geijutsu Senshō prize, his first literary award since 1950),
spurred Shimao on.

    Shi no toge is Shimao's best-known, and only best-selling, novel.[40] In
the months after it was published the novel sold an impressive one hundred thousand copies and established, in one critic's flowery words,
Shimao's position as a "shining symbol of Japanese pure literature."[41]
Shi no toge is advertised as a love story, a "lurid" "human document"
that probes to the depths the questions of "what are the bonds between
husband and wife, and what is love." As Okuno puts it:

> In all of literature there has been no novel which questions so fundamentally,
> or pursues to such lengths, the essence of [the relationship between] husband
> and wife.[42]

Critics have expended much energy debating the extent to which *Shi no
toge* is or is not an I-novel, exposing in the process how unfixed and
shifting the definition of this "genre" is, and the ways in which Shimao's
Catholic beliefs are reflected in the work. Reading it as religious in turn
has led to debate by critics (and Shimao himself) over the question of
literature as an act of atonement.[43] Others have seen the novel as a con-

tinuation of Shimao's attempts to soothe his wife's condition. While this may have been one of the side effects of his composition of the *byōinki*, by the time Shimao began writing *Shi no toge*, Miho was no longer ill.

Critical writing on the novel has thus tended to one of two extremes. The first is to universalize it as a religious, or existential, statement about questions of human relations, sin, and belief. The second is to personalize it, in a traditional I-novel reading, unproblematically equating Toshio and Miho with the real-life author and his wife and viewing the work as principally important for fleshing out the chronology of Shimao's real life.[44] Although the novel follows the main outline of events in his life, it is clear that Shimao took what was in real life a longer, more diffuse course of events and compressed it into a more compact unit. This seems particularly true of the two most dramatic events of the novel—the outbreak of Miho's madness and the confrontation with Toshio's lover.[45] Japanese commentators have ignored much of this evidence and, in fact, have blithely constructed their chronologies of Shimao's life based on the novel. For instance, they have ignored his own statements that his wife was already having mental problems in the "middle of the summer" of 1954, far before the sudden outbreak of her illness in the fall depicted in *Shi no toge*.[46]

Universalizing or personalizing *Shi no toge* blinds us as readers to aspects of the novel that lend it its power. The novel tells us much about the role of women in postwar Japan and the connection between madness and the female role. In *Shi no toge* Shimao builds on the depiction of Miho's condition in "Ie no naka," and for the first time allows the wife full voice, making the work a powerful exposure of the inequalities that mark the postwar nuclear family. The reversal of gender roles that Miho's madness demands underscores these points, because with the husband now playing the female role, he, too, begins to question his sanity. With its subtext of the war, *Shi no toge* also reveals the victim mentality of postwar Japan, and the history of victimization during the war that has, even to the present, been conveniently ignored. Underlying the husband-wife struggle are deep-seated resentments of wartime mistreatment in which the husband is implicated. The novel is a portrait, too, of a person (Miho) who is the product of a culture, the southern islands, whose madness is also triggered by a kind of cultural incongruity. Ultimately, her cure is found in a return to her native cultural zone. This in turn exposes the postwar myth of a homogeneous, single-culture Japan, and the history of victimization that historically existed—and continues to exist—between mainland and the periphery.

Women and Madness

Shi no toge covers a period of approximately ten months (late summer to late May or early June) in the lives of one family, whose last name is given only as S. The narrator, Toshio, is the familiar aspiring novelist and former naval officer. His wife, Miho, is from the island where he was stationed in the war, and their children are named Shin'ichi (just entering first grade) and Maya, age four.[47] The bulk of the novel is set in Koiwa, Edogawa-ku, in the eastern part of Tokyo; the rest takes place in Sōma, Fukushima Prefecture, Sakura, Chiba Prefecture, and Ikebukuro and the hospital Toshio and Miho are admitted to at the end of the story.[48]

Van Gessel speaks of the opening pages of *Shi no toge* as full of "holes in the logic of the narrative."[49] His point is that there is no logical reason for the extreme reactions of Toshio, the fear and anxiety he feels at the rather mundane scene he finds in the house—the dishes piled up and his inkpot spilled. Gessel is right, of course, but only if one reads *Shi no toge* in isolation from all of Shimao's previous work. Readers who had followed *Garasu shōji no shiruetto*, the late 1954–early 1955 stories, the *byōinki*, "Tetsuro ni chikaku," and "Ie no naka" will *not* find Toshio's reactions here, his feeling that the "day of judgment had finally come" as unexplained by the scene around him. The question is not so much *why* this "day of judgment" has come as it is why it has taken so *long* in Shimao's fictional world to arrive at this point—namely, the moment at which Miho goes mad.

As with the *byōinki*, the primary focus of *Shi no toge* is Miho's madness. The novel concludes by telling the reader she is not, as is sometimes thought in the course of the story, schizophrenic, but rather suffering from a "psychogenic reaction." Medically speaking, a psychogenic reaction is triggered by a specific experience or environmental factor; thus it is distinguished from neurosis, in which personality disorders play a greater part. In general it is thought that if the cause of the reaction is traced and removed, the psychogenic reaction will abate; unlike schizophrenia, then, there is much more hope for a cure. This is not to say, however, that personality does not play a part, because it does: the outbreak of the disorder is often closely linked with "hypersensitive" personalities. The types of psychogenic reactions vary, ranging from "acute stress response" to paranoia and persecution complex, depression, and "prison psychosis." And the causes can be as varied as a seemingly small incident, perhaps one in which a person feels slighted or that his rights have been infringed, to the death of a loved one or the experience of a natural or man-made catastrophe (such as war).[50] In Miho's case, the immediate specific cause is, as mentioned earlier, her husband's diary entry, which, although never fully revealed, one assumes reveals a lack of affection for her and/or the depth of his feelings for another woman. One psychiatrist familiar with Shimao's work calls Miho's reaction "jealousy delusion" *(shitto mōsō)*, an extreme jealous reaction usually perceived in Japan as that of a wife directed toward her husband. This state is characterized by such behavior as the wife investigating the husband's personal effects (his underwear, for instance) for traces of sexual encounters, and strong demands for sex with him.[51] In fact, early in *Shi no toge* one finds Miho arriving home with new underwear for Toshio to replace his old (along with a new pen), and repeated scenes of Miho "testing" Toshio with her body, enticing him sexually.

But the main characteristic of Miho's madness is a series of repeated, ruthless interrogations of her husband, where she forces him to dredge up every detail of his affairs with other women, in particular his current lover. Miho calls her "Aitsu" (perhaps best translated as that person), the other woman who comes to play an important, but muted, role in the novel.

The beginning of the novel is complex and highlights several aspects of the narrative of *Shi no toge*. The story opens as follows:

> From that night on, we stopped using the mosquito net. Because there weren't any more mosquitoes. My wife and I didn't sleep for three nights. I don't know if that is possible or not. We might have slept a little and didn't notice it, but I had no memory of sleeping. In November you will leave the house, in December you will kill yourself. That's your fate, my wife was strangely convinced. "That's definitely what happened to you," she said. But the day of judgment came earlier than that, on a day at the end of summer. (7)[52]

The narrator, Toshio, is already somewhat removed (although how much is unclear) from the events he is relating. The paragraph that follows is a flashback to the day he returned home to find his wife and children gone, "ink . . . spattered on the desk, the tatami and the walls like bloodstains," and his diary "sordidly discarded in the midst of it all."[53] The next few pages are a second flashback to the three days of interrogation hinted at in the opening paragraph, the lengthy dialogue between Toshio and Miho. Toshio (in other contexts in a constant state of anxiety about what will happen at home in his absence), rushing home so he will not be "too late" for the "transformation" about to occur, is, here, at the crucial moment of the transformation—his wife's outbreak of madness—absent. The same holds true for the readers, because as the plot summary in the appendix indicates, we, too, are denied the crucial, transformative experience of Miho's change from sanity to insanity. If Shimao had continued writing in the style of "Ie no naka," one would expect at this point a detailed scene of Miho alone, discovering the diary, reading it, and flying into a mad fit—a scene along the lines of the one quoted at the beginning of this chapter. In this point one sees the difference between "Ie no naka" and *Shi no toge* and can understand the effects of excluding the former from the novel. The opening of the novel is thus indicative of an epistemological stance by Shimao that has as least two aspects. First, unlike his earlier depictions of Miho's condition, here readers are totally excluded from the interior of her consciousness. We can know her through concrete exterior evidence—her words and actions—but her consciousness remains ultimately unknowable. Second, this crucial gap in the narrative—the scene of the outbreak of madness—is indicative of the nature of trauma in general. Traumatic moments are experiences that elude language; language can circle around them but cannot fully recoup them. In the context of *Shi no toge* this produces an endless repetition, specifically the interrogations by Miho, which (although often bringing up the subject of the diary, even at times mentioning fragments of it) never fully confront the question of the final spark that drove her into madness.

The opening paragraph of *Shi no toge*, above, in compact form, sets the tone for the entire narrative. The mundane (here, putting away the mosquito net at the end of summer) is juxtaposed with the abnormal (Toshio's and Miho's three days without sleep). Toshio's knowledge of events is always limited, circumscribed. He, like the reader, is left unable to pin down what really happened—that is, whether they did or did not stay awake for three days is left undecided. Readers find themselves through the course of the novel in much the same position, unsure at times of the real or imagined nature of events. Probably the most memorable example is the finger-cutting scene in chapter 6. In this gruesome scene Toshio pledges to cut off a finger as proof of his sincerity, but the reader is left unsure of what actually took place. Miho takes over before Toshio can cut himself, and makes him close his eyes until she is "done" and has swathed his finger in a bandage. He feels pain, but it is unclear what, if anything, has occurred. (The reader learns in a later chapter that his finger was not really cut off.) The bandage itself, and the mystery of what lies beneath, is in a way symbolic of the entire text and the readers' often frustrated desire to uncover the "truth" of what actually takes place and what is imagined. The text itself is, as it were, covered with a similar gauze.

In light of the discussion of Shimao's *byōsaimono* as the projection of the dream world onto reality, the opening paragraph of *Shi no toge* raises the question of waking and sleeping in such a way as to blur the boundary between them. Perhaps Toshio *did* stay up for three days, and the lengthy interrogation is a transcription of what was actually said. But the possibility is left open that the interrogation is a mixture of dream and the real. Unlike the confident, supposedly stable stance of the typical *shishōsetsu* (I-novel) narrator (for whom the distinction between reality and dream is unproblematic), this narrative, despite its outward resemblance to a *shishōsetsu*, leaves the reader from the beginning with the uncertain feeling that there is no stable ground from which to maintain a clear distinction between actual occurrences and the imagined or dreamt. Readers view the world through Toshio's eyes, and his view of the world is subtly skewed just enough in the direction of the ambiguous to plant seeds of doubt in our minds.

Miho's "strange conviction" that Toshio will kill himself is unsettling. Unlike the chronology of events around it, the statement is not tethered to any time reference; when and under what circumstances it was made remain unclear. Assuming it is a statement made before the onset of her madness, one might see Miho's madness as, in part, a last-ditch effort to forestall or preempt her husband from fulfilling his "fate." In "Ie no naka" the wife fears her husband's death most of all and desires to put a halt to the downward spiral of his life, yet hesitates to take the "next step"—that is, confronting him directly. Unlike "Ie no naka," however, in *Shi no toge* Toshio is confessing to a knowledge, well before the onset of Miho's madness, of her profound misgivings about his future, yet he continues passively to let events unfold. Or does he? In "Ie no naka," despite his feeling that he is being dragged by forces beyond his control, Toshio is actively desirous of bringing on a crisis in his household in order to put an end to the "stagnation" in which his self is "rotting." In that story this desire takes the form of active nonresistance to an "invasion" of his house by outsiders, although a side of him loathes them. In the opening of *Shi no toge*, however, one might ask if Toshio has not taken an even more resolute step toward instigating the crisis. Why does he so carelessly leave his diary open, at an entry bound to enrage his wife? Assuming he is not stupendously dull, this action is explicable only as the deliberate design of one who wishes to provoke a crisis.

Miho's interrogations of Toshio, which continue to the end of the novel, open up an area heretofore little explored in Shimao's earlier *byō-saimono:* the past. Contrary to one's expectations, however, they serve less to reveal in I-novel fashion any sordid details of the narrator's sexual affairs (readers learn very little of substance in this area) than to open up the notion of the past as an object of discourse. When Miho raises what has been suppressed in their lives, what begins to be subtly uncovered is much more than her husband's past infidelities. The past has been hinted at in some of the early stories, but in the *byōinki* the past surfaces only in the most oblique ways. Here in *Shi no toge*, however, the past explodes into Toshio's and Miho's consciousness, and a pattern begins to take shape in the narrative: Miho's insistence that the past be revealed running straight into Toshio's equally strong plea that they "forget the past." Much of the "past" here involves Toshio's neglect and mistreatment of his wife, and the novel can easily be read in terms that may be called feminist. At the same time, however, the notion of the past raises issues of their entire past relationship, experiences in the war, power between Miho's island village and the military that Toshio led, and between the mainland government in World War II that directed the fate of the periphery and used these areas as buffer zones and its people as sacrificial victims. And ultimately the "past" revealed here is the history of the southern islands vis-à-vis the mainland, a relationship that is very much one between victim and victimizer.

In this novel, on the immediate level the victim is Miho and the victimizer Toshio; concern with the past takes the form of her husband's infidelities, which she relentlessly pursues. Miho's "attacks" (*hossa*) are really twofold in nature: complaints about Toshio's mistreatment of her coupled with demands that he reveal every detail of his outside affairs. At times her demands are what one might expect. She forces him to list all the women he has gone out with (8, 312)[54] and where he has taken them. Her questions are at times cruelly probing, demanding confessions of intimacy—whether Toshio has ever taken a bath with his lover, whether he has made her "happy" (i.e., made her achieve orgasm), whether he and the woman have had an illegitimate child (312). At other times, her interrogations border on the laughable:

> As my wife changed her underwear, her attack raised its head. List the color of each and every pair of underwear you gave that woman, she told me, but I couldn't remember if I'd given her any or not. She said she followed along and saw me give the woman a set of a dozen pairs of underwear, all different colors, and I felt it strange I couldn't recall. . . . If I said I couldn't recall, she wouldn't accept that, and would tell me she wanted me to remember no matter what. It didn't matter, really, about the colors, she said; what she wanted was to grasp hold of proof of the sincerity of her husband who pledged himself never to tell the smallest lie.
> "I am not *mugari* [having an attack]. I feel like I'm losing myself. Please, try to remember for me," she said entreatingly. I couldn't recall the truth, and I couldn't just list a lot of colors; I tried to turn her attention to something else, but she held on and wouldn't let it go.
> "If you don't tell me, I'll wait until you remember." (292)

And a while later she laments, "Just once before I die I'd like to wear all those colored panties" (293).

The supply of questions, however, is not endless. Miho's later grillings become an endless repetition of what has been detailed in the first chapter. Toshio notes early on that "[t]here was nothing left for me to add, but my wife wouldn't accept this, saying I was still hiding something" (71). After the first chapter, the term *hossa* becomes shorthand for an act that endlessly repeats these known contents. The chapters that follow bring less revelation of new facts about Toshio's affairs than the emergence of a pattern: Miho's *hossa* occur, Toshio struggles to survive her grilling (the details of which the reader already knows), or, as time passes, to preempt these attacks by violent acts against his person that at first seem calculated, then uncontrollable.

A second aspect of the *hossa* that readers infer in later chapters from information provided in the first revolves around Miho's "confession" of all she has hitherto remained silent about. One critic has said of Miho that she has the most "intense individualism" found in any female character in postwar literature;[55] surely Miho's explosion of pent-up emotion is remarkable as one of the most concentrated explosions of a woman's repressed emotions found in recent literature. Very early in the novel Miho catalogues the frustrations she has kept hidden for some ten years. The operative word is *gaman*—forbearance that she is no longer able to display. Her complaints are myriad: Toshio's own "bad illness" that plagues him; her fear that he will kill himself; her hatred of his father, who treats her and the children as outsiders; Toshio's inability to provide enough money for their family to live on; her disgust with his "artistic" activities and status as "hack writer." She has been treated as a "maid," she says. "Is this what a wife is? Was I ever treated as a wife? You never did anything for me" (9).[56] She demands more money and extracts a promise from him that he will provide "family service" (*katei no hōshi*, i.e., take the family out on the town occasionally). Toshio, she continues, thinks only "dirty thoughts," the result of learning "dirty things" while in the military.

Miho's initial long "confession," spread over three days of interrogating Toshio, sounds to him like a "long epic poem" (12). With the spilling of his inkpot, his lifeblood as a writer, which signaled the outbreak of her madness as she wreaks havoc on the family, there is a transformation in Miho. Toshio, the writer in the family, is no longer the only "voice" to be heard, because Miho is also now a writer in a sense, composing the "epic poem" of her life and their past. There is much in Miho's complaints that is banal, and the juxtaposition of these with the vehemence of her attacks somewhat justifies Shimao's own contention that the novel should be read as portraying a situation that borders on the humorous.[57] Yet a more serious reading of the text is justified, one that would emphasize Miho's madness as the inevitable outburst of what was seen building up in Shimao's earlier stories—the suppressed aspirations of women.

Indeed one of the most neglected areas in critical writings on the novel is the topic of the connection between women and madness. Phyllis Chesler, in her work, *Women and Madness*, sees madness in women as inevitably linked with socially imposed roles women must play. Madness, she writes, is an "intense experience of female biological, sexual, and cultural castration, and a doomed search for potency." Likewise, Barbara Rigney views madness in women as a political event explainable by the "oppression of women in a power-structured, male supremacist society." As Carol A. B. Warren writes in her 1950s study of women mental patients in the United States (paraphrasing Chesler)—the time of Miho's story—"The traditional housewife role contains the structural potential for going crazy, for feeling locked up, smothered, and unable to get out by any means short of madness."[58]

Male critics are often quick to acknowledge how the situation depicted in *Shi no toge*, despite its extreme nature, remains a possible scenario for all families; the madness of Miho lies as a dormant possibility in all women, they imply. Yet they fail to explore the reasons that make this true, namely that the role of women in postwar Japan—despite liberation from the *ie* (the legalized extended family) and the restraints it imposes on women, the democratization of society, and the new Civil Code guaranteeing equality of the sexes—is still one in which personal aspirations are much more circumscribed than for men. Although they acknowledge the potential for madness just below the surface of the family, critics such as Mishima at the same time seem bewildered by *Shi no toge*, wondering what the fuss is over a mere outside love affair. Mishima's position is interesting for its combination of blindness and insight. It exposes the inevitability of conflict in the family due to the suppression of women—so that Miho comes out looking like a fairly typical representative of modern women—while simultaneously failing to question the attitudes that produce an explosion of madness, that is, the bland acceptance of inequality and double standards.[59] Japanese critics almost universally downplay the importance of Toshio's sexual affair in instigating Miho's madness; it is merely the *kikkake* ("last straw," perhaps) that pushed her over the edge. Instead, while viewing her on the one hand as representative of women, critics attempt to defuse her status as representing any larger trend by leaving largely unanswered the question of *why* she goes mad, implying that the reasons lie more in an inborn, personal propensity toward madness than in any larger social forces. These critics, in short, fail to see the obvious point that, while indeed Toshio's affair may be merely the final straw, it is symptomatic of larger forces, of the inequality of relations between the sexes that leads to pent-up frustration and rage.

Chesler calls women's madness a "cry of powerlessness," and for all who have followed Shimao's stories to this point there could be no more apt description of Miho's condition. Miho's desire to be treated as a "wife," along with her lament in "Ie no naka" that it has been a long time since she was "treated as a human," make clear the nature of her stance. Far from rejecting the role of wife, she seeks its redefinition so that the social role of "wife" and of "human being" are no longer incompatible. Shimao, as always, works with a limited palette, never making explicit the ways in which the Toshio-Miho relationship is emblematic of sexual inequality in Japan. The world of *Shi no toge* is squeezed into the narrow confines of Toshio's limited vision and the conflict between one man and one woman, yet to dismiss the story as simply an

I-novel account of marital discord between two quirky, atypical characters is to miss entirely the ways in which it is one of the more powerful depictions in postwar Japanese literature of the position of women.

Miho's search for "potency" takes many forms. Much attention in *Shi no toge* is focused on forms of address, for instance, and the ways they signal hierarchical status. Miho's shifting attitudes toward her status vis-à-vis her husband are clearly reflected both in the way she addresses him and the way she demands to be addressed. In the *byōinki* we have seen the exaggerated forms this takes as Miho demands that Toshio use comically exalted forms of address, and similar scenes are found in the novel. In *Shi no toge*, in the throes of her first fit, for example, Miho insists that he call her exaggeratedly polite *anatasama*, rather than the rough term *omae:*

> "So you [*omae*] are planning to die?"
> "I don't want you to call me *omae*. Don't mistake me for someone else."
> "Should I call you by your name then?"
> "I can't believe how insensitive you are. How calmly you use my name. Call me *anatasama*."
> "So are you [*anatasama*] really planning to die?" (9)

Besides the almost ludicrous spectacle of two people worried about forms of address when one of them is contemplating suicide, the reader also notes the incongruity of elements in Toshio's last sentence (*Anatasama, dōshite mo shinu tsumori ka*), where the switch to an exalted form of address is at odds with the much more familiar grammatical form of the end of the sentence. These contesting elements within the sentence work well to illustrate Toshio's own divided self concerning Miho's madness: on the one hand he is obedient to her wishes, on the other, antipathetic toward them. A few pages after this scene, Miho suddenly addresses him as *Otōsan* (Father). This is every bit an indication of a respite in her attacks as is her later demand to be called by the name of his lover a sign of how deeply disturbed she can become at times.

At first glance sexual matters are apparently absent from *Shi no toge*;[60] it is not that they are entirely missing, but that they are "cleverly hidden." Indeed, at first reading, the novel, ostensibly centered on the consequences of marital infidelity, seems remarkably reticent about sex. A closer reading, however, reveals Miho's and Toshio's ongoing concern about their own sexual relationship, and also a changed Miho, more aggressive in seeking to reestablish her sexuality. Key terms in this regard are *nikubanare* (the physical, sexual estrangement Toshio says they have experienced for most of the past ten years) and *kokoromi* (test), the way Miho is constantly using her body to "test" Toshio in bed. One result of the outbreak of Miho's madness is the closing of a physical gap in their relationship: no longer do they sleep in separate rooms, but spend each night side by side on the same futon. (One can only assume that this is at Miho's insistence.) Paralleling the new sleeping arrangement, much of Miho's concern revolves around a recovery of her sexuality, a desire, it should be noted, that contrasts strongly with the imagery Toshio uses to describe the "new" Miho: whereas she wants to recover her body, he sees her as less human and increasingly more "machine."

From the opening pages of the story, the novel is remarkable for its concern over Miho's body. Toshio feels her body has, with her madness, changed from soft to hard, from "plant" to something "hard and metallic" (13). Miho decries how, for the sake of Toshio's body, she has had to watch her own be "shaved away" layer by layer until she is now thin and weak (14). Miho's body has become a "lie detector," Toshio feels, recording everything he says (18). And in one memorable scene at night, Toshio is surprised to find Miho putting on makeup (which, he notes, she is doing badly) and preparing an especially comfortable futon, usually reserved for guests, for the two of them. The scene is open to several interpretations—the makeup application, for instance, may actually be poorly done because of Miho's disturbed mental state, or may only appear so to Toshio in contrast to his more sophisticated lover. Nevertheless, it is clear that Miho is attempting to entice her husband sexually, to bridge the gap of *nikubanare* that has separated them and, on a very practical level, win his attention back to herself. The passage ends ambiguously, as do so many in the novel; one can assume Toshio reluctantly sleeps with her.

In fact, this scene is indicative of a pattern that binds together many disparate scenes in the story, namely Miho's sexual advances and Toshio's confusion in the face of them. Here readers witness a reversal of the situation found in "Ie no naka," because there it was the wife who consistently refused the husband. In that story, when the wife rebuffed her husband's sexual advances one night, he feels "the sand beneath his feet collapse a little,"[61] and, as was seen, the story ends with Miho's admonition, "Don't touch me!" which makes the husband "tremble" and "droop." In *Shi no toge*, their stances are to a great extent reversed, with Miho the aggressor, the one whose sexual advances Toshio often resists—a move that deepens her depression (344). It may be too simplistic to say that Miho and Toshio have completely exchanged sexual roles, although much evidence points in that direction. She is now the one who demands respect, whose voice is the one with "authority" (282, 291). She is the one for whom *he* works, cooking, cleaning, taking care of the children, the one whose words have the force of commands (Miho: *Ocha!* [Tea!] Toshio: *Hai hai!* [Coming!]) (283). In short, the focus of activity in the home is no longer the husband, his work, and welfare, but *Miho* and *her demands.* One sees in her situation more than a hint of what Chesler calls the "double standard for mental health," namely, that the kind of behavior "considered normal or desirable behavior for men is thought to be neurotic or even psychotic for women," because in many ways Miho's conduct is little different from that of a typical Japanese male. Despite the abnormally tenacious quality of her interrogations concerning her husbands affairs, one can see in them the sexual double standard turned on its head. The typical husband would be allowed to "fool around," while any transgressions on the wife's part would be dealt with severely. Here, in a radical move that works to expose the double standard, it is the husband whose transgressions are disallowed and the sexually aggressive wife who sees to his punishment.[62]

In subtle ways, the story links female sexuality and self. For Miho, the loss of sexuality is connected not just with the loss of her husband's affection but with the loss of her body, with the loss of her self, and with death. Her interrogations about Toshio's sexual activities become both a ferreting out of every detail of the past—the lie detector part—and a way of inserting herself back into a sexual relationship in order to gain a sense of identity. One particularly remarkable section is the one quoted in chapter 1 of this book, the dream Miho relates to Toshio. I will argue later how this key passage relates to the intended wartime mass suicide on the island and Miho's status as southern islander. Here, let us consider what the passage reveals about Miho, sexuality, and the self:

> "Last night I returned to the islands [Miho says]. The sky was so very clear and blue, but *since my body was like this,* I couldn't bring myself to go into my home."
> My wife deliberately avoided looking into my face, and continued slowly.
> From the *jouguchi* (front door, in her island dialect) she looked out at the garden and saw a huge hole there, with many people crammed inside. Maggots crawled out of the hole to the outside. The maggots squirmed and the hole was full of people. From out of the crowd of people in the hole she saw

the bloodless, horribly pale faces of her dead mother and father. She was so startled she stopped breathing—"*Anmai!*" she cried out, and ran to the hole in order to save them, but *Anma* said, "Don't come here," waving her away with a scary face she'd never seen before. "If you don't escape from your distress, *Anma* and *Jū* won't be able to crawl out of this hole. You still want to return to the islands? It's not the time for you to return. You poor thing." *Jū* was emaciated, with his beard covering his cheeks and chin—only his eyes were the same as they used to be, gentle. "*Anma* told me to go to the evacuation hut. I understood very well what she meant. I'd done something terrible without giving it a second thought. During the war I didn't know when you might come visiting from your naval base, and *Jū* got in the way. So I made him go to live alone in that hut. He could die for all I care, I thought. *Anma* was trying to make me go there. I did go, and broke down in tears. I cried and cried, and the tears wouldn't stop. My eyes ended up all puffy and I couldn't open them. And *meanwhile the lower half of my body rotted away*. It's all Heaven's punishment, all punishment for what I did. I sacrificed *Jū*, who was like a god, and picked you, and now look at the horrible things you've done to me." (104; emphasis added)

The dream continues with *aitsu*, Toshio's lover, appearing, together with Toshio and a "living thing like a puppy," the bastard offspring of their adultery—all of whom have followed Miho back to her island home:

> "That was your child, wasn't it?" [Miho asks]
> I turned pale and couldn't answer.
> "I shuddered and tried to run away from there but my legs were stuck and I couldn't. Demons one after another came to me, and whispered all kinds of things. But in an instant those demons changed into one of the customers at the Rubicon, who told me that no matter who sleeps with him he will *cure their rotting body*." (104; emphasis added)

Let us consider the italicized portion about Miho's body. This passage is highly suggestive: for a start, Miho has been forced into the isolation of their tiny house in Koiwa—her own "evacuation hut" of sorts—where she finds herself rotting, dying, much as, in her dream, her parents are attacked by maggots. Significantly, the dream suggests that the way to cure the "rotting lower half" of her body—and avoid the fate of her parents—lies in following the very path Toshio has taken, the release of sexuality in an adulterous relationship. The Rubicon, the reader learns later, is the bar where Miho briefly worked.[63] The name Rubicon, with its implication of a decisive act, reveals her unconscious desire to regain her sexuality through the bold step of sleeping with another man. In an earlier story, "Tsuma no shokugyō" (My wife's work, 1953), one sees only the husband's reactions to his wife's working outside the home—the deterioration of his physical and mental health when placed in the same situation she was in for so long, waiting in vain for her spouse to return. Here in *Shi no toge*, in Miho's dream one catches a suggestion of *her* side of the story, what it meant to her to be able to be free of the home, to work outside and come in contact with other people. This was, the dream suggests, more than just the opportunity to go out and enjoy herself. It was the difference between life and death.

Miho's dream, then, is that of a woman suffering the effects of powerlessness, including sexual repression, who dreams of sexual freedom equal to that of a man. As seen before, one of the "symptoms" of the mad Miho is the return of sexuality, a sexual aggressiveness more "normal" for a man than for a woman. Toshio's confusion and fear in the face of Miho's newfound sexuality are not unexpected, nor is his linking of this with madness, because as Elaine Showalter makes clear, male fear of female sexuality has a long history. The nineteenth-century British psychiatric establishment for instance, concluded that "uncontrolled sexuality seemed the major, almost defining symptom of insanity in women."[64] In her study of the medical establishment's treatment of female insanity, Showalter notes the extremes to which the profession went to "manage women's minds by regulating their bodies," an example being the Victorian practice of clitoridectomy, the surgical removal of the clitoris.[65] I have discussed some of the medical profession's treatment of Miho as depicted in the *byōinki* and will touch on this topic again shortly. Suffice it to say that although the 1950s Japanese medical establishment is beyond such cruelty, the therapy proscribed for Miho—electroshock, insulin shock, and so on—although not so crudely linked to the suppression of women's sexuality, nevertheless has the effect of returning her to passivity and compliance in all senses of the terms.

One of the more cryptic yet suggestive passages in the novel also hints at a problem of a sexual nature. It comes in a scene where Miho, as she does several times in the course of the story, confronts her husband with what he has written in his diary. "In your notebook it says, 'wife: impotent'—what does that mean?"[Miho asks] but I had no idea what she was talking about.[66] As with all passages concerning the black hole of the fateful diary, the full details of what Toshio has written are never revealed, and we learn only fragments of what is clearly a focus of Miho's rage and disgust. What Sparling translates as "impotent," the word *fugu*, has several meanings. Usually the word refers to a disabled condition of the body—being crippled in an accident, for example. Sparling's choice of "impotent" is intriguing, because it reveals an interpretation of Miho's plight not unlike my own. In this reading I would flesh out the sentence to have Toshio writing, "My wife is impotent." Yet the fragment is open to other readings, including the possibility that Toshio means that *he* is the one who is impotent when with Miho, presumably through lack of desire for her.

Like many scenes in the novel, this one, which seems critical to an interpretation of the problems that confront Toshio and Miho, is left in ambiguity. The first meaning—namely (assuming that these words were written by Toshio), that Miho is viewed by Toshio as a "cripple" in some way—accurately captures what has driven Miho mad: the impotence and powerlessness, in all senses of the terms, that her role as wife forces upon her. For the reader alert to one of the mysteries of the novel—what exactly it was that Toshio wrote that drove Miho insane—this passage comes closer than many to providing a clue. Another possibility one should consider—especially in light of the letters from the other woman, which the reader soon realizes are for the most part written by Miho herself—is that Toshio's inability to understand the meaning of the words stems from the simple fact that this "diary entry" and many (but not all) of the others mentioned in the novel might not be the work of Toshio, as first assumed, but of *Miho*. Typical of much of Shimao's fiction, readers are left to make a choice of interpretation in an ambiguous passage.[67]

To see Miho's madness as a successful rebellion or liberation from the role that has confined her, however, is to forget the truth of Chesler's contention that the "cry of powerlessness" that is the madness of women is always "mercilessly punished." If the novel is read merely as showing Toshio's often passive acceptance of Miho's condition and her successful reversal of household roles, one fails to see the institutional reaction to the outbreak of female madness detailed by the novel—a far from passive reaction operating on the assumption that a "cure" is found when the woman again accepts in silence the role that drove her mad in the first place. In this regard readers need to consider both the medical profession's reaction to Miho's madness—the more one-sided attempt to suppress the "past" that troubles her—and Toshio's, which, as is true of other aspects of his character, is more fascinating for its divided nature. Toshio, in short, can see both sides of the argument and thus is torn between a desire for control over Miho and a desire for her madness to continue.

The decision to take Miho to see a doctor comes rather late in the book, at the end of chapter 6, after Toshio has given up attempting to care for Miho alone. This decision comes at a supreme point of incongruity, even absurdity, in which Toshio attempts yet again to strangle himself, then decides it is *Miho* who needs medical attention. The reader is struck by the deterioration of Toshio's condition to the point where, as in this scene, he seems as much in need of help as she. A broader consideration of their situation reveals why Toshio is progressively unable to control his own fits. It becomes apparent to the reader, if not Toshio, that *he* is now placed in a position analogous to the one *she* endured and is himself now experiencing the powerlessness and impotency that leads to madness.

In a novel of such glacial slowness, what is striking about Miho's medical treatment is the swiftness with which she is diagnosed and processed by the psychiatric establishment once Toshio finally decides to take her to the hospital. Toshio expects at most to receive a prescription for sleeping medicine for Miho's chronic insomnia, but in the space of a few hours Miho is diagnosed as schizophrenic, given electroshock therapy (hereafter ECT), and told to prepare for hospitalization in a locked psychiatric ward. She is examined twice by doctors, first in private and then in a group consultation with the head doctor and interns. In the first session Toshio reluctantly feels compelled to reveal not only Miho's symptoms but the cause as well: the fact that he had an affair. When he does, Miho explodes in fury, slapping him and calling him "shameless" to reveal their private affairs to others. Similarly, in the second session she screams that Toshio is a liar, that she is not sick, and that he is trying to trick her into being locked away. The irony is that it is less Toshio who tricks her than the very medical establishment to which she is appealing, because she is prepared for ECT while being told it is "just a shot." The scenes reveal other points as well: Miho's insistence, up to this point, that their problems be kept secret from others, even close relatives; her violent reaction to the thought of being hospitalized; and the doctors' rush to judgment—labeling Miho a possible schizophrenic and calling for her hospitalization in a locked ward. As Toshio tells one of the doctors soon afterward, this was the first time Miho had ever been violent in front of others. Up to this point she has been remarkably able to turn off her attacks in the presence of others (and re-start them as soon as she and Toshio are alone again)—a fact Toshio uses to his advantage by deliberately inviting friends and acquaintances over and insisting that they spend the night in order to stave off the re-turn of Miho's fits.

Toshio fails to understand, however, that this abrupt change in Miho's reactions at the hospital is directly attributable to the fact that this is *not* Miho's first encounter with psychiatrists and their treatment of the mentally ill. As is soon learned, Miho has seen the effects of the control techniques used in hospitals, particularly ECT, and is both frightened and determined not to be part of them. Pleading with a nurse, she says, "Please don't do electric shock to me. I'm so afraid of it. I know about it. Because I saw a friend of mine who always used to get it done" (211). Who this friend is and what the circumstances were, we do not find out, but a few pages later we do learn that both she and Toshio have already experienced the aftereffects of this treatment. In a crowded recovery room, taking care of the unconscious Miho after her ECT, Toshio re-calls a time when Miho and he were in just such a room, presumably looking after the friend Miho has mentioned. In one corner, he remem-bers, a young girl kept repeating, "No! No! . . . I'm not crazy," while

> one man stood there in trousers and *tabi*, a baby strapped to his back with a red *nenneko* [a kind of cloth baby carrier] and another child by his side, gaz-ing fixedly at the sleeping face of his wife. My wife looked at him steadily and whispered in my ear, "When I go crazy, will you take care of me like that?" (213)

The preponderance of female patients is notable, suggesting that in mid-1950s Japan, as in the West, ECT was more often given to women than men. As Showalter writes, "[T]he available statistical evidence shows that in England and the United States women to this day out-number men as ECT patients by a ratio of two or even three to one."[68] Showalter quotes one doctor, a firm opponent of the therapy, who "ar-gues that women more often receive this treatment because they are judged to have less need of their brains."[69] Miho, in short, knows full well the medical profession's reaction to madwomen, and is fearful of falling victim to it herself. "If you force that on me," she tells Toshio, "I really *will* die. You understand?" (210).

Toshio, in his often ineffectual way, hesitatingly asks the doctor and nurse in charge of Miho's case not to administer ECT, but he is rebuffed by both. The doctor ignores him and turns to another case, while the nurse, who reassures them they will just give Miho a shot, lies, because the shot turns out to be the combination short-term anaesthetic and muscle relaxant administered just prior to ECT.[70] Finally, the male attendant who delivers the injection brusquely admonishes Miho to hold still as she struggles to avoid the shot.

Readers, much like Toshio, are left in shock themselves at Miho's treatment at the hands of the medical profession. The staff is callous, prevaricating, and ready after only the briefest of observations to declare her schizophrenic, perform ECT, and lock her up. Showing no interest in the possible causes of madness in a woman, the doctors immediately restrain any woman who threatens to be out of control, thus preserving tranquility for *men*. In Miho's case this seems particularly true, because the doctors not only respond to Miho's violent act against a man (slapping her husband) with violence (namely ECT) against *her*, but also emphasize to Toshio the advantage to *him* in having her locked away (205, 211).

In a similar vein, the question of controlling women is raised later in the novel. After Miho has been hospitalized alone the first time and is no longer thought to be schizophrenic, the attending doctor emphasizes to Toshio the need for him to control Miho. In the hospital, he says, she is obedient, and thus concludes that hers is less a "medical problem" than one of "human relations between husband and wife" (242). It is a problem of the "husband's ego" (*goshujin no shutaisei*), and until Toshio can "recover [his] ego," Miho cannot be "cured" (250, 252). In other words, Toshio must regain an ego unafraid to victimize others if he is to recover his dominance over his wife. Despite the doctor's comments that her madness is no longer a medical problem, he in essence urges Toshio to reproduce at home the basic conditions of control over women established in the hospital. One wonders whether the doctors' downgrading of Miho's condition from schizophrenia to psychogenic reaction is the result of further observation that has shown her condition to be less severe than originally thought, or rather the passivity brought about in her repeated "treatment." In other words, the doctors have not now discovered the "truth" about her condition, but instead have *created* her present state—one that can now be controlled by the husband, provided his ego is as hardy and implacable as they hope.

Toshio is caught in that most Shimao-like of binds: feeling pain at

contemplating the moment Miho awakes, when she is once again beyond control, yet equally fearful that communication between them has
been cut. Up until now, during every attack he feared just such an irrep-
arable cleavage, but always afterward communication returned:

> But now I was frightened by the anxiety that, like a flame on a burner being
> sucked into the hole and disappearing when the gas main is shut off, the inte-
> rior of my wife's brain would be shut off and all traffic with it pull back. (216)

In the final scene after the first ECT treatment, Toshio gives Miho
sleeping medicine, and all is finally quiet around him. But the end of her
attacks does not bring with it any respite from the constant anxiety that
assaults him:

> *Now that silence felt like death*, and made me terribly lonely. I should have let
> her talk to her heart's content; the image of her as she talks, like a praying
> mantis with raised head clung to my eyes and would not disappear.
>
>   My wife was neither human nor animal, but had become like a demon
> who's settled in one spot, and *the deep fissure between talkativeness and silence
> which appeared before me made me feel I, too, would go mad.* (217–218; emphasis
> added)

What Toshio fears most is silence, the silence that leaves him back in
a monologic world, a silence that feels "like death." Just as in the beginning of the novel he is nostalgic for a return to the "peaceful" family life he remembers before her initial outburst, a sense of nostalgia for
the earlier, dialogic phase of Miho's madness increasingly comes to
pervade the narrative. "Talkativeness and silence"—at first glance
opposites—in the world of Toshio and Miho have now become nearly
the same. Awake and talking, asleep and silent, Miho is no longer en-
gaged in a dialogue with her husband. As she goes further and further
to a "place where [he] cannot reach," Toshio is once more in solitude,
cut off from dialogue. Quite simply, an end to dialogue—both for Miho
and Toshio—is associated with a deepening of madness. One might
even say that the only healthy aspect of their entire relationship was the
stinging, relentless days of dialogue they experienced, the demand for
total honesty about their past and present. Only now, when they are
again in "inescapably solitary consciousnesses," are they both beginning to be truly mad.

Toshio's relationship with the past is complex and subtle. The novel
traces the move from his more simple desire to put an end to the past
(that Miho will just "seal off the past and thrust it aside")[71] to a grudg-

ing realization that he cannot avoid confronting it. This is the greatest difference separating *Shi no toge* from Shimao's previous work—the conclusion that we not only should, but *must*, confront the past directly.[72] Through most of the novel Toshio seldom wavers in his goal of putting an end to the past, to cut himself off from it, yet under the influence of Miho's relentless attacks he begins to conclude that the only way to overcome the past is by confronting it. The past for him becomes likened to an oozing, pustulent "wound" that Miho's attacks never allow to heal; yet in order to stop her attacks, he must allow her to open up this wound. The paradox becomes that of a wound that heals only when it is picked and gouged at. He himself fails to understand completely why he cannot stand having the past brought up over and over (331) and finds his "body cannot take" having the past "rehashed again and again"(327). The pain of having this wound constantly reopened leads Toshio to devise strategies to deflect a direct confrontation with the past, as he struggles both to suppress the past and bring it to the surface of his consciousness.

And what is the content of the past? As in the *byōinki*, the past in *Shi no toge* includes, but is not limited to, Toshio's infidelities. Toshio's affair with another woman *is* the primary focus of Miho's anger and hurt, yet as I have indicated, his infidelity is merely part of a larger pattern of neglect and mistreatment to which she has fallen victim.[73] Miho is depicted as a mistreated 1950s urban Japanese housewife, but in *Shi no toge* she is delineated as something more—a native of a locality in Japan, the southern islands, whose residents bear a history of having been victimized at the hands of the mainland. And when she raises what has been suppressed in their lives—the past—this opens up much more than just her husband's infidelities. It raises the issue of the entire past they share, including the war.[74]

Shi no toge, the War, and Responsibility

Shi no toge abounds with subtle, and less than subtle, references to the war experience, and the reader is justified in viewing Toshio and Miho as later manifestations of the lieutenant and village girl of Shimao's numerous war stories. When Toshio strikes Miho, for instance, he recalls the feeling of striking the soldiers under his command in the war (19); he recalls, too, walking over the mountain path in uniform during the war to see her (240). Their present battle with Miho's madness, too, is often described in military terms. Toshio sees the world around him filled with "mines" ready to explode at the slightest touch, and wonders why Miho won't "cease hostilities" when he has "unconditionally surrendered" to her (72–73). One scene in particular illustrates the overlap of the war experience and their present battle with madness. Unable to stand Miho's relentless interrogations, Toshio is about to rush out of the house, when she stops him at the door and grabs him:

> She enfolded her husband with both arms as though she were clinging to a pillar. Then she slid down his body to the floor.
> "I nurtured and formed these hands and feet. You would have died a long time ago if I hadn't worried about feeding you properly. I don't want to give you to anyone else. No one. No one! But you ignored me and did whatever you wanted. And not just for one or two months. For ten years. I've tried and tried to endure it, but I can't go on anymore."
> Half in tears, she chanted the words like a rehearsed monologue. She sat on the floor, alternately stroking her cheek, all the while weeping out of control.
> Suddenly I thought of the war days. I was stationed at a naval base near her home. Late at night when I went to see the still youthfully plump girl, she had groped in the darkness for the stars on my uniform, run her hands along my jacket, and knelt to stroke my combat boots. The memory persuaded me that the aroma of beach crinum had wafted all the way to this backstreet house in a corner of the capital. I'm not sure what combination of circumstances made me grow distant from my wife in the turbulent chaos after the defeat. But I couldn't help seeing in the tiny figure of my wife sobbing at my feet an image of the past that was an irrefutable part of my experience.[75]

If Miho's madness is in part a healthy questioning of all Toshio has suppressed up until now—the ways in which the cloak of being a "victim" can be used to mask one's own victimization of others—what exactly does victimization entail in this story? The subtext of the war experience takes this novel beyond the level of marital problems between one couple and into the realm of the experience of the Japanese in the war. Shimao's war experience, I have argued, made of him a liminal figure who recoded the traumas of war and its aftermath in his early fictional dream stories. It is easy to see his literature, as Okuno does, as "literature of the victim" (*higaisha no bungaku*). Okuno, writing in 1954, speaks of the Shimao protagonists' "persecution complex" as a trait all Japanese share, since "society is an evil victimizer against our lives and freedom." In Shimao's dream stories Okuno finds a representative of ordinary postwar Japanese wandering aimlessly in a world devoid of meaning, a state made particularly poignant for Shimao due to the emptiness and meaninglessness of the *tokkōtai* experience.[76] As Oda argues, however, a reading such as Okuno's buys into a dangerous assessment of the mental state of postwar Japanese:

> [O]ur sense of victimization was too pervasive and too seductive. We took refuge in our feelings of victimization to avoid the perils of true autonomy, finally nurturing those feelings into what amounted to a full-fledged persecution complex. This complex precluded a parallel awareness of our own complicity as victimizers. . . . In fact, . . . we were entirely unable to realize that we ourselves may have been guilty of victimizing others.[77]

Shimao's early dream stories *do* reveal a victim of war struggling to recover and come to terms with his experience. However, at the same time that they reveal an impotence and sense of powerlessness in war, they expose a potent side as well—the "parallel awareness" of the victim also as victimizer. In these stories one sees the protagonist's complicity in the wartime sacrifice of the southern islands to save the mainland, the power of life and death he had over the islanders, hints of wartime mass suicides of civilians, and an overarching sense of guilt over wartime actions that call for punishment. The wandering motif, too, is not simply the aimless wandering of a victim of war; a wider reading of Shimao's early work reveals a pattern in the apparent randomness. The Shimao protagonist is not merely wandering among the ordinary, mainstream citizens of Japan, all of whom, as Okuno would have it, are victims. Instead, he is on a search for the marginalized of postwar Japan, the true victims on the margins of postwar society: white Russians and outcastes ("Tandoku no ryokōsha"); Eurasians and the poor (especially women) ("Chippoke na aventure," 1950); unemployed "juvenile delinquents," lepers, victims of the atomic bombings, and "half-breed" children ("Yume no naka de no nichijō").

With its doubled structure of the past constituted by both a marital relationship and the war experience, *Shi no toge* overlays a simple I-novel format with something of greater significance. The layered nature of the novel rises to the surface most clearly in the dream Miho relates to Toshio—a dream that simultaneously accuses him of neglecting his wife and attempts to articulate wartime trauma. Let us review part of this crucial passage:

> From the *jouguchi* [front door, in her island dialect] [Miho] looked out at the garden and saw a huge hole there, with many people crammed inside. Maggots crawled out of the hole to the outside. The maggots squirmed and the

hole was full of people. From out of the crowd of people in the hole she saw the bloodless, horribly pale faces of her dead mother and father. She was so startled she stopped breathing—*Anmai!* she cried out, and ran to the hole in order to save them, but *Anma* said, "Don't come here," waving her away with a scary face she'd never seen before.

The dream image of the mother and father, dead among crowds of villagers in a huge hole dug in the ground, is nothing less than Miho's horrified reaction to a submerged memory, the way her villagers were commanded to assemble in trenches built in part by Toshio's troops to commit mass suicide *at his command.* Miho's madness accords well with Ōshiro Tatsuhiro's reading of postwar southern islander (specifically Okinawan) mentality. Unlike mainlanders, for Okinawans the war continues to be a prime source of anger, specifically because it is linked so closely to continuing discrimination. And many southern islanders hold a strong desire to see mainlanders repent of their wartime actions. Citing one of the more infamous cases of enforced wartime mass suicide, for instance, Ōshiro notes the rumor circulating at the time in Okinawa that the lieutenant who ordered the massacre had entered the Buddhist priesthood to atone for his actions.[78] For Miho, too, the war and her husband's actions continue to be a similar source of anger, one that in part accounts for the vehemence of her attacks.

Shimao's message to postwar Japanese is best read thus: it addresses Oda's contention that many survivors of the war have far too quickly developed an explanatory narrative for the past in which a clear-cut dichotomy emerged with themselves as victims and *something else* (the military regime, especially) as victimizer. As Oda notes,

> Countless records of wartime experiences have appeared in the twenty-one years since the war, but all are reconstructed from the point of view of the victim. The accounts of students, soldiers from rural areas, evacuated school children, and repatriots [sic] from overseas are all filled with tragic victimization. Together they have contributed to *a situation in which the term "wartime experience" is synonymous with "experience as victim."* [79]

Critics such as Okuno who see Shimao's early work as depicting the victim only miss what is clearly present as early as "Shutsu kotōki"—the divided nature of the protagonist as both victim (his role as *tokkōtai* leader about to die on his mission) and victimizer (of his lover, his men, the entire village.) This is not to say that Shimao's early stories are not deeply imbued with a sense of the protagonist as victim. Indeed they are. But what separates these stories from *Shi no toge* is the latter's insistence on ruthlessly bringing to light the other side of the coin—the protagonist as victimizer. Critics who rejected Shimao's early *byōsaimono* (in particular the *byōinki*) on literary grounds as a stylistic "retreat" from the avant-garde surrealism of his early dream stories were rejecting not just what they saw as a stylistic shift—a regression from a progressive antirealism toward a conservative realism. They were also rejecting the *content* of the *byōsaimono*—the exposure of the victimizer side of the "victim" that shatters the narrative construction that sees the Japanese people solely as victims.

In the view of Takeda Tomojū, it is not just postwar Japanese literature, but modern Japanese literature as a whole, that takes as its starting point the consciousness of the victim.[80] The literary ego is victim of all outside it—family, society, organizations—and literature itself is energized through its resistance to these outside forces. What separates Shimao's *byōsaimono* from the mainstream, he argues, is its characterization of a person "tortured" by his "consciousness of being a victimizer"; for Shimao, the "victimizer is always oneself, not another."[81] Shimao's genius, Takeda concludes, lies in clearly depicting how the positions of victim and victimizer are not fixed. In the case of *Shi no toge* one witnesses how Miho, the victim, begins to be a victimizer, while Toshio, the victimizer, often is the victim (and how the two of them combine at times to victimize others—their children and the other woman in particular). Takeda writes at length of what has troubled so many readers of the novel, the question Mishima and Karatani addressed: why does Toshio refuse to run away from this terrible situation he finds himself in with Miho? Takeda concludes that the novel reveals Toshio's gradual realization that the only way out of this living "hell" is to assume full responsibility for the consequences of his actions, for his collapsing family and sick wife. Here Takeda's analysis turns religious, with Shimao seen as primarily a religious writer. Takeda argues that the difference between the *byōinki* and *Shi no toge* is explained by Shimao's 1956 conversion to Catholicism, which colors the latter work. In this view Shimao exhibits in *Shi no toge* a "Christian view of existence," exploring what is in essence "original sin," namely, the power to victimize others that exists in all humans, and the meaning of salvation, which is liberation from victimization of others. Ultimately, Takeda argues, Shimao's works are "metaphysical" attempts at "self-liberation" that "go beyond the character of times or society, and in fact rejects these." Shimao's work takes him "beyond the category of postwar literature" as he becomes an author who "listens attentively to the eternal groans of distress of human existence."[82]

Thus Takeda, who so accurately pinpoints the dynamics of *Shi no toge*, unfortunately ends by removing the novel and the author from their particular historical situation. By talking of unproblematic "universals" of human experience, Takeda in effect defuses anything Shimao could be telling us about actual postwar Japanese society and the experience of the war. *Shi no toge* and its characters, however, must be repositioned in the historical setting in which they belong. Toshio is an example par excellence of the postwar Japanese "victim" mentality of which Oda speaks. Miho, in her madness, exposes the entire ten-year period of their marriage (which overlaps precisely with the entire postwar period up to that point, 1945–1955) as one of deception of others (Toshio deceiving Miho) and of *self*-deception—of Toshio playing the victim while below the surface struggling to contain his past, which threatens to expose another side. Toshio has "almost recovered" his "ego," only to have it threatened by Miho's insistence on facing the past and his victimization of herself and others.[83] Significantly, the period depicted in *Shi no toge*—the mid 1950s—is the time when Japan, as a nation, had successfully suppressed its wartime past and, owing to the bolster of the Korean War, had begun the long climb to economic recovery. Paralleling Toshio, the national "ego" was almost recovered. But at what cost?

The *byōsaimono*, *Shi no toge* in particular, forcefully drag to the surface *not* something that has been entirely absent—guilt, the sense of being a victimizer—but something that has been there all along, submerged. Even in the most dreamlike of Shimao's early stories the protagonist is plagued by a profound sense of guilt, hardly what one would expect of characters who are pure victims. Yet this sense of guilt, as with most elements of these surrealistic stories, is often unfocused, or directed at characters in what is, at least on the surface, an improbable situation. In *Shi no toge* Shimao takes the dream world into the real by combining dream techniques with a fictional world based closely on real-life situations. The result is far more than an adjustment in literary technique. The effect is to bring the unconscious into the world of the conscious, to take the diffuse sense of guilt that works itself out in the symbolic imagery of the early stories into the light of a hyperrational

interrogation and attempt to trace its sources—and possible cures—
in the *real world*. If indeed madness is a "state in which unconscious
processes dominate our consciousness,"[84] the outbreak of madness in
Shimao's world finds the suppressed unconscious breaking to the surface in the *byōsaimono*. Toshio's and Miho's world becomes one in which
this unconsciously suppressed past erupts into, and comes to dominate,
the conscious real world.

Sparling has spoken of the power of Shimao's *byōsaimono* as lying in
how they "represent a commitment, rare in Japanese literature, to life
and the responsibilities it brings."[85] The struggle of Toshio coming to
grips with his responsibility is indeed one of the reasons *Shi no toge* is
powerful reading, yet this responsibility should not be read as ending
with a husband caring for an ill wife. Responsibility is linked with the
past, with both Toshio's mistreatment of his wife and his experiences of
the war, which were, in essence, those of failed victim and victimizer of
both Miho and her people. Thus the ending of the novel is, in a way,
full of hope. Because despite the ever-present temptations that tug at
Toshio to lock Miho away alone, to lock away the "image of the past"
she is to him, Toshio abandons all—work, children, home—to join her
behind the locked doors and barred windows of the mental ward. The
novel, then, is both *byōsaimono*—"sick *wife* story"—and *byōfumono*—
"sick *husband* story," because although the ostensible reason for their
hospitalization is to seek a cure for Miho's madness, Toshio's decision
to confront the past is made as much to seek a cure for himself. Much
as Sakaguchi Ango, in his influential 1946 essay "Darakuron" (trans.
1986, "Discourse on Decadence"), argues that the early postwar Japanese must reach the bottom before they can regain their humanity, Shimao insists on confronting the past, taking this confrontation to the
very "abyss," and climbing out again. Only in this way can Toshio—
and Japan—begin to enter a healthier world.

The Amami Connection: Miho and the Southern Islands

If the character Miho is viewed only as a typical urban housewife whose
husband's infidelities push her over the edge to madness, one is missing
half the story. Miho is very carefully positioned as coming from a culture outside the mainstream, namely the islands south of Kagoshima.[86]
In most readings of the novel her origins in a marginalized area of Japan

(one with a history of victimization at the hands of mainlanders, World War II being the latest episode) are treated as no more than an interesting sidelight, the assumption being that Miho is a fully integrated, modern urban woman.[87] Such readings, however, which focus entirely on the fragility of the postwar nuclear family, fail to do justice to the deep link between Miho, her condition, and her position as a southern islander.

Early in the novel the reader is sensitized to Miho's position. In chapter 1 Toshio goes off to watch a movie one day, remarkable in itself as showing the occasional breaks in the intensity of their conflict. The movie depicts the lives of natives deep in the jungles of Brazil. Back home, describing the film to Miho, Toshio flinches as he uses the word native; the implication is that he recognizes, and is sensitive to, her position as "southern island" native and all the prejudices directed at such people (22–23).[88] In earlier stories ("Kisōsha no yūutsu" and "Tetsuro ni chikaku") the wife's desperate condition, her outbursts of sadness, and her suicide attempts are all intimately linked with her parents and her island home. The stories paint a picture of a person driven by a profound nostalgia for the world she came from, with her mad screams primal cries for a return to the island. Such points are driven home in *Shi no toge*. Here there is an even more intimate connection between the island and her madness, particularly its language: mad attacks bring on a switch from standard Japanese to the Amami dialect (94, 193). The pain of having been betrayed and victimized brings forth a rush of emotions that can be expressed only in language that for her exists at some deeper and basic level than the overlay of standard Japanese with which she functions on a daily level in Tokyo. It is language that reaches, in Okamoto Keitoku's words, "the core of her personality."[89] And it is as if the dialect words she uses, often untranslated, are as out of place in the text as Miho is in Tokyo.

Further, although Miho sometimes calls herself *kichigai*—standard Japanese for "crazy"—throughout the novel she refers to her madness in dialect words. She is like a *gudoma*, a shellfish that shuts itself particularly tight, she is attacked by *unima*, evil spirits that possess her, she is *mugari* (a term whose meaning is not entirely clear, but indicates that she is having an attack). And more than in any previous story, her dead parents (always referred to in the dialect terms *Jū* and *Anma*) become spirits of the islands themselves not only to which she appeals, but which she sees as dictating her actions in prophetic dreams and visions. I have noted the dream of *Jū* and *Anma* that seems so crucial to understanding Miho's feelings and return to this a final time. Soon after relating this dream, Miho informs Toshio that her father, *Jū*, came to her and told her not to badger her husband anymore. "Let's all ask *Jū* and *Anma* to let us build a happy family" (115). In the critical scene in chapter 5 where Toshio comes closest to committing suicide, it is *Jū* and *Anma* who hold Miho back from joining him: "I can't kill myself," she tells Toshio. "*Jū* came and told me not to" (149). And finally, Miho tells her husband that *Anma* and *Jū* "warned [her] every night" that Toshio is still lying (225).

For his part, Toshio comes to realize how out of place Miho is in Tokyo and how profound the differences are between their backgrounds:

> If you go a little ways outside of Tokyo there is, all the way to Tohoku, a taciturn smell of flesh which arouses a homesickness in me. I was born in the city, but had Tohoku blood from my parents; my wife had her hometown far away, in an island rather close to Okinawa. The crisis we were now facing might have some connection with this fact. (114)

Listening to her talk on about her dead father, Toshio notes,

> I thought it would be like a grandchild listening to his grandmother telling old tales *(mukashibanashi)*, but it wasn't like what I'd experienced as a boy, filled with the workings of Tohoku; it was instead an emotional tale of a southern island, shadowless under the white sun. (288)

As one might expect, and as the characters grow to realize, a cure for Miho's madness lies both in a renewed, intimate relationship of caring and in a return to her island home—because in great part her madness results from a deep sense of incongruity with her surroundings in the mainland city, feelings that can be relieved only by returning to Amami.[90] Toshio is the first to suggest such a return, an idea Miho at first opposes (128). Later, however, she considers the idea of returning on her own (224), and gradually the idea comes to them that the only solution is a permanent move of the entire family to the island. Thus as *Shi no toge* draws to a close, Toshio and Miho ship their belongings to the island and prepare to send their children to live with Miho's aunt there. The unspecified period of treatment in the mental hospital depicted in the *byōinki*, one understands, will be followed soon after by the decisive move to faraway Amami.

Read together with the *byōinki*, the imagery in *Shi no toge* used to contrast the mainland and the island overlaps in interesting ways with images of Miho's madness, and reinforces the notion of the island as a place of cure. Miho's condition in the story parallels changes in the seasons in an interesting way. The outbreak of her madness comes at the end of the summer, or the beginning of a return of the cold. As the days grow shorter and winter deepens, so does her condition worsen. Time, too, in the story parallels her deepening madness, as the chapters progressively cover shorter spans of time (chapter 5 covers ten days; chapter 6, six to seven days; chapter 7 only one day). Chapter 7, appropriately entitled "Hi no chijimari" (The shortening of the days) comes at the height of winter, the end of January, when the days are indeed at their shortest and Miho's condition has worsened to such an extent that Toshio finally must take her to see a doctor. Thus the sense of "frozen time" (145) brought on by Miho's madness is reflected in the gradual slowing of the narrative, which itself is paralleled by the gradually shrinking days of winter. As seen in the *byōinki*, Miho's madness is described as a frozen world, an icy plain she and Toshio must traverse; respite is found only when the ice melts, when the plain turns from winter to spring and life returns. What is needed is warmth, and in this sense the tropical island stands as the very place to provide both the physical and spiritual warmth she seeks to "melt" away her madness. Likewise, in *Shi no toge* Miho's attacks are described repeatedly as a shadow *(kageri)* that clouds her features; as Toshio grows to realize, what Miho needs to dispel this shadow is her home—a place *without* shadow *(kageri no nai)* (288).[91]

Several commentators, most notably Yoshimoto Takaaki, have noted an aspect of Miho that reveals her as separate from the mainland urban setting in which she is placed. This is the part of her that is of "ancient" *(kodaiteki)* Japan, namely the ways in which her actions and powers resemble those of a shamaness. Sparling has neatly summarized how this image of the female protagonist as shamaness is apparent in the first story Shimao published after the war, "Shima no hate." Writing of Toë, the native girl who is a prototype for the later Miho, Sparling notes:

> It is easy to associate the Toë of "The Farthest Edge of the Islands" with the village shamaness. One hereditary group of Shamanistic priestesses (and more rarely, priests) in the Amami Islands was called *yuta*. They traditionally lived alone, like Toë, in an isolated sacred dwelling, suggested by Toë's garden of roses, often located near a sacred grove, suggested in this story by the "ancient trees, from whose branches hung many roots, like beards," trees that

"stood as if shoulder to shoulder, strangely encircling the village," giving off
a mysterious scent, bearing "flowers whose buds opened secretly, quietly,
only at night."[92]

Sparling notes the "special respect" accorded the *yuta*, which Toë seems
to be afforded: "Among the people of the village," the story tells us,
"both children and adults, there were many who thought that Toë was
fundamentally different from themselves. This was simply because for
a long time Toë's family had been thought of in such a way." She notes,
too, Toë's "extraordinary auditory and visual powers" and the way in
which, much like a shamaness serving as a spiritual medium, she has the
power to feel what others feel.[93] In the story "Yoru no nioi," too, the
lieutenant imagines his lover "possessed by the *yuta* spirit."

In Yoshimoto's reading of the *byōsaimono*, Miho's move to Tokyo, the
capital city, which for most people brings an increase in status, indicates, rather, a *fall* in status for Miho. The shamaness-like figure welcoming the *marebito* protector of the island (the lieutenant) depicted in
"Shima no hate" becomes a frail housewife in unfamiliar surroundings,
whose greatest anxiety is the result of her having been uprooted.[94] Yet,
like the remnants of her dialect that occasionally surface, aspects of her
former status and powers reveal themselves: her vision of what is none
other than an *ikimaburi* in "Kisōsha no yūutsu" (a spirit of one about to
die), her prediction ("strange conviction") of Toshio's impending suicide on the opening page of *Shi no toge*, and her prophetic dream of
meeting the other woman in Suidobashi followed by the arrival of a
letter from the woman telling how she waited in vain for Toshio at
that very place (24–25). The notion, too, that her interrogations are
less to uncover facts she does not know than to reconfirm what she already knows (because concerning Toshio she *knows everything already*)
at the least hints at the sort of extraordinary knowledge possessed by a
shamaness.[95]

One interpretation of Miho's madness is that it is a last resort, a
weapon she turns on Toshio in an attempt to cure him of his downward
spiral, which she prophesies will lead to his death. ("In November you
will leave the house, in December you will kill yourself.") This makes
sense, of course, if she is viewed as a sort of shamaness, because as
William Lebra notes, the main role of a shamaness—a *yuta*—is to rem-
edy such misfortune:

> The *yuta*, with preternatural powers of seeing, hearing, and possession, are
> regarded as uniquely equipped to discern the causes of misfortune and to

suggest or direct remedial action. They are commonly called upon when misfortune strikes or when any unusual, and hence seemingly ominous, events transpire.[96]

Obviously the Miho-Toshio relationship is not that of the usual *yuta*-client relationship in which a person, usually in ill health, consults a *yuta* in order to find a cure. Yet there are indications that Toshio has indirectly sought a crisis, a confrontation with Miho, in order to escape the stagnated and rotting life he sees himself leading in the mainland.[97]

There is, however, another aspect of Miho's madness that must be considered, one that returns to Yoshimoto's comments on her fall in status. Yoshimoto argues that in some of Shimao's stories (he highlights "Ie no naka") the wife's sufferings are similar to those of people, the vast majority women, chosen to be *yuta*—that Miho's madness, in essence, is the agony associated with *initiation* into becoming a *yuta*. To follow Yoshimoto's logic, we would have a woman who is, in the island, already a *yuta*, who then undergoes *initiation* as a *yuta* later—an illogical reversal of events.

Instead, Miho is suffering the agonies of *refusing* to be a *yuta*, a refusal that brings on *tatari* (or *kamidatari*), retribution from the gods, and

> strikes prospective *kaminchu* (community priestesses, kin group priestesses, or shamans) who reject their destined role, or established *kaminchu* who shirk their ritual obligations. Although almost any kind of misfortune afflicting a *kaminchu* may be labeled *tatari*, most frequently it assumes the pattern of a genuine psychosomatic disorder . . . [including] physical weakness or sickness, inability to perform normal routine work, lack of appetite, auditory and visual hallucinations, disturbing dreams, [and] periods of dissociation.[98]

Miho's madness, then, is not the agony of someone becoming a *yuta*, but of a woman trying to dissociate herself from the island and her roots in order to create a successful marriage and family in urban postwar Japan, a woman who has come to understand how she cannot cut herself off from her roots and still survive. There is a terrible price to pay for cultural alienation in a country that, as Shimao reveals, is marked by suppressed diversity. One recalls the physical symptoms that first manifested themselves in "Ie no naka"—the stomach pains, the headaches, the gaps in memory—followed by the chilling outburst of her attacks. To return a final time to the dream section in *Shi no toge*, Miho's unconscious reveals a desperate desire to return to the island as the root of her problem. This section deals with women's sexuality, and wartime mass suicide. It also contains elements of what Yoshimoto calls "ancient" imagery, in particular that of the ancient Ryukyuan custom of *fūsō*, exposure of dead bodies to the elements.⁹⁹ More important, Miho's dream reveals her relationship to and need for the island, and the conditions of her return:

> *Anma* said, "Don't come here," waving her away with a scary face she'd never seen before. "If you don't escape from your distress, *Anma* and *Jū* won't be able to crawl out of this hole. You still want to return to the islands? It's not the time for you to return. You poor thing."
> [Later, Miho speaking]: "And meanwhile the lower half of my body rotted away. It's all Heaven's punishment, all punishment for what I did. I sacrificed *Jū*, who was like a god, and picked you, and now look at the horrible things you've done to me." (104)

Having abandoned the father (the island) for Toshio (life on the mainland), Miho suffers. She must complete the cycle of "distress" she is in, "Heaven's punishment" for having sacrificed her Father, a "god," before (1) she can return to the island, and (2) *Jū* and *Anma* can "crawl out of the hole" and return to the land of the living. For turning her back on the island, and her role as *yuta*, then, Miho is suffering *tatari*, the retribution of the gods *(kami)*.

This need not be read as taking the reader into the religious interpretation I eschewed at the beginning of this chapter, as substituting a somehow more authentic local religious tradition (instead of, say, a Christian reading) as interpretive paradigm. As will be seen in the next chapter, Shimao found the motif of wife-as-*yuta*-healer a productive shorthand for larger concerns, namely the role of the southern islands and their identity vis-à-vis the dominant culture. In the final analysis, Shimao is concerned with the discovery of difference and cultural diversity, the seeds of which he discovered first on a personal level in his wife's condition. On one level Miho is angry at Toshio for his ill treatment of her, but in a very real way, too, his crime lies in having removed her from all that supports her, from an environment and culture that is very much *not* that of modern urban Japan. As Okamoto (an Okinawan reader) sees it, *Shi no toge* as a whole must be read from the perspective of the margins: as an uncovering of the importance of *place*, specifically the island, in Miho's well-being and recovery.¹⁰⁰ Further, Okamoto writes:

> [A]s depicted in *Shi no toge*, the direct cause of Miho's madness is "Toshio," but in the background we can see the complex of Miho, from the islands, which manifests itself particularly in an incongruity *(iwa)* with the people around her; granted this, tracing the origins of the complex which Amami

people, indeed all southern islanders have, and groping for a way to dispel this, became pressing problems for Shimao.[101]

In the next chapter we will see how Shimao dealt with these "pressing problems"—both on a fictional and non-fictional level. It is to Amami and the southern islands, to the margins of Japan and the place they occupy in Shimao's literature, that we turn next.

FoUR

Island Dreams: *Yaponesia* and the Cultural Unconscious

> Every time I see a papaya tree, whether its
> leaves are full or fallen, I feel my wife's limbs;
> whether its fruit is ripe or unripe, there I see
> my wife's form; when I eat the fruit, thinking
> it's delicious, somehow I get the feeling I'm
> eating a part of my wife's body. What could
> this mean, I wonder.
>
> Shimao Toshio, "Niwa ue no papaya," 1963

FROM THE late 1950s through the 1970s
Shimao was absorbed in two projects: the fictionalized account of his
wife's mental illness that became *Shi no toge* (see chapter 3), and the depiction of his relationship with his island home, which is the topic of
this chapter. To divide these two projects, however, is to risk missing
how they are in many ways one. As noted at the end of chapter 3, Shimao's *byōsaimono*—his twenty-year literary study of his wife and her
madness—is in large part a study of a native of Amami, of a woman who
could not adjust to life away from her island home, whose profound
sense of incongruity drove her back to the southern island. As I examine in this chapter, Shimao's myriad essays on the islands (numbering
some 170 from 1954–1978) and his "Yaponesia ron" (Theory of *Yaponesia*) are both an attempt to trace the origins of this complex of southern
islanders vis-à-vis the mainland, and a move to dispel it by helping instill

160

a sense of cultural identity, even pride, in a people historically deprived of such. Through these writings Shimao became known to southern readers perhaps less for his fiction than for the issues he raised in his essays: the historical and present-day relationship between the center and the peripheral regions of Japan (one in which the latter have been victimized), the possibilities of a multicultural Japan, and prospects for maintaining diversity within one nation. As I will argue, Shimao's fiction and essays are mutually reinforcing, and a full understanding of either depends on knowledge of both projects.

One particularly intriguing way that fiction and essays overlap is found in connections between *Yaponesia* and Shimao's fictional preoccupation with the unconscious. In rediscovering and bringing to the forefront marginalized geographic and cultural zones, Shimao uncovers what he views as Japan's cultural unconscious. His fictional depiction of encounters with these zones, in turn, is shown as a journey toward the edges of consciousness, indeed to the unconscious realm itself. And this fictional meeting of conscious and unconscious is conveyed in the distinctive style he develops from the mid-1950s onward, one that subtly brings the two worlds together.

After examining Shimao's *Yaponesia* essays, I will discuss *Shi no toge* and several stories—which I call Shimao's "island stories"—written at the same time the first half of *Shi no toge* was composed (1959–1965), and, in the conclusion, the two books *Hi no utsuroi* and *Zoku Hi no utsuroi*. All set on an island (except *Shi no toge*)—usually but not always identifiable as Amami—these stories are connected by two common elements. The first is their depiction of the familiar Shimao male protagonist (and in three stories the wife), now after the wife's madness has subsided, back in the island. The second is the husband's search for knowledge of the island, which to a large degree comes to him filtered through the medium of the wife, who as an island native is privy to an insider's viewpoint he is never allowed to share fully. The wife represents the closest the narrator can get to the island—she is, arguably, a symbolic substitute for the island—yet, despite the narrator's attempts to get "inside," both the island and the wife remain Others who are more often than not unknowable and ungraspable. Traces of madness remain in the wife, but she has shifted from madwoman to guide, even healer, of the husband who, because he is "out of place," is the one who is ill. The male protagonist is forever the perpetual outsider, but one who, despite his sense of incongruity toward the island, is profoundly drawn to it and its people. To understand fully these island stories and *Shi no toge* and its sequels—indeed all of Shimao's fiction—one must first grasp *Yaponesia*.

A clear split in public perception of Shimao Toshio continues to separate readers on the mainland from those in the southern islands. For Tokyo-based writers and readers, Shimao was an aspiring writer who, unlike many of the writers in the informal circles in which he moved during 1952–1955, failed to win the coveted Akutagawa Prize[1] (one key to launching a literary career) and who, because of his wife's illness, soon removed himself from the center of literary activity. Shimao, in short, is seen in Tokyo as a writer who continued to remain a highly respected, although somewhat distant, voice in modern fiction. In contrast, in Amami and Okinawa Shimao came to the attention of many students and intellectuals more through his essays on the southern islands. I refer in particular to those dealing with *Yaponesia*, which he began to write in the early 1960s (just after he commenced work on *Shi no toge*) and which came into prominence around 1970 with the reversion of Okinawa to the mainland. As Okamoto puts it, for Okinawans such as himself, gradually disillusioned with the reversion movement and concerned that the distinctive character of Okinawa would be "lost as it was homogenized into the mainland," there was a desperate need for a "conceptual basis for supporting . . . the special character of Okinawa." For Okamoto, this need began to be filled in 1970 when he heard Shimao lecture in Okinawa; he discovered in *Yaponesia* and "Ryūkyūkō" (the latter another term for the Ryukyu Islands) "a revelation in the concept these beautiful words presented."[2] Shimao's ideas helped work to confirm the "special nature" of Okinawan culture; one could find a basis in it to "assert in strong terms the meaning of the existence" of that culture.

This dichotomy of Shimao as novelist on the one hand and cultural critic on the other appears in clear relief in summaries of his career found in special issues of magazines appearing in the last decade of his life. In the December 1978 issue of *Kaie*, a Tokyo journal, only four of the twenty-three articles on Shimao, confined to the very end, concern his study of the southern islands. In the spring 1987 issue of *Shin Okinawa Bungaku*, published soon after his death and devoted to his relationship to Okinawa, an entirely different picture emerges. The bulk of the issue is devoted to a reexamination of Shimao's *Yaponesia* ideas, with studies of his fiction taking second place. Even the short studies of his fiction that are included, however, work to reinterpret his literature in southern terms. Uehara Nario's analysis of *Shi no toge*, for instance, brings a fresh, "southern" perspective to the novel. For Shimao, writes Uehara, the southern islands underlying the novel are a "mythic space" where "actual time [time expressed as the present only, the idea of living one day at a time] can be grasped." Shimao's confrontation with Miho becomes a confrontation with an "alien culture," a "maternal society" with female-centered religious institutions (*noro* and *yuta* shamanism) from the past to which he was an outsider.[3] Of *Shi no toge*'s Uehara concludes:

> With Nyūin ["Nyūin made," the last chapter] *Shi no toge* has arrived at a conclusion of sorts. Now Toshio must set off on a journey to the southern island time and space within Miho.[4]

Thus while the mainland literary establishment saw Shimao primarily as a writer of fiction, readers in Okinawa viewed him as both an essayist concerned with the identity of the southern islands and as a writer whose fiction demanded to be read in light of these concerns. As for Shimao himself, he viewed his two projects—fiction and essays—and the influence of his twenty-year Amami residence on both as a complex mixture of mutual influences. Of the relationship between his fiction and Amami experience, he writes,

> I don't think I consciously try to write about my Amami experiences [in my fiction]; instead I want them to naturally come out as I write. . . . I don't feel like writing about my Amami experiences the way they actually occurred. So my Amami experiences and my writing might seem to be separated, but *the underside of my stories is dyed with this experience. Even though I don't write about it directly, if you took Amami out of my works, my stories themselves would be no more.*[5]

The *Yaponesia* Essays, 1954–1970

In 1972, the year Okinawa reverted to Japan, the Okinawan novelist Ōshiro Tatsuhiro wrote of many Okinawans' fear that their islands would be inundated with less than desirable aspects of the mainland culture. "One can easily imagine it," Ōshiro writes, "like polluted water flowing in."[6] Ōshiro's words express a shift in Okinawan opinion from an unproblematic early postwar desire for reversion to a widespread questioning of the impact of such a political change as the reversion became a reality. Despite the negative effects of the American occupation, one positive legacy for Okinawans is that "only by being discarded by Japan did [they] finally awaken to their identity."[7] This awakening, Ōshiro notes, should be viewed as part of a gradual historical shift in relations between Okinawa and Japan from a desire on the part of Okinawans for assimilation (*dōka*) to, by the time of the reversion, a desire for "*dis*similation" (*ika*). At this juncture, the need for defining Okinawan identity was crucial. Such identity, Ōshiro maintains, can be constructed only through a thorough examination of the "cultural" (i.e., latent) tendencies underlying current political and economic trends, and through "cultural creativity" (*bunkateki sōzō*)—that is, an active stance that seeks to confront common feelings of inferiority vis-à-vis the mainland.[8] In the face of the expected cultural flood from the mainland (which was vastly superior materially), confronting these feelings and constructing the basis for a sense of self-worth became vital issues for the people of Okinawa.

As the debate over the meaning and impact of the reversion intensified in the late 1960s–early 1970s, many Okinawan intellectuals discovered, and were greatly influenced by, Shimao's *Yaponesia* writings. What, then, is *Yaponesia?* As I outline below, *Yaponesia* begins with a conception of an underlying cultural bond linking mainland Japan and the Ryukyus, but gives way in Shimao's later writings to the broader notion of difference and cultural diversity. An unspoken assumption of Japan as a natural entity, and of an underlying oneness of Japanese culture, in other words, shifts to the uncovering of a plurality of cultures within the confines of the nation we call Japan. Shimao's early *Yaponesia* writings can be criticized for making exotic Ryukyuan culture and for subordinating the Ryukyus to the role of utopian "savior" of the mainland. In his later work, however, Shimao points in the direction of autonomy not just for the Ryukyus, but for all of what he calls the "anti-Japan" elements suppressed in the creation of the modern state.

Shimao first coined the term *Yaponesia* in the 1961 essay "Yaponesia no nekko" (The root of *Yaponesia*).[9] *Yaponesia* begins with a deceptively simple reversal of commonsense beliefs about the nature of Japan. If Japan is part of Asia, Shimao believed, is it not just as much a part of the South Pacific?

> I felt this about Amami, that in thinking about the identity of Japanese culture we might be too conscious of the [Asian] mainland. In other words, we think too much about the influence from places like China and India. If we look at the map we can't escape the fact that Japan is an island country. Island

countries are surrounded by the ocean. The Pacific Ocean is a particularly broad ocean, with myriad islands in it. Especially there are many islands in the South Pacific. The lives of the people in those islands must share similar characteristics. And isn't Japan one of them, too? In the South Pacific you find the islands of Polynesia, Micronesia, Melanesia, and Indonesia, and in the same way I saw the Japanese archipelago as a clump of South Pacific Islands. And I gave it the name *Yaponesia*. (Vol. 16, 217)[10]

The influence of Yanagita Kunio's 1960 *Kaijō no michi* (The ocean path), with its argument for a prehistoric migration from the South Pacific into Japan, is evident. The power of Shimao's work lies in its combination of the general with a profoundly committed personal statement. When "Yaponesia no nekko" is read together with the next essay he wrote on the topic, "Furusato o kataru" (Talking of one's home, 1962), one sees the ever-present combination in Shimao's work of two concerns. If "Yaponesia no nekko" seeks to answer the question (to quote Shimao), "What is Japan and the Japanese?" "Furusato o kataru" asks the question, "Who am I? What are my roots?" The interplay of these two strands, the questioning of national identity always intermingled with the search for a personal identity, makes these writings particularly compelling.

Shimao's interest in the southern islands was naturally enough aroused by his experiences during the war when he was stationed in Kakeromajima in Amami; preceding this, however, was a childhood interest in the islands sparked by reading Bakin and others. This experience molded an image of a Shangri-la in his mind located somewhere to the south.[11] The strongly positive image of a southern island as, if not exactly utopia, at least a partial refuge from, and antidote to, the "poison" of modern urban life, continued to inform his work. Shimao's first wartime impressions of the southern island, recalled in later writings, were entirely positive. Amami was

> cut off in the mist of ancient times. Buddhism and Confucianism, I felt, weren't able to cover this island. In the bottom of my wicker trunk I had a copy of the Iwanami edition of the *Kojiki*; when I re-read the book in Amami, I forgot that it was an ancient text. The life written about in it was exactly that lived out there in the reality of the island and wrapping itself around us.[12]

In the midst of this "ancient" lifestyle still remnant in Japan, Shimao found the antithesis of mainstream mainland culture with which he felt ill at ease:

> In the middle of the Pacific War, when I was first assigned to a naval squadron stationed in one of the islands of our archipelago, I noticed there, somewhat

vaguely, in the culture of the island, none of the hardness concocted out of tension and stiffness you feel in the mainland. And since ten years ago when I came to live in one of the islands that feeling has deepened even more. It's hard to put it in a word, but I have discovered here a naive vitality hidden in the life of the islands of the Ryukyu chain, in the actions of the people a "gentleness" forgotten in the Japanese mainland. I say this hesitantly, but a fully human life breathes here, a medieval or ancient life unpoisoned by civilization. (Vol. 17, 46)[13]

In later writings Shimao seldom wavers from these first impressions, but he modifies and appends them in several ways. After 1967, when he began to concentrate on the ways outlying regions of Japan, in particular his own ancestral home, Tōhoku, and Amami were related, he began revising these "first impressions." His wartime encounter with Amami becomes less one of surprise at finding the remnants of a unique "ancient" lifestyle existing only in the south than a return to something he had already experienced: "I felt somehow like I was returning to my hometown in ancient times," Shimao wrote in 1970. "I thought that this island preserved the roots of Japan *(Nihon no ne)* more simply and purely" (vol. 17, 175).[14]

[S]omehow it felt like Tōhoku to me. . . . Naturally the language was different, and many other things were very different, but deep down there was a feeling like that of a Tōhoku village. It was a deep emotion, *as if I were visiting the land of far away ancestors whom I'd never seen before.* (Vol. 17, 386)[15]

It is understandable for Shimao to have contemplated Amami during the war and after his move to the island in 1955, because this was the environment that surrounded him. Significantly, however, even during the period in between, during his stay in Tokyo, the southern islands remained an active alternative to the urban world around him. In October 1954, just as the crisis with his wife was worsening, Shimao published the first of his numerous essays on the southern islands, "'Okinawa' no imi suru mono" (What gives meaning to Okinawa). It was remarkable as his first statement on issues he would continue to deal with for the rest of his writing career.[16] Besides attempting to articulate what attracted him to the islands, the essay is a critique of the relationship between the islands and the mainland. It touches on the "tragic history" of the islanders as victims of the mainland, the islanders' forms of resistance to this, and the mainlanders' way of dealing with the islanders by either suppressing knowledge of the islands or by making exotic southern island culture. The essay is noteworthy as well for the even-handedness of its criticism of the islanders themselves for their own prejudices.

"'Okinawa' no imi suru mono" attempts to answer the question of Okinawa's appeal by viewing it in contrast to what is wrong with the alternative—the culture and life of mainland Japan. Shimao writes:

> *In this country of Japan there is a despairing poisonous element contained in the sleep-inducing uniformity of the nature and the history of the people.* To say Shangri-la or something is to invite misunderstanding, but what I want to say is that, believe it or not, there is still an island in this barren archipelago in which exists what we have long forgotten, the *"fresh emotions of amazement at life."* In Japan, no matter where you walk you see the same faces and monotonous words that, if you pay just a little attention, you soon understand. This leads to stagnation and a rotting away of everything. All that holds sway there is a meddlesome impudence and that which suppresses people. And an unpleasant self-complacency and exclusivity. We have been left behind by the energy produced when different things collide, built up each others' bones and put on some abundant flesh. That is, until we discover Okinawa. (Vol. 16, 11–12; emphasis added)

And what does Okinawa have to offer? In contrast to the mainland, mere knowledge of the "existence" of the island makes one's "mind free and easy." Okinawa brings a needed "diversity" to Japan; a "wonderful place [like Okinawa] in our country where [Japanese] isn't understood" can "rescue our stagnant history" (vol. 16, 13). "We tend to believe that a history based on official documents full of falsehoods is history," Shimao cautions, the implication being that the "falsehood" is the assumption that there is but one narrative of Japan. There is not one narrative, Shimao implies, but many, and the uncovering of these is the key to rescuing Japan from "stagnation" and "rot."[17]

"'Okinawa' no imi suru mono" focuses on an exhibition of Okinawan folk arts. Here his discussion centers on what in his later essays become the preeminent examples of the expression of southern island uniqueness—southern *minyō* (folk songs) and folk dance.[18] He takes to task both the mainland audience at the exhibition and attempts to extract expression from context. Taken out of context, set down in the "smug atmosphere" of the mainland hall, Okinawan *minyō* and dance become mere "spineless" "shells." The dancing, with its whistling and wild gyrations, leaves "Yamato people" (i.e., mainland Japanese) "dumbfounded" (vol. 16, 12–13). Expression of any kind must be contextualized to be appreciated and understood. The dances do remain full of meaning, however—a meaning that can be read as directed specifically toward the mainland audience, but one they cannot appreciate. The dances are "full of the close intimacy of the Okinawan people for each other, and adhering to them is a rebellion against their unfortunate history" (vol. 16, 13). The "wild" dance movements, so unlike mainland folk dances, thus can be seen as symbolic expressions of the frustration of these people who have "tasted the bitterness of history" (vol. 16, 15). One can view them as expressions of rage and, perhaps, symbolic physical violence directed against the very people who sit before them—the mainlanders whose past and present actions have caused their suffering.

Mainlanders' reactions to things Okinawan, such as these dances, is twofold: either they attempt, quite successfully, to suppress any discourse about Okinawa (speaking of it only in "whispers") or they appropriate it, wrench it from its cultural context, and turn it into "exoticism." If, for instance, mainlanders studied Okinawan folk arts themselves, the enterprise would have "nothing to do with Okinawa" since "for [the mainlanders] Okinawan folk arts are ornaments suspended in midair"; "mainlanders cannot seem to escape the narrow confines" of seeing everything related to Okinawa as exotic (vol. 16, 13). Shimao clearly seeks to break this impasse, while ultimately concluding he is fighting a losing battle.[19] He speaks of the experiences of the Okinawans as victims having "tasted the bitterness of history," which makes them capable of providing a "blood transfusion" to a Japan suffering from "hardening of the arteries."[20] This transfusion will come about when Okinawa is no longer treated as a "sideshow review," when there is a genuine "collision" and "confrontation" of local differences within Japan, properly contextualized, producing an energy to revitalize mainstream Japan. For Shimao, Okinawa consists of a curious mixture of this energy (the partial result, he implies, of its history as victim) and calm:

> What "Okinawa" possesses in this country of ours, at least for me, is a fortunate sense of peace found amid the ruins. We must respond to "Okinawa" not with whispers or as some hobby, but must be the same recipients of the tragic history Okinawa has followed. Losing sight of Okinawa will dry us up. (Vol. 16, 16; emphasis added)

Shimao's thoughts on the mainland-island relationship are always a mix of the personal and the communal. At the same time that he speaks in broad terms of the need to rescue Japan from "stagnation," he is clearly concerned with finding his own position within this discourse and within Japan. Not surprisingly, he locates himself *in-between*, pulled

in the direction of the "victim," the islanders whom he views as historically victims of the mainland. He can never fully occupy that spot, however. In fact, one grows aware in "'Okinawa' no imi suru mono" of how
Shimao's own speaking position is itself unstable: at times he speaks
from the position of a mainlander, at other times from one closer to an
islander, at still other times somewhere in between.[21] Shimao notes his
pride at sometimes being mistaken for an Okinawan and how, by coincidence, his own last name sounds "southern" (vol. 16, 16). Replace the
second character "o" with the related character "shiri" (to make the
common island surname Shimajiri), he writes, and it would be even
more fully of the south.[22] His own name, then, partly "southern" but
not fully so, becomes an appropriate metaphor for his own position. If
mainlanders must be the "same recipients of the tragic history" of Okinawa but have yet to be, he himself, in the context of his own life, has
accomplished this, but only in part. His wife, he notes, is from Amami
but is originally of Okinawan descent; although he regrets not being
born in Okinawa himself (a fact he views as "decisive" in his life), Shimao writes:

> At least I am satisfied that my children have Amami Ōshima blood mixed in.
> [Through them] I have gained half the same position . . . as victim. (Vol. 16,
> 14; emphasis added)

A key word, naturally, is "half," because despite the obvious desire to
approach closer to the islands and their people, Shimao's assimilation
is never complete. Okinawa does and will continue to "occupy a large
spot" in Shimao's "spiritual landscape" (vol. 16, 16), yet the reader of
his essays (and of course stories) is struck by the tension in his position
"in-between." His continuing efforts to serve as spokesman for those
whose voices have seldom been heard is always tinged by the facts of his
birth. He is not, and cannot be, an Okinawan (or Amami islander). Shimao's later attempt to link Tōhoku and Amami is a project to find communality between local regions cut off by official histories and central-
ized political power, but it is also a more personal quest to locate his
own "native" place. Just as the folk arts of Okinawa must be placed in
their cultural context to be anything more than a "shell," we find the
Shimao of his essays (and the protagonist of his stories) concerned with
a search for his place, for the context out of which "creative energy"
springs.

The 1954 "'Okinawa' no imi suru mono" is directed as much at the southern islanders as it is at the "stagnant" mainland. Shimao's essays, even this early one written in Tokyo, were part of an ongoing discourse in the 1950s, then 1960s and 1970s, within the southern islands over several broad questions that (much like Shimao's own private search) boil down to a question of identity: what is Okinawa? (and Amami, etc.?) What distinguishes the islands from the mainland, and from each other? How does one balance the strong pull of a materially advanced center to the north (producing an understandable desire for a share of the wealth denied to the islanders) with a more nebulous cultural side, a loss of certain values, and a lifestyle more easily felt than articulated? In short, could the islanders maintain a culture distinctiveness while sharing in an increasingly uniform, affluent society? The questions, certainly, are not unique to Japan, or even to the southern islands, but took on increasing urgency as the date for Okinawa's reversion drew near.

In the context of this essay, Shimao's comments directed at the islanders can be read as a clear-eyed recognition of opposing forces acting on them. A large number of Amami people, for instance, desire nothing more than assimilation into mainstream Japanese society. Thus they move their family register (*seki*) to Tokyo or elsewhere on the mainland where they have moved and obscure their origins in the island by insisting that they are from "Kagoshima" (which is technically correct, as Amami is part of Kagoshima Prefecture). They try also to circumvent the single-character surnames forced on them during the Edo period by the Satsuma-han (as one of a series of policies to control the islanders) by means of what Shimao calls a "humorous resistance." Parents in Amami have taken to adding an extra character to their sons' names when registering them so that the child may better pass as a mainlander. For example, the 福 *(Fuku)* family might add the character 田 *(ta)* to the given name 利男 *(Toshio)* to come up with a name that, officially read as 福・田利男, could essentially be indistinguishable from the mainland name 福田・利男 (vol. 16, 15). This may be a somewhat "humorous" resistance on the part of Amami people to the historical discrimination against them, but along with the other strategies Shimao lists, it is clearly part of a more serious move to conceal differences, to smooth over what might hinder assimilation into mainland society. In short, while this may allow Amami people to shuck off a sign of stigma from the past, at the same time their solution aims at lessening difference, rather than fostering it, as Shimao would hope to do.

Whatever anger is present in this essay, however, is directed not at these tactics, but at relations within the islands. Islanders, Shimao tells the reader, have reproduced in their relations with each other their relation as a whole with the mainland. If they have been victimized and looked down on by the mainland, they turn around and misdirect their emotions at each other:

> [W]hat I really cannot bear is how Kagoshima people won't have anything to do with people from the islands [Amami], how Amami Ōshima people do the same with those from Naha, how Nafuanchu [Naha people] do the same with residents of Itoman and Hisadaka, a meaningless vicious circle going down [the islands] in order, which is making us suffocate. (Vol. 16, 13)

One is reminded of an exchange between Shimao and the Okinawan novelist Ōshiro:

> Ōshiro: Somehow I am only interested in [writing about] Okinawa.
> Shimao: That's fine, in fact if it wasn't that way there'd be a problem. Mostly [your work]'s taken as dealing with the victim side, I imagine.
> Ōshiro: The sense of being a victim is generally strong.
> Shimao: But it's possible to be a victimizer as well. It's possible to become a victimizer. Getting deeply into that is necessary for literature.[23]

Shimao, who found personal satisfaction by gaining a position as "half a victim" and who concluded "'Okinawa' no imi suru mono" with an admonishment to mainlanders to work to "receive" the "tragic history" of Okinawa—that is, for those historically in the position of victimizer both to acknowledge their position and attempt an understanding of the experience of the victim—is careful to remind the reader (islander or mainlander) of a dual nature at work. When he speaks of the victimizer, Shimao here goes beyond a simplistic dichotomy of island victims/mainland victimizers that occasionally seems at work on the surface of his essays. Victims, too, can quite easily turn into victimizers of each other. In light of what is known of his literature of this time (late 1954), with its developing thematics of the victimizer, it is interesting to see how the same themes pervade this essay, his first of many on the southern islands.

IN OCTOBER 1955, just released with Miho from the mental hospital, Shimao settled with his family in Naze (population around thirty thousand), the largest town in Amami Ōshima. A few months later his writings reveal a mixture of both resignation and optimism—resignation that he may "never set foot in the mainland again," and optimism that he had found a new, although not entirely unexpected, world opening up for him both as a person and a writer:

> The color of the sky, the roar of the waves, the shape of the island mountains, *the sufferings (juku) of the people closed up on this miniscule island*—all of this I must put into writing. (Vol. 16, 28; emphasis added)[24]

There is, in this tropical island, an element to "unthaw the frozen, barren Tōhoku part flowing in my blood" (vol. 16, 28). His Tōhoku background, it should be noted, is viewed as a negative element; by 1967 Shimao reverses himself to find in both Tōhoku and Amami a shared communality of suffering.

As Shimao's wartime memories of the islands run up against the realities of daily life in Naze, his writings on Amami in the mid- to late 1950s modify the early idyllic picture of the southern island. *Naze dayori* (News from Naze, serialized from 1957–1959), his summary of his first few years on the island, fascinated mainland readers with details of such typical aspects of Amami life as the *habu* vipers that roam the mountains and sugarcane fields, bullfighting, and the juxtaposition of Catholicism and shamanism. Yet the reader is struck by an undisguised sense of disillusionment and loss: disillusionment in finding his image of the island unrealistic (it is not quite the idyllic place of his imagination), and loss in that what he finds most distinctive and valuable about Amami was fast fading in the encroaching influence from the dominant mainland culture.[25] If in 1954 Shimao sought in the southern islands a diversity that could "rescue" the stagnant mainland, the center, after his 1955 move to Amami he sought to rescue this diversity from the overwhelming influence of the mainland. The desire for a "collision" and "confrontation" of mainland and southern islands gives way in the mid- to late 1950s to a desire to separate the two, to recoup "old" Amami through isolation.

The essays of this period are extremely personal. It is hard to imagine otherwise, because now Shimao, following the battles with Miho's mental illness, is looking to Amami as a personal refuge, a site of physical and emotional recuperation. What is most interesting is the emphasis placed on his own sense of incongruity with the mainland he retreats from, and how much this retreat to the island is for his sake. From the evidence of later essays of this period—"Tsuma e no inori" (A prayer to my wife, 1956) and "Tsuma e no inori: hōi" (1958; trans., "Postscript to a Prayer to My Wife")—it is clear that Shimao was neither loathe to discuss the details of Miho's illness nor to locate in it the focus of many of their troubles as a couple. Yet in other essays a quite different picture emerges—one of Shimao himself as frightfully ill-adjusted on the mainland. In the 1958 "Ritō no nagusame" (The comfort of a solitary island), Shimao equates the two years before the end of the war (his *tokkōtai* experience) with the year before he moved to Amami—that is, the year of crisis in Tokyo. He sums up his troubles in the term *gankabyō*, a sort of visual epilepsy in which his visual sense of the world was, for spells, severely restricted (isolating him further, one can imagine, from the world around him.) In addition to the restricted visual access to the world, the last year in Tokyo became a "blank in my own time," a "period when the flow of time was stopped," and he suffered from "migraines," which made it almost impossible for him to leave the house (vol. 16, 82).[26] The crisis he experienced (Miho is nowhere in evidence here) is potentially transformative, as his "ignorance up until then was sucked up by a bottomless silence" and became the inkling of a renewed strength that required isolation in order to be understood fully (vol. 16, 82).

And Shimao fairly revels in the isolated nature of this "solitary island," where nothing new can reach him and "only the old washes up on our shore." In the isolation of this "fossil group of islands," within which he is "locked up and cannot move," he discovers the "true nature" of his self and a sense of concentration impossible in the city:

> Right now the mail and newspapers from the mainland don't reach us everyday; there are two to three, even more, days between deliveries, and in this I find a sense of salvation. In the meantime, no matter how impatient you get, until the next ship arrives we cannot have modern relations with the world outside the island. This is a time of pleasant silence for me. In the interval I do what must be done. And that is only one thing—what life in this island has taught me. (Vol. 16, 83)[27]

As always, however, Shimao acutely detects both sides of the situation, finding in this transformative, regenerative isolation another face. Islanders are "caught in the vice" of conflicting emotions in which "[a]nyone who lives here feels a sadness that pierces your guts, and a burning desire to escape from the island" (vol. 16, 128).[28] Underlying all these early essays, too, is Shimao's understanding that the "isolation" he craves is no longer (if indeed it ever really was) a viable option. Even the small, far-off island of Amami is threatened by the homogenizing powers of the mainland culture—powers that bring a dissonance to the "harmony that can be found everywhere in the life of the islands, if only we look hard enough" (vol. 16, 129).

To give an indication of the portrait of difference Shimao wants to paint between island and mainland lifestyles, let us briefly examine two passages, both from 1962 essays. "Watashi no mita Amami" (The Amami I saw), a lecture delivered to a meeting of the town and village council in Amami, in part deals with Shimao's oft-repeated view of the history of Amami and the southern islands—views that can be summarized in two basic points. First, the southern islands have, throughout Japanese history, served as a stimulus for the mainland, with great historical changes often intimately connected with the southern islands. Second, the southern islands have been sacrificed time and again for the sake of the mainland. An example close to home for Shimao's audience was the history of the Meiji Restoration and Amami's little-discussed role in it. The economic power that propelled Satsuma to leadership during the restoration, Shimao argues, was in great part based on wealth derived from its control of the sugarcane production in Amami and other islands. To exploit this source to the fullest, Satsuma held the majority of islanders in a condition bordering on servitude, seeing to it that they were almost completely sealed off from access to economic or political power (vol. 16, 225). "You could say," Shimao concludes, "that Satsuma sacrificed the southern islands in order to be able to set the Meiji Restoration in motion" (vol. 16, 226). The modern Japanese state itself, in other words, was built through the exploitation of the ancestors of the people he is talking to. A second example, one more readily known to his listeners and thus abbreviated, is of course World War II, where, "through sacrificing the southern islands, the state *(kokka)* could move in the direction of finding peace" (vol. 16, 227).

But what is more interesting, especially from someone such as Shimao, who is the antithesis of a Marxist critic, is his reliance on ideas akin to the Marxist notion of alienation to explain the illnesses of life on the mainland. The dominant trend in modern civilization, he writes, one that must be resisted, is "fragmentation" of daily life and labor. He deplores the "extreme division" found in city life, and how it has spread to the larger realm of social life: "There are more and more people whose daily life has been cut to shreds and who have become scattered *(bara ni naru)*" (vol. 16, 211). One example of a recent train accident in Tokyo illustrates his point that modern life has fragmented to such an extent that people, in what might be called schizophrenic fashion, are able only to comprehend events as single, isolated incidents. A grasp of the flow and connection between events has been lost to them. In the rail accident a train engineer ignored a signal, but no one took any action to prevent disaster. No one could grasp a "total approach to dealing with the situation," Shimao writes. "They couldn't understand the situation and its consequences and their connection" (vol. 16, 211). Although it should have been obvious that another train would soon come from behind and a collision would occur, no one noticed; people should have had the sense, for instance, to burn a shirt with a lighter to act as a warning signal, but they did nothing. "The habit of thinking about things in their totality in daily life is steadily being poisoned," he writes. The fragmentation of life in the city makes it inevitable that one becomes "paralyzed" like the people in the accident (vol. 16, 211). Life on the island, although containing many "unfavorable conditions to be sure," resists fragmentation and preserves a more integrated approach to life. Division of labor is impossible because in Amami you "can't live just by doing one thing only" (vol. 16, 210).[29]

One of the more vital points to note here about Shimao's writing is that, as he fills in details of the island lifestyle, one by one he reverses the standard tropes of mainland discourse on the southern islands. As Alan Christy notes, in prewar mainland writing on Okinawa, "walking barefoot, Ryukyuan women's clothing, a preponderance of dialects . . . and Okinawan music were all taken together as the image of the 'loose Okinawan' and visible signs of their backwardness."[30] In his *Yaponesia* writings Shimao effectively rewrites each of these tropes and images of inferiority into a narrative of cultural distinctiveness and value. I have touched on music and dance, and will briefly discuss clothing and language below.

In another essay from the same year, "Shima no naka to soto" (Inside and outside the island) Shimao reworks the notion of walking barefoot quoted above. One day in early spring, he set off to work and encountered the following scene:

> On one of those days I was walking towards where I work. Rain hit then, too, the road was muddy and a northern wind was blowing from the direction of the harbor.
> I was hurrying along, chest thrust out, flushed inside my raincoat, and my blank feeling disappeared; it's a spring storm, I thought. My first reaction

was to excitedly tell this to my wife, when I looked up; right before me two women were walking barefoot. Their feet were bony and dark. The younger of the two was lifting up her well-worn skirt with her right hand, and I caught a passing glimpse of her knee. They wore neither overcoat nor raincoat, and carried no umbrellas. Wet in the rain, their unglamorous looking heels unhurriedly tramped the muddy road, one after the other. I felt that cold through the soles of my own feet. I was moved somehow, and couldn't take my eyes off the muddy bare feet of these women. This had to be the way island people dealt with the season from long ago, a way which one seldom sees in the town anymore. The long passage of time in this poor island far from the mainland, where no other way of dealing [with the rain] was conceivable, entwined itself around my body. . . .The weather always astir outside their minds and bodies was an environment they could do nothing about, one which manifested itself with nearly the weight of their entire lives. Thinking this, something obstinate and hard within me crumbled just a little. (Vol. 16, 200–201)

"After this," Shimao continues, "many of the scenes and customs of the island began to appear softened to me. Compared with Tokyo customs they may seem dull, rough, and irrational, but they took on an individuality, and particular local features (*chihōteki na yōbō*) were absorbed through my eyes and spread through my whole body" (vol. 16, 201).

One might expect Shimao to draw a conclusion, as he does in the earlier essay ("Watashi no mita Amami"), pointing toward a stark dichotomy of positive and negative poles, Amami on one end, Tokyo on the other, life in Amami "integrated," life in the city not. Yet he backs away from doing so directly. The scene he has just witnessed, and the repercussions of it for him, are valuable as they bring both Tokyo and Amami into sharper contrast, and it is not so much a hierarchy of worth he wants to emphasize as the difference between the two places. The "pull toward Tokyo . . . makes the life in the islands that much more distinct, not as something supplementary, but as a multi-layered, set form, like a fortress": it is by "assaulting this" that he hopes to gain a "means of expression" (*hyōgen hōho*) (vol. 16, 202).[31] "Shima no naka to soto" in fact anticipates a move some eight years later in Shimao's thinking on the relationship between mainland and the islands, one that aims not at a hierarchy but at a relationship between independent, autonomous, equal regions. In an essay in-between these periods, written in 1965, he also writes of Amami, in relation to Tokyo, as "one more local region" (*mō hitotsu no chihō to shite wa*), the fairly radical implication being that Tokyo, too, is "one more local region." No longer is the southern island something to be used to "rescue" the center; it is now "distinct, not something supplementary," and the center is no longer quite the center it was.

The image of the island women in the rain, of course, is a portrait of poverty, of a present impoverishment that has roots in the historical exploitation of the islanders. In this sense, the juxtaposition of the barefoot women with Shimao, the outsider warm in his raincoat, properly clad in shoes, becomes a miniature tableau of the history of relations between islander and mainlander. In other essays it is clear that Shimao, as amateur historian, was only too aware of this history and was forceful in his denunciation of the mainland's role in creating and maintaining the level of poverty on the island. Yet the image here is not of poverty and exploitation alone. The women, representing an older island tradition, deal with their physical environment in a way Shimao clearly finds surprising and exhilarating. Unlike Tokyo-ites, they do not circumvent the weather, shut themselves off, sequester themselves from their surroundings. Neither do they revel in it. They simply, unhurriedly, live in it. One can see them as victims—of poverty, of an unstable, unpredictable island climate; given half the chance, these women may well prefer to be as warm and dry as he is. Yet the image remains with him of the possibility the women represent: a relationship with one's surroundings that is not found on the mainland, a relationship not of resignation, even, but of a positive, complete integration into place.

This stands in sharp contrast to one of the first stories Shimao wrote after his 1952 move to Tokyo. If the women in the rain are symbolic of an integrated approach to life, a simple but profoundly connected life, in "Garasu shōji no shiruetto" (Silhouette on the glass screen) city dwellers in Tokyo are alone, cut off from both place and each other:

> You can't see the mountains anywhere. There's no feeling of being embraced by nature, the ground is bumpy and on the bumpy ground you feel the people are stretching out their feelers towards the sky, all groping in space and getting tangled up. So if you lower your eyes to look at what surrounds you, you feel you can depend on no one, that you have to stand alone on the ground.[32]

The concern with "standing on the ground"—with the physical point of contact between one's body and the earth that so moves Shimao at the sight of the women's feet—becomes in his *Yaponesia* essays a repeated image. In Amami, there is a "source of life" that "creeps up through the soles of your feet"; the discovery—or rather the recovery—of this "source" is the driving motive behind *Yaponesia*.

In the seminal 1961 essay "Yaponesia no nekko," one finds Shimao already working with metaphoric images of the body—his body in particular—laid out on the map of Japan:

> I discovered an invitation *(sasoi)* coming from the ocean that cannot be filled in even if one wanted to, *a feeling coming up from my feet* that cannot remain hidden. This island's small size and its position facing south pull my gaze from the Asian mainland and mainland Japan, towards the other islands. A definite feeling of vitality which has passed through numerous feelings of inferiority appears, and something, I'm not sure what exactly, calls out from someplace deep, from the south beyond the ocean." (Vol. 16, 191; emphasis added)

Daily life in Amami contains differences that leave him "intoxicated": the melody of folk songs, movements in group dances, ways people greet each other, vocalization of words. Together they are a "compound rhythm of life" that is not of a "foreign country," yet they are not of the mainland, at least the surface of mainland life. These elements are not entirely absent in the mainland, he argues, but are well hidden. There is something "in far off memory" that responds to them; they represent a "hidden, deep expression" that surfaces only in "drunkenness and *matsuri* [festivals]" to replace, if only for a moment, the "hardened faces" of daily life on the mainland (vol. 16, 192):

> [A]n idea began to unfold in my mind. *Maybe Amami is a clue to finding another face of Japan. Not something that is forced into the head and permeates it, but a source of life (seikatsu no ne) which creeps up through the soles of the feet.* The area of the islands is only thinly covered with scales from the mainland; it still has the smell of the land and the sea. (Vol.16, 192; emphasis added)

The fragmentation of "modern civilization" is less Shimao's target here than is the cultural influence on Japan from the Asian mainland—the influence, for example, of Confucianism and Buddhism. He sets up a clear dichotomy, using his physical imagery of "head" and "feet" to separate an intellectual part of Japanese culture, which is ultimately sterile, from a more visceral, physical element ultimately originating in the south. In his fiction, of course, Shimao finds a wealth of source material in dreams and the unconscious workings of his own mind; thus it is significant that we find the mainland and island lifestyles expressed in somewhat similar terms that suggest a dichotomy between the conscious and unconscious. The "other face of the mainland" that Amami represents is, in a sense, the unconscious of Japan, a "far off memory" that remains suppressed by the higher intellectual powers making up mainland Asian culture, manifesting itself only when the conscious part of the mind itself is suppressed by alcohol and the ecstasies of the festival (fueled, too, by *sake*.) Finally, although in the 1954 essay ("'Okinawa' no imi suru mono") the southern islands (in this case Okinawa) provide a potential difference that exists on the periphery of Japan, a diversity that could "rescue" the stagnant mainland, by 1961 this "southern" element is given a more central role. It becomes a difference that already exists within the mainland (and its people) itself—a kind of cultural unconscious that is suppressed, but may possibly be recovered.

Shimao calls for a rethinking of the map of Japan, a redrawing of it so that the "southern islands" (here he means the islands of the South Pacific), not the Asian mainland, are shown as the "subject" *(shudai)* — that is, the focus or center. (This point becomes visually compelling when one, as Shimao implies, reverses the map of East Asia and the South Pacific.)

> Then the figure of *Yaponesia*, made up of three bow-shaped flower designs *(hanakazari)* will clearly reveal itself. That image encourages me, and Amami looks to be the key to solving *Yaponesia*. (Vol. 16, 192)

This figure of a tripartite Japan is developed in later writings and is part of what eventually works out as a decentering of Japan. At this point in "Yaponesia no nekko," however, before Shimao can decenter Japan, he must first reverse the hierarchical dualism in order, in the end, to neutralize it. No longer is mainland Japan, with its East Asian continental culture, the "subject," because it has been replaced by the southern islands of Japan and the culture of the South Pacific.

The period 1962–1967 is one in which Shimao begins to reach out beyond the southern islands to link Amami with his native Tōhoku, the latter taking shape as a kind of personal spiritual base. Although clearly different, the two areas share a common "temperament of life" (vol. 17, 106, 108), a "simplicity," "straightforwardness," and an "extreme sincerity toward weakness" (vol. 17, 109). All of these Shimao finds valuable, as they underlie the "source of attraction *(sasoi)*" he feels for Amami, the ascertaining of which is the "same as ascertaining life" (vol. 17, 105–106).

Shimao's main focus thus remains Amami, although Tōhoku has taken on a new importance. In familiar ways he contrasts the mainland and the islands (here focusing on ways of wearing clothes), finding the island people's approach to clothing "rough-hewn" yet "generous," a "dry" way of wearing clothes that contrasts with the "depressing, gloomy craftsmanship" and "wet" way of the mainland (vol. 17, 105). In positioning Amami (actually Ryūkyūkō, literally "Ryukyu arc," a term he begins using at this point) as showing new "possibilities of expression" *(hyōgen no kanōsei)* for Japan and the Japanese, as a "window onto the world" for the "exitless" country of Japan, Shimao opens himself up to the charge of viewing the islands in the way he says he now opposes. He views them, that is, as something supplementary to the mainland—the islands, in other words, being positive only insofar as they aid the mainland. However, compared with earlier essays such as "Yaponesia no nekko," there is a subtle shift in focus, the glimmerings of an attempt to view the islands not in their relationship to the mainland, but as independent entities. Shimao writes, "I want this region [the islands], which compared to other regions has a strong, distinctive character, to express its individuality without inhibitions" (vol. 17,105). This shift of focus, from a supplementary to a more independent view of the islands, becomes more pronounced with time.

Shimao's claim in 1962 of a tripartite view of *Yaponesia* becomes clear at the end of the decade. In the 1969 article "Watashi ni totte Okinawa to wa nani ka" (What Okinawa is to me) he writes:

[R]ecently I can't help but think that my country, the country of Japan, is made up of three parts. Starting with the north, these are the three parts consisting of Tōhoku, the Central part [Chūō], and Ryūkyūkō. . . .
   [I]f we say that each of the three parts has its own heterogeneous elements, then these must be clearly brought out and faced directly. Not so that one part can dissolve into and assimilate to another part, but the opposite: *that each of the three parts, standing alone, [can be seen as] . . . carrying the fate of Japan.* (Vol. 17, 167–168; emphasis added)

And again one can see the mixture of identity on both personal and wider levels, because only by approaching the nature of the country in this way can both "Japan and I" be "set free" (vol. 17, 168).

As the debate and political movements centered on the reversion of Okinawa heated up the late 1960s, Shimao's essays adopted a more openly political phrasing. This period marks a decided shift in definition of *Yaponesia*. Shimao takes the idea of a link between Tōhoku and the southern islands—the shared "extreme sincerity toward weakness"—one step further. Sensitivity toward "weakness" in both regions,

he concludes, has historical roots and is the result of "having been excluded from the center of political power"; the two areas have historically existed "in the back alleys of politics" and have been suppressed by
the center (vol. 17, 176). As Okamoto argues, at about this time Shimao
begins to break with some basic past assumptions. In particular, Shimao
moves from an unproblematic view of Japan as a nation *(kokka)* (the
"historical epistemology which takes *kokka* as a given," in Okamoto's
words) to a questioning of the framework in which nation is structured.
Tōhoku and Ryūkyūkō move from distinctive heterogeneous areas excluded from power and history (which must be reexamined in order to
understand Japan and Japanese history) to cultural zones that should assert their independence and that, ultimately, have their own equally le-
gitimate and different histories.[33] The localities of Japan must stop "carrying the fate" of a single Japan and begin to assert their own destinies.

Although all of this becomes a move to decenter Japan, to see it less
as a country centered on the area from Kantō to Kyūshū than as a
grouping of three equal regions, Shimao stops short of envisioning the
independence and autonomy of the local regions as existing outside the
framework of the country of Japan:

> [Now is the time, more than ever] to re-acknowledge the position occupied
> by these islands in Japan, furthermore it is necessary for them to move from
> reliance on others to a feeling of independence. . . . [The islands need to be
> able to] express themselves, free of being bound by the mainland . . . and aim
> at an independent system *(jiritsu taiseizukuri)*. (Vol. 17, 171–172)[34]

> It's desirable for each region to wrap itself in more autonomy, or to put it
> more emphatically, in a strong independent character. Even Okinawa, though
> it's naturally desirable for it to revert [to the mainland], it shouldn't cling
> tightly to the mainland, but think about a direction in which it can firmly es-
> tablish Okinawan autonomy and independence. (Vol. 17, 189–190)[35]

By the early 1970s Shimao begins to use a new vocabulary. A common cultural base, which he now calls *Jōmon*, is overlaid in the "central
part" *(Wa)* by a later mainland Asian cultural layer *(Yayoi)*, which, as a
politically (and militarily) powerful entity, historically suppressed, con-
quered, and excluded the areas to its north and south, which he calls,
respectively, Tōhoku and Ryūkyūkō. Tōhoku and Ryūkyūkō, although
different, distinct regions, share "common elements," in particular a
feeling of incongruity with the people of *Wa* and their lifestyle. These
two "excluded" regions of Japan must become "heterogeneous," "anti-

Japan" elements[36] that are part of a nation that accepts all of its diverse elements as rightfully "autonomous" and "independent."

Despite calls for some sort of independence for such "anti-Japan" regions, it is important to note that throughout his writings Shimao seldom wavers from his seminal stance of a common cultural heritage whose roots are in the South Pacific that underlies all of the geographical area known as Japan. Before recorded history, Shimao writes, the entire Japanese archipelago must have had "shared experiences"; "and thus from any region of the Japanese archipelago it is possible to unearth a common memory" *(kyōtsū no kioku)* (vol. 17, 296).[37] Shimao's unwillingness to question fully this common cultural unconscious finally prevents him from envisioning real political autonomy of localities because despite their differences, the common culture of *Yaponesia* binds both periphery and center.

Critical Reaction to *Yaponesia*

Ironically, it was just about the time Shimao was moving away from using the word *Yaponesia*, and edging away from any role as spokesman for the islands—the early 1970s—that his ideas were discovered and taken up by other southern island thinkers, writers, and activists. Shimao's *Yaponesia* essays essentially lay dormant for nearly a decade until interest in them was sparked by a combination of three factors: two lectures he gave in Okinawa in the early 1970s; the enormous influence of Tanigawa Ken'ichi's 1970 article, "'Yaponesia' to wa nani ka" (What is *'Yaponesia'*?); and the heated debate in the late 1960s and early 1970s over the reversion of Okinawa.

Tanigawa's 1970 essay effectively synthesized Shimao's ideas scattered through essays of the 1950s, 1960s, and 1970s, and first put them on a more theoretical plane.[38] As with many intellectuals of the period, Tanigawa's unspoken concern was the deleterious effects of the emperor system, his desire, like that of Yoshimoto (who has written extensively on the Ryukyus), being to reveal the emperor system and modern Japanese state as historical constructs resting on the suppression of cultural difference. Until the advent of the modern state, Tanigawa argues, there was an unspoken acceptance within Japan of the view of the country as a multilayered cultural space (his definition of *Yaponesia*)—a mixture of old and new, modern and premodern. Japan's earlier rulers never insisted on one cultural stratum completely replacing another—

an organizing principle that led to a diverse, heterogeneous space. The modern Japanese consciousness has lost this sense of diversity, having been molded by the intolerance of the modern state, which, "twisting together a multi-layered heterogeneous time into a single strand" "glossed over . . . and fabricated in order to create the history of 'Japan.'" Embracing "*Yaponesia*—based on the premise that local histories have their own completeness and relative independence," Tanigawa writes, is a way of regaining this lost diversity. As with so many writers discussing *Yaponesia*, Tanigawa cannot resist a bit of word play. The modern Japanese consciousness sees itself and Japan not as "Poly-nesia, but Mono-nesia," not as "Micro-nesia, but as Macro-nesia."[39] It is the liberation of the "poly" and "micro" cultural elements that Shimao's *Yaponesia* encourages. For the past century, Tanigawa concludes, Japan has witnessed the "Japanization of *Yaponesia*"; what is needed now is the "Yaponezation of Japan," or the change from a homogeneous to a heterogeneous historical space—namely, *Yaponesia*.[40]

Clearly two conflicting definitions of *Yaponesia* are at work within Shimao's writings, and much of the debate over the significance of his work revolves around them. In its earliest manifestations, *Yaponesia* is mainly a shared culture, the common memory that underlies, and in a sense unites, all of the Japan. As Tanigawa (and Shimao in his later essays) would have it, however, *Yaponesia* is less the recovery of commonality than the discovery of cultural *difference*, an unearthing of the suppressed diversity of cultural zones in Japan. In this sense, the development of Shimao's *Yaponesia* writings parallel Ōshiro's summation of Okinawan-mainland history, the historical trend toward assimilation (Shimao's "common memory") giving way to a movement toward dissimilation. It is worth noting Shimao's reluctance in later years to use the term *Yaponesia*. According to the Okinawan poet Takara Ben, Shimao's strategic shift to other terms (*Jōmon* and Ryūkyūkō) reflects both his suspicion of those who would appropriate *Yaponesia* for immediate political ends, as well as his search for a deeper layer of significance beyond the politics of the day, a means by which to take a long-range view of historical relations between mainland and islands and thereby construct an autonomous position for the latter.[41] In this sense, despite his lingering attachment to the notion of a cultural commonality, Shimao in later years was clearly struggling for a way to express a quite different point of view.

In spite of the distance Shimao's thought traveled over some twenty years, for many concerned with the question of Okinawan identity his *Yaponesia* ideas remained problematic, either too inclusive or exclusive. Ōshiro viewed attempts to link Tōhoku and the southern islands as suspect, because Tōhoku is just one more part of the mainland toward which Okinawans feel ill at ease. Likewise, Takara, generally sympathetic to Shimao's *Yaponesia* ideas, warns against any that "bind Ryūkyūkō to the Japanese State."[42] Among those who see *Yaponesia* as too exclusive, Miki Takeshi criticizes Shimao for not discussing the Ryukyus sufficiently; he coins the term "Okinesia" to indicate his desire to explore more concretely the cultural links between Okinawa and the South Pacific. Similarly, Yamada Munemutsu argues against the potential narrowness of the *Yaponesia* idea, the fact that while it touches on the South Pacific islands, it focuses just on Japan, Okinawa, and Amami. He calls for an "Indo-Yaponesia" theory looking at Indonesia, the Philippines, Taiwan, the Ryukyus, and the Japanese archipelago as one region.

In a revealing discussion between Shimao and the novelist Nakagami Kenji (known for his fictional portrayals of *burakumin* outcastes in the Kishū Peninsula south of Nara), one can see that writers outside the southern islands who also struggled with the relationship between local regions and the center (here expressed as *Wa*), while sympathetic to Shimao's ideas, feel they were not sufficiently nuanced or radical. In the discussion Shimao concedes that his tripartite division of Japan oversimplifies the situation, because

> in the Japanese archipelago many different kinds of people came and went and cultures with different elements piled up. I want to examine this in detail. In the center were the *Wa*, the culture and country created by the *Wa* people, but even there many layers of culture existed. . . . I don't want to overturn *Wa*-like things, but want to consider that if *Wa* is one culture, then the southern islands and Kishū too have their own.[43]

Shimao is reacting to two of Nakagami's points: (1) that *Wa* is not the monolith that *Yaponesia* envisions (i.e., within the "center" there are other localities that are separate, non-*Wa* cultures). Nakagami contends that Kishū, his home, is the "reverse side of the central *(Wa)* culture"; and (2) Nakagami's desire to "overturn that culture (of *Wa*)." We see in the exchange two significantly different positions: Shimao calling for an acceptance of the cultures of other localities as equal to that of the center (with the understanding that they share a common cultural base), Nakagami hoping to overturn that center. Interestingly, Nakagami views *Wa* not only as a political center but as a force that unifies and controls the diversity of spoken language, the other local regions as a counterforce working against this standardization:

> [I]f you consider what makes culture decadent, it is not "spoken language" but "written language." What fascinates me about the southern islands is that there still exists a situation where "spoken language" has not completely shifted over to "written language," making for a rich culture.[44]

Despite criticism of his writings, on the whole Shimao's *Yaponesia* ideas have been more praised than criticized by residents of Okinawa and have proved immensely influential to this day. A 1978 roundtable discussion with Shimao and three Okinawan intellectuals on "'The *Yaponesia* theory' and Okinawa" illustrates the generally favorable response Shimao's ideas have generated—and continue to generate— among Okinawans.[45] Kawamitsu Shin'ichi, for instance, sees *Yaponesia* as providing a "strong support for us in Okinawa"; it showed Okinawans that "thought and literature" needed to be created to "strengthen the base for Okinawans to stand on." Unlike Nara and Kyoto, Okinawa had no resources to leave "tangible cultural monuments," thus there is little about Okinawan culture one can "see or touch"; *Yaponesia* provides a method by which Okinawans can begin to find the "intangible, abstract cultural ethos" of their land.[46] Likewise, Niikawa Akira maintains that *Yaponesia* demonstrates there is no absolute value adhering to the material side of Japanese culture so evident in the mainland. Shimao's ideas help destroy "absolute values" and may lead to the "autonomy" (*jiritsusei*) of local regions.[47]

Significantly, as with Shimao's discussion with Nakagami, the roundtable discussants end by focusing on the language of the southern islands. Standard Japanese, Kawamitsu says, is "intellectual," something Okinawans learn through reading, but it is not a part of the "emotions of one's own life" (*jibun no seikatsu no kansei*); "there are many emotional areas of our lives that are not those of the Japanese language."[48] The people's lives in Okinawa are different from those of "Yamato," and writers must work to express this difference, says Niikawa, but ultimately what distinguishes Okinawa from the mainland is Okinawa's "intangible cultural legacy"—its language.[49] Not surprisingly, Shimao was deeply concerned with preservation of this cultural legacy of language, working actively in researching local dialects, collecting and recording folktales of Amami and Tōhoku, and encouraging the activities

of Okinawan *shibai* (play) troupes. As with all his *Yaponesia* writings, Shimao's work on language, too, contains an intensely personal dimension.
His search was also for the roots of his personal expression, his "place"
of "spontaneous expression," a search that ultimately led him to a discovery of his own place, namely Tōhoku.[50]

In recent years Takara and others have identified the need for a
homegrown *Yaponesia*, that is, a stance toward Okinawan identity that
comes from Okinawa and Okinawans, rather than from outside. In this
sense, according to Akasaka Norio, the "first chapter" of the southern
island debate, one owing much to such outside intellectuals as Shimao
and Yoshimoto, is now giving way to a second chapter, one written by
Okinawans themselves.[51] In fact, much recent debate has concerned the
politics of naming and the construction of identity from within. Takara,
for example, prefers Shimao's terms *Yaponesia* and Ryūkyūkō to Yoshimoto's Nantō (Southern islands) because the latter implies the existence and privileging of the north and binds Okinawan identity to its
relationship to the mainland. Ultimately, Takara advocates the use of
locally constructed terms, his choice being *Uruma rettō*, taken from
Urumanoshima, an old term for Okinawa.[52] As Yoshimoto has likewise
commented, by constantly viewing their culture in comparison to that
of the mainland, seeing it, in other words, within a mainland frame,
Okinawans themselves are guilty of helping blur what is really distinctive and valuable about their land.[53]

It is debatable whether Shimao's *Yaponesia* essays help Okinawans
break out of this comparative frame; deciding whether or not they do
rests in great part on which *Yaponesia* one emphasizes—that of the earlier, or later, essays. In contrast to Yoshimoto's carefully argued, fact-
filled, intellectual essays, Shimao's *Yaponesia* writings are anecdotal,
suggestive rather than limiting, ambiguously shaded enough to serve
as catalyst to the reader—particularly the Okinawan reader—to fill in
the gaps the essays willfully create. To read Shimao's essays is to be, on
the one hand, frustrated by the ways his writing often pulls back from
definitive statements. At the same time, to read his work fully is to en-
gage in an active process of construction of meaning, a process akin to
what both Ōshiro and Okamoto advocate—the kind of "cultural" activity that actively seeks, and constructs, definitions and possibilities of
identity.

Shimao's *Yaponesia* writings must be placed not just in the context of
the reversion of Okinawa and attendant debates on Ryukyuan identity,

but in the larger context of modern Japanese social change and its expression in literature. Shimao's work and career are caught up in such notions as *jōkyō* (literally, going up to the capital, here signifying the post-Meiji Restoration movement of writers to Tokyo), the construction of the meaning of *kokyō* (one's home place), and, connecting both, the "metaphor of center and periphery" dominating post-Meiji conceptions of social change.[54] One can see in Shimao's early career the typical *jōkyō* move to the center, followed by aborted attempts to reconcile urban life with a growing sense of alienation and displacement. These feelings were captured well by Kobayashi Hideo some twenty years before: "I know that my life has been lacking in concrete substance. I do not easily recognize within myself or in the world around me people whose feet are planted firmly on the ground."[55] Shimao's dominant literature of his urban period, stories of an alienated protagonist wandering the blighted urban landscape are, to borrow Kobayashi's phrase, indeed part of a "literature of the lost home." And his subsequent abandonment of Tokyo for Amami is both a reversal of *jōkyō* and an attempt to construct the missing *kokyō*.

Shimao's early *Yaponesia* writings can be challenged as constructing a nostalgic, even utopian, vision of the southern islands as Japan's own lost home, an isolated spiritual haven where some purer, more authentically lived experience is still possible. Shimao, critical of mainlanders' making the islands exotic, risks repeating this move himself. A number of clear-eyed countermovements within his essays modify this conclusion, however, including the recognition of the impossibility of isolation, and of the islanders' own prejudices. Ultimately the *Yaponesia* essays are best read in the larger context of post-Meiji concerns and the notion of center-periphery. Shimao's reversal of the standard tropes of backwardness used in discussing the Ryukyus, plus his challenge to conventional readings of Japanese history that view the Ryukyus as a historical backwater, are important attempts to instill a sense of worth and cultural pride in a people historically deprived of both. As the later essays reach out beyond the Ryukyus to take in other marginalized regions (particularly Tōhoku), Shimao moves on to the larger question of ways to defuse and rewrite the dominant metaphor of center-periphery, and it is here that the lasting significance of his work is found. Not surprisingly for a novelist, Shimao considered many of the same questions in his writings on literature. In the 1965 essay "'Chihō bungaku' to iu koto ni tsuite" (On what is called 'regional literature'), Shimao discusses the relationship between literature produced in peripheral localities and the Tokyo-based literary establishment (the *bundan*). While recognizing the practical necessity of literature "directly or indirectly [to] pass through the *bundan*," at the same time Shimao envisioned a liberation of writing from just such a center-based establishment. Shimao viewed local literature as the means for reacting against the *bundan* and, ultimately, for dispensing with it, for dispensing with Literary History in favor of literary histories.[56]

As Okamoto argues in his book-length study, *"Yaponesia ron" no rinkaku* (Outlines of the theory of *Yaponesia*), a variety of experiences contributed to the development of Shimao's *Yaponesia*—everything from his undergraduate research on Chinese border regions to his foreign travels in Eastern Europe (and the discovery of various "border regions" therein, most notably Poland).[57] Underlying much of Shimao's statements on the southern islands, however, is his own feeling of being an outside "invader."[58] Statements in 1967 identifying himself as a descendant of Tōhoku stock, coupled with later essays specifically linking the southern islands and Tōhoku as disenfranchised, suppressed regions, Okamoto argues, are Shimao's way of dealing with what was a pressing personal problem. Simply stated, how can Shimao explain, and deal with, the feelings of incongruity both he and his wife felt toward mainland Japan, and his own mixed feelings of attraction and sense of incongruity (*iwakan*) toward Amami? Both he and Miho are Japanese, yet why did they feel so out of place in the "center" of Japan? Speaking of his own feelings vis-à-vis the mainland, and with Amami, Shimao writes:

> In the beginning I thought my *iwakan* was a problem of personality, that because my personality or character was that way I couldn't fit in well with my surroundings. . . . Even in Amami I feel *iwakan* towards various things, but along with the *iwakan* there's a strong feeling of lightness. When I came to Amami I felt I was a Tōhoku person, but even so there was a situation in Amami that could make me relax. This led me to start considering that there's something about Amami and Tōhoku that's the same.[59]

Although Shimao felt out of place in Amami and remained the eternal outsider, what drew him was a perceived similarity between himself and the islanders, which in his writings took the form of a shared sense of incongruity that they felt toward the center:

> My ancestors are from Tōhoku, and I grew up in Yokohama, then Kobe, and Kyushu. I always felt there something like a sense of *iwakan* toward society.

I thought this was because of my own disposition, but living in Amami I've found this is not because of one's disposition, but is more the *iwakan* that Tōhoku people have.[60]

The experience of living with the islanders allowed Shimao to see that the sort of incongruity of individuals—the sense of being out of place that both he and his wife experienced in Tokyo—should not be traced to problems of individual personality dysfunctions. Instead, it is the result of real differences that exist within present-day Japan at the level of regional, local culture, something shared by both Amami and Tōhoku.

Thus the two strands of his *Yaponesia* writings—personal and communal identities—are in the end uniquely bound to each other. At the individual level, Shimao begins with the question, Why was my wife unable to cope in the setting of urban, mainland Japan? Okinawan critics such as Okamoto are quick to link Miho's incongruity with a complex toward the mainland. For Shimao the intensely personal dimensions of this problem soon took on larger significance. Shimao began to understand that his wife was the product of a certain history and culture that he has not shared in directly, and which sets her and her people apart from other regions. The idea, for instance, that Shimao wrote *Shi no toge* primarily as a "cure" for his wife ignores the thrust of all of Shimao's concerns outlined above, namely with a "cure" for larger social groups. On the level of the southern island people, this "cure" takes the form of the *Yaponesia* ideas, which, as seen before, worked to strengthen both cultural pride and self-identity in a people whom the dominant discourse had always consigned to the margins. The fictional portrayal of the inability of one member of this group to cope with life on the mainland—the madness that is cured by a return to the place where she "belongs"—becomes a tale with significance far outside the boundaries of one family, and it speaks to all the southern islanders, and indeed to all Japanese. At the same time of course, it makes problematic the notion of "all Japanese."

As discussed above, Shimao contests the idea that a solution to the sense of *iwakan* felt by people from outlying localities lies in increased uniformity, in further homogenization of Japan and its people. His works thus act as rebuttal to the so-called *Nihonjinron* discourse of the 1970s and 1980s, which finds Japan's strength as lying in its already constituted cultural homogeneity. Shimao's entire *Yaponesia* project remains clearly a celebration of diversity. In a different context (discussing the fear of death) Shimao speaks of the "positive side" of fear; it is better, he maintains, to "face fear directly without running away." His own

literature he defines as the "restoration of fear."[61] Likewise his literature should be seen as a restoration of a positive sense of incongruity
with one's surroundings, with all the connotations this has taken on in
our discussion. Most readers, quite understandably, are inclined to read
Miho's madness in the *byōsaimono* as what it appears to be on the surface: a horrible condition that makes her and her family suffer terribly.
To deny these aspects is to ignore much of what Shimao is telling us.
Yet read together with what is known of his ideas on the southern islands and their culture, the outlines of something quite different take
shape. In Shimao's literature *iwakan* becomes a positive sign of difference and diversity both at the level of individuals and social groups.
Miho suffers through not belonging, through being "out of place"—yet
in her fevered cry to be taken back to her home we detect the glimmerings of a sign of health, of the recognition of the existence, and importance, of difference. And, in the so-called "island stories," the male
protagonist's sense of *iwakan* with his island surroundings, together
with the attraction these surroundings hold for him, parallel precisely
Shimao's *Yaponesia* discoveries—the sense of one's cultural place and
identity brought into focus by an exploration of difference.

Yaponesia and Shimao's Fiction: Writing *Yaponesia*

Shimao was always writing *Yaponesia*. His war stories, as we have seen,
are equally about the discovery of an Other within Japan—the island
and its people who act as antidote to the death-inducing dominant culture. No longer, I think, can one read Shimao's early dream fiction, as
mainstream critics have tended to do, as admirable but nearly impenetrable avant-garde creations. They are clearly symbolic expressions of a
yearning for the excluded, and of the guilt of one whose wartime role
was intimately linked with their oppression. And to label Shimao's *byōsaimono* as mere I-novels ignores how these stories, too, are statements
on dominant and marginalized cultures.

From his first published story, "Kotōmu" (Dream of a lonely isle),
Shimao is writing *Yaponesia*. We have seen how this dream-like story reveals the dirty secret of the Ryukyu campaign, how civilians became
sacrificial victims to allow the military to escape. Equally, however, the
story is an early expression of what was to develop into *Yaponesia*. The
narrator, who, in the midst of war, desires to preserve the uniqueness
of the island "through pen and camera," meets up with one islander
(a dentist) who has denounced his heritage in favor of assimilation with

the mainland. The narrator's loathing for this man overlaps with his fear that the island will soon "sink beneath the waves." In the wartime context we are to read this as meaning the island will be invaded and destroyed by the enemy. However, a second reading is possible: "sinking beneath the waves" is also an expression of fear that the island's cultural uniqueness will disappear in the face of a dominant mainland, and that someone must rush to save it. "Kotōmu" also anticipates by some thirty years sentiments expressed above concerning the southern islands' lack of "tangible cultural monuments." In the penultimate scene, the narrator leaves the dentist's office full of despair, only to find before him a huge gate. The gate, it turns out, is a remarkable symbol of the island: built without a single nail, it is reproduced on woodblock prints (which the narrator remembers seeing in the mainland), and in miniatures. The narrator buys one of these miniatures—like the gate itself, something "found only in this island." Far from lacking tangible monuments, the island provides the fearful and despairing narrator with one ray of hope. In the midst of the imminent collapse of the world, the gate will remain.

Shi no toge

Shimao began both projects—the *Yaponesia* essays and *Shi no toge*—at the same time, and continued to work on both over roughly the same period of time (1960–1976). Over the drawn-out process of writing the novel (composed, as with most of his works from 1957–1975 at night after his day job as Amami librarian), certain intriguing parallels developed between the fictionalized retelling of his wife's madness and his cultural analysis of mainland-marginal relations. Chapter 5 of the novel, written in 1963, just after Shimao first mentioned Tōhoku in his essays, is important for how it carefully positions Toshio as being from that region. If Miho's problems stem in great part from an inability to cope with life in Tokyo, chapter 5 reveals Toshio as equally not of the center, but the product of another marginalized region. Tōhoku is the only place he can find comfort, where memories of the past are ones of belonging to a community that welcomed him as a member. The landscape of Tōhoku has meaning for Toshio, although none for Miho; the two of them are, for the first time, portrayed not as rootless urban dwellers but as two individuals from vastly different backgrounds. And within the comfort of memories that being in Tōhoku brings, Toshio first begins to conceive the notion that a cure for Miho lies in returning her to the equivalent of his Tōhoku—Amami.

In the opening of chapter 8 (1964) Toshio for the first time admits the need to confront the past, a feeling that draws him closer to Miho's mindset. This newfound closeness—although strained as always by the demands of her madness—reaches a climax in chapter 10 (1967), where Toshio and Miho together attack Toshio's lover. Yoshimoto sees the world of Toshio and Miho as a closed one reminiscent of Japan itself during World War Two, when outsiders were expelled, foreign elements excluded.[62] Yoshimoto's ideas, however, are off the mark. To see Toshio and Miho as similar to the mainland Japanese during World War II ignores a vital point—how Shimao has carefully positioned the two of them as coming from areas historically victimized by the center. Indeed, as one reader puts it, Shimao's project is to reverse the wartime order—with the colonies now "invading" the mainland as defining cultural centers of their own.[63] Coming on the heels of his essays of the same year in which he for the first time is emphatic in seeing a communality between Tōhoku and Amami and is calling for greater autonomy for these regions, the dramatic scene of Toshio and Miho joining forces to beat the other woman (who as modern, urban intellectual is depicted as completely of the center) can be read as the localities' expression of that communality, the release of suppressed rage, and desire for independence directed toward the mainland and the culture of the center.[64] Read in tandem with the essays, then, the outlines of *Shi no toge* intersect with Shimao's *Yaponesia* ideas in interesting and suggestive ways. The growing consciousness of Toshio of himself as a Tōhoku person and Miho as a native of Amami, together with the sense of newfound closeness that draws them together to stand in opposition to the center, find parallels in Shimao's burgeoning *Yaponesia* writings.

In many interpretations, however, this positioning of Toshio as also not of the center is put aside. A recent feminist work, *Danryū bungakuron* (Theory of male literature, 1992), takes up issues of connections between *Yaponesia* and the story of Miho's madness. The three panelists whose discussions make up the book—psychologist Ogura Chikako, novelist Tomioka Taeko, and feminist writer and scholar Ueno Chizuko—cover a number of topics, from the meaning of madness to a discussion of "mad" elements of Shimao's prose style. In addition, they undertake an impromptu play in which they act out possible solutions to the couple's discord.

Before this, however, the discussants begin by questioning what they see as the typical male interpretive paradigm for dealing with Shimao's work, namely the notion that in the *Shi no toge* Miho-Toshio relationship is found the clash of two cultures—Miho representing an ancient, or premodern, island culture, Toshio representing modernity and contemporary Japan. This paradigm, most notably propounded by Yoshimoto, works well with the notion of Miho as healer of the troubled Toshio.[65] Ueno in particular questions this interpretation, instead viewing Miho's story as a more universal one of modern women's experience. To Ueno, Miho is neither *yuta* shamaness nor a woman who embodies a premodern culture, but is a typical modern woman "bound by the spell of modern love."[66] In other words, Miho is constricted by the structure of modern romantic love wherein women are condemned to believe in two things: (1) that their identity is completely relational, always dependent on their relationship with a man; and (2) that in the course of their passionate love they are able to have a measure of control over the interior *(naimen)* of another.[67]

This does not mean, however, that Miho has abandoned the role of healer. The paradox of modern sexual love, Ueno states, is that while woman is subordinate to man, she believes that by positioning herself as self-sacrificing wife—a self-sacrificing "martyr to love"—she can be his savior.[68] Miho's madness, then, is the anger of a woman in this structure who discovers that the Other is not completely knowable, that despite her sacrifice the man has an emotional space to which she will never be privy and which will remain unknown to her. Miho's cure, Ogura adds, which must be a self-cure, comes with the realization, and acceptance, of the fact that the same applies to her: that she herself constitutes an unknowable Other for the man.[69] When she rejects this structure of modern love, when she believes her identity can be found outside their relationship, and when she rejects the notion of herself as savior, her cure is complete.[70]

In the course of the discussion, Ogura raises some points about a lecture in Okinawa by Yoshimoto on his *Nantō-ron* (theory of the southern islands). Yoshimoto's idea, in short, is to privilege the southern islands as containing a culture that predates the Japanese state and emperor system; it thereby might serve to relativize these, to help mainland Japanese look beyond, and ultimately overcome, the emperor system and modern state. The audience of Okinawans, Ogura says, felt a great deal of incongruity *(iwakan)* toward Yoshimoto's ideas. For Ueno, this sense of incongruity is a reaction against Yoshimoto's "fantasy" of the southern islands; the point, she states, is that in much the same way Miho is fantasized and romanticized by critics such as Yoshimoto.[71]

Ueno's point is well taken, and it is clear that not just the critics have fantasized Miho; Shimao himself has. As seen before, in his essays Shimao gradually questions his original stance of seeing the islands as healers of a "sick" mainland. By the 1970s, Okinawa and the southern islands are to him no longer the healers of a mainland culture in relation to which they find their identity. Instead, the islands are seen as independent cultural entities whose task is, while maintaining a relationship with the mainland, to develop their identities outside such a framework. What is of particular interest here is that while in his essays Shimao gradually moved toward a more progressive stand in regards to the mainland-island relationship, his fiction emits contradictory signals. Whether we accept the notion of Miho as premodern or modern, shamaness or not, in the larger context of Shimao's entire fictional project Miho very much is a stand-in for the island; the Miho-Toshio relationship quite often parallels that of island and mainland, of healer and the ill. Miho may end up cured in the stories, but she never fully rejects the role of healer; and Toshio, for his part, clings to both her and the island in hopes of finding his salvation. There is a strong argument to be made that in Shimao's fiction, woman, while struggling to find her own voice and independence, more often than not is given meaning only in relation to man, her purpose to act as conduit for his ill-defined quest for fulfillment. Put in terms of the mainland-island relationship, then, Shimao's fiction tends to reinforce his earlier, rather than his later, views of *Yaponesia*.[72]

Such an argument is convincing, but rests on a narrower reading of the character Toshio than Shimao's texts allow. One must acknowledge the positioning of Toshio in *Shi no toge* as also not of the center. If in later fiction (most notably the island stories and *Hi no utsuroi*) the wife is indeed the "healer" of the male protagonist, one should read Shimao's fiction, and its relationship to his *Yaponesia* ideas, in a more positive light. That is, it should not be read as reinforcing the early *Yaponesia* notions of the marginal regions "rescuing" the ailing center, but as paralleling the entire *Yaponesia* project—the discovery of a shared commonality between differing marginalized areas, with the southern islands serving as guides to this discovery.

Five "Island" Stories (1959–1965)

In the late 1950s–1960s, Shimao increasingly used his island home as backdrop for his fiction. These stories, which I call his island stories, are in many ways a continuation of concerns found in earlier fiction and serve as dramatic illustrations of ideas found in the essays on *Yaponesia*. The unique island culture of "Kotōmu" and "Sotetsujima no jifu" combine with the utopian longings for a refuge found in "Chinkonki." Added to this are the figure of the now-healed wife of the *byōsaimono* as guide and mediator between island and outside, and the always-present incongruity and attraction the narrator feels for the island. As with the *Yaponesia* essays, the island stories depict an attempt to get at the heart of the island, to seek out an inner core. This journey, in turn, is depicted in terms of a falling away of the ordinary world and ordinary perception. Like the cultural unconscious the islands become for Shimao in his essays, in his fiction the journey to the islands core parallels a journey to the unconscious. Here I will examine five of Shimao's stories set in the islands: "Kawa ni te" (At the river, 1959), "Haishi" (Ruins, 1960), "Shima e" (To the island, 1962), "Sōsaiki" (A record of a search for my wife, 1964), and "Keiji no tsutome" (A day's work, 1965).[73]

"Kawa ni te" (1959)

"Kawa ni te" illustrates this journey to the unconscious clearly. Led by a local guide, the narrator journeys to the river at the hidden interior of the village. The river is the one spot where fresh water comes out of the ground and is the center of the village's daily life. There, women wash clothes and old men and women bathe together. Finding this river, however, is never easy. The narrator notes that

> it's hard to tell where the river is just by passing down the island highway running through the village and linking it with the neighboring villages at opposites ends. There were lots of side roads running at angles to the main road, but these branch roads were a maze, and you couldn't tell where they ended. [In the village] high coral walls surrounded the houses, and with the alleys and fences cut through the natural stone crags, it was impossible to see the whole of any house from the outside. . . . [I]t isn't easy to ascertain the location of the river, which exists in only one spot in the village. But in actual practice it isn't too hard to sense from the way the village is laid out which part contains the place that must be protected from the eyes of outsiders. *Where the real difficulty lies is in "approaching" that place you sense.* (311–312; emphasis added)

The physical description of the village is typical of traditional Amami villages and is one repeated in similar form in many of Shimao's stories. The village is a labyrinth of walls, alleys, and passageways that form a physical, as well as psychological, barrier to penetration by outsiders. A whole other life goes on beyond these barriers, but the contents of that life are impenetrable to the outsider without a guide.

The road to the river spirals downward, and the narrator feels he is approaching a boundary where there is "an inner logic which can never be explained outside of a state of drunkenness." "In a sudden feeling of guilt *(tsumi no ishiki)*" he notes, "my actions slowed down, and I began to wait to be judged" (314). The spot where the road to the river begins clearly marks a boundary of several dimensions. It marks the spot where an "inner logic" takes over. Perception of surroundings are altered as well, as soon as the narrator sets foot in it: the rain and wind he had felt up until then are now "outside [his] senses" (315), the brisk movements of people from a moment before are slowed, and everyone around him has shrunk in size. The sounds of the village are replaced by an "almost obscenely cheerful liveliness" from the bottom of the spiral path and by the perfume-like fragrance of the women who continue to pass them as they head back to the village.

Although he knows the river is a place where villagers wash clothes and themselves, and thus should present an everyday scene, for him, coming on this all of a sudden, it is a "shock, as if I were standing at the scene of a crime" (316). The crime he imagines involves death, because at the "scene of a crime" he senses a "sopping wet *goshiki no ito*" (315). The imagery itself is unusual: *goshiki no ito* (literally, five-colored threads) is the Buddhist concept of five colored threads (green, yellow, red, black, and white) the dying believer holds in his hand, physically connecting him to a statue of Amida Buddha, thus ensuring rebirth in paradise. Here this "sternness of primary colors that makes you look away" (316) is presumably triggered by the villagers' wet clothes stretched out to dry. The reader is startled by the incongruity of the description and his reaction to it; the river makes villagers visiting it calm, they have a wonderful fragrance, there is a lively sound coming from the river—yet the narrator is shocked by what he sees:

> People from outside the village shouldn't come to a place like this. A cold rejection, not allowing any reason for a visit by outsiders, radiated up from under the tolerant faces of the villagers there. If even one outsider comes there, dense waves radiate out and assault him, as if a fever lying just below the surface came in touch with a foreign object and was activated. (316)

Stripped naked before the villagers, ready to bathe with them, the narrator feels an overwhelming sense of guilt. Seeing them staring at him, he says, "When I saw the light in their eyes, I understood. The moment that was meant to come was already prepared, and it had surely come" (319). As with many of Shimao's narrators and their incessant feelings of guilt and waiting for judgment, one can understand the narrator's words as signifying that the moment of judgment has arrived. The three old men who sit facing him, indistinguishable one from another, call to mind the stern row of judges—usually three in number—of a typical Japanese courtroom. They possess an "ominous will" *(bukimi na ishi)* that is like the "tentacles of a jellyfish that continue to wrap around you and sting even after they're cut off" (320):

> Perhaps I should have asked the old men why they watched over me with such set expressions, and why they sprayed me with these questions whose intentions were far from clear. But the moment I set foot in the village I was haunted by that familiar sense of a guilty conscience. (321)

As he finishes bathing and leaves the river, the "normal" world and sense perception are recovered: "[L]ike a film that had been cut and now started up again, the wind and rain resumed. The feeling remained that only the river and the bathing spot were blankly left behind by the weather outside" (325). He remarks:

> Again I was beleaguered by the thought that weighed heavily on me, that as long as I live I could never become a villager. (325)

The nature of this "crime," however, goes beyond the present situation and the relationship of narrator to the villagers, to something in his—and their—past. Why does he feel, with this encounter, that "the moment that was meant to come was already prepared, and it had surely come"? A clue lies in the following passage (as he first encounters the women at the bath):

> In the dim, narrow interior [of the bath] the women's eyes, like those of animals, glittered, and were watching me. And, while chatting endlessly over things with those white teeth of theirs, those eyes surely would fall on me. *Surely my past will be exposed!* I thought. (317; emphasis added)

The narrator in "Kawa ni te" is not simply feeling the guilt of an intruding outsider, stepping for the first time into a place that rejects him, but is, in a very strong sense, returning to the scene of a crime. And this crime, as we have seen, is connected with death. The narrator is yet another manifestation of the former wartime *tokkōtai* commander who held the power of life and death over the village. And his past, of course, includes the powerful image of old men and women, collected together in one spot in the village, about to commit mass suicide.

"Haishi" (1960)

If the status of the narrator as former *tokkōtai* commander is somewhat veiled in "Kawa ni te," it lies exposed at the surface in "Haishi." Readers again see the encounter of outsider and islanders—protagonist and his past as it relates to the islands—here in the more familiar and clearly outlined form of the former commander and his wife, the former mental patient. The story is of special interest for an additional reason: "Haishi" is a return to origins, a physical pilgrimage back to the Ur-spot of Shimao's fiction—the *tokkōtai* base. Just after publication of this story, Shimao began to publish the first of what became the *Shi no toge* series,[74] turning his gaze backward further to tracing the origins of the situation depicted in the *byōinki*, that is, the months of illness leading up to the hospitalization. "Haishi" in part represents the opposite spectrum: the first of the post-*byōinki* stories tracing the lives of the husband and wife after the release from the hospital and move to Amami. In this, "Haishi" is the precursor of many Shimao stories in the 1960s and afterward dealing with the life of his protagonist and family on Amami.[75]

As with "Kawa ni te," here Shimao brings perception to the forefront and equates the encounter with the island with a transformation in consciousness. The narrator has trouble judging distances. Looking down at the waves pounding the shore, he feels he cannot judge how far away the scene is: "An ungraspable sound, the waves, or the wind, perhaps, enveloped me like a smell; though it was in my field of vision, a sense of distance beyond my grasp numbed my head" (363). This uncertain sense of distance is soon followed by an overlap of past and present:

> U Island, like a lid on the scene in front of me, stood squarely in the sea. I had thought it was closer, and smaller. The image I'd retained in my memory overlapped with what was before my eyes, and grew large, then small, then repeated this, wavering uncertainly. (363)

The pattern for the entire story is present in these lines, because as one discovers, the narrator, revisiting what is left of his former *tokkōtai* base with his wife, is constantly shifting between memories of the past and images of the present, so much so that they often overlap.

The first memory is striking: It is ten years earlier, during the war, when he was crossing the same path over the hill:

I remembered seeing a man, an island resident, with a crazy woman, walking over the red clay road of the mountain ridge. . . . As I always did when crossing over the mountains, I had my military sword over my shoulder, and as I neared them the man's quarrelsome voice and the entreaties of the woman came to an abrupt halt. They moved to one side of the narrow mountain path and waited for me to go by.

At the time, I felt a strong body odor from the life outside the squadron, so even the man's impoverished, pasty, dirty appearance made me feel an odor coming to envelope me. (364)[76]

After describing the background that led him to this spot during the war (the oft-repeated background of the *tokkōtai* commander), the narrator recalls:

I thought it would be best to pass by them without staring. But in fact, I wanted to get closer and take a good look at the crazed woman. I even felt envious of the man, for at the time I understood nothing about the mental illness of women. Their lives were stuffed full, overflowing, even. While I had not a single trace of life. (365)

While in the present, with his own wife (here called Kesana; recently released from a mental hospital) beside him, the narrator understands how misplaced his envy of the man he saw ten years before was. But what is also important is that, ten years before, the image of a man and crazed woman was symbolic of life, so to the narrator the image served as an enviable contrast to the situation of himself and his lover, Kesana, who had made a "pledge to die" that "would absolutely never be broken" (365). The irony, of course, is that his former envy has turned into reality (a reality he feels is a burden), because he and Kesana have become the man and crazed woman walking the path in the woods.

The narrator's conflicting desires both to keep his past hidden and expose it—the tension that energizes "Kawa ni te"—likewise prevail in "Haishi," as does the same question, Why does the narrator choose to go to the island? In neither story are the motives made explicit, yet in both we can see that he has decided the time is ripe for "digging up his body" again. This is not the trite metaphor of the past as "buried" and the act of recalling it one of "unearthing." The wording used here, and later on (at the base memories "come rising up out of the grave, overturning gravestones" [369]), should also be read in the literal sense, because the narrator's past is bestrewn with actual graves. The first is that of an American soldier who died on the island, the second that of Kesana's father, and the third—and here one gets closer to the absent cause of the narrator's sense of guilt—the "graves" of the villagers (i.e., the site of their near mass suicide). Speaking with the new village chief, the narrator thinks:

> I couldn't let go of a feeling of being on the defensive. I couldn't accurately grasp what influence the actions of the squad during the war had had on the villagers. Perhaps this intrepid, thin, unshaven man was trying to lodge a protest against the person responsible for the squad. Could I withstand that? Even if *all the hatred of the village from the time of the war until the defeat* rained down on me, there was nothing I could do to avoid it. (371–372; emphasis added)

Addressed at the end as "Commander" by the new village chief, the narrator feels like he was once again in wartime, making his way back to the spot where his base was. And that is a "somehow dirty feeling" (372).

Looking over the scene at the inlet, the narrator notes that "the past, which had started to decay and disintegrate, once more raised its head—a feeling that was hard to bear" (379):

> With the passage of ten years of time, N Bay had recovered its original repose. But the staring eyeballs at the entrances to the twelve caves were unchanged, as were the beak-like mounds of earth in front of them. The ocean waters had not touched the granite rocks that we had pounded into the beach so that the tires of the trailers carrying our five-ton launches would not sink into the sand. Gazing through narrowed eyes at the two tracks of granite that remained, I was swallowed up by an inexpressible feeling of desolation.
>
> The fading light of evening was preparing to trade places with the dark of night. We stepped back, making up our minds to take the mountain path to O Village. Kesana and I both hoped that we would be able to reach the cemetery under cover of darkness, unnoticed by the people of the village.[77] (380–381)

One aspect of the story that links it directly with other island stories is the narrator's desire to know more about the islands, and in the process to discover something more about himself and his wife. With the help of hindsight he recognizes now that his experiences in the island were vital to the person he has become. "From the houses in the inlet," he notes, "looking around the former base, detailed memories of things I'd forgotten one by one pushed over the gravemarkers, and rose up, pushing aside the dirt on the graves. I couldn't help but think that this was a place that had deeply determined the tone of my life" (369). But just as much, the island is the environment that shaped his wife, and it is this he wishes to pursue:

I had grown used to thinking with Kesana, and was trying, like a starving, thirsting person, to relive the environment that had helped shape her spirit. I wanted to take inside of me the island mountains, the inlet, the beaches, all which reflected her in younger days. In the past an unusual collective life had taken place here, but now that the odor of that life had been completely chased away, when all that remained was an inorganic concrete ruin, N Inlet, silent and washed by the wind and rain, was the perfect spot for Kesana and me to wander in order to cure our damaged nerves. (380; emphasis added)

Shimao's twenty-year literary preoccupation with *byōsaimono* and with pursuing his wife as a literary theme, and his research into Amami and the southern islands that took shape in his numerous essays are, as Fujii Reiichi has noted, unrelated projects only on the surface. At a deeper level, both are attempts to "relive the environment" that helped shaped Miho, to understand, in Fujii's words, "*Jū* [father] and *Anma* [mother], in other words, the essence of the southern island Amami." As another critic puts it, "For Shimao, journeying to the southern islands meant journeying to his wife." One might very well reverse these terms and conclude, to paraphrase, that it is within—and through—Miho that Shimao discovered the islands, and their sense of time and space.[78]

"Shima e" (1962)

"Shima e," Shimao's best-known story set in the islands, describes a three-day trip the narrator and his wife take to the island. Again, the male narrator has a military background clearly linked to the *tokkōtai*, which he feels ambiguous about exposing, and both he and his wife have experienced hospitalization in a mental hospital. Once more, perception is brought to the forefront, in this case the narrator's difficulty in seeing. This should be characterized less a physical problem and more the feeling that one cannot see:

I landed on the island and walked down the white roads, but couldn't see a thing. When I was on board the ship I couldn't see anything, either. To say I couldn't see anything doesn't mean I didn't recognize the island's position in the ocean, that the island itself existed, that it had bays and valleys, grass and trees growing, and coral reefs. *But I felt I couldn't see anything.* This was probably because I couldn't see any artificial structures which gave off the smell of humanity. Even so I felt I couldn't see anything. (235; emphasis added)

In contrast to his blindness in regard to the islands, the narrator can see his wife. He describes her kimono in detail and notes that her way of wearing it is unusual and seems the "re-enactment of a way of wearing kimono from somewhere else" (235):

> Feeling my wife's unbalanced way of wearing kimono, I thought of the weight surrounding her past. Even if she were wearing something other than kimono, it would reflect the scenery (*fūbutsu*) of the island and make her look beautiful. But another emotion was mixed in with this sense of incongruity (*iwakan*). The clothes she wore clung to my skin. (235–236)

The narrator, then, can "see" the island—its scenery and customs—but only as filtered through the medium of his wife. No matter what she wears, the wife has wrapped herself in the island, and by returning to it the narrator, unable to "see" the island on his own, is likewise enveloped. This "unbalanced" way of wearing kimono, a way foreign to the narrator, makes him feel both the familiar (to Shimao readers) sense of incongruity, but, importantly, also some other emotion as well. It is precisely this tension that energizes "Shima e" and much of Shimao's literature. Simply put, the narrator, like the narrators of "Kawa ni te" and "Haishi," is torn between the knowledge that he does not belong here and the desire to be one with the community of the island. He knows he should not expose himself, sensing nothing will come of it, yet he desires to penetrate to the core of the island, to find out what is hidden from him. In short, he wants to overcome the sense of Otherness he feels both toward the island (and its people) and his wife, who is the embodiment of the island for him. To put on the "clothes" of the island, in a sense, he must first take off his clothes—and expose himself.

Even more than in "Kawa ni te," where the narrator *did* succeed in touching, if only momentarily, the secret hidden core of the village, the narrator in "Shima e" finds the task of penetrating the surface of the island difficult, if not impossible, because he is rebuffed every step of the way. A word repeated so many times in the story, the verb *hajiku* (to repel), begins to take on an incantatory feeling; taken with the narrator's persistent vision problems, the conclusion is clear: he can neither "see" nor penetrate the island. This sense of being repelled by the island is highlighted even before the narrator and his wife actually make landfall. In the first part of the story, as they journey by ship to the island, they pass other islands, each with its own special shape and character, but all sharing a closed, hidden essence. There is an "inner part which is hidden," the narrator remarks of one island, and the life he can glimpse on another is like life seen in a movie:

The life unfolding there had a solid sense of existence like that on a movie screen, and like the brilliant life shown in a movie, which is there for an instant then disappears forever, denied my intervention. The seacoast was artificially hardened by cliffs and stone walls, the sea water pushed up against the cut-out walls, swelling up; the houses were mixed in among these, as if they were one part of the stone walls, and depending on the angle it looked like a fortress, or a floating castle. . . . If you were not born there you couldn't become a resident; the appearance of the houses took the rough edges off my heart, and then I couldn't see them anymore. (238)[79]

The island on which he and his wife make landfall, too, repels outsiders and the outside world. Its relationship with its ocean surroundings is antagonistic: it resists the ocean, cutting it so the ocean, wounded, "turns its white stomach inside out," with the island, too, receiving its "share of the pain" (239). The black limestone along the shore "stubbornly resists" people who attempt to land; as with the island as a whole, this resistance brings on suffering—the waves breaking on the offshore coral form a "halo of suffering" around the island. There must be a "place of rest" (*ansoku no basho*) somewhere on the island, the narrator feels, but it is like a mirage, because as soon as one looks for the spot it disappears. Villages are similar to the ones in "Kawa ni te"—one road goes straight through them and the entrances to the houses are shut tight, "repelling everything from the outside" (239). One cannot see the villagers—no people are visible—but ones feels one is being watched. Coral walls surround the houses, shutting out a view of the inside, but here, unlike the village in "Kawa ni te," there are no alleys to take you deeper into the heart of the place.

One of the more memorable scenes of "Shima e" takes place at a cape the narrator and his wife finally reach. Left alone as his wife goes ahead to check out a bus stop, the narrator undergoes a visual hallucination, described in great detail over several pages. He feels a dizziness and a "ring of light in a vague spot" somewhere between the "inside and the outside of his skull." He becomes aware of problems in seeing; he can see only the ground five to six meters in front of him, beyond which there is nothing:

I was filled with excitement as the thought crossed my mind that I was witnessing an extraordinary, rare phenomenon. I thought that I needed someone to witness this, and hoped that my wife would soon return, but the thought also occurred to me that perhaps my wife wouldn't be good as a witness. Slowly edging forward I feared my feet would collapse and be pulled down toward the void; I stuck my right foot out and tapped my heel on the ground, slowly moving forward. After a certain amount of continued tension, the ring of light inscribed on my eyes disappeared. The objects in the scenery I could perceive now with clear vision were the same as before. *I was able to escape the restrictions of the limited, dark world and could see a solitary expanse. Somehow the conclusive, fearful shadow had passed, and I was standing where the grass of a pasture spread out before me; new grass continued to be created and added on, and I felt like I could hear the merry whistling of the creator.* I thought that since this was a spot unknown on the map it should be marked with a dotted line, and though it was scenery right before my eyes, the sense of distance and size was unsure, and there was nothing to grasp on to. Decisively I stepped forward; I hesitated to put all my weight on it and walk, an exhilaration mixed with some fear held me, and I had to stay put. It was a sight I'd never experienced before, and thus couldn't deal with intellectually. The pain and pleasure after being struck all over with a razor blade remained, and I had a desire to bare my wound in that direction and eagerly await an even stranger phenomenon. (247–248; emphasis added)

Readers of the *Yaponesia* essays will understand the deeper significance of this scene. Again and again in the essays, Shimao remarks on the need to break out of the restricted, limited view of mainland Japan. "A voice keeps telling me to head south," he writes in 1962, "in the direction of the undeveloped periphery" (vol. 14, 76). Combined with the notion we have seen before—of the mainland ethos and culture as "dark" and death-inducing—this scene at the cape is symbolic of the sort of revelation Shimao found on the margins. Light, broad vision, creation—even life—is to be found in the island. "Shima e" highlights these possibilities, as the narrator ecstatically, albeit briefly, "escape[s] the restrictions of [a] limited, dark world."

At a village inn that night, the couple share a room with a young man with whom the narrator discusses the island. The young man tells him that "[t]here is a strong, submerged, conscious energy here. Like a will toward barrenness *(fumō)*. When I discovered that it frightened me. I hate this island" (252–253). Quite suddenly their room is transformed into the setting of a strange ceremony. "Intruders" enter, wearing black poncho-like outfits and beating drums. One man holds out his hands toward the young man, who looks downward docilely, and sprays water over him with his mouth. The ceremony is over as quickly as it began. The young man is revived, full of vitality, and the narrator is left excited yet irritated, feeling "warm" about having witnessed the young man's *dappi*—literally, a shedding of skin as of a snake, with the figurative meaning of a decisive break with something, particularly convention. The young man excitedly discusses the ceremony with the narrator, happily asking him if he noticed how the man performing the ceremony held his hands out toward him. This pose of hands stretched out, the young man explains, has special meaning:

> "That's the important part. It'd be terrible to miss seeing that gesture with his hands. You should keep it in mind. *In an emergency all you have to do is stretch out your hands.* Just imitate that pose. Just doing that has an effect. As long as you know that, you'll be all right."
>
> I looked deeply at his face, but there was no way I could know how his thoughts were organized. But *the image of both hands stretched out was one which drew me in, and the way the earth crumbled at the cape awhile ago came to my eyes.* (256–257; emphasis added)

In the final scenes of "Shima e" this notion of stretching out one's hands toward the island is rewritten into what becomes a favored motif: the narrator searching for his wife. These scenes revolve around three odd steeple-like buildings the narrator sees the next day. His wife becomes friendly with a man who lives in one of the steeples, and takes to visiting him. Meanwhile, the narrator finds himself thinking about the ferry boat that comes every two or three days, and how easy it would be for him just to board it when it comes, leaving the island. "Realizing how the thought occurred to me, everything went black before me, but I didn't know what could be the key to going deeper into the island. I couldn't change the fact that unless I were reborn in the island it was too late" (262). The wife returns from the steeple and her encounter with the man, and excitedly tells the narrator all about him. The man is a foreigner of unspecified nationality; the narrator remembers his skin, seen from a distance as lighter than his own, and imagines his pupils must be "as blue as the sea surrounding the island" (263). "Those somewhat threatened me," he notes:

> There was a sort of world projecting out there which effortlessly had obtained an individuality, a world facing me, beyond my reach, and not coming any closer. Out beyond the barrier reefs, too, the waves, their thoroughly sparkling bodies turning over white, played in the sun, but I could take no part in this. (263)

In the penultimate scene of "Shima e" the wife has gone out in the evening to see the man at the steeple again, while the narrator goes to bed alone. He cannot rid himself of thoughts of his wife, however; he feels desire for her welling up, and sees her smiling face and hears her voice—both as they were in her younger days. He gets out of bed to find her and walks through the village late at night. The scene of the narrator waiting for his wife, who has gone out to see another man, then setting off to roam the town is highly significant in light of what is known of *Shi no toge*. Quite simply, he has taken on her earlier role, and she his.[80] As he walks through the town, the narrator feels how "the village, far behind me now, began to swell up, and I felt it as if it were some unknown, warm, living creature covered with a bag and unable to move. If you tried to push your way in, the outer skin would cave in, but you wouldn't be able to open up the inside" (266). Having just passed through the "womb of the village" *(buraku no tainai)*, the narrator is suddenly afraid, not knowing where he is, or whether he is coming or going. Both the village and the steeple (and the sea surrounding it) reject his efforts to approach, and in typical Shimao fashion the narrator finds himself stuck between two alternatives, helpless and alone. And, as at the cape, he is limited to a small circle of vision, in this case the circle of his flashlight as it lights up a small portion of the deep darkness. "It was," he writes, "like walking through an unknown country" (267). He views his wife through the window of one steeple, apparently playing hide-and-seek with the other man. He enters the steeple and talks with the man, but his wife remains hidden. She eventually emerges, laughing, from her hiding place under a thick pile of clothes in the corner of the room. One recalls the opening of the story—the wife wrapped in a kimono containing the essence of the islands, and the only thing the narrator can "see." Here, wrapping herself again in clothes, the wife ends up hidden.

"Sōsaiki" (1964)

In the 1964 story "Sōsaiki" (literally, a record of a search for my wife), the theme of the wife who slips through the protagonist's grasp paralleling his desire to enter or grasp the island plays an even more crucial role. If the wife in "Shima e," with her game of hide-and-seek, threatens to slip through her husband's grasp, in "Sōsaiki" she eludes him completely, disappearing not once, but twice, in the course of the story.[81] As the title implies, the main action becomes her husband's search for her. Not surprisingly, her disappearances are set against the backdrop of the island of Amami (recognizable through references to *keihan*, a local delicacy); by the end of the story, however, the island is less backdrop than main topic of concern. In short, the narrator's search for his missing wife leads to the realization that it is the island, too, that has eluded him. At the same time, he discovers crucial "gaps in [his] consciousness," the inability to grasp the flow of time. The story, then, consists of a series of the narrator's failures to grasp his wife, the place he is in, and the present moment. In fact, "Sōsaiki" could be read as the antithesis of much of what one normally expects of fiction—a certain mastery over the three basics of time, setting, and character—because the story depicts the main character's continual failure to possess a single one of these elements.

The story is a series of vignettes taking place on a single day, and in each of the scenes one fact is brought home to the narrator—that he is in a place where he does not belong. No longer a short-term visitor to the island, the narrator has shifted to being an island resident. At a school where he has applied for work he is told his services are not needed. On the way back from the school, when he and his wife stop at a roadside fruit seller's stand, he ends up feeling he needs to "run away." At a farmhouse where he finds his wife after her first disappearance, he feels like a "trespasser." On the way home again the road is suddenly full of people. Although physically part of the crowd, the narrator is not a part of the shared experience that has brought them together— a school athletic meet. (Being in the "stream of people" makes him feel in "high spirits," yet a "restlessness" he doesn't fully comprehend drives him to push his way out of the crowd.) Finally, he reaches a bridge, where he stumbles and nearly falls off. The ornamentation on the bridge, which he has not noticed until then, brings the sudden realization that the town he thought he knew is "different" from what he imagined (107). The narrator's relationship with the island, in sum, is one of incongruity, a feeling of being unwanted and out of place, coupled with the exposure of his "knowledge" of the island as false.

At the same time, the narrator finds himself, despite a desire to record and capture certain moments that move him, unable to do so—unable, in a sense, to capture time. On the way back from the school, he and his wife run across a man and woman selling fruit by the roadside. Watching his wife approach the woman, the narrator is struck by the tableau; he detects in it a certain "harmony" he wishes to record and preserve with his camera. The "scene had died," however, before he was able to capture it. "I felt somehow discouraged," he says, "like I'd been trying to do something I shouldn't. I knew that instant was not something that could be captured, yet why did I put my hopes in a later chance, never learning from the repetitions that always end in failure" (98).

Like the harmony in this scene that escapes him as soon as he tries to grasp it, the narrator discovers crucial gaps in his consciousness, moments when continuity is lost, during which important changes take place. The first two occurrences are accompanied by his wife's disappearance. After taking the photos, he and his wife are walking by some storehouses in a village when a "vacant blank" is born in his consciousness and he finds himself unable to "link" the time his consciousness returns with what came before, because in-between there is nothing:

> I intended not to take my eyes off my wife even for a moment, but a vacant gap in my consciousness occurred, and the time when I realized this and my consciousness before this realization wouldn't connect up with each other; what occurred in the interval, I had no idea. And now, in the interval when I was assailed by this, again my wife had vanished somewhere. (98–99)

After he tracks his wife down at a farmhouse, they continue their journey home, the narrator carrying her piggyback style.[82] He carries on a conversation with her, only to turn around and find her gone once again. His hands are still cupped in a circle where he was carrying her, but she is nowhere to be found:

> I looked around for her but couldn't find her. A lightness remained in the sinews of my arms, and I felt like that feeling had been there for some time. Walking with her on my back I should have noticed the sudden lightness. If I'd turned around then, I would have been able to see how it was my wife slipped down, and capture the scene *(genba o tsukamaeru)*. (104–105)

Despite the frustrations of a long, fruitless search that occupy most of the story, "Sōsaiki" ends with the narrator determined to pursue to the full the twin, overlapping objects of his search—his wife, naturally, but also the island itself:

> The shape of this town, which had started to look completely different to me, pushed my life upward *(watakushi no sei o tsukiageru fū da)*. . . . I would go to "Keihan" [a restaurant's name] and if my wife wasn't there, go downtown, and walk the town from one end to the other in search of her. I'd have to check carefully in my brain to make sure I didn't miss a single place. Calmly, calmly. And accurately. (107–108)

The search for his wife and the grasping of the island are tandem pursuits. One ends the story with the conviction, as in none of the others set on the island, that the narrator is taking to heart the advice of the young man in "Shima e" to "stretch out [his] hands" toward the twin objects of his desire. Only by pursuing one will he grasp the other.

In similar fashion, the temporal dislocations, the gaps in consciousness the narrator suffers in "Sōsaiki," are at least partially overcome
at the end of the story. Standing, significantly, on a bridge, he feels
for the first time that "everything was connected with what came before" (107). This is followed by his resolute stance to pursue his wife
and the island. Thus the Shimao protagonist, if only briefly, is afforded
glimpses of a way out of a limited, "dark" vision (cf. "Shima e") and temporal fragmentation—the inability to connect one event to the next described in the *Yaponesia* essays as characteristic of the alienated life of
the mainland. The island holds the promise of reintegrating shattered
senses (space and time), of freedom from the restricted vision and fragmented sense of time that characterize the "poisoned" life of the mainland. Despite the sense of anxiety hovering over these stories (a sense,
one should recall, now read as containing a healthy sign of difference),
one can detect, in fleeting glimpses, a sense of what it would be like to
be one with the island community—to find one's "place" and live an
"integrated" life.

"Keiji no tsutome" (1965)

One formal element in "Keiji no tsutome" linking it with Shimao's fiction that will follow, especially *Hi no utsuroi*, is the protagonist's position, as Shimao's in real life, as head librarian—dispenser of knowledge
of the island to its people and outsiders. The protagonist, supposedly
privy to intimate knowledge of the island, lives in a constant state of in-
decision regarding this knowledge: how much do I know about the island? How can one go about knowing it? As head librarian the narrator
feels a great responsibility to provide as much and as accurate information as he can about the island, its customs, and history. He silently
scolds those on his staff who respond perfunctorily to the public's desire for knowledge (145), yet he begins to question the limits of his own
knowledge. One of his duties is to act as go-between for scholars from
outside the island who come on field trips, and he has decidedly mixed
feelings about their work and approach to the island. A recent symposium was held that, if only he had attended, could have filled gaps in his
knowledge; he is held back, however, by his own ignorance:

> I could just picture myself in front of these researchers, who pretended not
> to know much but really did, absorbed in talking on, all the while knowing
> how superficial my knowledge was. (146)

Knowledge can come, the narrator feels, only from the basic approach of the researchers, that is, walking the island paths and seeking out its villages, yet doubts remain in his mind about their methods. The scholars are able to grasp "academic knowledge" from field trips to villages (one village in particular becomes the focus of the narrator's concern) and discuss it abstractly, whereas the narrator cannot. "I had to admit that I did not have the ability to abstract and grasp the village myself" (149). Yet what he seeks, and what he sees as truly valuable, is less abstract notions borne of sociological surveys, interviews with informants, and the filling in of forms, than the observation of life as it is lived. In contrast to the outside researchers' knowledge of the village in question, he recalls a scene he observed in the same village of children playing in a spring:

> In the village spring just off the road that leads to the tip of the island, girls had gathered to splash in the water. Some of the girls were standing, some crouched down, others sitting with knees pressed together; each with their clothes still on, they scooped up water with buckets and splashed it over themselves, laughing loudly with joy. Their hair and clothes became plastered to their skin, and the soft outlines of their bodies became visible. They couldn't stay still for a second, and stood up, lay down, and just when you thought they'd settled down, two or three would get up and leave, only to be replaced by four or five others who'd come to splash water over themselves and each other. Like the celluloid chips in a kaleidoscope moving from one crystal pattern to the next, in every moment there remained a strange harmony, and an innocent will radiating outward. Finally they all started to remove their clothes, and in an instant were naked, yet their movements never showed signs of ceasing. The high noon sun reflected inside the water drops, swelled up, and danced with joy. The unaffected shouts as the girls splashed water pierced right through my heart. (149–150)

The narrator remains the outside observer, unnoticed by the girls. "I had a strange feeling," he says, "as if I were watching from the sidelines something from long ago." Images of the girls already "grown and married, even dead and placed in the white ruins of the cemetery" rise up in him. The statement echoes the underlying tone of many essays, that is, the sense of loss already in the present, as if what he observes is but a memory of an island lifestyle that is no longer.

As in "Chinkonki," the story that introduced this motif, and the first island story, "Kawa ni te," the most memorable scene in "Keiji no tsutome" involves villagers bathing. Although tension, a sense of being out of place, remains, to the narrator the scene evokes no guilt and fear about his "past" being uncovered; instead, it is a glimpse into the very life he seeks, the community he wants to join. The narrator journeys to a town on an outer island and wanders the streets in search of lodgings. The back streets and alleys, as in so many stories, become a maze in which he can only plunge ahead, uncertain how he entered and how he can get out. Suddenly he encounters an unusual sight:

> On both sides [of the street] there were bathtubs lined up, and naked men in the dim light were bathing, their copper-colored skin hidden. None of the bathtubs had partitions hiding them, and were lined up all in view. . . . [T]he men were all fairly old, sturdily built, their deeply chiseled faces in broad smiles, turning toward me while continuing to talk in loud voices with those beside them. . . . If I went a little farther I might run into the women's tubs. A tension like a shudder ran through my body. If only I could bathe here, I thought (the desire to bathe here welled up in me and was almost too much to suppress), but I was pulled up short by how terrible I would look compared to their coppery skin. And it didn't seem I'd be able to be a part of their rough-hewn, vulgar conversation. (157)

As he walks on, the narrator notices that the water outside the tubs has filled the whole street, rising up to his waist. He recalls having read in a "book on ethnography" about a village like this in which people bathe outdoors and the streets are filled with water, and realizes he has found the place described:

> At that time I couldn't picture it at all, but this is what it must be. A strange pride pierced my body that now, by accident, I had run across this unusual village and experienced that custom. Telling myself to treasure this experience, that I would observe this village even more, I walked on through the water. (158)

In the final scene, the narrator has left the village behind, and finds himself alone:

> I looked down at my feet and saw they were soaked, and some kind of vine was clinging to them. When I pulled off the vine and put it in my mouth, an indescribable sweetness spread out over my tongue. This place had been hoping I would come—the thought struck me like a sudden revelation. The sweetness of the juice of the vine made me remember something. I looked around me. It was dark, but I could make out a gently undulating hill before me, and a spring at the top which gushed forth, the flow making a stream; in the middle of the brook, on the banks, flowers with thick leaves blossomed, strewing about a sour smell. A warmth that was just right wrapped itself around me, the night sky at the hill's ridge line glowed faintly white, and for some reason that gentle undulation brought on tears. I was tired, and laid my

body down on the spot where I stood, the moss a luxurious bed spreading out. I couldn't see any houses or signs of people. A silence like death reigned. (158)

One is tempted to find in this story a summary of Shimao's relationship with, and hopes for, the island. "The villagers bathing" (or, like the girls at the spring, naked and splashing water), one comes to understand, is an archetypal image. Whether Shimao actually observed such scenes, imagined them, or saw them in dreams is beside the point. The island girls, joyous and innocent in a ceaselessly transforming harmony, and the men in the tubs, with their healthy good looks and uninhibited manner, become in Shimao's fictional world a clear set of ideals—ideals of the world of the southern island village that he desires to be a part of, but in which he can never fully participate. The naked bodies of the villagers are just that—the island stripped to its essence. The narrator can observe, hear, and see the sounds and sights of the village and the villagers so in tune with their surroundings, even wade in the water that cleanses them, but he can never be one of them. "Only people of the village could be invited to the banquet," as one essay puts it.[83] Yet as the final scene reveals, in the island the narrator finds a place of rest, an idyllic spot he has been looking for, and which has been waiting for him. Laying his weary body down, he has found his own spring in which to bathe.

From the world of the *byōinki* and *Shi no toge* narrator (for him the outside world is an ever-lurking threat, and he wants to erect walls between himself and others), Shimao has taken the reader to the protagonist of the island stories, who desires not to build walls but to penetrate them—to pass to the heart of the village and the island—and join the wider world around him. The outside world has moved from an object of fear to an object of desire.

Further, one detects a movement south, away from the center and urban society. Yonaha Keiko's penetrating reading of Shimao's early postwar stories captures this succinctly. In her reading of "Yume no naka de no nichijō" (1948), "Tandoku ryokōsha" (1947), and "Kotōmu" (1946), Yonaha examines the Shimao protagonist in terms of the paradigm established in the classic last scene of "Yume no naka" where the protagonist pulls his body inside out, reversing "*omote* and *ura*" (outer and inner realities). This reversal should not be written off as merely a "dream image," she writes; rather, it is a theme found in all of Shimao's literature. Like the protagonist of "Yume no naka" who reverses the *omote* and *ura* of his body, Yonaha argues, Shimao's fictional world depicts the desire of the protagonist, by a reversal of his surroundings, to overturn the *omote-ura* relationship maintained between mainland Japan and the "south." Again one might very well connect this move south with the ex-*tokkōtai* commander's desire to confront his past—his role in the war, the victimizer side of him he has suppressed in the *ura* of his mind (the unconscious).[84] But there is another movement afoot. As Yonaha suggests, there is a point to the protagonist's move south-ward—the desire not just to expose his past, but for the *ura* of Japan, found in the southern islands. The protagonist, she writes, is in search of a "place to find rest," and moreover, to find community.[85]

Afterword

                  ASKED IN 1981 whether he ever planned a sequel to *Shi no toge*, Shimao remarked, "I feel that I wrote about what happened afterward in *Hi no utsuroi*." *Shi no toge* is indeed continued in the 1976 *Hi no utsuroi*, translatable as "The changing [or passing] of the days."[1] The same cast of characters appears—the *tokkōtai* survivor husband/narrator, the wife, who is a former mental patient, the son, and daughter, Maya—now some years after the crisis of the wife's madness, living in Naze City on the island of Amami, the husband the head librarian depicted in "Keiji no tsutome."[2] *Hi no utsuroi* in a sense is also a continuation and extension of the story "Sōsaiki," because as its title suggests, time is a key element here, with the narrator, in his contacts with the island, recovering a sense of "ordinary" time—of connectedness and continuity.

    Hi no utsuroi follows a diary format that, from internal evidence, covers the period of April 1, 1972–March 31, 1973.[3] Based closely on events in Shimao's life, the book fits at best uneasily into existing genres, prompting critics to see it as everything from a *nikkitai shōsetsu* (a novel in diary form) to an avant-garde "anti-novel."[4] Shimao identifies in *Hi no utsuroi*—and even more so in its sequel—his "tendency towards an anti-structure" stance.[5] The problem remains as to how to define "structure" or the lack thereof (Shimao's comments can be taken to mean the intricacies of a connected plot, a "plot for plot's sake" attitude toward fiction), but it is important to note how this diary-cum-novel approach to writing, with its series of often marginally related vignettes held together largely through the framing device of a diary, came to dominate his writing at this time. As Shimao's only other literary production of note during the period consists of two diaries of dreams, it is fair to say that his literature of this entire period 1968–1976 (and considering *Hi no utsuroi*'s sequel, published serially from 1976–1985, even further) can be characterized as diary-like.[6]

Conceived as a sequel to *Shi no toge*, *Hi no utsuroi* is its mirror image.[7] Where *Shi no toge* depicts the struggle of the protagonist to come to terms with his wife's mental breakdown, *Hi no utsuroi* portrays the same cast of characters now dealing with the husband's illness—chronic depression. The husband's and wife's roles have been reversed, with the wife, the recovered madwoman, now taking the lead in attempting to relieve her husband's mental distress. If *Shi no toge* is primarily (although not exclusively) a *byōsaimono*—the story of a sick wife—*Hi no utsuroi* is very much a *byōfumono*—a story of a sick husband. What has been only hinted at in *Shi no toge*—the wife's *yuta*-like restorative powers—come to the fore as the setting shifts to the island. Read together, the two works, while telling stories of terrible suffering, combine to form a wonderful kind of symmetry: in the earlier book the wife is sick on the mainland and her husband attempts to aid her recovery, while in *Hi no utsuroi* he is the one who is ill on her island home.[8] This situation is only to be expected, because just as the wife is "out of place" on the mainland, so too is the husband on the islands. Yet, as one must also expect, for the husband the islands hold out the promise of something more.

In several powerful scenes, culminating in the wife's attempt to drag her husband off to a slaughterhouse to witness the slaughter of pigs, she attempts to bring him face-to-face with the realities of death, and the narrative reaches a climax of sorts after which is depicted his partial physical and mental recovery. That this recovery comes as the family begins to prepare for Easter allows a simple reading of the plot as a religious narrative of resurrection from death, or more accurately, the fear of death. In the text, however, the husband's recovery is linked less with religion than with his growing awareness of, and contact with, the island.

As in *Shi no toge*, dreams play a crucial role in *Hi no utsuroi*. A telegram arrives announcing the death of the husband's relative in his hometown, and the wife recalls her dream of the night before, which now seems prophetic. In the dream this same relative reached out to her with a cold, pale hand like that of someone dead. This dream in turn reminds her of the prophetic dream she had during the war that foresaw her meeting her husband:

Oh, how cold Kiyono's [the dead relative's] hand was, she said. She instinctively tried to brush the hand away and woke up, her cheek twitching as she spoke. The same thing happened in the past. That was less than a month after *Anma* [the wife's mother] died. Then my wife dreamed that at Tifadaki Cape a naval officer she didn't know, tall with large eyes, confessed his love for her. That officer put his hands on her shoulders and said "I love you," she said. And several months after that dream, at the same spot, my wife received the same words and actions from me that she saw in the dream. It was a shock, she said [to hear about the relative's death], and she remembered that dream, a strange feeling. I'd been made to listen to that dream any number of times. *Anma* had gone out to collect shellfish and died in the sea at the entrance to Nominoura inlet. It seems her figure could be seen, *tiru* basket on her back, cane in hand, swaying in the sea. Three times my unit was set to attack, but in the end never set off from the base in Nominoura—all due to *Anma* standing in the inlet as a human sacrifice (*hitobashira*), my wife firmly believed. And the dream in which my wife met me was also *Anma* telling her in advance what was going to happen; my wife couldn't be persuaded otherwise.(37)

As in Miho's dream in *Shi no toge* of *Jū* and *Anma* dead in the hole in the ground, her parents—archetypal spirits of the island—remain guides to the island. Here, however, they have shifted from guides to her recovery to those for her husband, with the implication of her relating this dream being: my mother was a human sacrifice so that you, my husband, could live during the war—so why are you allowing yourself to be paralyzed by depression?

Despite the wife's efforts in the first half of the book, the reader is tempted to see her intervention as a failure, because her husband's depression remains unabated as her role as healer fades in importance. Finally, however, in the closest thing to a climax to which this rambling narrative comes, the reader learns she has not failed, because the husband is put on the road to recovery by a confrontation with the island itself (of which the wife is symbolic). This climactic encounter with the island, too, is prefaced by a dream. In retrospect the prophetic quality of the dream compels the reader to wonder whether the narrator, in his search for the heart of the southern island, has not taken on some of the characteristics of the islanders—specifically the wife's *yuta*-like prophetic powers. In the dream, the narrator finds himself wandering in a southern island village, his body "captured by the strange sort of rhythm" of a melody coming through loudspeakers. The music is not an Okinawan melody, but neither is it like the "wet, meandering melodies

of the mainland." The singer sings in a way "allowed only to natives";
"people from outside are not allowed to participate" (197). Wandering
farther, he finds unlighted houses, with no people in sight, yet he hears
voices. He comes upon a banyan tree with an iron tub set up at its base;
the voices come from inside:

> Voices came from inside that, it seemed. And the wet sound of water splash-
> ing. A man's voice and a little girl's were mixed, probably a father and his
> daughter taking a bath together. What was that single emotion which over-
> flowed inside me? Like nostalgia, with despair mixed in. Oh! This is an Oki-
> nawan village! I thought, unsure of how I understood this. The reason de-
> spair was hidden in there was that *I was nothing more than a passerby. I couldn't
> hold that little girl, inside that bathtub.* I stood still for a while in the darkness,
> listening carefully to all the sounds I could hear coming from there. Fearing
> I might be noticed and driven away by them, I felt an itchiness as countless
> intimate, silent feelers stretched out towards me from the houses hidden in
> the dark—less houses than huts with thatched roofs. Even though I wanted
> to stay still there forever, I was agitated and couldn't relax, and felt like I had
> to leave soon. But I was confused, for I had no idea where else I should go.
> (199; emphasis added)

Bracketing this dream—the imagery of the village bathing so prototypical, it is now known, of the encounter with the exposed essence
of the island the narrator is forever seeking—are other dreams linked
by the motif of rebirth: one a dream of Christ crucified (170), the second a bizarre dream of dead people inside mirrors coming back to life
(209). These elements soon combine in the narrator's real life, as an encounter with the island much like the one in the dream brings about the
transformation he has hoped for—his own rebirth out of the depths of
depression.

The climax of the story—the narrator's momentary but critical
transformation—comes as he prepares for bed one night, the sole guest
in a small inn in an island village—as physically close to the heart of the
village as this book ever takes us. Here "an unexpected phenomenon
occurred. It was completely unexpected" (247). Much like his earlier
dream, he hears, but cannot see, a father next door bathing his children.
"How much I envied that father's position. But it was no doubt true that
he himself was unaware of how happy he was" (247). A short while later
he hears what are presumably the same children in their room working
aloud on their homework:

> In the midst of all this the clear voice of a girl practicing very earnestly a song
> she learned at school. A strange emotion pulled me in as if I remembered

something I'd long forgotten, or rather what I had given up for lost had been revived. I felt like maybe I'd been taken to a place where time had gone backwards some fifty years. The brother and sister practiced their music for a while, then turned to reading aloud from their Japanese textbooks. That was when a completely unexpected phenomenon took place. Something inside me passed through me, pushing something else out, and I found myself returned to a bracing feeling, as when anger dissipates. *What I had been thirsting for all this while—the recovery of the very ordinary, commonplace, everyday.* It is nothing but a commonplace sense of peace of mind *(yasuragi)*, but I had lost it for a long time and had grown weak. I had been irritated, for it was as if this feeling had withdrawn to a corner of some other dimension and could not be recovered. You could even say I had nearly lost hope that I could ever recover it. But an unexpected opportunity had brought it back quite easily. . . . [Y]*ou might say this is a kind of miracle.* (248–249; emphasis added)

Significantly, this feeling of being on the road to recovery is soon followed by his expressed need to ascertain his position as being in the island:

To make sure of my feelings, I looked out at the garden again. What I saw first were the banana, papaya, gum, and phoenix trees. Usually I just don't notice these plants, but I must come to realize [these plants are here] because I am at the edge of the south. *I'm living now on an island way to the south, I have to make sure to tell myself, and tell my heart.* (266; emphasis added)

Such sentiments—the narrator's need to ascertain his being in the island as a way to confirm the feelings of recovery—are underscored in a later scene as, following a brief lecture trip to the mainland (Kagoshima), he boards a ferry back to the island. Feeling he is facing death when setting off toward the mainland, upon returning he feels as if he is "being grabbed from behind by the god of death" (314). The passage at first is puzzling. Why is death behind him, and not in front? Is not death waiting in front of us—in the future? To readers familiar with Shimao's *Yaponesia* ideas, however, the passage makes perfect sense: for the narrator a cure lies in shedding connections with the mainland, with mainland thinking, and penetrating to the heart of the island. This "god of death" lies in front of him when he faces the mainland, behind him when he faces Amami. And, in the context of the entire Shimao saga, readers come to understand that a return to the mainland is a return to a life of fragmentation of time, and alienation from life. In contrast, the only hope to recover what he seeks most—the return of a "normal" sense of the flow of time, of a recovered sense of *hi no utsuroi*, the passing of the days—lies in the island.

To be truly "reborn," the narrator decides, he must cast off the physical and mental baggage that adheres to him and lay himself bare. One by one he strips away connections with the mainland, turning down writing offers and invitations for trips to the mainland. Significantly, what writing he does undertake is the reconstruction of *mukashibanashi* folktales of Tōhoku; memories of his grandmother and cousins in Sōma produce a "warm" feeling of "nostalgia" for what is perhaps the only place he ever really *belonged*. This stripping away of contractual and social relations with the mainland is accompanied by a parallel physical stripping that exposes him to the gaze of the islanders, produces an affinity and empathy between them, and reveals to him the "old island" lying beneath the new.

Finding that his hopes that the week in Kagoshima would lead to some way out of "stagnation," he discovers instead that the "layer of stagnation" has grown. He abandons thoughts of modern medicine helping, and is pulled instead by something more ancient: "I began to think that the treatment left that might cure me is an implausible, primitive method" (317).

The method turns out to be *okyū*, moxa treatment, in which moxa is placed directly against the skin and burned, producing a sensation hovering just at the edge of pain:

> I began to think that I must discard everything that clung to me and begin all over again from the deepest starting point *(soko no shohatsu)*. (317)

The moxa clinic has none of the "brightness" of a modern hospital, but rather an "atmosphere of a dark, hidden room" where one participates in a "secret religious ceremony"; there the other patients look at him "with the undistanced, natural gaze of fellow sufferers—no, rather they might just have removed all defenses." The narrator, in the treatment room open to the gaze of all, strips down and receives his treatment, a "strange feeling of friendship" welling up in him toward the islanders around him (317–318):

> The moxa clinician had all the weird generosity the town showed deep down; mixed in with this was the acceptance and endurance of the patients— all producing an atmosphere which made for a healing power that covered and softened my wounds. Today the number of spots where he applied the moxa increased, reaching down to near my intestines or my bladder. My skin had the burn marks left on it by all these places, but that smell of my own flesh burning made me feel *a slight, tangible sense of being a sacrifice, and that*

might very well have brought about a sense of peace of mind (yasuragi). (323; emphasis added)

The clinic becomes a "place of leave taking" *(ridatsu no basho)* for him, producing feelings of "nostalgia for all the scenery" around him (326).

In *Hi no utsuroi* the whole process of "stripping away" described by the narrator is a symbolic rebirth in the island, a way of shucking off all remnants of the mainland, which is a place of stagnation, fragmentation, alienation, and death. The connection with these final scenes and the archetypal bathing scenes in the island stories becomes clear: baring oneself works both ways, because the bathing scenes reveal not only the essence of the island, but work to strip the narrator as well. He undergoes the "sacrifice" of his bared body, "beginning all over again at the deepest starting point," this "secret religious ceremony" under the gaze of other "sufferers"—all in a "place of leave taking."

The word translated as "leave-taking"—*ridatsu*—is significant. Asked years later what he meant by the title of the first chapter of *Shi no toge*—"Ridatsu"—Shimao came up blank.[9] Now, however, nearing the end of Shimao's literary saga, we can supply the answer. Miho's madness marked the beginning of break, a critical, decisive rupture in Toshio's world that plunges him into a variety of discoveries. Miho's madness, the emergence of the unconscious into the conscious (marked by a stylistic shift in Shimao's writing that mirrors the merging of these two worlds), brings to the surface the margins of postwar Japanese life— that which has been shunted to the side in the course of constructing a dominant identity. These margins include a number of things—women's aspirations, the insane, war responsibility, and, looming largest in Shimao's concerns, Japan's cultural unconscious, the suppressed diversity he discovered in Amami, Okinawa, and the whole southern islands.

I have at times characterized Shimao's writing as that of a wanderer, a person who never discovered his place. If in *Hi no utsuroi* Shimao has depicted the recovery of a sense of time, by the year of his death and his last full-length work, *Zoku Hi no utsuroi* (Hi no utsuroi continued, published as one volume in 1986), Shimao at last was ready to define his place in the cultural unconscious. In the latter book, as the character (now named Toshio) travels to Tōhoku ostensibly to gather material on the poet Miyazawa Kenji, his search becomes equally one for his own origins in the same region. Interspersed with visits to places associated with Miyazawa are visits to (Toshio's) parents' hometown, and memories of childhood days spent there, memories that remain "submerged deep inside my body."[10] Later on Toshio takes his wife to Tōhoku, where they are thinking of moving permanently. Here the book—and arguably much of Shimao's saga—reaches a climax with Toshio's discovery that he was not, as official records of his birth maintain, born in Yokohama, but in his parents' hometown in Tōhoku:

> [I]f I was born in Sōma [and not Yokohama], then I most definitely shoulder its fate, and can declare without hesitation that it is my birthplace. But I had gone all the time up until the present, much more than half my life, without realizing this, and had been floating in a strange world of reprieve. I felt as if my life, built upon a temporary foundation, noisily collapsed beneath me. No—that's not right; it was a temporary illusion which disappeared, and now, able to grasp the real image firmly, *I underwent a kind of great transformation* and found twice as many possibilities open to me.[11]

Thus in a quite offhand fashion Shimao's saga reaches its climax. Having regained a temporal orientation, the Shimao protagonist has at long last situated himself spatially as well, pinpointing and ascertaining where—among the reemergent cultural diversity of Japan—he belongs. Shimao's literature can, and often has, easily fooled readers and critics. The closed-in, often suffocatingly narrow world it depicts veils an important reality: his writing was always a search for greater experience. Shimao may have characterized his own life as a failure to experience, but through his writings he opened up a vision of new possibilities of experience—rediscovering the excluded, recentering that which has remained on the margins. That his acknowledgment of his own place, and the transformation and possibilities inherent in this discovery, came so late in his life may appear to be a great irony. But let us not be fooled here, as well. The "fertile womb" out of which was born his means of expression came precisely in the process of this discovery.

Appendix: Plot Summary of *Shi no toge*

Chapter 1: Ridatsu

CHAPTER I involves approximately the first eight days of the ten months covered by the novel, from the first outbreak of Miho's madness.[1] The chapter title, meaning "separation" or "secession," implies that the sudden crisis in the family—the outbreak of Miho's mental illness—is the beginning of the process whereby Toshio and Miho separate, or "secede," from their former life, so much so that by the end of the novel they are about to enter the mental ward and be cut off from the outside world. The time is the end of summer, and Toshio returns from yet another night outside the home. The crisis, or "transformation," the male protagonist of earlier stories has been fearing and desiring has at long last materialized. He returns home to find the house locked; through the window he sees his ink bottle overturned on his desk. After using a piece of brick to break the glass and enter his home,

> I felt much like a criminal, and a shudder surged upward from the soles of my feet. Dishes lay untouched in the sink, and I knew that the day of judgment had finally come. My body and heart both felt as if they were suspended in midair. I walked from the entranceway through the two- and six-mat rooms and on into my study. As I stood frozen there, I felt as though I were examining the graphic scene of a crime. Ink was spattered on the desk, the tatami and the walls like bloodstains. And my diary, sordidly discarded in the midst of it all.[2]

The image of ink as blood is significant, because not only has his enclave, his study, been invaded by Miho, as in "Ie no naka," but she has attacked the very symbol of his work as writer—his ink, which for a novelist is in a very real sense his lifeblood. The reader is thrown into the midst of what becomes the main action of the remainder of the novel — the relentless interrogations of Toshio by Miho as she becomes the "ultimate lie detector," able to ferret out the slightest deception and prevarication on Toshio's part as she gruelingly forces him to reconstruct his past, in particular his activities with other women. Early on Miho is revealed as a complex personality, a divided self who is brutally, relentlessly cold, yet at the same time warm and affectionate. At one moment she will stare at her husband with the coldest expression imaginable, then turn to beg forgiveness and pledge her love (25–26). As in "Ie no naka," her fits bring on excruciating physical pain, and often the only cure is to plead with Toshio to douse her repeatedly with water and hit her on the head. Her body has numerous bruises and burns she cannot remember getting, which presumably resulted from falls during her fits. She has also had fits in the past that necessitated her being alone (on the banks of the Edogawa River, for instance) for them to subside — what the wife was doing in "Tetsuro ni chikaku." Another aspect of Miho that is highlighted in chapter 1 is her uncanny ability to predict events — what some commentators have called the shamaness side of her. Despite the intensity of the first chapter, which sets the tone for the rest of the novel, there are respites in the Toshio-Miho battle. Fearful that Miho will run away or kill herself the moment he takes his eyes off her, Toshio still finds the time to go alone to the public bath and the movies. And, in the sort of scene Shimao is so skilled at writing, the changing moods of the household are reflected in the words and actions of the children, who often serve to mitigate or soften the intensity of the exchanges between Miho and Toshio. At the end of chapter 1 Maya is playing with her dolls:

> Maya talks to herself when she plays with her dolls. *Daddy's stupid, I don't like my house anymore, I went to another house.* Every time things started up, we sat and talked. We talked about so many things. The first time we'd done so since our marriage. I might have been getting used to this. But it worried me that my wife's dark expression didn't fade at all. The pain she had at working hard to keep up with the housework came through to me, but whenever I drew near her the body odor of the past wafted up and my feelings were severed *(bunri suru).* (25–26)

Yet at times when Miho says she loves him and says, "I'm sorry. Forgive me. I feel so embarrassed for you to see me like this" (25), tears well up in Toshio's eyes and the tension drains from his body. At times like these Maya decides that

"Daddy's not such a bad person" . . . and the two of us burst out laughing.
So I felt that the situation was ever so gradually congealing in a good direction. (26)

The "split" feelings Toshio has as he draws near Miho—the attraction
he feels for her always at odds with something in her that pushes him
away—is the cycle of the centripetal and centrifugal forces tugging the
Shimao protagonist toward and away from the home. Here, however,
they are focused less on the abstraction of the "stagnant" home than on
the concrete figure of his wife. Finally, with Toshio's comment that they
"talked about so many things" in their past they had never discussed before, an element is introduced into the configuration—the past—that
plays a crucial role in the novel.[3]

Chaper 2: Shi no toge

The second chapter begins the day after the first and covers an unspecified number of days. The reader soon learns that the optimism expressed at the end of chapter 1 is unfounded, because Miho's condition
is unchanged. Unlike chapter 1, however, much of the action takes
place outside the home, with Toshio visiting both an editorial office in
search of work and a group of writers with whom he is associated. Anxious to return home, he rushes back to discover Miho gone. He worriedly rides all over Tokyo in search of her, first to her uncle's house,
then to the home of his lover, whom he fears Miho might kill. The
"other woman," unnamed in the novel, appears only twice—here and
in the dramatic confrontation in chapter 10—yet plays a critical role
not only as the immediate cause of Miho's condition, but as the focus of
the cloud of paranoia covering the novel. In this sense the other woman
becomes symbolic of the entire world outside that threatens Toshio and
Miho. Toshio tells the woman he must not see her again, but she clings
to the hope that they can maintain some sort of contact. Toshio rules
out any further meetings or letters, but agrees to send her copies of the
magazines in which his short stories appear. Toshio returns home, as
does Miho, who is determined to leave him for good. Instead, they repeat the three-day ordeal of intense interrogation. Miho reveals having
paid ¥70,000 to a detective to investigate the other woman, an enormous sum considering their circumstances.[4] She maintains that she already knows everything, but just wants Toshio to confirm it, which he
resists; this is a pattern repeated through much of the novel as Miho

insists on digging up the past while Toshio demands that they forget it. Chapter 2 reveals the first evidence of the household's lifestyle change and the gender role reversal that makes this novel so unique in postwar literature. Toshio is the one who cleans the house now, and family life is centered not on the husband's job, but on the wife and children, all of whom must accompany Toshio whenever he goes out. Toshio finds himself "creating a new role" for himself, giving up all his "old habits."

Chapter 2 ends with the first of what becomes a series of fits on Toshio's part, as he runs around the room, banging his head on the *fusuma*, followed by Miho's demand that he put his thumbprint on a "sworn statement" that he will never see the other woman again. Thus by the end of the chapter a pattern of events has developed that is repeated throughout much of the rest of the book: Miho's relentless interrogations, followed by Toshio's own "mad fit" as he reaches the limits of endurance, ending with a "pledge," often written, that Miho demands of him as proof of his good faith.

Chapter 3: Gake no fuchi

"Gake no fuchi" (The cliff's edge) opens with Toshio's statement that he has "learned how to pretend to be mad" as a way to deal with his wife's attacks. As the chapter progresses, however, it seems more likely that his own fits are less pretense than the beginnings of a madness not unlike Miho's; he "pretends" to be mad as a way of keeping Miho's mind distracted from her own problems, yet he soon loses control of his actions. The chapter reveals more about the changed lifestyle of the family, with Toshio sweeping outside and shopping with Miho (for the first time in their marriage), all the while anxious about how to support his family with his writing. He makes a radio broadcast at a friend's studio and hands in a manuscript of a short story—enough to tide them over for the time being but not enough to allay his fears that they will "starve to death" unless he can continue his work as before (78). Miho continues to interrogate him about his diary and again extracts a pledge from him. The chapter is bracketed by desperate calls for help. At the beginning, in the midst of yet another interrogation Toshio cries out, "Tasukete!" (Help!), which Miho interprets as a call to the other woman; at the end of the chapter Toshio runs out of the house to commit suicide, first by attempting to leap into the river and second in front of a train. In this dramatic concluding scene it is Miho who cries out for help, from a passerby, to save her husband from destroying himself. Toshio realizes he cannot kill himself (although he continues to try throughout the rest of the book!) because he is "weak and cowardly" (97). The chapter ends with Miho and Toshio walking back home, Toshio sobbing uncontrollably.

Chapter 4: Hi wa hi ni

"Hi wa hi ni" (Day by day) covers the last few days of December to January 9. Toshio again attempts suicide, this time by hanging, and again Miho pulls him back from the edge of death. The chapter revolves around several menacing letters and telegrams, ostensibly from the other woman, demanding that Toshio "chase Miho out" and stating that she will come to visit their house. In order to escape the woman's visits, the family tries to stay away from home as much as possible, first going to a temple in Narita on New Year's Day, then staying overnight at a friend's house, finally going on a day excursion in Tokyo. The paranoia of Toshio and Miho vis-à-vis the woman and her imminent appearance is contagious, and readers find themselves drawn into what is possibly the most suspenseful section of the novel, anxious and on edge regarding events to come. At the end of the chapter, however, when Miho greets Toshio (who had gone out for five minutes to buy something) with the news that the other woman had come to their house, readers begin to suspect that much of what they have been attributing to the other woman—the letters and telegram—may be partly, or entirely, the work of Miho.[5] As with many Shimao stories, however, the scene is left hanging. Finally Toshio makes the decision to sell their house and move away; he briefly considers Miho's hometown on the "southern island," but decides to go instead to his parents' hometown, Sōma, in Fukushima Prefecture. At the end of the chapter the four of them are on the train to Sōma as Toshio contemplates the scenery, the childhood memories the trip evokes, and what he perceives as the changed nature of Miho's attacks: no longer are they able to communicate their feelings to each other, because Miho now simply talks ceaselessly and is no longer interested in his replies. Following the pattern established, the chapter ends with Miho again extracting a written pledge from Toshio.

Chapter 5: Ryuki

"Ryuki" is an obscure compound meaning "exile," a fitting title to describe the fate of this family who now, with their house up for sale, are teetering on the edge of homelessness. The chapter makes clear, however, that it is not some entirely foreign venue to which they have been exiled, because the ten-day visit to Sōma covered here is, for Toshio, a trip back in time to his childhood, to the closest he can come to finding his roots. Much of the chapter revolves around the overlap of past and present as places and scenery set off memories of childhood, of quarrels with other children, of village festivals, and of the relatives to whom he felt closest—his mother and maternal grandmother. More than in any previous chapter, landscape plays an important role, less as objective background than as a projection of Toshio's feelings. The climax of the chapter depicts yet another suicide attempt by Toshio (this time by hanging himself from a tree), his feelings about death, and his continued failure to die—a failure made more telling by the juxtaposition of this scene with one at his mother's grave. One senses that Toshio's death wish, if it can be called that, is tied in with an unarticulated desire to merge with both these "native" surroundings and to join the ones he loves most who are now themselves in their graves. Economic concerns are again brought to the forefront, with the question of how Toshio can support his family without continuing his writing leading him to apply for a teaching job. He travels alone by train to the prefectural capital to apply for the position's test and is once again drawn into the complex mixture of emotions witnessed so many times before: anxiety at what might happen in his absence coupled with a feeling of liberation at being on the move away from home. Instead of waiting the two weeks before the teacher's exam, Toshio decides abruptly that they should return to Tokyo; the question of whether they will move permanently to Sōma or not is left unresolved. In the final scene of the chapter, the morning of the day they will return to Tokyo, Toshio awakens to find Miho missing, and, fearing she has killed herself on the railroad line, pedals his bicycle furiously over the countryside in search of her. He finds her not by the railroad tracks, but sitting quietly by the river. The chapter ends as they return to their house in Koiwa.

Chapter 6: Hibi no tameshi

With this chapter (literally, the precedent of the days) the narrative begins to slow down. Chapter 5 covers ten days, chapter 6 covers approximately one week, chapter 7 only one day, and chapter 8 one day and part of the next. "Hibi no tameshi" covers the period January 20–26. It is now five months from the beginning of Miho's madness, and with Miho's condition worsening, Toshio decides to have her examined at a hospital. Readers learn in a flashback that Toshio had already consulted with a doctor once—the previous November, when Shin'ichi had scarlet fever. Miho's complaint was insomnia, for which she was given shots, but the symptoms were alleviated only temporarily. Talking to a cousin of theirs who also suffered from insomnia but was cured with sleeping pills, Toshio is encouraged, thinking Miho's troubles may be relieved through similar means. The chapter includes more mad attacks by Miho, including the lament that she will change herself, if only Toshio will tell her what he doesn't like about her. Toshio contemplates moving to the southern island, but will wait until April to see his test results for the teacher's position. The need for money is again highlighted, with Toshio and family visiting a publishing house in Akihabara and the friend B's radio station in search of writing jobs. In the most gruesome scene of the novel Miho again demands that Toshio make a pledge to her, and he decides to sever one finger as proof of his sincerity. They go out to buy a sharp knife, and Miho insists on doing the job herself as Toshio keeps his eyes closed. The reader learns in a later chapter that the finger was not actually cut, but here the result is left entirely ambiguous, and one is at a loss to decide what really occurred. The chapter ends with Toshio and Miho in a frenzy, struggling with each other, Miho attempting to strangle herself and Toshio smashing the *fusuma*. Miho ends up in great pain—from the same stomach ailment in "Ie no naka," but here she claims the pain is the result of pregnancy and demands ¥10,000 from Toshio. (This is the amount she mentions elsewhere that Toshio paid when he hospitalized his lover, presumably for an abortion, and one can assume this is what Miho has in mind for herself.) Hearing this, Toshio gets up to strangle himself, is stopped by Miho and Shin'ichi, and then decides that he's "got to take her to the hospital." The reader is left wondering at this point whether it is not Toshio who needs medical help as much as Miho.

Chapter 7: Hi no chijimari

"Hi no chijimari" (The shortening of the days) is appropriate in that it covers the shortest amount of time—only one day. The action takes place almost entirely in K Hospital, where Toshio has taken Miho for her first thorough psychiatric examination. Toshio again contemplates the changed nature of Miho's madness, as she no longer insists that he answer her questions but instead has become a *katarite*, reciting a litany of questions over and over. The reader notices a change in Toshio as well, one hinted at in the previous chapter, in that he is less anxious when out of her sight than relieved. His thoughts lead him to imagine permanent flight from her and his feelings if she were to kill herself. He decides that their situation is totally without hope. Miho is examined by two doctors, the first one concluding she is deranged and must be hospitalized promptly, the second identifying her illness as schizophrenia and also calling for immediate hospitalization. The diagnosis of schizophrenia, which the doctors tell Toshio is incurable, sends him into despair, and throughout much of the rest of the novel he struggles with the varying diagnoses of doctors who conclude she is, then is not, schizophrenic. Miho accuses Toshio of trying to put her away permanently in a mental ward, a thought that has, indeed, crossed his mind. Yet talking with the doctors Toshio realizes he has "grown used to" their life of madness and has trouble contemplating a life outside it (212). Finally Miho is given electroshock therapy, which puts her out cold for several hours. Gazing at her sleeping face, which he finds beautiful, Toshio contrasts his present relief with his fear of what will happen when she awakens. As much as he fears Miho's renewed attacks, however, he fears even more that the treatment will permanently alter her, putting an end to any communication between them. Back home, however, nothing has changed, as Miho, a sort of "demon," violently throws objects and berates her husband.

Chapter 8: Ko to tomo ni

In "Ko to tomo ni" (With the children) Miho is mostly absent, because she has already been hospitalized. The chapter opens with a remarkable sequence in which Toshio explores the workings of his own consciousness; in doing so he touches on his anxiety that he, himself, is becoming schizophrenic. Much of chapter 8 revolves around Toshio as sole provider for the children and his increasing problems with them. Shin'ichi and Maya fight each other, and Maya throws away her overcoat and continues to prevaricate about her actions. It is clear that their parents' crisis has begun to affect the children in ways Toshio can only begin to understand. The three of them visit Miho in the hospital, where she looks "beautiful" and "listless." Her attacks are far from over, however,

as she berates Toshio again, saying he is trying to get rid of her and contact the other woman. And again there is confusion over what the medical nature of her problem is. One doctor diagnoses her condition not as
schizophrenia but as a "psychogenic reaction," while yet another is convinced she is indeed schizophrenic, but says he would need half a year
of observation to be sure. The chapter ends with Toshio's thoughts
about schizophrenia and the possibility of locking Miho away permanently, and with a mysterious phone call from Miho telling him she is
to be released. Toshio, understandably confused, wants to rush off to
the hospital to learn what is going on.

Chapter 9: Sugikoshi

"Sugikoshi" (Passover) sees Toshio constantly moving from one place
to another, first to the hospital, then to the homes of various friends,
then to a psychiatrist for a private consultation. For much of the chapter (which covers about eight days) he communicates with Miho only by
telephone; it is learned later that her doctor has ordered strict separation from Toshio as part of her treatment. She calls him one day to say
she has escaped from the hospital with another woman. Toshio tells her
to return to the hospital, rushes over to check that she did, and is confronted by the doctor, who is upset that Toshio has visited without per-
mission and thus has upset his treatment schedule. During the long
discussion that follows the doctor tells Toshio that their problem is
less medical and more one of "human relations" between husband and
wife. "You must control her," he urges Toshio. Miho runs away from
the hospital again, this time back to Koiwa. Despite her assurances that
she is fine, the following day she has her usual attack, and Toshio takes
her back to the hospital. Toshio visits four friends and tells one that
he is thinking of quitting writing altogether.[6] Later, he again talks with
the doctor in charge of Miho's case, who tells him the problem is Toshio's ego, and announces that Miho will be released in five to six days.
Meanwhile a nurse in the hospital has advised them to visit a local
shamaness to help cure their problems; after Miho's release they do so,
and perform a ceremony to purify their house. Finally, they visit a psychiatrist in his home, and Miho, as she did the first time she was examined at the hospital, slaps Toshio. He is thrown into despair at this
change in the nature of her symptoms, because unlike before, when she
suppressed her attacks when outsiders were present, she is now prone to

have fits regardless of who else is there. The psychiatrist tells Toshio he will recommend a good psychotherapist for Miho to work with as an outpatient.

Chapter 10: Hi o kakete

In this chapter[7] (which covers about one week) Toshio and his family move from Koiwa to a large house in the town of Sakura, in Chiba Prefecture. The chapter depicts the house and town and discusses the move and the packing involved. After the move Miho continues her successive attacks, takes sleeping medicine to combat insomnia, and makes twice-weekly visits to a hospital for psychotherapy. Toshio cuts his ties with society even more, but finds there is no real escape. He has no sense of the future and can see only "two or three days ahead." Hoping their new life will create a "new past" for them, he takes his family on a Sunday outing to Inba Swamp, a broad expanse of water visible from much of the town. The outing is described in great detail, and for the second time (the first being the scenery in chapter 5) the landscape plays a significant role in the novel. The chapter details more problems with the children, Miho's constant attacks, and Toshio's inability to continue his writing, as well as a visit by Toshio and Miho to the psychiatric ward of D Hospital, where they are finally admitted at the end of the novel, and which is the setting of the *byōinki*. Toshio is troubled by what appears to be a mild case of tuberculosis, for which he is X-rayed while Miho undergoes her session with the doctor. On the way back to Sakura they stop in Koiwa to bid a final farewell to their neighbors and to visit the shamaness again. In Sakura they perform a second ceremony designed to undo the "blockage" making their home impure. The climax of the novel occurs when the "other woman," in only her second appearance in the book, pays a sudden, shocking visit one night, bringing Toshio and Miho *mimaikin* (condolence money for sick people) she claims his writer friends have contributed. In a lengthy and dramatic scene Miho berates the woman for having "destroyed" her home, forces Toshio to slap her, then herself beats her. When the woman attempts to escape, Miho chases her into the garden and wrestles with her, forcing Toshio to hold the woman down. Finally the battle is interrupted by a young tuberculosis patient (sister of the owner of Toshio's and Miho's house, who lives in a separate wing of the house) and soon afterward by the arrival of the police. The chapter ends with the police taking care of the woman and warning Toshio they may have to call him down to the station. Trying to put a good face on the incident in front of Miho, Toshio wants to see it as the "shock" she needs to recover.

Chapter 11: Hikkoshi

"Hikkoshi" (The move) opens with Toshio and Miho being called to the police station, where the police explain the legalities of the situation; Toshio agrees to pay a small sum of money to the woman as compensation, and he and Miho agree to write a formal apology for the incident. However, despite urging by the police, Toshio refuses to see the woman. Much of the remainder of the chapter traces the outcome of the incident, with Toshio and Miho taking a present to one of the police officers involved, and, finally, when they realize they cannot live in Sakura anymore, packing up to move once again. Toshio has decided to hospitalize Miho and is waiting for the most convenient time; in the meantime, they have decided their future lies in Miho's southern island home, where they send most of their belongings and plan to move after her treatment is completed. Several scenes depict their twice-a-week visits for Miho's "free association" therapy, including one scene quite similar to the opening of "Ware fukaki fuchi yori." Toshio, worried about what is to become of them, is severely depressed and has fits of his own. The chapter ends with Miho's relatives helping them pack for their move to her cousin's tiny three-mat apartment in Ikebukuro.

Chapter 12: Nyūin made

"Nyūin made" (To the hospital) is the chapter linking *Shi no toge* with the *byōinki* to form one long saga. The story alternates between the cramped quarters in Ikebukuro, where first Shin'ichi, then Maya, come down with the measles, and the hospital, where Miho continues to undergo psychotherapy. Her doctor plans to hospitalize her, and it becomes merely a matter of a few days before she is admitted. In the meantime Toshio is kept busy taking care of the children, seeing to their luggage, and dealing with what is, in the last few pages, a noticeably deteriorating Miho. Her attacks seldom let up, she wants "revenge" now on the other woman, and Toshio admits that "all the progress I thought we'd made with this illness has now collapsed." At the hospital (as read-

ers already know from the *byōinki*) Miho's treatment will consist of
"sleep treatment," and Toshio looks forward eagerly to the liberation
this will provide him. Before she is hospitalized, however, Miho demands that Toshio retrieve every letter he has ever written to the other
woman; since this would involve visiting her, however, Toshio is hard
put to understand Miho's desire. Miho's condition worsens even more,
and she berates him night and day, refusing to eat. For his part, Toshio
again feels something is "terribly wrong" with himself as well. The story
ends with Toshio going back alone to Ikebukuro to retrieve the bedding
they will need in the hospital (because he will be put in the ward with
her), and his thoughts are the usual complex mix of freedom at the
thought of being apart from her, even for a short time, and anxiety at
the same. In the end he thinks:

> That image of my wife—a woman thrust down into a desolate hell when the
> only man she ever loved betrayed her—gripped my soul and tugged at my
> body, which was about to fly away, refusing to let go. My wife was in a men-
> tal ward, awaiting my return. I could not imagine that I had any other work
> to do than to live together with my wife in that hospital room. . . .
>
> My chest began to pound with anxiety after being separated from my wife
> for even a short time, and I could not relax. I had to see her again, even if it
> meant being caught up in another of her attacks. I felt we might even be able
> to start out on a new life *(atarashii shuppatsu)* if we were in our asylum room
> separated by locked doors from the outside world. Though a dark shadow
> was cast over that hope because I could not think of a way to dissuade my wife
> from trying to get back those letters.[8]

Notes

Introduction

Unless otherwise noted, all Japanese books are published in Tokyo.

1. Shimao Toshio, *Shimao Toshio zenshū* (Collected works of Shimao Toshio, hereafter Collected Works), vol. 13 (Shōbunsha, 1981–1983), 121.

2. Van C. Gessel, *The Sting of Life: Four Contemporary Japanese Novelists* (New York: Columbia University Press, 1989), 31. Besides three of my own articles on Shimao, two published studies of Shimao's works exist in English, the first being Gessel's *The Sting of Life*, which devotes chapter 4 to Shimao; the second is Mark Williams' article, "Life after Death? The Literature of an Undeployed Kamikaze Squadron Leader," *Japan Forum* 4(1) (April 1992): 163–179. In addition, Kathryn Sparling's interpretive commentary in her translation, *"The Sting of Death" and Other Stories by Shimao Toshio* (Ann Arbor: Michigan Papers in Japanese Studies no. 12, 1985), is an important resource. Seven of Shimao's short stories are available in English translation: six in Sparling's book, the seventh, "With Maya" (by Gessel), in *The Shōwa Anthology: Modern Japanese Short Stories*, vol. 1, ed. Van C. Gessel and Tomone Matsumoto (Tokyo: Kodansha International, 1985), 196–217. Another English resource is the extensive chapter on Shimao as a Christian writer in Mark Williams' "Shadows of the Former Self: The Influence of Christianity on Contemporary Japanese Literature," Ph.D. dissertation, University of California at Berkeley, 1991.

3. Morikawa Tatsuya, *Shimao Toshio ron* (Shinbisha, 1965).

4. David Harvey, *The Condition of Postmodernity* (Cambridge and Oxford: Blackwell Publishers, 1989), 47.

5. Ueno Chizuko, Ogura Chikako, and Tomioka Taeko, *Danryū bungakuron* (Chikuma shobō, 1992), 87.

6. For remarks on Shimao's dream stories, see Karatani Kōjin, *Imi to iu yamai* (Kōdansha Bungei Bunko, 1989), 67–108. For remarks on his war literature and Mishima, see Karatani Kōjin, *Kindai Nihon no hihyō: Shōwa hen*

(Fukutake shoten, 1991), 73. Karatani confirmed his assessment of Shimao and Mishima to me in personal conversation, August 1991, in Tokyo.

1. Self Apocalypse: Tales of the *Tokkōtai*

1. The appellation kamikaze, a term never used officially by the Japanese, is based on an alternate reading of *shinpū*, or "divine wind," in the full name *Shinpū Tokubetsu Kōgekitai*, or Divine Wind Special Attack Force. See John W. Dower, *War without Mercy: Race & Power in the Pacific War* (New York: Pantheon Books, 1986), 232, and Ivan Morris, *The Nobility of Failure: Tragic Heroes in the History of Japan* (New York: New American Library, 1975), 289, for discussion of the difference between the readings.

2. Kyoko and Mark Selden, eds., *The Atomic Bomb: Voices from Hiroshima and Nagasaki* (Armonk, N.Y.: M. E. Sharpe, 1989), xxv.

3. Morris, *The Nobility of Failure*, 329. One must temper this observation, however, with another: news of the *tokkōtai* attacks was withheld by the Allies for nearly half a year. Civilians in the United States first heard of them in April 1945 (Dower, *War without Mercy*, 52). One can speculate that Allied leaders were initially fearful that the reaction in the West might have been the one anticipated by the Japanese.

4. Dower, *War without Mercy*, 232. As Dower adds, as the war situation worsened still, a new slogan was devised to further this sense of public identification with the *tokkōtai* and for the citizenry at large to view themselves as a "collective suicide unit." "Ichioku Tokkō, the new slogan went: 'the hundred million as a Special Attack Force.'"

5. Yasuo Kuwahara and Gordon T. Allred, *Kamikaze* (New York: Ballantine Books, 1957), 36, 48.

6. Morris, *The Nobility of Failure*, 310. A similar image of the *tokkōtai* is projected in the Time-Life book series on World War II, especially *The Road to Tokyo* and *Return to the Philippines* (Alexandria, Va.: Time-Life Books, 1980). A typical comment from this uncritical look at the *tokkōtai* says, "Japan tapped its one plentiful resource: thousands of young volunteers, ill-trained but devoted to the Bushido code and ready to lay down their lives for the Emperor and the homeland" (*The Road to Tokyo*, 140).

7. Interestingly, the seeds of Morris' view are already found in the final pages of *Kamikaze*, in which the defeated *tokkōtai* pilots raise their *sake* cups as one proclaims, "We have lost a material war—but spiritually we shall never be vanquished. Let us not lose our spirit of brotherhood and let us never lose the spirit of Japan" (*Kamikaze*, 186).

8. Saburō Ienaga, *The Pacific War 1931–1945* (New York: Pantheon Books, 1978), 184.

9. His chapter, "If Only We Might Fall," is based on the haiku by a *tokkōtai* pilot—"If only we might fall/Like cherry blossoms in the Spring—/So pure and radiant." As Dower notes, "The First Special Attack Forces unit . . . took the name Divine Wind . . . and was divided into four groups whose names all derived from this seventeenth-century poem: 'The Japanese spirit is like mountain cherry blossoms, radiant in the morning sun'" (Dower, *War without Mercy*, 232).

10. Ienaga, *The Pacific War 1931–1945*, 183. A recent Western attempt to find a balance between the various views of the *tokkōtai*—fanatic, victim, hero— is found in Haruko Taya Cook and Theodore F. Cook, *Japan at War: An Oral History* (New York: The New Press, 1992). Two interviews with survivors of the *kaiten* corps (*kaiten* are manned torpedoes) present first the image of selfish devotion and strong camaraderie among the *kaiten* pilots, and second a story of the deception played on "volunteers" to hide from them the realities of the *kaiten* until it was too late for them to back out (306–319).

11. Several of these weapons, including frogmen, bomb-laden motorboats (both manned and unmanned—in the latter the pilot would jump overboard before impact), and small submarines, had been developed earlier by the Italian special assault teams and used with some success in battles against the British in the Mediterranean. (See the Time-Life World War II series book *The Mediterranean*, 116–129.) Along with a full-scale *kaiten* (featured prominently in Kōno Taeko's short story "Tetsu no uo"—trans., "Iron Fish"), the war museum next to Yasukuni Shrine in Tokyo contains one painting depicting the *shinyō* in action. Typical of wartime paintings, it shows the *shinyō* in heroic, wave-pounding glory, cutting through the sea in much the way Shimao originally imagined them. Several full-scale *shinyō* models were constructed for the 1989 movie *Shi no toge*, shot partly on location in Kakeromajima. One such *shinyō* is now prominently displayed outside a government office in Koniya, across the channel from Kakeromajima.

12. The information on the *shinyō* and other weapons is taken from Shimao Toshio, *Uchi ni mukau tabi: Shimao Toshio taidanshū* (Tairyūsha, 1976), 217–218. The estimates are probably overly high, but they give some indication of the relative effectiveness, or lack thereof, of the various *tokkōtai* weapons. See Cook and Cook, *Japan at War*, 317, for a discussion on the number of effective *kaiten* raids and losses. Shimao mentions another weapon, a *shinyō*-like boat called the "Maru-re," which was an army weapon, not a navy one. Rather than an attached explosive charge, the Maru-re had two depth charges on board. (See Shimao Toshio and Yoshida Mitsuru, *Tokkō taiken to sengo* [Chūkō Bunko, 1981], 69.)

13. Shimao Toshio, *Gyoraitei gakusei* (Shinchō Bunko, 1985), 99.

14. In addition to the very real danger that their wake would be spotted by enemy planes either during the day or at night, Shimao mentions the possibil-

ity that the *shinyō*, battered by rough seas, might self-destruct or explode long before reaching the battlefront (*Uchi ni mukau tabi*, 243).

15. These stories include: "Hamabe no uta" (1946), "Kotōmu" (1946), "Nikutai to kikan" (1947), "Shima no hate" (1948), "Tokunoshima kōkaiki" (1948), "Asufuaruto to kumo no kora" (1949), "Rongu rongu agou" (1949), "Shutsu kotōki" (1949), "Sotetsujima no jifu" (1950), "Yoru no nioi" (1952), "Asa kage" (1952), "Ritō no atari" (1953), "Tatakai e no osore" (1955), "Hoshi kuzu no shita de" (1955), "Haishi" (1962), "Shuppatsu wa tsui ni otozurezu" (1962), "Sono natsu no ima wa" (1967), and "(Fukuin) Kuni yaburete" (1986). In addition, see Shimao's full-length works *Gyoraitei gakusei* (1985) and *Shinyō hasshin* (1987).

16. Yoshimoto Takaaki, *Yoshimoto Takaaki zen chosakushū 9: Sakkaron: Shimao Toshio* (Keiso shobō, 1975), 51; Okuno Takeo, *Shimao Toshio* (Tairyūsha, 1977), 146. I discuss some of the dream-like or surrealistic stories involving the war in chapter 2.

17. Although composed over a nearly forty-year span, it seems clear that the four stories discussed here were meant to form one complete narrative. Thus I have labeled them a novel. In the collection of war literature by various writers, titled *Shōwa sensō bungaku zenshū* (Shūeisha, 1965), for instance, the stories "Shutsu kotōki" and "Shuppatsu wa tsui ni otozurezeu" are combined into one story, with the title of the first given to the whole. The lover's name, given as N in the original version of "Shutsu kotōki" and Toë in "Shuppatsu wa tsui ni otozurezu," is given as Toë throughout this combined version. (See Okuno, *Shimao Toshio*, 194–195, for a discussion of these points.) While most other works are arranged in chronological order of publication, in the final Collected Works the three stories "Shutsu kotōki," "Shuppatsu wa tsui ni otozurezu," and "Sono natsu no ima wa" are put together at the end of volume 6—a clear indication that Shimao meant them to be read as a whole. Interestingly, however, the lover's name in "Shutsu kotōki" has been changed back to the original N.

18. Yoshimoto notes similarities between this title and that of the biblical "Exodus"—in Japanese "Shutsu Ejiputo ki" (literally, record of leaving Egypt)—and speculates on what Shimao may have drawn from the biblical story. Yoshimoto, *Zen chosakushū 9*, 64–65. Williams translates it as "Exodus from the Solitary Island" ("Shadows of the Former Self," 153).

19. The time of composition accords well with Shimao's often desultory pace of composition. *Zoku Hi no usturoi*, a diary-cum-novel covering six months, took over seven years to complete, while *Shi no toge*, covering nine months in his life, took over sixteen years to finish. Shimao spoke often of his "anti-structure," "anti-*monogatari*" (tale) bias, and this leisurely, open-ended approach to writing, evincing little concern for closure, marks much of his oeuvre.

20. Yoshimoto, *Zen chosakushū* 9, 84.

21. More precisely, however, only in 1962 is Shimao able—in a *realistic* mode—to write of these events, because earlier, in the 1949 "Asufuaruto to kumo no kora" (Asphalt and the baby spiders), he already dealt with the moment of surrender in inimitable, dreamlike fashion. (See the discussion of this story in chapter 2.) It is interesting to note that the first chapter of the novel, "Shutsu kotōki," although winning a major literary award in 1949, was never anthologized until Shimao's first edition of collected works in 1962. One must conclude that Shimao's reluctance to anthologize the story is evidence of how the author viewed the story as incomplete.

22. Although the island lover is called only N in "Shutsu kotōki," her name is Toë in the second and third stories. See note 17 above.

23. Sparling, *"The Sting of Death,"* 51.

24. Ibid., 41.

25. Ibid., 56.

26. Shimao mentions this term in an interview with Okuno Takeo in *Uchi ni mukau tabi*, 86. Ōe Kenzaburō analyzes the term in more detail in his article, "Shimao Toshio 'kuzure' ni tsuite," *Gunzō* (September 1972): 216–227. For Shimao's remarks on war see the interview with Tsuka Kōhei in *Subaru* 8(4) (April 1986): especially 262–263.

27. Yoshimoto, interpretive commentary *(kaisetsu)* in Shimao Toshio, *Sono natsu no ima wa/Yume no naka de no nichijō* (Kōdansha Bungei bunko), 281–282.

28. Ōe, "Shimao Toshio 'kuzure' ni tsuite."

29. Shimao Toshio, *Yume no keiretsu* (Chūō Daigaku shuppanbu, 1971), 222.

30. Ibid., 223.

31. All page references to Shimao's war novel given in the text are from the Collected Works, vol. 6.

32. Karatani, *Kindai Nihon no hihyō*, 77. The word *kokkei*—comical or ridiculous—is one that is also scattered throughout the text.

33. It also revives images of an earlier event—the explosion of the firing charge on one of the boats that fortunately did not set off the main charge.

34. One critic refers to this as "seeing the Other as scenery" *(fūkei to shite no tasha)*. See *Kanshō Nihon gendai bungaku, vol. 29: Shimao Toshio/Shōno Junzō*, ed. Sukekawa Tokuchika (Kadokawa shoten, 1983), 88.

35. Linguistically, this is reflected in Shimao's writing style. As scholars have noted, the novel is filled with an abundance of verbal negatives, all of which gives the novel a sense of constant denial. See Sukekawa, *Kanshō Nihon gendai bungaku*, 87, for a discussion of Shimao's grammar. Shimao's prose is characterized as containing an unusually high number of "negative auxiliary verbs," with "Shuppatsu wa tsui ni otozurezu" having an extraordinarily high number.

36. Naoki Sakai, "Return to the West/Return to the East: Watsuji Tetsuro's

Anthropology and Discussions of Authenticity," *Boundary 2* 18(3) (Fall 1991): 187. Sakai writes, "The history of modern Japan is nothing but a history in which a national community was formed as the community of 'unnatural' death."

37. Oda Makoto, "The Ethics of Peace," in *Authority and the Individual in Japan: Citizen Protest in Historical Perspective*, ed. J. Victor Koschmann (University of Tokyo Press, 1978), 154–170.

38. One can argue, of course, that Private Tamura, in his mindless murder of a Philippine woman, is as much victimizer as victim. The tenor of the novel, however, in its exploration of his descent into madness and cannibalism, is one of victimization of this ordinary, although apparently well educated, lowly private.

39. See, for instance, Okuno's discussion with Shimao of this point in *Uchi ni mukau tabi*, 57–58.

40. Shimao Miho discusses this in a joint interview with her husband in *Uchi ni mukau tabi*, 229.

41. "Ryūkyūkō no kyūinteki miryoku," in Collected Works, vol. 17, 295. Kinjo Shigeaki, the survivor of the Tokashiki mass suicide quoted below says much the same, noting that, after surviving the massacre and discovering the Japanese military unharmed, "Our sense of unity with the military—dissolved completely afterwards. Now, the Japanese more than the Americans became the object of our fears" (Cook and Cook, *Japan at War*, 366).

42. Ota Masahide, "War Memories Die Hard in Okinawa," *Japan Quarterly* 34(4) (January–March 1988): 10–11.

43. Cook and Cook, *Japan at War*, 364.

44. Ibid., 366.

45. Iwaya Seishō, *Shimao Toshio ron* (Kindai bungeisha, 1982), 141–142.

46. Shimao, Collected Works, vol. 17, 229.

47. Ibid. The essay "Ryūkyūkō no kanju" discusses the trenches the villagers built and how they were planning not to kill themselves, but to have the remaining troops blow them up. See Shimao, *Nanpū no sasoi* (Tairyusha, 1978), 114.

48. Sparling, *"The Sting of Death,"* 181; emphasis added.

49. For discussion of this point, see Yokoyama Nobuyuki, "Shimao Toshio 'Shi no toge' to sensō," *Kindai bungaku shiron* (June 11, 1973): 53.

50. Ōe makes a similar point in "Shimao Toshio 'kuzure' ni tsuite," 216–227.

51. All page references to this story are from the translation in Sparling.

52. In the 1967 story "Shuppatsu wa tsui ni otozurezu," the lieutenant sleeps with his sword beside him, the implication being that after the surrender he must protect himself against his *own men*, not the enemy (Collected Works, vol. 6, 331).

53. Collected Works, vol. 6, 330; emphasis added.

54. Sparling, *"The Sting of Death,"* 49. And thus he feels a "phony." One key word picked up on by many commentators to describe the early postwar Shimao protagonist is indeed this very word—phony *(nisemono).* See also the title of Shimao's only *kakioroshi* novel (one published first in a single volume, not in serialized installments), *Nisemono gakusei* (The phony student, 1950).

55. This is particularly the case with "Hamabe no uta," which seems to have been deliberately written so a child could understand it. The reader realizes how simple the style is when the child's (Keko) letter appears in the text; its childish vocabulary and syntax do not stand out much from the rest of the text.

56. The 1949 story "Rongu rongu agou" (Long, long, ago), not covered here, fits quite well into this "pastoral" group by its very title and the use of the song from which this is taken, all of which produces a sense of narrational distancing.

57. Kawamura Sō, interpretive commentary in Shimao, *Hamabe no uta/Rongu rongu agou* (Kōdansha Bungei Bunko, 1992), 303–306.

58. The story is dedicated to "Iwai Keiko [the little girl in the story] and her teacher," the real-life Shimao Miho. Shimao Miho recalls the circumstances behind the composition of this story, which she classifies as a *dōwa,* or children's story, and her receiving it ("I received it from Commander Shimao on a beautiful moonlit night in May, 1945") in "Ai no ōfuku shokan," *Marie Claire* 97 (December 1990): 192.

59. Nineteen sixty-two, of course, is the year he completed "Shuppatsu wa tsui ni otozurezu," and, some would contend, finally confronted the events of the surrender, war responsibility, etc. "Hamabe no uta," however, was included in Shimao's final Collected Works. The editing principle for this edition was to include every published piece—fiction and non-fiction—Shimao had ever published.

60. Page references for "Hamabe no uta" are from *Hamabe no uta/Rongu rongu agou,* 7–28.

61. Sparling, *"The Sting of Death,"* 6. All translations from this story (unless noted otherwise) are from Sparling.

62. Ibid., 6.

63. Ibid., 11.

64. Sparling's excellent discussion of Toë as shamaness raises the question of the distinction between *noro* and the *yuta.* The former are the "priestesses of hereditary nobility" Sparling refers to, while *yuta* is the term generally used to refer to people (most often, but not always, middle-aged women) struck by the "*yuta* spirit" who, it is believed, possess certain shamanistic powers. In my discussion of *Shi no toge* and other works, I do not strictly distinguish between the two terms. As I conclude in chapter 3, I believe the wife in Shimao's *byōsaimono* is depicted as a kind of hereditary shamaness; as the term *yuta* is used to describe her in most critical literature, I follow this in my own discussion.

65. Sparling, *"The Sting of Death,"* 151.

66. Ibid.

67. Ibid., 6.

68. Text references for "Yoru no nioi" are from the Collected Works, vol. 3.

69. This is a technique Shimao used sparingly. See several sections of *Shi no toge* and the stories "Kisōsha no yūutsu" and "Hoshi kuzu no shita de."

70. Indeed, as Kiji gazes at the "dull, dark skin" of Rie, he suddenly recalls his subordinate and the man's island lover, and what happened to them (379).

71. The book was winner, for chapter 4, of the Kawabata Prize for Literature (1983), and as a whole of the Noma Arts Prize (1985).

72. Here I refer only to the best-known chapter, "Wannai no irie de" (Inlet in the bay), for which Shimao won the Kawabata Prize.

73. Page references for "Tatakai e no osore" and "Hoshi kuzu no shita de" are from the Collected Works, vol. 5; page references for "Sotestsujima no jifu" are from vol. 3.

74. Shimao and Yoshida, *Tokkō taiken to sengo*, 81.

75. It is listed as incomplete, and as such was excluded from Shimao's first (1962) collected works edition.

76. Alan S. Christy, "The Making of Imperial Subjects in Okinawa," *positions* 1(3) (Winter 1993): 611. As Christy notes, Okinawans knew enough to boil the fruit to extract the poison. Okinawa, he also writes, was known as "sotetsu hell" to prewar Japanese visitors. Shimao's use of *sotetsu* as the slipcover decoration on his Collected Works can be seen as yet another of his determined reversals of the standard tropes by which Okinawa and the Okinawans were known in prewar times. For more on this, see chapter 4.

77. Shimao, *Yume no keiretsu*, 255.

2. Dreams and the Alphabet of Trauma

1. Tsuge Teruhiko, "Shimao Toshio no hōhō," *Genten* 2 (Fall 1983): 77. Tsuge lists "Shima no hate" as one of these dream stories, although it is usually classified as a war story. Although there is general agreement as to which stories belong in the "dream story" grouping, clearly some disagreement exists. Only one of Shimao's dream stories has been translated into English—"Yume no naka de no nichijō," translated as "Everyday Life in a Dream," in Kathryn Sparling's *"The Sting of Death" and Other Stories by Shimao Toshio*, 57–70.

2. Okuno Takeo, *Shimao Toshio*, 218. Okuno contrasts early Shimao dream stories with his series of *byōsaimono* begun in 1955. Okuno sees the latter as a literary "retreat" from experimental fiction into mainstream I-novels *(shishōsetsu)*; one could argue, however, that the dream stories, linked fragments of actual dreams, as records of a single consciousness, are the epitome of the I-novel.

3. The term "writer's writer" is borrowed from Sparling, *"The Sting of*

Death," 1. One former colleague of Shimao's at the Kagoshima Prefectural Library branch in Amami related to me Shimao's anger at being told that his works were "difficult" (personal conversation, Naze City, December 1990).

4. The question of which literary "group" to place Shimao in—the *Sengoha* (Postwar writers) such as Abe and Mishima, or the *Daisan no shinjin*—is a fairly contentious one. Morikawa Tatsuya, for instance, rejects the notion that Shimao, despite his close friendship and working relationship with the *Daisan no shinjin* writers, belongs with that group (personal conversation, Tokyo, spring 1990).

5. Tom Wolfe, "Stalking the Billion-Footed Beast," *Harper's Magazine*, November 1989, 53.

6. Shimao Toshio, *Uchi ni mukau tabi: Shimao Toshio taidanshū*, 289.

7. Martin Greenberg, "Art and Dreams," in *Franz Kafka*, ed. Harold Bloom (New York: Chelsea House Publishers, 1986), 66.

8. *Kanshō Nihon gendai bungaku, vol. 29: Shimao Toshio/Shōno Junzō*, ed. Sukekawa Tokuchika, 44–45.

9. Greenberg, "Art and Dreams," 64.

10. Critics have discussed Shimao as falling into a "daydream" in which the unconscious is more accessible as prerequisite for his method of composition. See Shimizu Tetsu's commentary in Shimao Toshio, *Yume no naka de no nichijō* (Shūeisha Bunko, 1979), 254–255. For Shimao's own comments on his methods see *Uchi ni mukau tabi*, 289.

11. Shimao Toshio, *Zoku Hi no utsuroi* (Chūkō Bunko, 1989), 484.

12. It is not known if Shimao had read this Kafka story before writing his own story, although it seems clear he had read parts of "The Trial" before writing "Yume no naka de no nichijō." (See Sukekawa, *Kanshō Nihon gendai bungaku*, 44.) For an interesting comparison of Shimao's writing and that of Kafka, see Tachibana Kengo, "Shimao Toshio no Kafuka juyō," *Fukuoka Daigaku Jinbun ronsō* 16(2) (November 1984): 969–993.

13. "Freudian cartoon" is Greenberg's phrase, "Art and Dreams," 71.

14. Ibid., 70.

15. "Yume to tabi nado," lecture at Kwassui Women's College, Nagasaki, Japan, November 11, 1982.

16. Shimao, "Yume to watakushi," in *Sugi yuku toki no naka de* (Shinchōsha, 1983), 68–69.

17. "Yume to tabi nado."

18. Shimao, "Yume to watakushi," 66.

19. Shimao, *Uchi ni mukau tabi*, 290–292.

20. Shimao, "Yume to watakushi," 74.

21. Shimao, Collected Works, vol. 2, 74.

22. Kawamura Sō, commentary in Shimao, *Hamabe no uta/Rongu rongu agou*, 303–306.

23. Okuno refers to Shimao as the "most avant-garde writer in Japan" for his use of a "surrealistic style" in such works as "Yume no naka de no nichijō" (Okuno, *Shimao Toshio*, 174). The quote about the nightmarish quality comes from *Introduction to Contemporary Japanese Literature: Synopses of Major Works 1956–1970*, ed. Kokusai Bunka Shinkōkai (University of Tokyo Press, 1972), 321. The interpretation of connections between Shimao's prose and the *shutai-sei* debate comes from Tsuge, "Shimao Toshio no hōhō," 74–75. Some critics, such as Shimizu, see the constant transformation inherent in the stories making "meaningless" the attempt to construct a "story" from them; see Shimao, *Yume no naka de no nichijō*, 258.

24. Okuno's attempt to deal with these stories in terms of a "literature of the victim" is a possible exception, although as I discuss below it engages only part of Shimao's project, ignoring the victimizer side (see Okuno, *Shimao Toshio*, 9–23). A more definite exception to the silence on war trauma is Mark Williams' article, "Life after Death? The Literature of an Undeployed Kamikaze Squadron Leader."

25. Elaine Showalter, *The Female Malady: Women, Madness, and English Culture, 1830–1980* (New York: Penguin Books, 1987), 170.

26. Ibid., 172.

27. One notes, for instance, the recurrence of condoms in Shimao's work (e.g., "Yume no naka de no nichijō" and "Kizashi") and how the narrator rejects them. Being impotent, one takes it, he has no need of them.

28. Showalter, *The Female Malady*, 172–173.

29. Kali Tal, "Speaking the Language of Pain: Vietnam War Literature in the Context of a Literature of Trauma," in *Fourteen Landing Zones: Approaches to Vietnam War Literature*, ed. Philip K. Jason (Iowa City: University of Iowa Press, 1991), 226.

30. Ibid., 227.

31. Ibid., 224.

32. Ibid., 224.

33. As mentioned above, Shimao's literature as that of a victim is discussed in Okuno, *Shimao Toshio*, 923. The discussion on records of war experience is from Oda Makoto, "The Ethics of Peace," in *Authority and the Individual in Japan: Citizen Protest in Historical Perspective*, 154.

34. Michael Gallagher, the translator of *Umi to dokuyaku*, says in his introduction that "Endo is the only major Japanese novelist who . . . has confronted the problem of individual responsibility in wartime." Shusaku Endo, *The Sea and Poison* (New York: New Directions Books, 1992), 7.

35. Page references to these stories are from the following editions, and are given within the text: "Kotōmu," from *Sono natsu no ima wa/Yume no naka de no nichijō* (Kōdansha Bungei Bunko, 1988), 175–184; "Matenrō" and "Sekizō aru-

kidasu," from the Collected Works, vol. 2, 74–82 and 55–63, respectively; and "Asufuaruto to kumo no kora," from *Shima no hate* (Shūeisha Bunko, 1978), 112–131. Page references to "Yume no naka de no nichijō" are from Sparling's translation.

36. The notion of structures, especially mysterious and inexplicable ones, dominating the dream stories is discussed by Okuno in *Shimao Toshio*, 195. The 1963 story Okuno discusses, "Kataku na konnichi," opens with a description of construction and a makeshift bridge the narrator and others must cross. Okuno sees this as symbolic of the alienated and unstable situation of contemporary Japanese.

37. Shimizu likens the stories to cinematic fade-in/out and montage effects (Shimao, *Yume no naka de no nichijō*, 258).

38. "Kotōmu" in its opening line reveals itself to be a dream: *"Yume no naka de wa . . ."* (In a dream . . .); "Matenrō" does this through its "eyes closed" opening lines and later references to dreams.

39. Okuno sees the story as linked to the later war story, "Tokunoshima kōkaiki" (1948) (Okuno, *Shimao Toshio*, 137). The basic outline is similar, namely the journey to a nearby island during the war.

40. In the 1952 dream story "Kizashi," discussed later in this chapter, the *tokkōtai* torpedo boat—in this case more a torpedo than a boat—does not launch itself into the water as it is intended to do, but unexpectedly transforms into a kind of drilling machine, boring down deep into the ground.

41. See Collected Works, vol. 16, 15, for a discussion of how Amami islanders manipulated this phenomenon of names for the purpose of passing as mainland Japanese. I discuss this in chapter 4.

42. The sense of superiority and pride that continues to vie with fear and despair throughout the story comes to a head when the narrator considers naming the island after himself (182).

43. Shimao refers to this in a variety of ways, although never, as far as I can ascertain, actually using the word "unconscious." (The closest he comes is when he writes of a Japan slipping up from below unconsciousness [*ishiki shita*]. See Collected Works, vol. 17, 122.) The Ryukyus contain something from "far off memory" and a kind of "deep, hidden expression" that mainland Japanese can call up to the surface only in drunkenness or the ecstasies of the *matsuri*. (Shimao, "Yaponesia no nekko," Collected Works, vol. 16, 192.) Later he writes of the possibilities of unearthing a "shared memory," the notion of a shared racial memory that lies closer to the surface in the southern islands (see Collected Works, vol. 17, 296).

44. For an excellent discussion of the doppelgänger motif in postwar fiction, including its use in Shimao's fiction, see Van C. Gessel, "The Voice of the Doppelgänger," *Japan Quarterly* 38(2) (April–June 1991): 198–213.

45. See *Shinyō hasshin* (Shiode shuppan, 1986); "(Fukuin) Kuni yaburete" appeared in *Gunzō* (42)(1) (January 1987): 248–255. This edition of *Gunzō* is one of a number of memorial editions dedicated to Shimao.

46. See Takeda Tomojū, "'Shi no toge' de purofuindesu—Shimao Toshio ron," *Mita Bungaku* (63)(4) (April 1976): 28–44.

47. Besides a variety of essays, both "Tandoku ryokōsha" and "Yume no naka de no nichijō" are partially set in a city based on Nagasaki, as is the 1950 novel *Nise gakusei*.

48. Okuno, *Shimao Toshio*, 264.

49. Collected Works, vol. 6, 240.

50. For Shimao's comments on this sort of erasure as stylistic choice, see his extended interview with Ogawa Kunio, *Yume to genjitsu—rokkakan no taidan* (Chikuma Shobō, 1976), especially 189–190.

51. Shimizu, in *Yume no naka de nichijō*, 260.

52. Tal, "Speaking the Language of Pain," 232.

53. Tsuge, "Shimao Toshio no hōhō," 61.

54. Haniya Yutaka is quoted in Tanaka Masato, "Shimao Toshio Matenrō," in *Shimao Toshio kenkyū*, ed. Aeba Takeo (Tōjusha, 1976), 318. For more on "Matenrō," see this article and the interview with Shimao, "Yume no naka de no nichijō—'Matenrō' o megutte," in *Uchi ni mukau tabi*, 283–314.

55. "Sekizō arukidasu" was originally titled "Muchū shigai," translatable as "Streets of dreams," a title usurped somewhat by the story the following year, "Yume no naka de no nichijō."

56. Tsuge, "Shimao Toshio no hōhō," 80.

57. One notes a similar buildup of tension in other stories, with a simple event or image escalating to catastrophic proportions. In "Oni hage" (1953), for instance, the protagonist is urinated on, the urine turning to rain and, finally, a flood.

58. Yonaha Keiko, "'Yaponesia ron' no sobyō," *Genten* 2 (Fall 1983): 71. Yonaha also points out that in linking the *tokkōtai* defender of the southern islands to the defender of the north, Shimao is making an early symbolic connection that later became one of the main thrusts of his *Yaponesia* writings, namely the links he saw between Tōhoku and Amami.

59. Okuno, *Shimao Toshio*, 137.

60. Sparling, *"The Sting of Death,"* 70.

61. Ibid., 57.

62. The critic, whose allegorical reading I borrow, is Katsumata Osamu in "Sei ni tachimoru michi: Shimao Toshio ron," *Gunzō* (October 1978): 192–210; see especially 198–200.

63. Sparling, *"The Sting of Death,"* 66.

64. Sukekawa, *Kanshō Nihon gendai bungaku*, 50–51.

65. Ibid., 46–47.

66. Kōno Kensuke, "Shimao Toshio/Yume no naka de no nichijō," *Kokubungaku* (33)(4) (March 1988): 47.

67. Sparling, *"The Sting of Death,"* 154–155.

68. Ibid., 69.

69. Kōno, "Shimao Toshio," 47.

70. Sparling, *"The Sting of Death,"* 63–64.

71. Ibid., 66.

72. See, for instance, the 1953 essay "Tobi koenakereba," in which Shimao, discussing his writings up until then, sums them up as the "books of one who failed to die" *(misui no shisha no hon)* (Collected Works, vol. 13, 122).

73. Yonaha Keiko, "Ura to omote no gyakuten—Shimao Toshio shoki sakuhin no shudai," *Shin Okinawa bungaku* 71 (Spring 1987): 72.

74. Juliet Flower MacCannell, *Figuring Lacan: Criticism and the Cultural Unconscious* (Lincoln: University of Nebraska Press, 1986), 9. My use of Lacanian ideas is taken from MacCannell.

75. Sukekawa, *Kanshō Nihon gendai bungaku*, 153–154 (a discussion of Yoshimoto Takaaki's ideas). See also Yoshimoto, *Zen chosakushū* 9, 128.

76. The story was collected in the dream story collections *Yume no naka de no nichijō* (1956) and *Yume no keiretsu* (1971), and in the 1974 war story collection *Shutsu kotōki—Shimao Toshio sensō shōsetsushū* (Shimao Toshio war story collection). Shūeisha's three 1978–1979 paperback collections of Shimao's stories are divided into one volume each of war stories ("Shima no hate"), dream stories ("Yume no naka de no nichijō"), and *byōsaimono* ("Ware fukaki fuchi yori"). "Asufuaruto to kumo no kora" is in the war story volume, and page references are from this edition.

77. That he is an officer is made abundantly clear by the sword and pistol he carries and the memory he has of ordering others around.

78. The word used for this "separation" *(ridatsu)* is, interestingly, the same one Shimao used for the title of the first chapter of *Shi no toge*. For more on this, see the afterword of this book.

79. Okuno comments that here, four years after the end of the war, Shimao is able to begin to confront directly an "overpowering reality" (Okuno, *Shimao Toshio*, 146).

80. Tsuge, "Shimao Toshio no hōhō," 76–77.

81. For this reading of *Shi no toge*, see Okamoto Keitoku, "'Shi no toge' ron nōto," *Ryūkyūdaigaku hōbungakubu kiyō: Nihon tōyō bunka ronshū* 1 (March 1995): 27–46.

82. Pages references for "Chinkonki" are from the Collected Works, vol. 3.

83. Robert Jay Lifton, *Death in Life: Survivors of Hiroshima* (New York: Basic Books, 1967), 409; emphasis in original.

84. Okuno, *Shimao Toshio*, 140.

85. As Sparling notes, the controversy over this story led to a split of the

Shin Nihon bungaku members into moderate and radical groups (Sparling, *"The Sting of Death,"* 9–10). For more on this controversy, see Makise Kōji's letter in the June 15, 1950, edition of *Akahata* and the two articles in response to this: Nakano Shigeharu's "'Chippoke na aventure' no koto de Makise shi ni kotaeru" and Kubota Masafumi's "Hitotsu no tosho ga dono yō ni atsukawareta ka" (both in the September 1950 issue of *Shin Nihon bungaku*). Shimao's bemused response, "Kokkei na ichi kara," is found in the May 1951 issue of *Shin Nihon bungaku*. It is important to note that despite this controversy, Shimao continued to publish stories in this journal.

86. One should note Shimizu's interpretation of the story, the notion of the final scenes representing an "allegory of the avant-garde" (Shimizu, in *Yume no naka de no nichijō*, 259).

87. Page references for "Kizashi" are from *Yume no keiretsu*, 101–137. The quote here is from page 137.

88. Page references for "Ōbasami" are from of the Collected Works, vol. 4; for "Nenokichi no shita" and "Kisōsha no yūutsu" the references are from vol. 5.

89. The translation of the last title is from Van C. Gessel, *The Sting of Life: Four Contemporary Japanese Novelists*, 148.

90. With inevitable backsliding, naturally; the 1954 story "Oni Hage," is a case in point.

91. The formal device of framing a story as a dream, incidentally, is one Shimao used sparingly. The only other example I know of is from the 1946 story "Kotōmu," which begins: "In a dream, I . . . " One should note, too, the beginning of "Ōbasami"; it is a series of short sentences depicting what must be fragments of a dream, which the rest of the text expands on:

> The moon was out that night.
> There was a small, round pond on top of a low hill.
> I was led by the devil to the pond.
> I was afraid of approaching the devil.(70)

This opening is particularly reminiscent of many entries in Shimao's dream diaries, *Yume nikki* and *Ki mu shi*. See also the discussion of "Tetsuro ni chikaku" in chapter 3; this story depicts the protagonist awakening from a dream. For a different and intriguing reading of "Ōbasami," see Kamiya Tadataka, "Shimao Toshio *Ōbasami* no akuma," *Genten* 2 (Fall 1983): 38–41.

92. It is interesting to note the playfulness at work in Shimao's stories regarding characters' names. In *Garasu shōji no shiruetto*, for instance, the children in one story ("Nyanko") are named Maya and Rokko, after two mountains in Kobe; while Maya is a common name (and the name of Shimao's daughter), Rokko is less plausible. In the last two stories of the expanded edition of the same collection ("Ani to imōto" and "Ensoku"), the protagonist's family name

is Shima*jiri*, not Shima*o*; the last two elements of each go together to form the word *shippo*, "tail." In "Kisōsha no yūutsu" the daughter's name is Tama, the name of the family cat in *Garasu shōji*; probably the most common name for a cat, it is also used in *Shi no toge*. One should note in passing that the name Maya, used in *Shi no toge* and elsewhere, is also "cat" in Amami dialect and that the daughter Maya in that work (and in one story in *Garasu shōji*) is nicknamed Nyanko, a child's word for cat. The name of the character Date Suteo in "Sōwa," an early story (1948) I will not examine, is perhaps the most amusing. The first element, the family name Date, is a homonym for "affected," and Suteo is written with characters that mean "discarded husband." No doubt this background of playfulness is what prompts critics to read into "Nenokichi no shita" and "Kisōsha no yūutsu" various interpretations of the characters' names. Gessel, for example, comments that the husband's name in the latter story—Kannō Miichi—is a "bizarre, emblematic name . . . written with characters that seem to mean 'a serpent that curses God,'" and that *kannō* has homonyms meaning "carnal pleasures" and "answers to prayers" (Gessel, *The Sting of Life*, 149). In a more extended treatment of "Nenokichi no shita," Urata Yoshikazu sees in the names a rich weave of connotations. First, the "Ne" in Nenokichi and "Mi" in Miichi refer to the zodiac signs *nezumi* and *hebi*, rat and snake. See Urata Yoshikzau, "Shimao Toshio ni okeru 'ie'—'Nenokichi no shita' o megutte," *Shin Okinawa bungaku* 71 (Spring 1987): 64–70. (See 68–69 for the discussion of names.) While Urata identifies these as gods in some folktales, it is interesting to note a more obvious connection he fails to mention: the two animals' relationship as natural enemies, with the snake preying on the rat just as Miichi causes his son's injury. On the other hand, Urata writes, Nasu, if read as meaning "eggplant," is symbolic of a woman's womb or sexual organs, and as a homonym for the word *nasu* (to give birth), is related to the *ne* in Nenokichi, which is written with the character meaning child. Since Nasu is also described as being "busy as twenty mice," she is again linked with her child, who is a "mouse" (the same word meaning both rat and mouse.) As this last sentence suggests, the overlap and linkage between parent and child is crucial to understanding the dynamics of "Nenokichi no shita." Nenokichi's body, in short, is the medium onto which parental discord is inscribed.

93. Sarah Kofman, *The Enigma of Woman: Woman in Freud's Writings*, trans. Catherine Porter (Ithaca, N.Y.: Cornell University Press, 1985), 43.

94. Critics were quick to grasp the shift in Shimao's style at this point, although not its full implications—i.e., that he had not abandoned dream in favor of transparent I-novels. The amusing story is told of the critic Hirano Ken, who, soon after the publication of "Nenokichi no shita," worriedly asked Shimao how his son was now, after the accident. Shimao replied that he had "taken what happened to a chicken and changed it into a story about a child." See Katsumata Osamu, "Sei ni tachimodoru michi: Shimao Toshio ron" *Gunzō*

(October 1978): 198. Hirano's reply to this (more of a brief aside) is recorded in a roundtable discussion of Shimao's work, "Shimao Toshio: Sono shigoto to ningen," in Aeba, *Shimao Toshio kenkyū*, 481. Hirano comments that "'Nenokichi no shita' might actually have been about a chicken, but at the root of it, it's not just simply about a chicken." Indeed.

95. This is a reference to Psalm 130, which begins, "Out of the depths have I cried unto thee, O Lord." See Van C. Gessel, "Voices in the Wilderness: Japanese Christian Authors," *Monumenta Nipponica* 37(4) (Winter 1982): 450. As Sparling notes, the image of the abyss "permeates the 'sick wife' stories" (Sparling, *"The Sting of Death,"* 175).

96. Shimao, *Sono natsu no ima wa/Yume no naka de no nichijō*, 281.

97. Translation from Gessel, *The Sting of Life*, 149–150.

98. Ibid., 150.

99. That the opinions of neighbors troubles Miichi is borne out in the later scene at the brothel. About to leave, and obviously recognized by both the prostitute and the brothel owner, he worries that this visit will "surely become the stuff of rumors and be spread around" (130).

100. Significantly, in *Hi no utsuroi*, the following day the wife hears the news about Kawabata Yasunari's death and tells her husband about it (*Hi no utsuroi*, 20).

3. Out of the Abyss: The "Sick Wife Stories"

1. Although most standard chronologies of Shimao's career (for example, Okuno Takeo, *Shimao Toshio*, 266) date the onset of Miho's condition from the fall of 1954, Miho's 1959 essay stands in direct contradiction to this, pinpointing the beginning of her condition in the spring of 1954. Critics have generally ignored this essay, instead using the chronology of the novel *Shi no toge* as transparently reflecting the order of real life events. Likewise, as discussed below, the chronology of real-life events in 1955—the quarrel with the "other woman" in Sakura and the length of the Shimao's stay in a locked mental ward—have generally been viewed as following the timeframe set out in Shimao's fiction. Recent investigations, however, have thrown into doubt the correspondence between fictional and real events. See notes 7 and 45 below. Concerning Shimao Miho, one should note that her mental distress was not entirely over until the late 1950s; two decades later she launched her own career as writer. Her 1974 collection, *Umibe no sei to shi*, won the Tamura Toshiko Prize for women writers.

2. From "Sakuran no tamashii kara yomigaette," 1959. Quoted in "Kaisō no Shimao Toshio," an interview with Shimao Miho in *Ōru Yomimono* (November 1990): 185.

3. The term *byōinki* refers specifically to the nine stories, beginning with "Ware fukaki fuchi yori"(trans., "Out of the Depths"), written between 1955

and 1957, based on the Shimao's 1955 stay in the Kōnodai mental hospital. As such, the term is usually used by critics to describe a subset of Shimao's *byōsaimono* ("sick wife stories") as well as to mark the beginning of this larger grouping of stories, although at least a few stories (the last three stories in *Garasu shōji no shiruetto,* and "Kisōsha no yūutsu") that predate the *byōinki* arguably belong in the larger grouping of *byōsaimono.* Besides their publication in literary journals, the stories have appeared in several books as well: the first three stories in the short-story collection *Ware fukaki fuchi yori* (December 1955), two other stories in the collection *Shi no toge* (October 1960), and three in the collection also titled *Shi no toge* that appeared in November 1963. All nine stories were collected for the first time in their present order—"Ware fukaki fuchi yori," "Kyōsha no manabi" (Lessons of the insane), "Aru seishin byōsha" (A mental patient), "Omoi niguruma"(A heavy piggyback ride), "Chiryō"(Treatment), "Nogare yuku kokoro" (trans., "The Heart that Slips Away"), "Tensō" (Forwarding), "Nemuri naki suimin" (The sleepless sleep), and "Ichijiki" (A period of time)—in the 1962 edition of Shimao's collected works. At the time of his 1962 collected works (when only four of the chapters of *Shi no toge* were complete), Shimao considered the *byōinki* and the *Shi no toge* series one long novel divided into two parts. The first depicts the characters in the hospital without revealing the reasons they were there; the second (the *Shi no toge* part) takes the story back to the time before the hospitalization and describes the reasons they ended up in a mental ward. Although the two sets of stories can be read this way, they were never again published in one volume, except for their inclusion in the same volume of the 1962 edition. And it seems clear that Shimao increasingly began to view the *Shi no toge* series as a separate, and more consuming, project.

4. Dennis Keene's translation of the term *byōsaimono* is "sick-wife-novels." Keene, in his work on Yokomitsu Riichi, calls the *byōsaimono* a "staple" of the I-novel genre, which might "also be considered a literary genre in itself." Keene cites Yokomitsu's acount of his wife's illness and death, "Haru wa basha ni notte" (1926), as the most well known prewar example, and Kanbayashi Akatsuki's "Sei Yohane byōin nite" (1946) as a classic early postwar story of the genre. To these must be added the postwar stories of Hara Tamiki on his wife's death from tuberculosis, as well as the poetry of Takamura Kōtarō collected in his *Chieko shō* (1941). For a discussion of Hara's work, see John Treat, "Atomic Bomb Literature and the Documentary Fallacy," *Journal of Japanese Studies* 14(1) (1988): 27–57.

5. He did publish two essays in this period: "Fuan e no sasae" (April 1955) and "Kishima Hajime 'Yottsu no mushi no monogatari'" (September 19, 1955); he also composed three of the *byōinki* stories while in the hospital.

6. Okuno Takeo, *Shimao Toshio,* 266.

7. The first is that he maintained his home in Sakura not for just one month (April–May 1955), but for six months from April to October, and that he and

his family were in Sakura at various times during the summer. In addition, the dramatic confrontation between Miho and Shimao's lover (chapter 10 of *Shi no toge*), which in the story occurred some time in April, might actually have occurred much later, possibly September. See Takahira Naomi, "Shimao Toshio *Shi no toge*: Sakura o chūshin to shite," *Rakuda* 21 (August 1990): 34–58. Takahira, who studied Shimao's time in Sakura, concludes that it was after this September confrontation that Miho and Shimao were hospitalized. This leaves the strong impression that Miho's treatment consisted of a longer period of outpatient care, with the two of them commuting to the hospital from Sakura and only being hospitalized at the end of the summer. The impression is reinforced by internal evidence of the *byōinki*, which, despite Toshio's claim that they had been in the hospital for "half a year," leave the reader remembering only the depictions of the end of summer, as if the hottest part of the summer had been elided.

8. Quoted in Okuno's review of *Ware fukaki fuchi yori*, originally in *Fujin kōron*, February 1956. Reprinted in Okuno, *Shimao Toshio*, 216–218. The quote is on 216.

9. Interview, *Bungaku jihyō* 39 (January 10, 1990): 4–5.

10. Page references are from the Collected Works, vol. 7; the *byōinki* are on pages 7–204.

11. The reasons are never clearly given, but Toshio and Miho are from the beginning an anomaly in the ward because they constitute a female patient-male attendant pair, while the ward is one for male patients and their female attendants (usually mothers or wives).

12. Kathryn Sparling, *"The Sting of Death" and Other Stories by Shimao Toshio*, 128.

13. Torii Kunio, "Sengo ni okeru shishōsetsuteki ishiki—*Shi no toge* o chūshin ni," *Kokubungaku* (March 1966): 58.

14. So convincingly that critics have unquestioningly based their chronologies on events depicted in the stories.

15. Sparling, *"The Sting of Death,"* 7.

16. Ibid., 115.

17. Ibid.; emphasis added.

18. Ibid., ix.

19. My discussion is a summary of Kawamura Jirō's commentary in Shimao Toshio, *Ware fukaki fuchi yori* (Shūeisha, 1977), 233–238. See especially 233–234.

20. Translation in Sparling, *"The Sting of Death,"* 113.

21. The image of Toshio as puppeteer himself, one should note, suggests the dual nature of their relationship at this point; with the treatment making Miho gradually more placid, Toshio is still her "servant," but as "puppeteer" he may be able to manipulate her as he was not able to before.

22. This is the military term used in Shimao's war stories to indicate the state of heightened readiness the *tokkōtai* squad was placed on.

23. Although I will not expand on this point here, the notion of a "power outside the sphere of human life" naturally lends itself to a discussion of Shimao as, in great part, a Christian writer. See Mark Williams, "Shadows of the Former Self: The Influence of Christianity on Contemporary Japanese Literature," Ph.D. dissertation, and the chapter on Shimao in Van C. Gessel's *The Sting of Life: Four Contemporary Japanese Novelists*, for discussion of Shimao as a Christian writer.

24. Mishima Yukio, "Mateki na mono no chikara," in *Shimao Toshio kenkyū*, ed. Aeba Takeo, 30–31; originally in December 1962 issue of *Bungakukai*.

25. Karatani Kōjin, "Yume no sekai: Shimao Toshio to Shōno Junzō," in *Imi to iu yamai*, 95, 84.

26. Thus one might say "Yume no naka de no nichijō" is less "Everyday Life *in* a Dream" than "Everyday Life *is* a Dream" in the sense that Karatani defines dreams as sites of no freedom or critical distance.

27. The word is *ishikure* (stones), but one is naturally reminded of the incident with the stone *jizō* statue in "Jizō no nukumi."

28. Sparling's translation, *"The Sting of Death,"* 114.

29. Ibid., 118.

30. Ibid., 119.

31. The therapeutic use of community dances in mental hospitals has a long history. Showalter notes their widespread use in England as far back as the 1840s. She speaks of the disquieting "illusion of normality" Victorian era "lunatic balls" presented, and how to many these dances were the "demonstration *par excellence*" of the mental asylum's "exercise of disguised control," with the dancers seemingly free but actually "obeying the commands of the keepers." See Elaine Showalter, *The Female Malady*, 49–50. A century and a half later, in present-day Japan, dances are still a part of the social life of even the most up-to-date mental hospitals, although less popular than *karaoke* singing, which in the words of one doctor is the patients' "greatest pleasure." An 1848 lithograph of a "lunatics ball" Showalter describes shows the "slogan 'Harmony' ironically presid[ing] over a scene in which each dancer seems to keep his or her own time." A similar irony is found in at least one present-day Japanese mental ward in which the names of individual ward rooms (*Jiyū*, "Freedom"; *Tabidachi*, "Departure") contrast with the barred windows and bolted doors and by the fact that the patients, some of whom have been hospitalized for decades, are neither free nor about to depart for anywhere. (These observations were made at the locked mental ward of the Horikawa Hospital, Kurume, Japan, March 29, 1991. The remarks about the ward patients are made by Dr. Mutō Kunihiro, psychiatrist at the hospital.)

32. Sparling, *"The Sting of Death,"* 124.

33. Ibid., 125.

34. "Kyōsha no manabi" is mostly about Oshō, while the next story, "Aru seishin byōsha," is almost entirely about Hanio.

35. Collected Works, vol. 13, 204.

36. "Tetsuro ni chikaku," the first proto-*Shi no toge* story (in the sense that it examines the period of the wife's full-blown madness prior to the hospitalization), was the second, and last, of Shimao's stories to be nominated for the coveted Akutagawa Prize. Possibly the critical recognition this story received (none of the *byōinki* stories, for instance, were ever nominated) may have been an impetus to Shimao to continue the project, which eventually became the novel *Shi no toge*. Page references for "Tetsuro ni chikaku" and "Ie no naka" are from the Collected Works, vol. 5.

37. At least one critic agrees with Shimao that "Tetsuro ni chikaku" stands at a critical juncture in his writing. Ishida Tadahiko argues that the story is "metafiction," "Shimao's declaration of a change from the literature of escape to that of staying put." Ishida's failure to discuss the *byōinki* is hard to fathom, because these stories—with the husband's decision to join his wife in the mental ward—display the "staying put" *(todomaru)* tendencies to an amazing degree. Be that as it may, his analysis is cogent, because in "Tetsuro ni chikaku" one sees from the beginning what has already been suggested by the ending of such stories as the 1955 "Kimo no chiisai mama ni": the centrifugal movement of the protagonist away from the home is replaced by its opposite, the centripetal forces pulling him back. What Ishida's analysis does not take into consideration is the role of the *female* character. As we have seen throughout the *byōinki* in Toshio's slavish devotion to Miho, Toshio and Miho are in the process of switching roles, and this is an important feature of "Tetsuro ni chikaku" as well. It is not so much "escape" and wandering that have ceased than that the *person* escaping has, because it is now the wife, Miho, who escapes the "pain" of being stuck in the home, neglected and lonely, and wanders the nighttime Tokyo landscape. And just as Miho in *Shi no toge* feels certain her husband's life of wandering will lead to his suicide, the husband in "Testuro ni chikaku" is convinced that his wife's "escape" from the home will bring about her death. To take Ishida's analysis one step further, it is only with *Shi no toge*, despite numerous "escapes" by the two characters, that Toshio and Miho acknowledge the need for both of them to move from fleeing their situation to "staying put." They need to accept responsibility for who and what they are and work together to overcome their problems.

38. The story "Ie no naka" exists in two versions. The original 1959 version, which appeared in both the 1960 and 1963 *Shi no toge* collections and the 1962 edition of Shimao's collected works, was written in first person and consistently placed in these collections to be read as the first chapter of the burgeoning *Shi*

no toge. The 1960 *Shi no toge* contained the following stories: "Ie no naka," "Ridatsu," "Shi no toge," "Chiryō," "Nemuri naki suimin," and "Ie no soto de." The 1962 edition of Shimao's collected works (vol. 4) contained all nine of the *byōinki* stories in the order discussed in note 3, followed by a second section containing "Ie no naka," "Ridatsu," "Shi no toge," "Gake no fuchi," "Tetsuro ni chikaku," and "Hi wa hi ni." The 1963 *Shi no toge* collection contained, in order: "Ware fukaki fuchi yori," "Chiryō," "Nogare yuku kokoro," "Ie no naka," "Ridatsu," "Shi no toge," "Gake no fuchi," and "Hi wa hi ni." In the completed *Shi no toge* published in 1977, "Ie no naka" is excluded and "Ridatsu" becomes chapter one. In subsequent interviews Shimao indicated that he planned from the first to make "Ridatsu" the beginning of the novel, but from the evidence of the three collections above, until the appearance of the novel, readers were justified in considering "Ie no naka" an integral part of the *Shi no toge* series. See the interview with Hariu Ichiro, "*Shi no toge* no dodai," *Shin Nihon bungaku* 34(2) (February 1979): 40. In Shimao's Collected Works, "Ie no naka" appears in its second version, rewritten in third person, with some minor revisions and at least two mistakes, where the original first person voice was not edited out. The husband and wife are unnamed.

39. As mentioned in note 38, in both the 1960 and 1963 collections, as well as the 1962 edition of Shimao's collected works, the story "Ie no naka" was positioned as the first story in the developing *Shi no toge* series, but was dropped from the final full-length novel. In addition, in the 1962 collection, "Tetsuro ni chikaku" was positioned between "Gake no fuchi" and "Hi wa hi ni" (which became chapters 3 and 4, respectively, of the 1977 novel). Thus Shimao originally conceived of "Ie no naka" and "Testuro ni chikaku" as chapters 1 and 5 of *Shi no toge*.

40. In its final version *Shi no toge* is Shimao's most celebrated novel, winner of two major literary awards. The final 1977 version, the one I use here, consists of the following twelve chapters (each with date of original publication in periodicals indicated): "Ridatsu" (1960), "Shi no toge" (1960), "Gake no fuchi" (1960), "Hi wa hi ni" (1961), "Ryuki" (1963), "Hibi no tameshi" (1963), "Hi no chijimari" (1964), "Ko to tomo ni" (1964), "Sugikoshi" (1965), "Hi o kakete" (1967), "Hikkoshi" (1972), and "Nyūin made" (1976). Three editions of the novel are readily available: vol. 8 of the 1981–1983 Collected Works, the paperback edition published by Shinchōsha (1981), and the 1977 hardbound version, also published by Shinchōsha. The Shinchōsha boxed, hardbound version was reprinted in 1990 after the critical success of the film version of *Shi no toge*. All page references are from the 1977 Shinchōsha edition.

41. Okuno Takeo, *Sugao no sakkatachi: gendai sakka 132 nin* (Shūeisha, 1978), 17.

42. This quote from Okuno about *Shi no toge* is taken from the advertis-

ing obi (a paper band placed around books that includes short quotes from critics or experts). It is an interesting, and very Japanese, form of extra advertising.

43. The title of the novel is taken from 1 Corinthians 15:55–56:

"Where, O death, is your victory?
Where, O death, is your sting?"
The sting of death is sin, and the power of sin is the law.

(*The NIV Study Bible*, Grand Rapids, Mich.: Zondervan Publishing House, 1995, 1760). The aspect of the novel as an act of atonement is delineated in Shimao's reply to Niwa Masamitsu's open letters: "Niwa Masamitsu e no henji: bungaku to shokuzai unnun no koto" (Collected Works, vol. 14, 13–19; originally published in *Sakka* 141 [June 1960]). Shimao's reply to Niwa's assertion that his *byōsaimono* are written as acts of atonement acknowledges a "strong sense of sin" behind his writing, but rejects the notion that literature should be written primarily as an act of atonement. "If there are clearly parts in my novels that are gestures of atonement for sin, then that's because the novels are no good" (18). Shimao also notes how he was happily surprised to see how it helped his wife's condition to read the *byōinki* stories; he makes it clear this effect on his wife was a *result*, but not his intention in writing the stories (19).

44. Concerning the extent to which the novel follows real life, Shimao Miho, asked years later to give an example of the fictional elements of the novel, cited the conversations, claiming they are mainly fictional and that she never berated her husband so vehemently in real life (personal interview, January 6, 1990). As these "conversations" (Miho's interrogations of Toshio) form the backbone of the novel, this claim makes a substantial part of the novel something other than an I-novel "true" recounting of events. One should note, however, that Shimao himself, speaking of the "created" nature of the novel, specifically cites the conversations as recountings of words he actually had heard spoken. See the interview with Shimao in *Genten* 2 (Fall 1983): 27.

45. As mentioned earlier, there is evidence that Shimao's stay in Sakura lasted much longer than depicted in the novel. In *Shi no toge* (chapters 10 and 11) the family is in Sakura for only about twenty-five days (approx. April 9–May 3), with the visit of the other woman taking place ten days or so after their move to the town. As mentioned above, however, recent scholarship suggests that the Shimao's were resident in Sakura off and on throughout the summer of 1955 and that the incident with the woman took place not in April, but in mid- or late September. These points are made in Takahira, "Shimao Toshio *Shi no toge*," 34–58. In a second article, written in part to answer some of the questions I posed to her after reading the first, Takahira backs away from her earlier conclusions of a discrepancy between novel and real events, concluding that the standard June–October scenario is sound. See Takahira Naomi,

"Shimao Toshio *Shi no toge* to Sakura," *Rakuda* 23 (November 1991). Despite her intriguing detective work, then, Takahira unfortunately retreats to a position much like that of other critics who read *Shi no toge* as transparent reflection of a real-life chronology.

46. Okuno, *Sugao no sakkatachi*, 17.

47. As with much of the novel, the names of the characters are almost, but not quite, those of the real-life Shimao family. "Toshio" is written not in the usual Chinese characters but in the *katakana* syllabary, and the son's name has been changed from the real-life Shinzō to Shin'ichi.

48. Readers who followed Shimao's work closely had already, at various times before and during the sixteen-year composition of the novel, been given what amount to outlines of the plot in essays and interviews that, in retrospect, indicate where the novel follows real events. The most prominent of these is the May 1956 essay, "Tsuma e no inori" (A prayer to my wife) (*Fujin kōron*, May 1956). The text here is from the Collected Works, vol. 13, 167–185. This essay covers the period of Shimao and Miho's life from the first examinations in the hospital and electroshock treatment (covered in chapter 7 of *Shi no toge*, "Hi no chijimari"), her first hospitalization alone (chapter 8, "Ko to tomo ni"), discussions with doctors about her problems (chapter 9, "Sugi koshi"), their move to Sakura (chapter 10, "Hi o kakete"), and the decision for the two of them to move into the psychiatric ward (chapters 11 and 12.) The essay briefly touches on their stay in the hospital and treatment there, the time covered in the *byōinki*, and takes the story further, discussing a subject Shimao never used in his fiction—the one-week trip by ship back to Amami. Thus well before Shimao began writing *Shi no toge*, readers were aware, in outline form, of the events, and even several of the more moving scenes, of Shimao's real life, which served as the foundation for the latter half of the novel. Taken together with the stories "Tetsuro ni chikaku" and "Ie no naka," one is left with the strong impression of Shimao slowly but steadily inching both backward and forward in his review of events of Miho's madness. The 1956 essay gives details of Miho's illness and treatment prior to the hospitalization, but does not discuss the critical period of the initial attacks. "Tetsuro ni chikaku" depicts one day's events some time after the initial attacks and prior to the hospitalization. And "Ie no naka" takes the reader back to the point of crisis, but cuts off before the nature of her madness is revealed—her relentless interrogations of her husband. A May 1961 interview with Shimao and Miho (after Shimao had published the first four chapters of *Shi no toge*) covers much of the same ground, but adds the background to the beginning of the novel: Shimao's own worsening health after their move to Tokyo; Miho's attempts to maintain his health by studying nutrition at a school; their financial difficulties, which forced her to sell off her possessions (the cultured pearls her father gave her); and Shimao's lifestyle in which, for the first year after their move to Tokyo, he rarely returned

to sleep at home. Miho, we are told, knew about Shimao's love affair, but felt she could stand it if it "helped his work." But finding his diary one day, she found that his "soul had been snatched away by that devil," and thus began her physical and mental symptoms that eventually forced her into the hospital. See "Shi no toge no ai" (Love in Shi no toge), Shufu no tomo (May 1961): 103–104. This interview, conducted soon after Shimao won the Geijutsu Senshō award for the first Shi no toge collection, also reviews events that Shimao had not yet written about, in particular the dramatic visit of the other woman to Sakura depicted in the 1967 "Hi o kakete." A companion piece to the 1956 essay, "Tsuma e no inori: hōi" (Postscript to a prayer to my wife), was published in the September 1958 issue of Fujin kōron as "Yomigaetta tsuma no tamashii" (The revived soul of my wife). A complete translation is in Sparling, "The Sting of Death," 181–187.

49. Gessel, The Sting of Life, 160.

50. Hinobara Shigeaki, general editor, Kango no tame no rinshō igaku taikei (Clinical medicine series for nursing), vol. 16: Seishin igaku (Psychiatric medicine) (Jōhōkaihatsu kenkyūjo, 1983), 134–136.

51. Conversation with Dr. Mutō Kunihiro, Horikawa Hospital, Kurume City, March 29, 1991.

52. All page references in the text, as noted above, are from the 1977 Shinchōsha edition of the novel.

53. Translation in Gessel, The Sting of Life, 159.

54. A demand that, as the page numbers reveal, brackets the entire narrative and works to underscore Toshio's words that all the treatment she has gotten has been for naught, because her condition, far from improving, has actually worsened.

55. Satō Junjirō, Shimao Toshio: Miho no sekai o chūshin to shite (Okisekisha 1983), 83.

56. I am reminded of Jared Taylor's characterization of the typical modern Japanese housewife:

> Japanese wives have to fend for themselves the way a single mother does in America, except that they do not have jobs and have to look after men who show up at odd hours expecting a meal and a bed. The wives are the first to get up in the morning, the last to go to bed, and are perhaps the best example of gaman to be found in Japan today. (Jared Taylor, Shadows of the Rising Sun [Tokyo: Charles E. Tuttle, 1983], 199)

57. The novel as "humorous" is discussed by Shimao in an interview with the playwright Tsuka Kōhei in Subaru 8(4) (April 1986): 252–268. Shimao sees as "funny" the way Toshio "performs these comical things for all he's worth" (254). In remarks soon after winning one of two literary prizes for the novel, Shimao writes that he is "relieved that the novel is read now not just as something serious but as having comical parts as well" ("Nihon bungaku taishō

jushō no kotoba," originally in *Shinchō* 75(7) (July 1978), here taken from the Collected Works, vol. 15, 437). One might add that Sparling's comments on Shin'ichi's role, and the implication of the term *"katei no jijō,"* may be off the mark and fail to capture what could be an aspect of the humor of the novel. She writes of

> Shimao's creation of a subgenre of more or less autobiographical fiction — dubbed *katei no jijō shōsetsu* ("domestic exigency novel"). This terminology derives from the five-year-old Shin'ichi's refrain in Shimao's "The Sting of Death." Whenever his parents begin to fight, Shin'ichi shouts, "Here we go with domestic exigencies" *(katei no jijō ga hajimatta),* "Stop your domestic exigencies!" *(katei no jijō wa yamero).* (Sparling, *"The Sting of Death,"* 1)

Sparling provides no clue as to where Shin'ichi may have picked up this phrase, but this may well be the point. According to one source, the phrase is taken from a well-known 1950s radio routine of a popular comedian and emcee, Toni Tani, whose skits often included a character claiming "katei no jijō" as a way of explaining his way out of tight spots. Thus the usage of it in the novel, and its usage in the "subgenre" label, are inseparable from this humorous background (Prof. Tsuge Teruhiko, personal conversation, Tokyo, May 1990).

58. Carol A. B. Warren, *Madwives: Schizophrenic Women in the 1950s* (New Brunswick and London: Rutgers University Press, 1987), 38.

59. Mishima's remarks are in his well-known review of the *byōsaimono,* "Mateki na mono no chikara," in Aeba, *Shimao Toshio kenkyū,* 30–31.

60. Shimizu Tōru, "Kokoro no michi: Shimao Toshio shiron," *Chūō kōron* (February 1977): 267.

61. Collected Works, vol. 5, 330.

62. Miho's new-found sexual aggressiveness is tinged, however, by pathetic promises at times that she will change to please Toshio if only he will tell her how he wants her to, and by demands to know whether Toshio likes her body or not (*Shi no toge,* 92).

63. Readers of Shimao's entire oeuvre will recognize this as the same place mentioned in the story "Tsuma no shokugyō" in *Garasu shōji no shiruetto.*

64. Showalter, *The Female Malady,* 74.

65. Ibid., 75.

66. Sparling's translation of *Shi no toge,* 66 (Sparling, *"The Sting of Death,"* 108).

67. If Toshio actually wrote this, it shows an early awareness of their problems; Miho's reactions then may be interpreted as showing she understood his recognition of her "impotence" but did not do anything about.

68. Showalter, *The Female Malady,* 207.

69. Ibid., 207.

70. A typical scenario for an ECT session would consist of the following: the patient "'lies on a bed or couch with the pillow removed and the usual pre-

cautions (e.g., removal of false teeth, spectacles, etc.) observed. He is then given an intravenous injection of a short-acting anaesthetic . . . and through the same needle, a dose of muscle relaxant. . . .' Respiration is controlled by an anesthetist with a face mask and a pressure bag. When the patient is unconscious, 'two electrodes, dampened with a bicarbonate solution to prevent skin burns at their points of contact, are applied to the anterior temporal areas of the scalp. . . . A gag is inserted in the patient's mouth to prevent him from biting his tongue. An electric current, usually eighty volts . . . is given which results in a 'modified' convulsion. . . . After the convulsion, the gag is removed, the patient is turned on his side. . . . Within five to twenty minutes the patient gradually returns to full consciousness although he may feel sleepy. . . .' Among the most frequently noted side effects are short-term and partial amnesias." This is Showalter quoting Anthony Clare's *Psychiatry in Dissent* (London: Tavistock Publications, 1976), 228–229 (see Showalter, *The Female Malady*, 207). Showalter goes on to note that "[a]lthough this clinical description of ECT . . . uses the male pronoun," as we have noted above, the vast majority of patients are female.

71. Sparling, *"The Sting of Death,"* 85.

72. Thus I come to the same conclusion that Yoshimoto Takaaki reaches, mentioned earlier, that only through the experience of dealing with his wife's illness was Shimao able to begin to confront—in a more direct fashion—such traumatic experiences as the final day of the war and the aftermath of the surrender. Obviously I do not conclude here that Shimao's earlier work excludes consideration of the past.

73. One of the ironies of her madness, of course, is that, understandable though her rage may be, it makes her repeat the role she abhors, i.e., the victimizer. Not only her husband suffers, but her innocent children do as well, not to mention, of course, the other woman who, in chapter 10, is roundly beaten by Miho as Toshio first looks on, then helps his wife.

74. One aspect of the novel that is little remarked on is the connection between present-day events and Toshio's childhood. A subtle subtext involving Toshio's childhood that crops up at various spots in the novel parallels the Toshio-Miho story and suggests that they are replaying in the present the marital discord of his parents in the past. There are, scattered throughout the story, references to both Toshio's and Miho's parents. In the case of Toshio's parents, the implication is clear that Toshio is associated with his father, Miho his mother. Miho calls him cold and selfish, and likens him to his father (10); by himself at a hospital, Toshio himself feels he is just like his father (289). In the public bath one day, Toshio hears his wife's voice (which reminds him of his mother's) from the women's side and is suddenly drawn into reveries of his long-dead mother's voice (120). Similarly, Miho rubbing his back to help him relax overlaps in his mind with his mother, who did the same for him as a boy

(291). On top of these comes the partially reconstructed story of Toshio's parents and their problems: Toshio's mother was unhappy with her husband and ran away, just as he fears Miho will do (see 11 and 228). Other scattered memories of his mother include her struggling to keep up with her husband as he dashed for a train to take them back to Sōma ("My fat mother ran behind, staggering. Poor mother" [138]), and how his mother's bones, in her father's family grave, were "mixed in among people she didn't even know" (147). Brief as these references are, a picture emerges of a woman who has suffered, and for whom Toshio is more than a little sympathetic. In addition, the reader learns that his mother had a fiancé other than his father. Walking in Sakura, Toshio passes an old stationery shop, the sight of which makes memories "swell up." He has a sudden vision of his mother as a young girl passing by, dressed like a young lady in a *hakama* with hair done up, "deep in discussion with the cousin of the fiancé her parents had picked for her" (269). This passing vision would not hold readers' attention except that we learn, in two places in the novel, that Miho, too, had a fiancé other than Toshio and thus again is linked with his mother. "And she [Miho] told me she wanted to meet Masaaki, the fiancé she broke her promise to in order to be with me and who was crazy about her, and cry her heart out to him telling him, 'I would have been happier if I'd been with you'" (93). Much later, in the last chapter, Miho again talks about her fiancé, begging Toshio to "send her back" to him (344). What emerges from all this is the outline of a portrait fitting both Miho and Toshio's mother. Both are women who had other marital options, but who found themselves in marriages in which they suffered. In Toshio's mother's case, this led to her fleeing to her hometown alone. Miho, one learns, is increasingly nostalgic and homesick for her own hometown and her parents who so lovingly raised her, and her frequent attempts to flee, connected with threats to die, seem in many cases irrational attempts to return to her hometown. Several of Shimao's other stories from the period just prior to his beginning the novel touch on childhood memories and the story of the male protagonists parents' unhappy marriage. Stories of childhood memories have not been entirely absent from Shimao's writing up to this time, but two stories from 1959—"Ie no soto de" and "Mittsu no kioku"—flesh out what is suggested in *Shi no toge* about the outlines of Toshio's childhood. These stories suggest quite strongly that, as with himself and Miho, his father and mother had serious marital problems, prompting attacks of hysteria on her part and a profound sadness and disgust with their marriage.

75. Translation in Gessel, *The Sting of Life*, 163.
76. Okuno, *Shimao Toshio*, 18.
77. Oda Makoto, "The Ethics of Peace," 157.
78. Ōshiro Tatsuhiro, *Dōka to ika no hazama de* (Shio shuppansha, 1972), 11–14.
79. Oda, "The Ethics of Peace," 158; emphasis added.

80. Takeda Tomojū, "'Shi no toge' de purofuindesu—Shimao Toshio ron," 28–44. Takeda's thinking has been a great influence on this book.

81. Ibid., 30–31, 32.

82. Ibid., 43.

83. *Shi no toge*, 25.

84. Lillian Feder, *Madness in Literature* (Princeton, N.J.: Princeton University Press, 1980), 5.

85. Sparling, *"The Sting of Death,"* ix.

86. The name Amami seems never to be used in the novel; Miho's island home is always referred to in more ambiguous terms, such as a "far away island near Okinawa" for instance. Early on, however, Miho is shown wearing a "formal *aizome* Ōshima kimono" (15), a clue that she is, like the real-life Shimao Miho, a native of Amami. (Shimao Miho is from Kakeromajima, the island just south of Amami Ōshima.)

87. For an interesting reading in this vein that focuses on the structure of modern love relationships, see Ueno Chizuko, Ogura Chikako, and Tomioka Taeko, *Danryū bungakuron*, 63–132, which I discuss in the next chapter. Obviously my reading in this chapter of Miho's madness and its relationship to the contemporary female role could be accused of similarly defining Miho as unproblematically a modern, urban housewife. She is, as I hope to show, a multifaceted character of whom this is but one part.

88. We see a similar dislike of the term native used for the southern islanders in later essays Shimao wrote on the islands.

89. Okamoto Keitoku further subdivides the daily use of dialect by Miho into her calls in dialect to her mother, the latter "signifying that the core of Miho's personality is supported by the island home she was raised in." See Okamoto Keitoku, "'Shi no toge' ron nōto," 27–46. (For the quote here, see 42.) It appears that Shimao was not always consistent in correct use of dialect terms. According to Okamoto's sources, actual island dialect is mixed with words that are probably not correct island dialect (Okamoto, 46).

90. Okamoto's essay is one of the few critical readings that makes this point. Okamoto believes the novel as a whole should be read as showing the process whereby the importance of the island to Miho's well-being is uncovered (Okamoto, "'Shi no toge' ron nōto," 45).

91. Miho's condition in the story, too, parallels changes in the seasons in an interesting way. The outbreak of her madness comes at the end of the summer, the beginning of a return of the cold. As the days grow shorter and winter deepens, so does her condition worsen. Time in the story also seems to run parallel with her deepening madness, with the chapters progressively covering smaller and smaller spans of time. Chapter 7, appropriately titled "Hi no chijimari" (The shortening of the days) comes at the height of winter, the end of January, when the days are indeed at their shortest and Miho's condition has

worsened to such an extent that Toshio finally must take her to see a doctor. Thus the "frozen time" sense (145) brought on by Miho's madness is reflected in this gradual slowing of the narrative, which itself finds parallels in the gradually shrinking days of winter.

92. Sparling, *"The Sting of Death,"* 151.

93. Ibid.

94. Yoshimoto, *Zen chosakushū* 9, 92–107.

95. The novel does provide certain "rational" hints to explain these powers of foresight and knowledge, the most obvious being the knowledge of Toshio's actions she has gleaned from the report of a detective she said she hired to follow her husband. Yet even this notion seems suspect, since she claims to have paid an enormous sum of money for the detective's services, then threw away his report. As in many cases, Toshio accepts her claims without questions, whereas the reader is left wondering what really happened and who should be believed. Thus the idea that Toshio would meet the woman at a certain spot on a certain day becomes less mysterious than it might at first seem. Nevertheless, the way in which she couches her statements, coupled with Toshio's comments on her stance as an "infallible judge" full of "authority" (282, 291), leads the reader to see her as something more than just an "ordinary" woman.

96. William P. Lebra, *Okinawan Religion: Belief, Ritual, and Social Structure* (Honolulu: University of Hawai'i Press, 1966), 79.

97. This idea is expanded in chapter 4.

98. Lebra, *Okinawan Religion,* 37.

99. Yoshimoto, *Zen chosakushū* 9, 154.

100. Okamoto, "'Shi no toge' ron nōto," 45.

101. Okamoto Keitoku, "'Yaponesia ron' no rinkaku 1," *Shin Okinawa bungaku* 72 (Summer 1987): 214.

4. Island Dreams: *Yaponesia* and the Cultural Unconscious

1. He was nominated twice, both before and after his Tokyo period.

2. Okamoto Keitoku, "Watashi ni totte no Ryūkyūko," *Kaie* (December 1978): 281, 278.

3. Uehara Nario, "*Shi no toge* iron," *Shin Okinawa bungaku* (Spring 1987): 56–63. Uehara's notion about fully grasping time, of course, links up with my analysis of the final section of "Sōsaiki" and the protagonist's ability to connect moments of time that were heretofore separate.

4. Ibid., 63.

5. Shimao Toshio, "Watakushi no bungaku ron," *Sugi yuku toki no naka de* (Shinchōsha, 1983), 35; emphasis added.

6. Ōshiro Tatsuhiro, *Dōka to ika no hazama de* (Ushio shuppansha, 1972), 23.

7. Ibid., 19.

8. Ibid., 23–24.

9. Fujii Reiichi tells how originally Shimao wanted to title the article "Ya-ponesia no shippo" (The tail of *Yaponesia*). Shimao said, "[B]ut since I thought it would give an unpleasant feeling to the people of the island, I decided to make it *nekko* (root) instead." Fujii notes how, in a 1974 symposium in Amami, Shimao mistakenly said that he *had* used the term "shippo" in an early article; Fujii concludes that in this mistaken remark one can glimpse the process whereby in Shimao's twenty-year residence he found a home on the island. Shimao moved, in other words, from an early stance of fear of offending the is-landers to being able to use a potentially offensive word because he was no longer a complete outsider. Fujii's book, itself entitled *Yaponesia no shippo*, con-cerns itself in part with this process whereby Shimao, both in his personal life and in his writings, found roots in Amami. Although "Yaponesia" is the closest romanized equivalent of the word Shimao writes out in *katakana*, other spel-lings exist: On the cover of Shimao's *Yaponesia josetsu* (Sōjusha, 1970), for in-stance, the word "Japanesia" is written in romanized form. Likewise, in the only full translation of any of his *Yaponesia* essays, the essay "Neglected Islands" (*Japan Quarterly* 14[1] [January–March 1967]: 72–75), the word is romanized as "Japonesia."

10. "Watashi no mita Amami," Collected Works, vol. 16, 217. Throughout the rest of this chapter, page references in the text with both volume and page numbers are from Shimao's essays on the southern islands in the Collected Works; the first number refers to volume—either 16 or 17—the second to page number.

11. "'Okinawa' no imi suru mono," Collected Works, vol. 16, 11.

12. Shimao Toshio, *Naze dayori* (Nōsagyoson Bunka Kyōkai, Ningen Sen-sho 10), 9.

13. From the essay "Amami—Nihon no nantō."

14. From the essay "Amami—Okinawa no kosei no hakkutsu."

15. From the essay "Ryūkyūkō no kanju."

16. The article was published in the magazine *Okinawa* and thus was pre-sumably written largely for an audience of Okinawan readers. The date of com-position is unknown, but since at this time Shimao was hard-pressed finan-cially, one can assume he could not afford the luxury of having unpublished manuscripts lying around and wrote this article on specific assignment from the magazine not long before its publication. One should note how Shimao (who admits to never having been to Okinawa—he would not visit until 1964, ten years later), while writing of Okinawa, attempts to link it with Amami and the other southern islands in a common cultural background and history, yet is sensitive to the issue of each island's local uniqueness. The question of finding a communality between the islands—while maintaining their individuality—is one Shimao continued to work on throughout his essays.

17. At this point, however, Shimao does not yet point to multiple narratives, but to two only—that of Okinawa and the mainland.

18. In the 1970 essay "Minzoku no katsuryoku," Shimao writes, "In these dances we find an unfaded energy *(katsuryoku)* hidden at the root of Japan" (vol. 17, 173).

19. Shimao soon concludes that fully contextualized expressions of cultural differences—at least as far as Okinawan folk arts are concerned—may be no more than unrealistic, wishful thinking. He feels "despair" over the commercialization of Okinawan culture and the fact that being an "exoticism" is the only course left for it; perhaps the only course remaining, he writes, is for "Okinawan feeling *(jōcho)* as a product" to "overwhelm Yamato completely" (vol. 16, 13).

20. Specifically, Shimao mentions a "blood transfusion" to "Japanese literature," but since the tone of the rest of the article is a more general examination not of literature but of culture in general, the statement can correctly be read as dealing not exclusively with literature.

21. When he says, for instance, that "losing sight of Okinawa will dry us up" (16), he is clearly identifying with the "rotting" culture of the mainland. In an earlier spot, where he speaks of the "meaningless vicious circle" of prejudice within the islands that is "making us suffocate," the "us" here points less to the mainlanders than to those either of the islands or, as in his case, in some way connected to them.

22. One should recall the first two third-person vignettes Shimao wrote after moving to the island, "Ani to imōto" and "Ensoku," in which the protagonist was given this very name, Shimajiri.

23. This exchange is from the 1967 interview with Ōshiro, "Uchinānchu wa Nihonjin da," in Shimao, *Yaponesia kō: Shimao Toshio Taidanshū* (Ashi shobō, 1977), 75.

24. "Amami Ōshima kara."

25. "What I noticed [after moving to Amami] was that 'My Amami' had swelled up and was too bloated. It probably doesn't overlap with the real island." Still, he expects to find something different from the mainland, a positive element: "I can't put it in a word, but I felt in the smell of the wind and the land, the dense relations in the temperament of the people I had never experienced before" (*Naze dayori*, 11).

26. "Ritō no nagusame." For a discussion of the actual visual problems Shimao had and their relationship to his literature, see Yoshimoto Takaaki, "Shimao Toshio *Hi o kakete*," in his *Zen chosakushū 9*, 221–225.

27. "Ritō no nagusame." What the island "taught" him, one understands, is to put the health and well-being of his family above everything else.

28. "Minami no shima de no kangae," 1959.

29. I am reminded of the situation even today in Amami regarding practi-

tioners of *shima uta* (island folk songs). Although Amami singers won the national folk song contests two years running (1989 and 1990), according to informants on the island there are no professional singers of *shima uta* in Amami; singing, instead, is a more integrated part of daily life. The most recognized practitioner, for instance, Tsuboyama Yutaka, is a marine carpenter who spends much of his day singing as he builds boats.

30. Alan Christy, "The Making of Imperial Subjects in Okinawa," 613.

31. This last expression, one should note, is Shimao's shorthand for a theme that weaves its way in and out of various essays of the period, namely his relationship, and that of others, to the islands as a *writer*. He is often concerned with finding a source of "energy" of a creative sort, a means of locating and securing a relationship between writing and place so that the one is rooted in the other. A somewhat later essay that deals more directly with both literary production and the relationship between center and periphery is the 1965 "'Chihō bungaku' to iu koto ni tsuite" (On what is called 'regional literature'). This essay is an attempt to liberate writing from the necessity of having to pass through the *bundan*.

32. Collected Works, vol. 7, 243–244.

33. I am particularly indebted to Okamoto's readings for these insights, especially parts 9 and 10 of *"Yaponesia ron" no rinkaku* (Naha: Okinawa Taimusu sha, 1990).

34. "Amami wa uttaeru," 1970.

35. "Ryūkyūkō kara," 1970.

36. Shimao uses the term "anti-Japan" *(han Nihon)* in the essay "Amami no shima kara" (1971), vol. 17, 258.

37. This is from the 1974 article "Ryūkyūkō no kyūryokuteki miryoku."

38. The article is reprinted in *Yaponesia no josetsu*, ed. Shimao Toshio, 61–66. Page references are from this reprint. The article originally appeared in *Nihon dokusho shinbun*, January 1, 1970, edition.

39. Tanigawa Ken'ichi, "'Yaponesia' to wa nani ka," in *Yaponesia no josetsu*, 63.

40. Ibid., 65.

41. Personal conversation with Takara in Naha, Okinawa, July 11, 1995.

42. These comments, as well as those of Yamada, Ōshiro, and Takara, are summarized in Miki Takeshi's *Okineshia ron* (Osaka, Kaifūsha, 1988), which is Miki's own attempt to trace a common cultural heritage between Okinawa and the islands of the South Pacific and countries of Southeast Asia; see 30–36. Miki's comments on Shimao emphasize that the Ryukyu chain should be viewed as connected with these areas outside Japan. Shimao's ideas, for him, are too narrow, since they merely discuss the southern islands as an Other in Japan that adds diversity to Japanese life. Miki wants to view Okinawa less as the root of what makes Japan than as something else entirely.

43. Shimao Toshio, *Heiwa no naka no shusenjō: Taidanshū* (Tōjusha raibu-rarii, 1979), 178–179.

44. Ibid., 178.

45. The other panelists were poet Kawamitsu Shin'ichi, Okamoto Keitoku, and Niikawa Akira, managing director of the *Okinawa Times*. "Ryūkyūkō to Yaponesia," in *Shin Okinawa bungaku* 71 (Spring 1987): 105–121. I recognize that Shimao's presence on the panel might tend to skew the comments of the other panelists, but the statements made on the panel are in keeping with the tenor of the partcipants' comments elsewhere.

46. Kawamitsu, et al., "Ryūkyūkō to Yaponesia," 115, 113.

47. Ibid., 115.

48. Ibid., 121.

49. Ibid., 119, 121.

50. Collected Works, vol. 17, 132–133.

51. Akasaka Norio, "Nantō ron, aratanaru taidō," in Yoshimoto Takaaki, et al., *Ryūkyūkō no kankiryoku to nantō ron* (Kawade shobō shinsha, 1979), 141.

52. Takara Ben, "Uruyu ron josetsu," in Yoshimoto, *Ryūkyūkō no kankiryoku to nantō ron,* 198–199.

53. Yoshimoto Takaaki, "Izoku no ronri," in *Jōkyō* (Kawade shobō shinsha, 1970), 248–249.

54. James Fujii, *Complicit Fictions: The Subject in the Modern Japanese Prose Narrative* (Berkeley: University of California Press, 1993), 101. I am indebted to Fujii's discussion of these three notions.

55. Paul Anderer, *Literature of the Lost Home: Kobayashi Hideo—Literary Criticism 1924–1939* (Stanford: Stanford University Press, 1995), 49.

56. Collected Works, vol. 14, 182–186.

57. Okamoto Keitoku, *"Yaponesia ron" no rinkaku.*

58. See Okamoto, *"Yaponesia ron" no rinkaku,* especially chapter 8.

59. "Amami bunka no kiso o ninshiki," *Yaponesia kō,* 247–248.

60. Nineteen seventy-one interview, "Nihon minzoku no genten," quoted in Okamoto, *"Yaponesia ron" no rinkaku,* 31; emphasis added.

61. "Yume ni tsuite," 1980, in *Sugi yuku toki no naka de* (Shinchōsha, 1983), 63–64.

62. Interview between Yoshimoto and Ayukawa Nobuo in their book *Taidan: Bungaku no sengo* (Kōdansha, 1979), 113–114.

63. These ideas are from a conversation with Prof. Asai Kiyoshi, Tokyo, July 1994.

64. There is much, naturally, that works against an interpretation of the novel as paralleling the development of Shimao's *Yaponesia* ideas, relations between Tōhoku, Amami, and the center, etc. The essays reveal an early enthusiasm and acceptance of Amami (which borders on the naive at times), followed by a later revision, as Shimao backs away from his earlier claims to knowledge

of the island. Arguably, *Shi no toge* depicts an opposite movement: the early shock and confusion at Miho's madness gradually tending toward a greater understanding and closeness. Any interpretation that sees the novel or the essays as reducible to such simple trends, however, threatens vastly to oversimplify what is a complex interweaving of often opposing tendencies and lines of argument.

65. The idea of the southern islanders as the ones who potentially can restore the mainland to a kind of wholeness is argued by Shimao's and Yoshimoto's intellectual predecessor, Yanagita Kunio. As Alan Christy notes, in the work of Yanagita, "It is the Ryukyuans who mediate for the Japanese primitive character," a character that can ameliorate the historical amnesia of the mainland. See Alan Christy, "Ethnography and the Assimilation of Okinawa," unpublished manuscript, 7–8.

66. Ueno, Ogura, and Tomioka, *Danryū bungakuron*, 73.

67. Ibid., 91.

68. Ibid., 113–114.

69. Ibid., 102.

70. As touched on in my introduction, despite reservations that the whole work is entirely Shimao's own attempt at self-cure, Ueno argues that the literary accomplishment of Shimao in *Shi no toge* lies in his depiction of an "absolute Other," a stance that separates his work from that of I-novelists (*Danryū bungakuron*, 86, 96).

71. Ibid., 109–110.

72. Another reading of Shimao's work worth mentioning is Oguri Kōhei's 1989 film version of *Shi no toge*. For commentary on this film, see Linda C. Ehrlich, "Water Flowing Underground: The Films of Oguri Kohei," *Japan Forum* 4(1) (April 1992): 145–162; and my own "*Shi no toge*: Eiga to shōsetsu no aida," *Genten* 10 (1990): 114–119.

73. Page references for "Kawa ni te" and "Haishi" are from the Collected Works, vol. 5; for "Sōsaiki" and "Keiji no tsutome" the page references are from vol. 6. Page references for "Shima e" are from *Sono natsu no ima wa/Yume no naka de no nichijō* (1988).

74. The next story Shimao published was "Ridatsu," which eventually became chapter 1 of the full-length *Shi no toge*.

75. One should note, however, Shimao's abortive attempt soon after he moved to Amami to start a second series of short sketches (*hahen shōsetsu*) as a sequel to the stories in *Garasu shōji no shiruetto*. He completed only two stories, "Ani to imōto," and "Ensoku." The date of composition is unclear, but since Shimao states that he wrote these soon after moving to Amami, they can most likely be dated to late 1955 or early 1956. Shimao himself was never sure if these were broadcast over the radio as planned, and they made their way into print only in 1972, in *Kanna*, a Kagoshima coterie magazine.

76. One is struck by the similarity of the line, "At the time, I felt a strong body odor from the life outside the squadron," to that of the opening line of "Ie no naka" (long considered by Shimao as the opening chapter of *Shi no toge*, published only two months before "Haishi"): "At the time, my heart was outside the home" (Collected Works, vol. 5, 326). Just as the husband in "Ie no naka" is having an affair outside the home, the commander in "Haishi" slipped away from his duties and went outside the *tokkōtai* squadron to rendezvous with his lover from the village.

77. The translation is Van Gessel's, from *The Sting of Life: Four Contemporary Japanese Novelists*, 133.

78. Fujii Reiichi, *Yaponesia no shippo: Shimao Toshio no genfūkei* (Hihyō sha, 1979), 17–18. The second comment is by Nakasato Susumu in the 1987 roundtable discussion, "'Yaponesia ron' to Okinawa: Shisōteki na imi o tou," in Takara Ben, *Hatsugen/Okinawa no sengo gojū nen* (Naha: Hirugi sha, 1995), 69. The paraphrase of Uehara is from his comments found earlier in this chapter.

79. As Yokoyama Nobuyuki puts it, the image of life in the islands as like that of a movie allows one only to watch, but never participate. This comment could serve for many of the island stories. See Yokoyama Nobuyuki, "Shimao Toshio 'Shi no toge' to sensō," *Kindai bungaku shiron* (June 11, 1973): 59.

80. Iwaya makes this point as well. See his *Shimao Toshio ron* (Kindai Bungeisha, 1982), 162.

81. No given names are used in the story.

82. Traces of madness still exist in her (thus he must "carry" her as he did in the *byōinki* story "Omoi niguruma"), although the reader is far removed from the Miho of the *byōinki* and *Shi no toge*. Here, madness seems more like a game to the wife: "My wife liked to make her face expressionless and pretend to be mad *(kichigai)* sometimes" (100). Still, the narrator remains anxious about her condition. As he explains to the unseen farmers whose property they have invaded, his wife's actions are the result of her being "a little strange." He regrets having said this, as "[t]hat's a matter just between my wife and me, not something I should tell strangers" (100). As the wife continues not to budge from the farm, her eyes "showing no concern" for him at all, the husband thinks "gloomily" that "maybe she really has become this way" (101).

83. Collected Works, vol. 17, 192–193.

84. This is a move seen in "Haishi."

85. Yonaha Keiko, "Ura to omote no gyakuten—Shimao Toshio shoki sakuhin no shudai," 76.

Afterword

1. Shimao, "Watashi no bungakuron," *Sugi yuku toki no naka de*, 38. As the name of the work—*Hi no utsuroi*—indicates, the passage of time is a key con-

cept in this novel. In this the work is not alone, because as many have pointed out, the word "hi" (day) appears in many other Shimao titles in the *Shi no toge* series: "Hi wa hi ni" (1961), "Hibi no tameshi" (1963), "Hi no chijimari" (1964), and "Hi o kakete" (1967). Writing in 1973, before either work was completed, Wakasugi Satoshi writes that "*Shi no toge* and *Hi no utsuroi* look like twins whose ages are quite different." He goes on to speculate that the task remaining to Shimao is the depiction of what is elided in the two works (that is, the works as they appeared in 1973)—namely the ways in which madness is cured:

> In both *Hi no utsuroi* and *Shi no toge* Shimao has presented to us his and his wife's depression *(utsu)*, but both are lacking the part depicting a recovery. Shimao is shouldering a great, incomplete task. . . . I think from here on we have reached the place which really counts, where it is all that much harder for [Shimao] to put his hand to the task (see "Tabi e—Shimao kun no utsu," in *Gendai no bungaku 15: Shimao Toshio* [Kōdansha, Geppō 27], 2–3).

Wakasugi's idea is that perhaps the two works—both depictions of depression, in his reading—will somehow, in later installments, be "linked" in some "skillful way."

2. The first-person narrator, the husband, is named Shimao, the wife is unnamed, and the son and daughter are given the real names of Shimao's children—Shinzō and Maya.

3. The internal evidence consists of the reference to Kawabata Yasunari's death in April 1972 (20). The book is notably sparse when it comes to verifiable references to the world outside of Toshio's small circle of acquaintances. The entire book was serialized over a period of four years, from June 1972 to September 1976.

4. The *nikkitai shōsetsu* remark is from Matsuoka Shunkichi, *Shimao Toshio ron* (Tairyūsha, 1977), 320; the "anti-novel" one from Okuno Takeo, *Shimao Toshio*, 106. I am eliding, obviously, the question of to what extent the *shōsetsu* and novel are synonymous—an important question. For more discussion of this point, see Edward Fowler's *The Rhetoric of Confession: Shishōsetsu in Early Twentieth-Century Japanese Fiction* (Berkeley: University of California Press, 1988) and Masao Miyoshi's "Against the Native Grain: The Japanese Novel and the 'Postmodern' West," *The South Atlantic Quarterly* 87(3) (Summer 1988): 525–550. One should note Shimao's own interest in "old-fashioned *zuihitsu*." In the same year *Hi no utsuroi* was published, Shimao published his own translation into modern Japanese of one of the *zuihitsu* (essay) classics of premodern literature, *Tsurezuregusa*. It is interesting to note, too, some of the superficial similarities between *Hi no utsuroi* and Sōseki's 1915 *zuihitsu* work, *Garasu dō no naka* (Behind the glass door). Although the title reminds one more of Shimao's 1972 collection *Garasu shōji no shiruetto*, Sōseki's work is closer in content to *Hi no utsuroi*. Both depict writers recovering from illness, often bothered by un-

invited guests, and both works deal early on with the death of an animal, which stimulates thoughts of the ephemerality of life and human mortality.

    5. *Zoku Hi no utsuroi* (Chūō bunko, 1989), 484.

    6. Evidence is found in his serialized diary of a 1967 trip to Eastern Europe, *Yume no kage o motomete* (Seeking the shadows of dreams), published over the period 1968–1974, and more surprisingly, even in *Shi no toge*. The novelist Hino Keizō has identified chapter 11 of *Shi no toge* ("Hikkoshi," 1972) as a break from the earlier chapters—the beginning, even, of a new set of *rensaku* (linked stories). While Hino identifies this break with such elements as the establishment of Toshio's "will" and "subjectivity," his desire at last to begin a "new life," one may identify a different, structural feature that marks the chapter as a break with what came before—the move to a more diary-like format. Chapter 11, in particular the last ten pages or so (consisting as they do of a series of short vignettes, the majority beginning with the marker "Tsugi no hi . . . "—The next day . . .), is nearly indistinguishable from the format of *Hi no utsuroi*, which was begun in the same month chapter 11 was published (April 1972). Shimao's published dream diaries are *Ki mu shi* (1973) and *Yume nikki* (1978), serialized in the Kagoshima coterie magazine *Kanna* from 1973–1976.

    7. Page number references in the text are from the 1976 Chūō kōronsha edition of *Hi no utsuroi*.

    8. I speak of *Shi no toge* as the earlier work, as the bulk of it (eleven of the twelve chapters) was published before *Hi no utsuroi* began to be serialized; the complete *Shi no toge*, however, came out a year after the publication of the one-volume *Hi no utsuroi*.

    9. Shimao Toshio and Ogawa Kunio, *Yume to genjitsu: Rokkakan no taiwa* (Chikuma shobō, 1976), 251.

    10. *Zoku Hi no utsuroi*, 242.

    11. Ibid., 445–446; emphasis added. Here I should mention that, in interesting ways, the published Shimao "saga" continues. Shimao's son, Shinzō, a photographer and essayist, recently published a memoir of his childhood on Amami, *Tsuki no kazoku* (Shōbunsha, 1997), which has been advertised as providing glimpses into the "*Shi no toge* family." At almost the same time, Miho Shimao authorized publication of Shimao's complete wartime diary, which appeared in the September 1997 issue of *Shinchō*, 186–197. Portions of the diary have appeared before, but this was the first time the entire diary was published. And most recently, three previously unpublished stories and essays by Shimao appeared in the February 1998 issue of *Shinchō*.

Appendix: Plot Summary of *Shi no toge*

    1. "Ridatsu" was not Shimao's first choice as a title. At first he intended to title the opening chapter "Iku do me ka no iyami" (perhaps translated as some-

thing like "How many hatreds"). (See reproduction of original first page of Shimao's manuscript, with this title crossed out, in *Kanshō Nihon gendai bungaku*, ed. Sukekawa, 147.) In later years Shimao himself expressed puzzlement at what "Ridatsu" meant in the context of the novel (see Shimao and Ogawa, *Yume to genjitsu*, 251.) See the afterword of this book for the meaning of the word as it appears in *Hi no utsuroi*.

2. Translation in Van Gessel, *The Sting of Life: Four Contemporary Japanese Novelists*, 159.

3. The word used here to describe Toshio's feelings *(bunri suru)* also harkens back to the chapter title, because both *ridatsu* and *bunri* mean "split off from" or "secede."

4. To give some indication of how large an amount it is, after selling their house near the end of the story, they have a savings of only ¥100,000.

5. Gessel writes, "The reader eventually catches on to the fact that the letters are written and placed in the mailbox by Miho herself, but Toshio never seems to realize this." See Gessel, *The Sting of Life*, 166.

6. Identified only as F. Okuno has said F is based on himself, which makes sense in light of F's remarks that he would be in a "fix" if Toshio quit writing, because he was the one critic who praised Toshio's writing the most. Okuno is well known for his statement that he "staked the future direction of Japanese literature on the direction Shimao's literature takes" (Okuno Takeo, *Shimao Toshio*, 182).

7. The title is difficult to translate. Sparling renders it "Taking Our Time" (Sparling, *"The Sting of Death" and Other Stories by Shimao Toshio*, 10.) "Kakete" is written with a character that can mean to "tie," "connect," or "join" something, or to "anchor" something. The implication is of a "tying" down of days or of time, a connecting or linking of time.

8. Translation from Gessel, *The Sting of Life*, 176–177. The phrase translated as "which was about to fly away," left out of Gessel's translation, has been added.

Bibliography

Works in Japanese

Aeba, Takeo, ed. *Shimao Toshio kenkyū* (Tōjusha, 1976).

Akasaka, Norio. "Nantō ron, aratanaru taidō." In Yoshimoto Takaaki, et al., *Ryūkyūkō no kankiryoku to nantō ron* (Kawade shobō shinsha, 1979), 140–149.

Akiyama, Shun. "Commentary." In Shimao Toshio, *Garasu shōji no shiruetto* (Kōdansha Bungei bunko, 1989), 191–202.

Awazu, Norio. "'Shi no toge' o megutte." *Kaie* (December 1978): 58–63.

Ebii, Eiji. "'Tsumi' o ikiru mono no kijutsu: *Shi no toge* ron." *Josetsu* 3 (1991): 50–58.

Fujii, Reiichi. *Yaponesia no shippo: Shimao Toshio no genfūkei* (Hihyōsha, 1979).

———. "Shimao bungaku no genkyō to Shimao Toshio," in *Shin Okinawa bungaku* 71 (Spring 1987): 32–39.

———. *Nantō bungaku no joron* (Kaifūsha, 1987).

———. "Shimao Toshio ni miru Amami/Okinawa." *Shin Nihon bungaku* 81 (Autumn 1989): 90–93.

Haniya, Yutaka. Postscript. In Shimao Toshio, *Garasu shōji no shiruetto* (Sōjusha, 1972), 211–214.

Hankichi, Mitsuo. "Genjitsu no seiyaku to yume." *Kaie* (December 1978): 154–158.

Hino, Keizō. "Nichijō no hikari: 'Hikkoshi' ni tsuite." In Aeba Takeo, ed., *Shimao Toshio kenkyū* (Tōjusha, 1976), 146–156.

Hinobara, Shigeaki, gen. ed. *Kango no tame no rinshō igaku taikei*, vol. 16: *Seishin igaku* (Jōhōkaihatsu kenkyūjo, 1983).

Hiyane, Kaoru, et al. Roundtable discussion. "'Yaponesia ron' to Okinawa." *Shin Okinawa Bungaku* 71 (Spring 1987): 14–26.

Horii, Kenichi. "Shi no toge." *Kokubungaku. Kaisetsu to kanshō* 39(9): 182–183.

Hoshika, Terumitsu. "Shimao Toshio ron." In Aeba Takeo, ed., *Shimao Toshio kenkyū* (Tōjusha, 1976), 227–252.

Iijima, Koichi. "Nantō ron o yomu." *Kaie* (December 1978): 252–257.

273

Imai, Mieko. "'Shi no toge' o yomu." *Shinchō* 75(1) (January 1978): 200–203.
———. "Kijutsusha no tsumazuki." *Kaie* (December 1978): 94–103.
Ishida, Tadahiko. "Nigeru, tobu, todomaru." *Josetsu* 3 (1991): 7–20.
Isoda, Kōichi. "Taicho no shokuzai." *Kaie* (December 1978): 165–169.
———. "Shimao Toshio ron." In Aeba Takeo, ed., *Shimao Toshio kenkyū* (Tōjusha, 1976), 92–96. (Originally in *Kyūshū daigaku shinbun*, August 25, 1966.)
Isogai, Hideo. "Shimao Toshio: *Shi no toge* o shiza to shite." In Aeba,Takeo, ed., *Shimao Toshio kenkyū*, (Tōjusha, 1976), 172–178. (Originally in *Kokubungaku* [February 1969]: 36–41.)
———. "Shimao Toshio." *Kokubungaku. Kaisetsu to kanshō* 40(8) (July 1975): 150–151.
Iwaya, Seishō. *Shimao Toshio ron* (Kindai bungeisha, 1982).
Kaga, Otohiko. Interview. "Tennōsei, nōshi, gendai bungaku." *Bungaku jihyō* 39 (January 10, 1990): 45.
Kaikō, Ken. "Ryūbō to rōjō." *Bungei* 7(5) (May 1968): 276–286.
Kamiya, Tadataka. "Shimao Toshio 'Ōbasami' no 'Akuma.'" *Genten* 2 (Fall 1983): 38–41.
———. "Shimao Toshio." *Kokubungaku. Kaisetsu to kanshō* 39(8) (July 1974): 101.
Kanehisa, Tadashi. *Amami ni ikiru Nihon kodai bunka* (Shigonsha, 1978).
Karatani, Kōjin. "Yume no sekai: Shimao Toshio to Shōnō Junzō." In Karatani Kōjin, *Imi to iu yamai* (Kōdansha Bungei bunko, 1989), 67–108. (Originally published by Kawade shobō shinsha, 1975.)
———. *Kindai Nihon no hihyō: Shōwa hen* (Fukutake shoten, 1991).
Katō, Norihiro. "Shimao Toshio." *Kokubungaku. Kaisetsu to kanshō* 40(13) (December 1975): 148–149.
Katsumata, Osamu. "Sei ni tachimodoru michi: Shimao Toshio ron." *Gunzō* (October 1978): 192–210.
Kawamitsu, Shin'ichi. "Mirai no Jōmon." *Kaie* (December 1978): 261–269.
Kawamitsu, Shin'ichi, Okamoto Keitoku, and Niikawa Akira. "Ryūkyūkō to Yaponesia." *Shin Okinawa bungaku* 71 (Spring 1987): 105–121.
Kawamura, Jirō. "Commentary." In Shimao Toshio, *Ware fukaki fuchi yori* (Shūeisha 1977), 233–238.
Kawamura, Sō. "Commentary." In Shimao Toshio, *Hamabe no uta/Rongu rongu agou* (Kōdansha Bungei bunko, 1992), 300–312.
Kimura, Yukio. "Kateizō no henyō to bungaku." *Kokubungaku: Kaisetsu to kanshō* 25(5) (April 1980): 105–110.
Kuroi, Senji. "Shikata nai mono nee . . . " *Gunzō* 42 (January 1987): 281–283.
Matsubara, Shin'ichi. "Shimao Toshio no byōsai shōsetsu to genjitsu." *Shūkan dokushonin* (July 29, 1968).
Matsuoka, Shunkichi. *Shimao Toshio no genshitsu* (Sanbunsha, 1973).

———. *Shimao Toshio ron* (Tairyūsha, 1977).

Miki, Takeshi. *Okineshia ron* (Osaka: Kaifūsha, 1988).

Mishima, Yukio. "Mateki na mono no chikara." In Aeba Takeo, ed., *Shimao Toshio kenkyū* (Tōjusha, 1976), 30–31. (Originally in *Bungakukai* [December 1962].)

Morikawa, Tatsuya. *Shimao Toshio ron* (Shinbisha, 1965).

Nagashima, Takakichi. "Kaku koto, ieru koto." *Genten* 7 (Spring 1987): 166–167.

Nakahodo, Masanori. "'Irie no uchi' kara 'Irie soto' e: Shimao Toshio no 'sensō' sakuin." *Shin Okinawa bungaku* 71 (Spring 1987): 488–495.

Nakayama, Masamichi. *Shimao Toshio ron/hoka* (Kindai bungei sha, 1989).

Niikawa, Akira. "Ryūkyūkō to Shimao Toshio." *Kaie* (December 1978): 283–287.

Niwa, Masamitsu. "Bungaku wa shokuzai kōi ni wa naranai: Shimao Toshio san ni." *Sakka* 118 (June 1958).

———. "Shimao Toshio ron." In Aeba Takeo, ed., *Shimao Toshio kenkyū* (Tōjusha, 1976), 207–227. (Originally in *Sakka* [April 1961].)

Odagiri, Hideo. *Gendai bungaku shi gekan* (Shūeisha, 1975).

Ōe, Kenzaburō. "Shimao Toshio 'kuzure' ni tsuite." *Gunzō* (September 1972): 216–227.

———. "Taiken to kuzure." *Shinchō* 84(1) (January 1987): 201–203.

Ogawa, Kunio. *Kaisō no Shimao Toshio* (Ozawa shoten, 1987).

Okaba, Noboru. "*Shi no toge* ron." *Subaru* 34 (April 1978): 230–242.

Okamoto, Keitoku. "Watashi ni totte no Ryūkyūkō." *Kaie* (December 1978): 278–282.

———. "'Yaponesia ron' no rinkaku." Serialized in *Shin Okinawa bungaku* 72–83 (Summer 1987–Autumn 1989).

———. *"Yaponesia ron" no rinkaku: Shimao Toshio no manazashi* (Naha: Okinawa Taimusu sha/Taimusha sensho II:3, 1990).

———. "'Shi no toge' ron nōto." *Ryūkyū daigaku hōbungakubu kiyō: Nihon tōyō bunka ronshū* 1 (March 1995): 27–46.

Ōkubo, Minoru. "Shimao Toshio: Hi no chijimari." *Kokubungaku: Kaishaku to kyōzai no kenkyū* 15(11) (August 1970): 97–101.

Okuno, Takeo. *Shimao Toshio* (Tairyūsha, 1977).

———. *Sugao no sakkatachi: gendai sakka 132 nin* (Shūeisha, 1978).

Ōshio, Tatsuya. "Yaponesia ron no shukudai." *Kaie* (December 1978): 270–277.

Ōshiro, Tatsuhiro. *Dōka to ika no hazama de.* (Ushio Shuppansha, 1972).

Sakaguchi, Hiroshi. "Shi yo, omae no toge wa izuko ni aru." *Josetsu* 3 (1990): 58–64.

Sasaki, Kiichi. "Kakegai no nai shishitsu." *Gunzō* 42 (January 1987): 278–280.

Satō, Junjirō. *Shimao Toshio: Miho no sekai o chūshin to shite* (Okisekisha, 1983).

Satō, Yasumasa. "'Shi no toge' no buntai." *Kokubungaku* (November 1977): 140–141.

Sekine, Kenji. "Ryūkyūkō no naka no Yaponesia ron." *Shin Okinawa bungaku* 71 (Spring 1987): 40–46.

Sekine, Kenji, et al. Roundtable discussion. "Ryūkyūkō to Yaponesia." *Shin Okinawa bungaku* 71 (Spring 1987): 105–121.

Shimao, Miho. "'Garasu shōji no shiruetto' e no omoi." In Shimao Toshio, *Garasu shōji no shiruetto: hahen shōsetsu* (Kōdansha Bungei bunko, 1989), 185–190.

———. "Kaisō no Shimao Toshio." *Ōru Yomimono* (October 1990): 178–187.

Shimao, Miho, et al. *Shimao Toshio, Kataribe sōsho 25* (Miyamoto kikaku kan, 1989).

———. *Shimao Toshio II: Kataribe sōsho 30* (Miyamoto kikaku kan, 1990).

Shimao, Toshio. *Yume no naka de no nichijō* (Gendaisha, 1956).

———. *Ritō no kōfuku, ritō no fukō* (Miraisha, 1960).

———. *Watakushi no bungaku henreki* (Miraisha, 1966).

———. *Hi o kakete* (Chūō kōronsha, 1968).

———. *Yume no keiretsu* (Chūō Daigaku shuppanbu, 1971).

———. *Garasu shōji no shiruetto: hahen shōsetsu* (Sōjusha, 1972).

———. *Hi no utsuroi* (Chūō kōronsha, 1976).

———. *Uchi ni mukau tabi: Shimao Toshio taidanshū* (Tairyūsha, 1976).

———. *Yume to genjitsu: muikakan no taidan* (Chikuma shobō, 1976) (with Ogawa Kunio).

———. *Shi no toge* (Shinchōsha, 1977).

———. *Naze dayori* (Nōsagyoson bunka kyōkai, Ningen sensho 10, 1977).

———. *Yaponesia kō: Shimao Toshio taidan shū* (Ashi shobō, 1977).

———. *Shima no hate* (Shūeisha bunko, 1978).

———. *Nanpū no sasoi* (Tairyūsha, 1978).

———. *Yume no naka de no nichijō* (Shūeisha bunko, 1979).

———. *Heiwa no naka no shusenjō: Taidan shū* (Tōjusha raiburarii, 1979).

———. *Shimao Toshio ni yoru Shimao Toshio* (Seidōsha, 1981).

———. *Shi no toge* (Shinchō bunko, 1981).

———. *Shimao Toshio zenshū* (Collected Works), 17 vols. (Shōbunsha, 1981–1983).

———. *Sugiyuku toki no naka de* (Shinchōsha, 1983).

———. *Yume kuzu* (Shinchōsha, 1985).

———. *Zoku Hi no utsuroi* (Chūō kōronsha, 1986).

———. *Shinyō hasshin* (Ushio shuppansha, 1987).

———. *Sono natsu no ima wa/Yume no naka de no nichijō* (Kōdansha Bungei bunko, 1988).

———. *Tōmei na toki no naka de* (Ushio shuppansha, 1988).

———. *Gyoraitei gakusei* (Shinchō bunko, 1989).

———. *Garasu shōji no shiruetto: hahen shōsetsushū* (Kōdansha Bungei bunko, 1989).

Index

abyss, 5, 22, 24, 90, 96, 152
Akasaka Norio, 186
Akutagawa Prize, 162, 254n. 36
alienation, 6, 10, 21, 24, 33, 174
allegory: in "Kizashi," 86–87; in "Yume no naka de no nichijō," 70
Amami Ōshima, 100, 116, 163, 164, 165, 166, 169, 195; *bushidō* and, 47; dialect, 48, 50; division of labor in, 265n. 29; island mythology, 26; and Meiji Restoration, 174, 176; and Miho's position, 152–159, 160, 161; names, 170–171; political control of, 47; poverty of, 177, 188; in *Shi no toge*, 154, 262n. 85; in "Sōsaiki," 206, 215, 219, 221
Amida Buddha, 196
apocalypse, 19–20, 65–66
atomic bombings, 18–19, 21, 22, 29

Bakin (Takizawa Bakin), 165
bathing (communal), 81–82, 196–197, 210–211, 218
body: and anticipation of death, 22; Miho's in *Shi no toge*, 137–139; and *Yaponesia* essays, 177–178
Buddhism, 165, 178, 196
bundan (literary establishment), 71, 188
burakumin (outcastes), 184
bushidō (samurai code), 8, 34, 117, 236n. 6; and Amami, 47; and death, 45–46

byōinki (stories of a hospital stay), 103–121, 154, 155, 212, 233, 234; language in 108; Miho's attacks, 109–111; publication history, 250n. 3; plot summaries, 103–104; victimization, 111–113; war experiences in, 108, 115–116
byōsaimono (stories of a sick wife), 4, 5, 81, 190, 210, 216; elements which make up, 98; definition of, 100, 216, 251n.4. See also *byōinki*; *Shi no toge*

castration, symbolic, 93
Chesler, Phyllis, 134, 141
Chinese characters, 59; and Amami names, 170; and *Shi no toge*, 257n.47
Christianity, 107; *Hi no utsuroi*, 218; in "Matenrō," 61; Old Testament wrath, 64; in "Shima no hate," 39; *Shi no toge* and, 150–151, 158
Christy, Alan, 175, 268n. 65
Civil Code, 135
confession, 133–134
Confucianism, 178
Cuban Missile Crisis, 20

Daisan no shinjin (Third group of new writers): accomplishments, 52; and domestic drama, 91; members, 1
Danryū bungakuron (Theory of male literature), 192–194
death: and the body, 22; *bushidō* ethic of, 45; in *byōinki*, 116–117, 121; "glori-

Ōe Kenzaburō, 3; and nuclear age, 19; view on Shimao as contemporary writer, 19

Ogura Chikako, 192–193

Ōhira Miho, 12. *See also* Shimao Miho

Okamoto Keitoku: on *Shi no toge*, 153, 158–159; on *Yaponesia* essays, 162; "*Yaponesia ron*" *no rinkaku*, 168

Okinawa, 116, 166–171, 221, 264n. 16; culture and *Yaponesia*, 185–187; commercialization of Okinawan culture, 265n. 19

Okuno Takeo, 51, 115, 149; on "Chinkonki," 84; depicted in *Shi no toge*, 272n. 6; high evaluation of Shimao's work, 51; and humor in "Sekizō aruki-dasu," 69; on *Shi no toge* 126, 147–148

Ōoka Shōhei: *Nobi* (*Fires on the Plain*), 17, 25, 240n. 38

Ōshiro Tatsuhiro, 183; dialogue with Shimao, 171; and Okinawan mentality, 149; on reversion and Okinawan identity, 163–164

Other, 5, 45, 46, 79, 114, 117, 119, 120, 161, 190, 193, 202, 239n. 34

pastoral stories: dichotomy in, 35; romanticized view in, 35; style of, 32–33, 35

periphery. *See* margins; Other

post-traumatic stress syndrome, 56

Potsdam Declaration, 22, 23

rensaku (linked stories), 126, 271n. 6

"Reverse Course," 87

Ryukyu Islands, 60, 79; custom of *fūsō*, 157. *See also* Amami (Ōshima); Okinawa

Ryūkyūko (Ryukyu arc), 180, 183; definition of, 162

Sakaguchi Ango: "Darakuron" ("On Decadence"), 152; "Hakuchi" ("The Idiot"), 17, 25

Sakai, Naoki, 25

Sakura, 232

samurai. *See bushidō*

Satsuma, 174. *See also* Kagoshima

schizophrenia, 24, 100, 128, 142, 144, 230, 231

senchūha (wartime generation), 2

sengoha (Postwar writers), 71

sexuality: imagery in war stories, 22; male fear of female, 140; in *Shi no toge*, 136–141

shamaness, 231, 232. *See also noro, yuta*

shell shock, 55

Shimao Miho, 173; final conversation with husband, 50; islands and wartime suicide, 28; outbreak of madness, 99; own writing career, 250n. 1; and *Yaponesia*, 189

Shimao Shinzō: writing career of, 271n. 11

Shimao Toshio: Amami and writing, 163; assessment of own writing, 121; autobiographical details in "Yume no naka de no nichijō," 70; as avant garde writer, 4, 52; chronology of life 1954–1955, 101–102, 250n. 1, 251n. 7, 256n. 45; classification of his fiction, 2; compositional techniques, 243n. 10; conversion to Catholicism, 150; as critical of postwar Japan, 115; death of, 50; diaries and writing, 215–216; as "difficult" writer, 242n. 3; on dreams, 53–54; dream stories, 51–57; earthquake of 1923, 1; high school coterie magazine, 63; *Hi no utsuroi* and real life events, 215; as ill-adjusted on mainland, 173; involvement with other woman, 100; journal issues devoted to, 162–163; as librarian on Amami, 100; literary "retreat," 4, 150; metafictional discussion of writing in "Kizashi," 88–90; and modern Japan, 4; move from Kobe to Tokyo, 84, 90; move to Amami, 100, 171; name and southern connection, 169; new writing career in Tokyo, 89; physical incongruity in stories, 77–78; as postmodern writer, 2; public perception of, 52,

as, 115; in *Shi no toge*, 127, 132; and war, 153; in "Yume no naka de no nichijō," 74
victim mentality, 5, 12; and literature of the victim, 147; Oda Makoto on, 148; and *Shi no toge*, 151

Wa (central culture), 181, 184–185. See also *Yamato*
wandering, 55, 80, 113–114, 122, 187, 221; in *Shi no toge*, 187
war: apocalyptic, 19; and collective amnesia, 3; end of, 74; and history of victimization, 153; outbreak of new war, 66; and responsibility, 146–152; versus nature, 44–45. *See also* trauma
Warren, Carol A. B., 134
Wolfe, Tom, 52
women: depiction of in "Ie no naka," 124–126; and double standards, 135; inequalities and, 5; and madness, 128–146
World War Two. *See* war
writing. *See* language

Yamato, 167
yamatodamashii (*Yamato* spirit), 34
Yanagita Kunio: *Kaijō no michi*, 165, 268n. 65
Yaponesia, 3, 160; coining of term, 164–165; conflicting definitions of, 183; contrasted with Yoshimoto's essays, 186; critical reaction to, 182–190; essays on, 163–182; and *Hi no utsuroi*,

219; influences on, 188; and Japanese identity, 187–190; "Kotōmu" as early expression of, 60, 191–194; and map of Japan, 179; Miki Takeshi's view on, 184; move away from using term, 182; new vocabulary for, 181–182; *Nihonjinron*, 189; and Okinawan identity, 186; Okinawan intellectuals and, 185–187; rediscovery of essays, 182; romanization of, 264n. 9; and "Sekizō arukidasu," 246n. 58; and "Shima e," 204; and Shimao's fiction, 190–213; and *Shi no toge*, 191–194; and "Sōsaiki," 209; and Tōhoku, 179–180; tripartite view of, 180; tropes of mainland discourse, 175; two strands of, 189; and the unconscious, 161; word play and, 183; Yamada Munemutsu and, 184
Yasuoka Shōtarō, 1, 88
Yayoi, 181
Yonaha Keiko, 73, 212–213
Yoshimoto Takaaki, 100, 155–157, 182, 186, 192, 193
Yoshiyuki Junnosuke, 1, 52, 88, 100
yuta (shamaness), 163, 193, 241n. 64; in *Hi no utsuroi*, 216, 217; Miho in *Shi no toge*, 155–159; in "Shima no hate," 38–39, 155–157; wife's special powers in "Kisōsha no yūutsu," 97; in "Yoru no nioi," 156

Zoku Hi no utsuroi, 221–222, 238n. 19
zuihitsu (miscellanies), 270n. 4

About the Author

PHILIP GABRIEL received his doctorate in East Asian literature from Cornell University and is associate professor of Japanese literature at the University of Arizona. In addition to his work on Shimao Toshio, he is translator of the novel *Dream Messenger* by Shimada Masahiko, the novel *South of the Border, West of the Sun* by Murakami Haruki, and two short stories by Murakami that have appeared in ZYZZYVA and *The New Yorker*. He co-edited with Stephen Snyder the anthology *Ōe and Beyond: Fiction in Contemporary Japan*. He is currently at work on a study of Japanese fiction of the 1960s and 1970s and a translation of a novel by Kuroi Senji.